Introduction to Therapeutic Counseling

INTRODUCTION TO

THERAPEUTIC

COUNSELING

Jeffrey A. Kottler
Robert W. Brown
Oakland University

Brooks/Cole Publishing Company
Pacific Grove, California

Brooks/Cole Publishing Company
A Division of Wadsworth, Inc.

Printed in the United States of America
10 9 8 7 6 5

Library of Congress Cataloging in Publication Data

Kottler, Jeffrey A.
    Introduction to therapeutic counseling.

    Bibliography: p.
    Includes index.
    1. Counseling. I. Brown, Robert W., 1943–
II. Title.
BF637.C6K678   1985   616.89'14   84-19838
ISBN 0-534-04698-3

Sponsoring Editor: *Claire Verduin*
Editorial Assistant: *Pat Carnahan*
Production Editor: *Ellen Brownstein*
Manuscript Editor: *Meredy Amyx*
Permissions Editor: *Carline Haga*
Interior Design: *Wendy Calmenson*
Cover Design: *Koney Eng*
Art Coordinator: *Michele Judge*
Interior Illustration: *Lisa Thompson*
Photo Editor: *Judy Blamer*
Typesetting: *Kachina Typesetting, Inc., Tempe, Arizona*
Printing and Binding: *The Maple-Vail Book Manufac-
turing Group*
Part Opening photographs courtesy of: *Jim Pinckney*
Photo Credits
P. 24, Ethan Hoffman, © Archive Pictures, Inc.,; p.
84, The Bettmann Archive; p.70, Sybil Shackman,
Monkmeyer Press Photo Service; p. 94, The Bett-
mann Archive; p. 132, Randy Matusow, © Archive
Pictures, Inc.; p. 153, Mimi Forsyth, Monkmeyer
Press Photo Service; p. 184, Mimi Forsyth,Monk-
meyer Press Photo Service; p. 204, Les Mahon,
Monkmeyer Press Photo Service; p. 223, Michael
O'Brien, © Archive Pictures, Inc.; p. 265, UPI/The
Bettmann Archive

To R.M.K. and M.L.O.

JEFFREY KOTTLER studied at Oakland University, Harvard University, Wayne State University, and the University of Stockholm, and received his Ph.D. in counseling from the University of Virginia. He has worked as a psychologist, counselor, consultant, and educator in a variety of settings, including schools, clinics, hospitals, mental health centers, universities, and private practice. He has special interests in ethics, group work, and introducing counseling technology to developing nations.

Jeffrey is the author or coauthor of the books *Ethical and Legal Issues in Counseling and Psychotherapy*, *Mouthing Off: A Study of Oral Behavior, Its Causes and Treatment*, and *Pragmatic Group Leadership*. He is currently an adjunct associate professor at Oakland University and executive director of Woodcreek Clinic in Farmington Hills, Michigan, where he resides with his wife Ellen and son Cary.

ROBERT W. BROWN is an associate professor and chair of the Counseling Area at Oakland University in Rochester, Michigan. He received his Ph.D. in counselor education from Wayne State University and has worked as a teacher and counselor in schools, colleges, and universities. Bob is a licensed psychologist, and his clinical experience includes work in hospitals and community counseling centers. His specialty areas include group counseling, educational and psychological testing, and developmental counseling; his current research is in the area of adult transition. He publishes and lectures on these and other topics. Bob resides in Rochester, Michigan, with his son, Chris, and in his leisure time enjoys hiking and skiing.

Preface

We wrote this book out of a very personal need to create a student-centered introduction to our field. We've felt frustrated because at times the personalized warmth and sensitivity that are the basis of our profession have not been reflected in academic experiences. Too often education emphasizes theoretical knowledge and scholarly inquiry to the exclusion of student involvement. We hope that this book not only meets the stringent demands of traditional scholarship but also provides a lively and dynamic overview of therapeutic counseling.

Throughout the text we speak directly to students, challenging them to explore their personal motives for choosing the counseling profession, as well as helping them to personally integrate much of the research and theoretical concepts. We use case examples, personal experiences, practical applications, and humor to make the material informative and exciting.

Introduction to Therapeutic Counseling is designed for initial courses in human service programs with titles such as "Principles of Counseling," "Counseling Theory and Practice," "Introduction to Guidance," and "Human Resource Development." The book emphasizes the development of a professional identity, ethical standards, basic process skills, the therapeutic relationship, personal theory building, and understanding of meaningful research, as well as a contemporary focus on the practical realities of counseling. Particular attention is devoted to the major specialities and diverse settings in which counseling takes place, such as schools, clinics, and medical, industrial, mental health, and community agency settings. We quite deliberately made the size of the book realistic for a semester's work and planned the number and length of chapters to be manageable for the student struggling to digest a new world of terminology and technology. The book is organized in four broad focus areas: professional identity factors, theoretical and research foundations, counseling applications, and issues in therapeutic practice.

Whereas the first two sections (Chapters 1 through 9) help the student to learn the foundations of therapeutic counseling, the latter two sections (Chapters 10 through 16) apply these concepts to the various specialities within the field. The student is thus encouraged to master the basic theory and research of the field and become familiar with the generic therapeutic skills as well as to begin thinking about the realities of developing a flexible speciality, making oneself marketable, finding suitable employment, and staying passionately committed to the profession.

We acknowledge the assistance of the following people who were instrumental in the preparation of the manuscript: Barbara Jo Yardley, Brenda H. Damiani, Andi Swaab, Caryn Drasin, Mary Otto, Ellen Kottler, Gen Kennedy, Claire Verduin, Pat Carnahan, Meredy Amyx, and Ellen Brownstein.

Our thanks go to the following reviewers who provided constructive criticism and advice during the production of this book: Bianca Bernstein, Wayne State University; William A. Lewis, University of Missouri at Kansas City; Robert Micali, University of New Mexico at Albuquerque; Bill Richardson, North Texas State University at Denton; and Fred Stickle, Western Kentucky University at Bowling Green.

Jeffrey A. Kottler
Robert W. Brown

Contents

Introduction to Therapeutic Counseling

PART ONE
THE PROFESSIONAL
COUNSELOR

Chapter 1

Therapeutic Counseling:

What It Is and How It Works

Why Be a Counselor?

It is both interesting and useful to begin the systematic study of the counseling profession by initially exploring the motives and expectations of students. The decision to become a counselor is as complex and multifaceted as any concern with which our clients might wish help. We expect, even demand, that our clients be completely honest with themselves, that they confront their self-deceptions, ambivalence, motives behind actions. It is only fair that we attempt to be honest with ourselves.

Students enter the counseling field, as they do any other profession, for a variety of reasons. Some people genuinely wish to save the world; others, more modestly, wish to save themselves. Many persons, including the authors, quite deliberately chose this field because there are so many opportunities to apply classroom and book studies to our own lives. Other persons have quite unabashedly admitted that it was a toss-up for them between going to see a counselor for their own problems and becoming a counselor.

The personal motives behind our own career decisions are indeed important to examine as this introduction to therapeutic counseling begins. Such an understanding will permit a more thoughtful and clear-headed approach to the material presented. Within a typical class there are often students who see themselves as missionaries. They choose the counseling profession because they have a strong desire to help others, to make a difference in the lives of those who are suffering. They frequently have a kind of empathy that comes from personal experience. They suffered and were saved; now the roles can be reversed. They wish to make the world a bit more civilized. Perhaps this reason belongs, even if only slightly, to everyone who selects this path; after all, it can't be for the liberal financial rewards, lack of stress, and open job market.

Apart from altruism and idealism there are many other reasons why people choose counseling as a profession. The selection could be pragmatic: grades or GRE scores may have prevented a move into highly competitive programs. Or the time commitments required by some disciplines may have seemed excessive or overwhelming. Counseling seemed a reasonable compromise; the program can be completed in a year or two and then the credentials will permit practice in many attractive settings. Some writers feel there is a narcissistic motivation for entering the helping professions since the counselor is able to satisfy unfulfilled nurturing needs by rescuing people with problems, as well as participate in intimate relationships while always maintaining control (Robertiello, 1978; Herron & Rouslin, 1984). Some people are attracted to counseling because they enjoy the power they can wield in influencing other people's lives. Counselors and other therapeutic practitioners are, in fact, the real power brokers in our society. They have become the oracles, the witch doctors, the gurus, the wizards, the mentors. They listen with compassion and speak with authority. They have the answers and, although they won't reveal them directly, if clients behave and do what they are supposed to, they will be gently prodded to discover truth for themselves.

Students also select counseling for many of the same practical reasons that lead to any other career. They need the graduate degree for a pay raise or promotion. The courses are offered at convenient times. Tests are infrequent or the program doesn't appear too demanding. And indeed counseling does not, at first glance, seem as rigorous as training in engineering, nuclear physics, or neurosurgery.

⟨But don't be fooled. A counseling program is about the most challenging emotional experience a student can undertake⟩Although some counseling programs do not create intense academic pressure, all emphasize skill mastery and performance competencies.⟨Graduate counseling programs are usually less interested in your ability to succeed at academic tasks and more interested in your ability to translate book and classroom learning into action. The bottom line for success in a counseling program is what you can do and what you can deliver⟩

The pressure and inward journeys necessary for growth and counseling skill development are well worth the effort. This profession offers the student more advantages on both a personal and a professional level than almost any other field in existence. Where else can all life experiences, books, films, travels, relationships, fantasies, jobs, losses, disasters, and triumphs help the professional to be more effective?⟨Everything and everyone teaches a counselor to understand the human world better⟩to have more compassion, to be better a communicator, to comprehend more completely the intricate complexities of behavior.⟨Every experience allows us to teach from what we know⟩

What other profession teaches skills and competencies applicable to work that can be so easily applied to one's personal world? Counseling trains people to be more vibrant lovers and livers. Intensive training in observing nonverbal behavior, analyzing motives, handling confrontations, and reflecting feelings helps counselors to be more attractive human beings, experts at efficiently developing trusting, productive relationships. If counselors can do that in their offices, they can certainly do it with their friends, children, spouses, and parents.

⟨Counseling inspires the student to be a knowledgeable generalist, a Renaissance scholar, a devourer of truth in any palatable form⟩We are not restricted to our texts for learning. We read literature, history, anthropology, sociology, biology, biochemistry, education, psychology, and philosophy, and they are all beneficial, even necessary, if we are truly to understand this abstract thing called the human mind.

⟨Counseling permits practitioners to make a difference in people's lives and to see the results in their own lifetimes⟩One of the ways in which we attempt to confront our own mortality is by preserving our spirit long after physical death. Certainly the principal reward for a dedicated teacher, counselor, or therapist is the knowledge that a generation of clients will remember and use the help that was offered. Our profession allows us to productively face our own fears of death and nonbeing by leaving behind those who, because of our efforts, feel less pain. One counseling student confronted his own anxiety, fear, and despair with the realization: "I know only two things—one, that I will be dead someday, two, that I am not dead now. The only question is what shall I do between those two points" (May, 1983, p. 169).

❰Counselors become more wise and self-aware with every client they see❱ Each presented concern forces us to consider introspectively our own degree of stability. Every discussed problem reminds us of those problems we still have unresolved. A client complains of periodic urges to break out of the mold and run away, while the counselor silently considers his or her own rebellious impulses. A boring relationship, fear of failure, career stagnation, sexual frustrations, loneliness, parental dependence, all subjects that are commonly presented, force the counselor to resolve them, once and for all, in his or her own life. The profession thus continually encourages its practitioners to upgrade their personal effectiveness.

At this very moment it may be profitable for *you* to examine your personal motives for studying counseling. Although you may never fully understand all the factors, needs, interests, values, and unconscious processes that are influencing your decision, the quest is, nevertheless, valuable. It is likely that only years after graduation, perhaps after your own experiences as a client, will you ever have a focused picture of your honest motives. This process of self-inquiry, once begun, is self-perpetuating because of the growth it fosters. And the beginning is *now*.

❰We thus commence with the realization that practically all behavior is complex enough to defy a simple definition or easy solution. This premise certainly applies to an explanation of exactly what counseling is and how it works❱

Definitions of Counseling

Counseling is such an ambiguous enterprise. It is done by persons who can't agree on what to call themselves, what credentials are necessary to practice, or even what the best way is to operate. It is done with persons who aren't certain why they want to be helped, what counseling can and can't do for them, or what they want after it is over.

The authors went all the way through master's level programs and most of the way through doctoral programs in counseling without ever really understanding what the profession was all about. Naturally, we could recite textbook definitions that sound as if they describe what counselors do❰And most of our professors and fellow students would eagerly nod their heads in agreement, particularly when our explanations included key phrases such as "actualizing your potential" (whatever *that* is) or "helping people to understand who they are" (as if they might be someone else)❱

For a definition to be useful, practical, of any value whatsoever except as a professional prayer to memorize, it should have certain elements. At several points in his or her professional life—if not on comprehensive examinations then certainly with every astute client—the practitioner will be asked to define what it is that she or he does. This definition ought to be as specific as possible, describing in detail what counselors do, why they do it, and how it works.

A Definition of Counseling from A-Z

We believe that a definition, like counseling itself, should be a process—a process designed to stimulate thinking so that ideas can ferment, evolve, and grow into a *personal* conception. Textbook definitions, although elegant, incisive, and comprehensive, almost always lack one essential ingredient: personalized meaning. We hope you can take one step toward developing your personalized meaning by following our A-to-Z definition.

"Counseling is a profession
with a history and a set of standards and ethics, distinct from other related disciplines
and a process
that is ongoing, ever-changing, dynamic, and open; that is definable and operational with stages, steps, and resting points
that involves a relationship
either in a group, family, or individual format that is caring, honest, and open and that leads to constructive psychological contact
between persons
one of whom is a professional helper with the training and experience to aid the other person, who desires assistance in resolving a personal concern
and demands a special set of skills
in supporting, empathizing, reflecting, confronting, analyzing, and disclosing
and knowledge
concerning how people learn, change, and grow
that can be communicated
clearly, efficiently, powerfully, and in situationally specific language
to influence a client to change "
attitudes, feelings, thoughts, behaviors, skills, and circumstances in a constructive and self-chosen way.

The preceding definition is somewhat general and provides an overview of what counseling is. However, like many other definitions, it is too brief and does not really illustrate the many facets of the counseling encounter. Let us take a more detailed look at counseling and attempt to fill in the gaps above, toward a more fully developed definition that covers all the bases from A to Z.

Counseling, as differentiated from therapy and guidance, helps relatively normal individuals, as opposed to those labeled psychopathological, to

A. *Articulate their reasons for seeking help;*
they listen to themselves, hear their feelings reflected, and clarify underlying reasons.

B. *Formulate their initial expectations and goals for the treatment;*
they think concretely and crystallize options, preferences, and priorities.

C. *Learn the specific procedures, roles, and behaviors that are appropriate in counseling;*
they learn to value honesty, autonomy, and positive feelings, to build strength, and to experience self-responsibility.

D. *Develop a sense of trust and a favorable mind set for change*
by understanding confidentiality, privileged communication, and openness.

E. *Label the specific self-defeating behaviors they wish to change*
by exploring, analyzing, and confronting personal behaviors that are self-limiting.

F. *Explore their worlds*
to collect and catalog relevant data that may be helpful.

G. *Identify with a powerful model,*
such as the counselor, who presumably is more fully functioning.

H. *Share pent-up frustrations and concerns*
through catharsis and self-disclosure.

I. *Feel support from an accepting person*
who is nonjudgmental and respectful.

J. *Confront inconsistencies*
in self, language, images, and self-talk, thereby experiencing discomfort.

K. *Challenge operating assumptions that are invalid, inappropriate, or irrational*
about self, the world, other persons, and problems.

L. *Realize hidden and unconscious motives behind actions,*
the better to understand the implicit payoffs for behavior.

M. *Understand the maintenance system for preserving the status quo*
so that the key reinforcers behind inertia can be identified and challenged.

N. *Accept responsibility for their existence, suffering, and growth*
and make a commitment to change.

O. *Develop options and alternatives to self-defeating behaviors*
and become more intentional.

P. *Formulate a pragmatic plan of action*
that can be set into motion.

Q. *Take interpersonal risks;*
explore risk versus safety issues within sessions and outside.

R. *Test new assumptions against reality*
to determine if new assumptions are more relevant and accurate than the old, thus facilitating adaptive behavior.

S. *Receive constructive feedback*
from counselor and significant others; learn to listen nondefensively.

T. *Rehearse and practice new behaviors*
   through role playing in the session.
U. *Do psychological homework assignments*
   to reinforce learnings and test new behavior in the real world.
V. *Report on progress*
   to aid in evaluation and fine-tuning.
W. *Maintain themselves through self-reinforcement*
   so that new, more enhancing behavior can be internally controlled and
   chosen, resulting in greater personal autonomy and freedom.
X. *Leave without dependency,*
   owning at a personal level the benefits of the counseling and recognizing
   the central role of the self in change.
Y. *Generalize results to life*
   to upgrade and enhance personal behavior in all life arenas.
Z. *Teach what she or he learned to others,*
   to share mentally healthful learnings and behavior.

The above definition is comprehensive, although not exhaustive. It is
intended to delineate the specific behaviors associated with counseling so
that the beginning student may grasp, from the outset, how most counseling
is delivered and what the various aspects of the process are. Exactly why
counseling works is a problem of even more complexity since there are so
many conflicting hypotheses with supporting evidence.

Why Counseling Works

Although at this juncture the jury has not yet returned to deliver its verdict,
we do know that counseling probably works as a combination of factors that a
number of theorists find significant (see Chapters 5 and 6). Rogers (1980)
believes that the nurturing therapeutic relationship plays the biggest role in
facilitating change. Carkhuff (1969) thinks that change is more specifically
the result of the counselor's core helping skills. Freud (1924), naturally,
emphasized the release of unconscious desires, and Ellis (1973) claims
counseling works by teaching people to think more rationally, whereas Perls
(1969a) was convinced that the primary task was to integrate a person's
polarities. Gottman and Lieblum (1974) have evidence to indicate that
reinforcement processes, modeling, and structured practice make a difference. And so on . . . and so on. By now, it must have occurred to you that in
this first chapter (and in a beginning course) it is not likely you are going to
get a very acceptable answer to the question "Why does counseling work?"
Patience.

The process definition presented in this introductory chapter represents our attempt to integrate many of the factors that various schools of

thought find significant. Although there are changes that every experienced practitioner would wish to make in this definition, depending on theoretical preferences and personality style, most counselors would agree that the elements listed in the definition are more likely than others to lead toward productive change.

Counseling is less likely to be effective when the counselor is inexperienced, self-indulgent, and rigid and forces compliance to a personal agenda. Similarly, counseling is more likely to be helpful when the clinician's definition permits a role that is flexible, genuine, and accepting. Counseling effectiveness is often the result of the practitioner's use of self as an instrument of communication and treatment.

Significance of the Self

What counseling is and how it works are important concepts that can be defined and illustrated. But any explanation of counseling, however precise, exists only in a static sense. Life can be given to a definition, vitality breathed into a process, only in the context of a person—the self of the counselor. It is to this self that we now turn our attention.

The self is the crucial, the undefinable, and the most variable component of counseling. Yet it is the most therapeutic dimension of the counseling process. The need to integrate the richness of the person within the boundaries of the process is a major challenge for both prospective counselors—*you*—and counselor educators—*us*. It is not a challenge that either of us can take lightly. We must respect and prize one another's uniqueness, personal preferences, and individual values, remembering that our task is to preserve the salient richness of the self as we direct the learning of a profession. For your part, it is necessary that you are open, flexible, honest, and nondefensive as you work to implant the professional skills within your essential self. The goal is simple: growing toward increased effectiveness both as a counselor and as an evolving being. Necessary as it may be, the task of sharing our self, using it to perceive our clients, make sense of their actions, and communicate our reactions is also quite difficult.

Thomas (1979) explains that the functional purpose of self is to maintain the individuality of every creature, to mark off distinguishing features so that each organism can defend itself against the rest. It is therefore our uniqueness rather than our sameness that gives our self an identity. And the threat to our self increases proportionately to risks we take in joining with another—an experience that is both exhilarating and terrifying.

Perceptual Base of Effective Counselors

It is helpful to think of the self as the primary tool in therapeutic counseling. The idea of self-as-instrument (Combs, Avila, & Purkey, 1971) emphasizes the importance of humanness and the counselor's perceptions as essential to the counseling process. In a sense, the self programs how the counseling skills, once learned, are put to work. The perceptual base of the self also defines the texture of the counseling process>Personal attitudes and self-characteristics that are facilitative include perceptions about self, others, and purposes<Effective counselors tend to

✔ Perceive
   —from an internal rather than an external frame of reference
   —in terms of people rather than things
✔ Perceive Others
   —as able rather than unable
   —as dependable rather than undependable
   —as friendly rather than unfriendly
   —as worthy rather than unworthy
   —as helpful rather than hindering
   —as internally rather than externally motivated
✔ Perceive Self
   —as identifying with people rather than apart from people
   —as adequate rather than inadequate
   —as worthy rather than unworthy
   —as trustworthy rather than untrustworthy
✔ Perceive Purpose
   —as freeing rather than controlling
   —as altruistic rather than narcissistic
   —as concerned with larger rather than smaller meanings
   —as self-revealing rather than self-concealing
   —as involved rather than alienated
   —as process-oriented rather than goal-oriented [Combs et al., 1971, pp. 10–17]>

<Each of these characteristics provides for organizing personal reality and serves as a foundation from which the counselor's self mediates the counseling process> In a classic study Fiedler (1950) illustrated the importance of the self in the counseling process by comparing the quality of the therapeutic relationships in psychoanalytic, nondirective, and Adlerian therapies. He found that experts in each of the three approaches were more similar than different in terms of style and personal relationship. He also found that the nonexperts were more different from one another in relationship style than were the experts and, further, the nonexperts tended to be less similar than the experts in their own orientation. He therefore concluded that theoretical orientation was not the distinguishing variable separating expert from nonexpert therapists, but rather, the difference was more related to personal style independent of conceptual affiliation. It appeared that a common thread unified the expert therapists, particularly with regard to relationship variables. In those instances in which there is a difficulty creating an alliance in counseling it is due more often to the counselor's personality than to the client's motivation (Fromm-Reichmann, 1952).

Personal Characteristics of Effective Counselors

Those counselors who are expert at using the self as an instrument, who are powerful models with the capacity for influencing others, tend to cross theoretical boundaries. In spite of how they label themselves—as behaviorists, humanists, Adlerians, gestaltists, or rational-emotivists—the most dynamic practitioners are intensely aware of the potential influence their selves can wield: as modelers of personal expertness, as reinforcers of appropriate behavior, and as nurturers of warmth and support.

Thus the self is the most significant dimension in therapeutic counseling; what counseling is and how it works depends to a large extent on the personal characteristics of the counselor. The existentialist Rollo May believes that, because counselors work through their personalities and selves as the primary instruments of treatment, it is crucial that certain qualities be evident. According to May (1967), good counselors are at ease in others' company, are free of personal prejudices, have the courage of imperfection, enjoy the process of living, have developed self-understanding, and are spiritually attractive.

Many other authors, such as Maslow (1954), Corey and Corey (1977), Carkhuff and Berenson (1977), Trotzer (1977), Kottler (1983), and Patterson and Eisenberg (1983), have compiled lists of those qualities they feel are necessary for the counselor's self to be in proper operating condition. A composite of these personality characteristics includes self-confidence, high energy level, sense of humor, neutrality, flexibility, emotional stability, experience in risk-taking, analytic thinking, creativity, enthusiasm, honesty, and compassion.

In reading these lists of qualities the student cannot help but evaluate the extent to which he or she possesses them and to feel, upon reflection, how much personal growth lies ahead. Yet in counselor training the development of self as a more masterful being parallels the evolution of therapeutic skills. The self becomes refined and nurtured as a sensitive and operative component of the counseling process. As the self evolves, the counselor becomes more aware of personal assets and limitations, biases, and areas in need of upgrading. It also becomes necessary to understand one's history to put the present in perspective. As the history of each individual self is important, so too is the history of our profession.

Evolution of Therapeutic Counseling

The field of therapeutic counseling and its related disciplines of psychiatry, psychology, social work, and guidance have undergone an uneven progression of development. In the days of our paleolithic ancestors, the first mental health professionals were fond of drilling holes in a client's head to permit the demons to escape. Through the days of ancient Mesopotamia and Persia, the Classical Greek and Roman eras, and into modern times, early therapeutic counselors were primarily philosophers, physicians, or priests.

The primitive days of the nineteenth century spawned the first real counselors, the experts who attempted to heal by talking even if they did so in ways we now find a bit bizarre. It is incredible to think that a hundred years ago therapeutic counseling, as we know it, did not exist. And it has only been in the past fifty years that counseling emerged as a distinct field apart from its related mental health disciplines.

The "talking cure" is a concept that we take for granted today, yet a century ago it was a revolutionary idea that was not only unaccepted but held in disrepute, smacking of witchcraft and the occult. The cathartic method of talking out problems was pioneered by Freud at the turn of the century as a method for treating persons with psychological problems. Although the concept had existed for many years, it took Freud to build credibility for the technique. Today, most people agree that talking over problems is helpful, sharing feelings and concerns is useful, and professional helpers are reasonable alternatives for those faced with problems or difficult situations. Interpersonal communication and verbal interaction form the heart of therapeutic counseling, albeit in a substantially different format from what Feud envisioned. Counselors, clients, and the "person in the street" all accept the interactive therapeutic process and believe that constructive change can occur when a counselor and a client participate in a verbally-mediated therapeutic relationship.

At about the same time (1890–1930) that Freud was interpreting dreams in Vienna, several other significant contributions to the burgeoning profession of therapeutic counseling emerged. Our research base and emphasis on scientific methods, precise observation and documentation of behavior, and the systematic process of introspective analysis received attention because of Wilhelm Wundt's efforts to set up the first experimental laboratory for the study of psychology (1879) and John Watson's work (1900–1930) in founding behaviorism. While his contemporaries, such as William James, were taking a more analytic approach to figuring out why people behave the way they do, Watson introduced scientific and behavioral laws to explain human conduct. Naturally, the influences of both James's philosophy and Watson's science have helped to make counseling so useful.

During that same era (1895–1915), a completely different movement was taking place. Frank Parsons and several colleagues applied the new technology of testing and interviewing to help Boston's unemployed youth identify interests and abilities and to find suitable work. Thus the vocational guidance field was born, enabling counselors to specialize in a particular aspect of human conflict. It carved a niche for guidance personnel in educational settings; yet it also made more difficult the integration of the structured teaching model of vocational guidance into the mainstream of therapeutic counseling.

Freud also left many legacies to counselors that have been less than useful and have served as barriers rather than facilitators to improving the profession. The medical model implicitly espoused by Freud, with its emphasis on diagnosis and treatment of psychopathology, influenced the field for many years. During the Second World War Carl Rogers began to argue persuasively that the traditional doctor–patient pattern of interaction was not useful in counseling. He urged that the essential ingredient in effective counseling was the relationship between therapist and client. His thoughts, at the time, were considered heretical. He suggested changes in terminology that were unthinkable—substituting "client" for "patient"!

In spite of the initially cool reception to the ideas in client-centered theory, Carl Rogers emerged as a significant force in the field of counseling, changing previous thinking about the nature of the therapeutic relationship. In retrospect, it seems difficult to imagine counseling today without the impact of Rogers and his ideas about the importance of relationship variables.

Client-centered counseling became the theoretical focus of many counselor education programs during the fifties and early sixties. On the whole, Rogers was enthusiastically embraced and legions of counselors were trained in nondirective, client-centered techniques. In spite of the general acceptance of client-centered counseling, some concerns were emerging that questioned the nature of this approach and criticized its relevance for many client populations. Additionally, the operational difficulties involved in defining the tasks of the counselor and the difficulties in gathering empirical evidence to support the client-centered approach caused further questioning and exploring.

The sixties and early seventies saw much change and refocusing in the counseling field. The wide acceptance of the Rogerian approach came under increased scrutiny. Carkhuff and Berenson (1967) and Krumboltz (1966) wrote books that were very influential in challenging the field to move toward a more behavioristic slant, while Ellis (1962) and other cognitive therapists emphasized the role of thinking in the counseling process. Other theorists joined the defection: Gestalt, Transactional Analysis (TA), Values Clarification strategies, Reality therapy, and others all clamored for attention and vied for influence.

From this rich inquiry and challenge there seemed to emerge a focus that gained wide credibility in counselor education. Carkhuff (1969) imposed a systematic and generalist approach to the task of helping. He suggested that counselors must be skilled, reliable, and capable of delivering effective levels of core counseling skills. He defined the skills and developed methods of assessing effectiveness. By and large the work of Carkhuff is widely accepted, with much counselor training emphasizing the development of generic skills that provide a base for effective helping relationships. It should be noted that Carkhuff's "core conditions" were built directly on the work of Rogers, with more attention given to defining relevant skills operationally and developing a quantitative base for those skills. Today, therapeutic counseling is built upon the work of Carkhuff, who has developed a base for the skill-development process; Rogers, who emphasized the importance of the relationship dimension in counseling; and Freud, who gave credibility to the idea of treatment through talking.

✳ Table 1–1 summarizes the contributions of many individuals to the field of therapeutic counseling. In a sense, it represents the generic foundation for training in therapeutic counseling. To achieve maturity as a therapeutic counselor it is necessary to integrate the various approaches to counseling within the generic model used in most training. It is a mistake to assume that minimal generic skills will prepare a person to function as a therapeutic counselor. Therefore, in your training you will first learn the basic skills of reflecting, confronting, summarizing, attending, and goal setting (see Chapter 8), and will then expand upon this base from the diverse sources of theory and technique available to therapeutic counselors (see Chapters 5–7).

Therapeutic Counseling and the Helping Professions

It is sometimes confusing to think of all the various labels used for persons employed in the helping professions. Tell someone that you are a counselor and they often ask if you mean psychologist, social worker, or guidance counselor. Often, the inference is that you work with some type of mental illness. The distinctions among them, although professionally clear, are muddled in the public's eye. In this section we will explore some of the differences between counseling and other related helping professions.

There has been much debate concerning the relationship between counseling and psychotherapy. Many contend that there is no essential difference between them and that any distinctions drawn tend to be artificial, tend to focus on superficial rather than substantial aspects, and may present a barrier rather than a help to practitioners (Patterson, 1980; Pietrofesa, Hoffman, & Splete, 1984). The differences, then, may be only a matter of degree along a continuum of depth, emphasis, and usage (Hansen, Stevic, & Warner, 1977; Brammer & Shostrum, 1982).

The other side of the debate argues that counseling is a profession unto itself and that the services delivered, approaches used, and underlying assumptions are distinct from those used in psychotherapy (Belkin, 1981; Ivey and Simek-Downing, 1981). Psychotherapy, for example, tends to rest upon a psychopathological base in which the medical model—emphasizing diagnosis and treatment—is commonly used. Counseling, in contrast, often rests upon a developmental model emphasizing learning and adaptation in response to problem situations. Thus, many practitioners see clear differences between counseling and psychotherapy and believe that, although overlap may at times occur, the typical client interaction reflects those basic differences.

It is our position to deemphasize these issues in our daily practice. Although it is useful to have a clear professional identity, it is more useful for

✳ Table 1–1. SUMMARY OF HISTORICAL FIGURES IN THERAPEUTIC COUNSELING, WITH CONTRIBUTIONS FROM PHILOSOPHY, EDUCATION, MEDICINE, LITERATURE, AND SOCIAL SCIENCE

400 B.C. Hippocrates	*classified types of mental illness and personality disorders*
400 B.C. Socrates	*encouraged self-awareness as purest form of knowledge*
350 B.C. Plato	*postulated human behavior in terms of internal states*
350 B.C. Aristotle	*designed first rational psychology to manage emotions*
100 A.D. Aretaeus	*studied personalities associated with depression*
400 A.D. St. Augustine	*prescribed introspection to master emotions*
1250 Sprenger and Kraemer	*wrote text of psychopathology and symptoms of witches*
1500 Leonardo da Vinci	*combined science with art to recreate human reality*
1500 Niccolo Machiavelli	*brought attention to group dynamics and social interaction*
1550 Johann Weyer	*documented case histories of depression*
1600 Shakespeare	*created a literature of psychologically complex characters*
1625 René Descartes	*attempted to resolve dualism of mind and body*
1675 John Locke	*theorized that all knowledge originates from experience*
1675 Baruch Spinoza	*developed an integrative personality theory with the unconscious*
1800 Johannes Müller	*plotted the physiology of the nervous system*
1800 Philippe Pinel	*described various forms of neurosis and psychosis*
1800 Anton Mesmer	*used hypnotic suggestion to cure psychological symptoms*
1850 Fyodor Dostoyevsky	*wrote complex character studies of anxiety and dread in novels*
1850 Charles Darwin	*set forth an evolutionary theory of individual differences*
1850 Jean Charcot	*scientifically studied hypnosis to give it respectability*
1850 Søren Kierkegaard	*developed an existential concept of giving meaning to being*
1880 G. Stanley Hall	*began first child guidance clinic*
1880 Wilhelm Wundt	*founded first psychological laboratory*
1890 James Cattell	*coined the term "mental tests"*
1890 Jesse Davis	*became first school counselor*
1900 Emil Kraepelin	*systematized the classification of mental disorders*
1900 William James	*postulated comprehensive theory of emotions*
1900 Ivan Pavlov	*described behavioral theory of conditioned reflexes*

Table 1–1. Summary of Historical Figures in Therapeutic Counseling.
continued

1900 Sigmund Freud	*invented first systematic form of therapeutic counseling*
1905 Alfred Binet	*invented first intelligence test*
1910 Frank Parsons	*established field of vocational guidance*
1920 Carl Jung	*proposed theory of collective unconscious*
1920 Alfred Adler	*authored theory of individual psychology*
1920 J. L. Moreno	*invented psychodrama*
1920 John Watson	*propounded behavioristic notions of prediction and control of behavior*
1930 Robert Hoppock	*studied levels of job satisfaction*
1940 B. F. Skinner	*formulated theory of operant conditioning*
1940 E. G. Williamson	*published standard text on school counseling*
1945 Gregory Bateson	*emphasized family influences in psychological disturbances*
1945 Kurt Lewin	*used training group format for personal development*
1950 Eric Erikson	*proposed theory of personality development*
1950 Jean Piaget	*proposed theory of cognitive development*
1950 Viktor Frankl	*introduced system of existential therapy*
1950 Milton Erickson	*focused on linguistic aspects of therapeutic encounter*
1950 Carl Rogers	*proposed theory of client-centered counseling*
1955 Abraham Maslow	*studied self-actualized people*
1955 Donald Super	*introduced theory of vocational decision making*
1960 Joseph Wolpe	*devised systematic theory of behavior therapy*
1960 Jay Haley	*was representative of family counseling movement*
1960 Eric Berne	*introduced Transactional Analysis*
1960 Albert Ellis	*began Rational-Emotive Therapy*
1960 Albert Bandura	*researched modeling processes in change*
1960 Frederick Thorne	*made systematic attempt to create an eclectic system*
1965 Fritz Perls	*popularized Gestalt Therapy*
1965 George Gazda	*popularized methods of group counseling*
1965 Robert Carkhuff	*organized the skills of helping*
1965 Lawrence Kohlberg	*proposed theory of moral development*
1965 Jane Loevinger	*proposed theory of ego development*
1965 John Krumboltz	*published theory of behavioral counseling*

the practitioner to conduct an effective session with a client regardless of what it is called. ‹An unfortunate correlate of this debate is the implicit assumption that counseling is relatively "easy" while psychotherapy is relatively "difficult" and that therefore less skill is needed by "counselors," especially as compared to "psychotherapists.›We could not disagree more with this position. Working with clients, regardless of the labels applied, requires enormous skill. Period.

Counseling versus Psychotherapy

Although we do not stress differences between counseling and psychotherapy, we do believe that at the beginning of a training program it is beneficial to crystalize some of the salient differences and similarities between the two therapeutic approaches as a guide for developing a personal position in this matter, as we do in Table 1–2. If this issue sounds very confusing, it is because most of us are confused regarding whether, if it is indeed possible to distinguish between them, there is a meaningful purpose in doing so.

Allied Professional Groups

In addition to the debate between counseling and psychotherapy, there exists another arena of confusion in the field: that is, differences and similarities between counseling and allied mental health professional groups. Included in these allied groups are psychiatrists, clinical psychologists, counseling psychologists, social workers, family therapists, psychiatric

Focused on in Video tape Lesson #4

Table 1–2. Counseling and Psychotherapy: Some Distinctions

	Counseling	Psychotherapy
Clients	Persons from a variety of walks of life who are functioning and are able to maintain psychological autonomy in spite of concerns or problem situations. Are not classified as mentally ill.	Persons from a variety of walks of life who are often dysfunctional in their natural environment, tending to be over-whelmed by the problems and situations they experience. May be classified as mentally ill.
Coping Abilities	Tend to cope with issues, although they may expend much energy on coping at the expense of growth. Will normally resolve problems or problem issues without counseling, although at much greater personal cost and by sacrificing growth potential.	Clients tend to cope very poorly, feel overwhelmed, at times unable to re-spond. Are unlikely to resolve problems without outside help.
Length of Treatment	Generally short term.	Generally long term.
Approaches	Developmental, adaptive, growth oriented, help to increase personal mastery and sense of self-worth. Build upon strengths—teach new skills.	Psychopathological, remedial, diagnostic. Attempt to develop coping skills, sense of worth. Restructure personality, define skills, provide support.
Goals	To facilitate personal growth; to increase adaptive behavior; to master negative emotions and situations; to improve decision-making and problem-solving skills. To increase autonomy and improve relationship skills.	To develop basic coping skills; to establish some psychological autonomy. To resolve past issues. To manage emotions and initiate some constructive relationships. To cure mental illness.
Setting	Variety of settings with which people come into daily contact, such as schools, churches, adult education facilities, recreational facilities, government agencies; also mental health clinics.	Settings requiring referral or intentional contact. Mental health clinics, psychiatric hospitals, private practice.

nurses, clergy, and others> Table 1–3 compares some of these groups.< It is important to remember that counselors are *not* in competition with allied professional groups: each discipline reflects specialized skills and various professional competencies, which overlap, yet have distinctive components> For example, although clinical psychologists do counseling, their area of training and expertise is more centered on psychodiagnosis, psychotherapy with patients demonstrating psychopathological behavior, and the management of clinically significant mental illness. Counselors do not generally develop expertise in these areas as much as they specialize in briefer treatment modalities with less disturbed individuals.

It is useful to think of the allied professional groups as forming a mental health treatment team that responds to various clients who experience problems within their areas of specialization.< The team concept recognizes the responsibility of professionals to provide relevant services within their respective areas of competence, and further, demands effective communication and cooperation among professionals> Working toward increased professional recognition and cooperation of various mental health specialties reduces the negative effects of implied competition and presents a coherent public profile.

Professional Regulation

The question of licensing as a professional counselor is quite complex. As you may have guessed,< a license entitles its holder to more status, more recognition, and more power> It broadcasts a minimum level of training, defines the range of activities that may be performed, and is intended to protect the consumer against quacks (Fretz & Mills, 1980; Phillips, 1982). Perhaps most important, it permits the practitioner to receive third-party reimbursement from insurance companies for services rendered.

Depending on the state and political climate, licensing can be a counselor's greatest ally or public enemy #1. Some states are completely deregulated, allowing anyone from a palm reader to witch doctor to hang out a shingle, while others are so rigidly controlled that only psychiatrists and clinical psychologists are allowed to practice. Naturally, these extremes are very frustrating for counselors who feel they are qualified and competent experts, perfectly capable of functioning in any setting—be it hospital, school, or private practice.

< Fortunately, there has been a growing trend, one that is likely to continue, for more and more states to recognize the ability of counselors and pass laws to protect our rights> Nevertheless, the student should be aware of the interdisciplinary conflicts: many social workers and psychologists feel they belong to an exclusive club and have politically organized themselves to rebuff attempts to make licensing laws more flexible. The current status presents a varied assortment of licensing and certification possibilities,

✳ **Table 1–3. Allied Mental Health Professional Groups**

Group	Specialization	Clientele	Training	Degrees	License
Counselors	Developmentally based interaction with nonpathological clientele having problems in daily living, including career, education, family, marriage, and personal/esteem issues.	Normally functioning individuals with adjustment problems that typically do not retard daily functioning.	Minimum 1–2 year program with practicum and internship.	M.A. M.Ed. Ph.D. Ed.D.	Professional Counselor (some states)
Clinical Psychologists	Psychodiagnosis, psychotherapy, intervention with persons evidencing psychopathology, clinical management of cases.	Persons with psychopathological symptomology who are often dysfunctional in normal, everyday living.	Minimum 2-year program with practicum and internship.	M.A. Ph.D. Psy.D.	Psychologist (most states)
Psychiatrists	Medical and psychiatric management of clients with clinically significant psychological problems. Provide psychotherapy, pharmacological therapy, hospitalization services to clients.	Persons with psychological symptoms that either are psychopathological or require medical management, including drug therapy. Persons are often dysfunctional in everyday life.	Minimum 3-year residency following medical school and medical internship.	M.D.	Physician
Social Workers	Social casework, family relations, social impact of client problems, organize and structure social resources for clients. Mediate clients' relationship with social structures, including schools, government, and health care facilities.	Persons who are experiencing problems and need to gain access to social services system. Persons who experience problems managing or responding to demands of society or social systems.	Minimum 2 years postgraduate training with internship.	M.S.W.	Social Worker (most states)

allowing master's-level counselors in many states to pursue options as "licensed psychologists," "licensed marriage counselors," "licensed professional counselors," "certified clinical mental health counselors," or "certified marital and family therapists."

Over the next decade, until regulations become better standardized and more equitable, counselors will be well advised to keep fighting for rights, to become more politically active, and to go about our business of proving our competence by the legions of people whom we help. While you should certainly keep yourself informed of the situation in your state, and work toward continuing recognition of your profession through political action, we sincerely doubt that having or not having a particular license will make a significant difference for those who are energetic, motivated, and exceptional practitioners. It is our job, and that of your professors and supervisors, to help you become the best skilled counselors you can be. It is your responsibility to assertively and enthusiastically get the most from this text, your counseling coursework, colleague and professor relationships, and your roles as student, intern, and finally professional counselor.

Summary

In this chapter we have explored the decision to enter the field of counseling from a personal perspective. Honesty and self-awareness are themes that you will encounter again in this book and on a daily basis in the field; they need to be applied at the onset of your studies. The energy, vitality, and commitment you bring to this introductory course, and ultimately to the field, will begin with increasing your personal awareness and understanding of the motives and payoffs for choosing counseling as a career objective.

In this relatively young profession there are many opportunities for creative individuals to make an impact. However, this flexibility of roles also results in confusion among people as to exactly what counseling is, how and why it works, and how it is different from other mental health disciplines. It will therefore become necessary for the beginning counselor to define the counseling process and profession assertively, both to carve out a useful identity and to provide a realistic and explicit portrait for clients who wish to know what services can and will be delivered.

Suggested Readings

Benjamin, A. (1974). *The helping interview* (2nd ed.). Boston: Houghton Mifflin.
Carkhuff, R. (1969). *Helping and human relations* (Vols. 1–2). New York: Holt, Rinehart & Winston.

Combs, A. W., Avila, D. L., & Purkey, W. W. (1971). *Helping relationships: Basic concepts for the helping professions.* Boston: Allyn & Bacon.

Pietrofesa, J. J., Leonard, G. E., & Van Hoose, W. (1978). *The authentic counselor* (2nd ed.). Chicago: Rand McNally.

Shertzer, B., & Stone, S. (1980). *Fundamentals of counseling.* Boston: Houghton Mifflin.

Whiteley, J. M. (1980). *History of counseling psychology.* Washington, D. C.: AACD Press.

Chapter 2

Counseling:

By Chance or by Choice?

Ants leave nothing to chance. All their acts are intentional and deliberate. There are no random movements in their scurrying to find food, wage war, or build the hill.

> Everyone says stay away from ants. They have no lessons for us; they are crazy little instruments, inhuman, incapable of controlling themselves, lacking manners, lacking souls. When they are massed together, all touching, exchanging bits of information held in their jaws like memoranda, they become a single animal. . . . One thing I'd like to know most of all: when those ants have made the Hill, and are all there, touching and exchanging, and the whole mass begins to behave like a single huge creature, and *thinks,* what on earth is the thought? [Thomas, 1979, pp. 10–11].

Ants and their behavior are a perfect metaphor for understanding the difference between choice and chance. Ants are totally predictable, reliable, and consistent in their behavior. The quality of their efforts leaves out the possibility that chance could ever make a difference. For every footstep that wipes out their hill, they will labor to set things right.

Young King Arthur's tutor, Merlyn, frequently changed his student into other living forms so that he might learn his lessons directly from Nature and experience the laws of the universe that apply to all living things. Such intimate knowledge of, say, the ant world would later aid the future king in ruling his own subjects.

> But we need not go on about ants in too much detail—they are not a pleasant subject. It is enough to say that the boy went on living among them, conforming to their habits, watching them so as to understand as much as he could, but unable to ask questions. It was not only that their language had not got the words in which humans are interested—so that it would have been *impossible* to ask them whether they believed in Life, Liberty, and the Pursuit of Happiness— but also that it was dangerous to ask questions at all. A question was a sign of insanity to them; their life was not questionable: it was dictated [White, 1939, pp. 127–128].

Unlike ants, human beings have the opportunity to rule their lives not only by choice but by a series of deliberate, conscious, individual decisions about their lifestyles, mates, homes, and occupations. Although chance variables occasionally enter the picture, humans have, for better or worse, the capability to control much of their own destiny.

It is not by accident, a random throw of the dice by fate, that a student decides to explore counseling as a career. Perhaps many different factors, such as those noted in Chapter 1, coalesced to get the student's attention or to introduce the student to the field. But the decision to be a counselor has so many far-reaching consequences that the student must take responsibility for that choice every day.

In all cultures, therapeutic counselors are empowered to act as models of wisdom, serenity, and guidance.

To Be a Counselor

The action of choosing counseling as a career sets into motion a chain of events and leads to a series of direct and indirect consequences, the impact of which is often initially unclear. The choice to be a counselor, for example, not only will dramatically affect the education, training, and molding of the student who made the decision but will also affect family, friends, and clients. Choosing to be a counselor means opening oneself to feedback, self-assessment, scrutiny, and personal growth. It creates a context in which vulnerabilities are explored, limitations examined, strengths identified, and behavior changes implemented. New awareness will be developed and personal standards modified, often in the direction of increased rigor and effectiveness. All these changes emerge as the consequence of simply selecting graduate studies in counseling and are capable of significantly influencing one's life. A number of other implications flow from choosing to be a counselor:

Making a Commitment

To be a counselor means making a commitment to a profession and a lifestyle.

For every spectacular success there are also failures. Counselors must learn not only to temper their exhilaration after witnessing phenomenal change but to cope with the frustrations of resistant clients, rigid institutional policies, overworked administrators, irate parents, and confusing laws. While there are few greater victories than the feeling of knowing that a person has been helped as a direct result of one's efforts, oftentimes clients do not accommodate our wishes or cooperate with our interventions. They may stubbornly insist on staying miserable in spite of our best attempts at helping them to find another way.

There are times when a counselor will do everything perfectly: patiently build a trusting relationship with a client, gently lead her through the successive counseling stages—exploring, reflecting, analyzing, interpreting, and confronting—and then, finally, the time comes for action. Let's say the client agrees that a divorce is imminent. The marriage has become destructive, her husband abusive. She realizes she cannot grow further while handcuffed. She has worked through her guilt over deserting him, her fear of disapproval by mutual friends, and her fear of making it on her own without a man to lean on. She is ready—or so she says. But time is up for this week's session. She will do her homework and be prepared by next week to make the commitment to beginning her new life as a single woman.

Eagerly, the counselor awaits the report next week. He tries hard not to pat himself on the back because he *does* feel proud. He has done good work. The next week arrives. The counselor waits in his office. And waits. The client doesn't show. She doesn't show! He calls her only to receive the cold announcement, without any explanation, that she will no longer be returning for sessions. That's it. Before the counselor can sort out the mess there is a knock on the door. His next client is waiting impatiently for the session.

Striving for Excellence

To be a counselor means taking responsibility for one's own growth, striving for excellence in one's personal behavior. Every client presents a novel challenge. Five persons who are depressed will act differently as a result of the symptoms they may call depression. Even though there are a dozen major problems that most frequently present themselves to a counselor, there are endless variations on those themes. In order to be maximally helpful to each client it is desirable for the counselor to understand the problem thoroughly and to have had some experience in handling it.

Whereas a male counselor cannot directly relate to the struggle of a female client considering an abortion, and can never have worked it through himself, it is likely that this counselor has accumulated rich personal experiences in resolving similar value conflicts. And although a female counselor can never know the shame of her male client who is impotent, she does know the awful dread of being unable to perform adequately.

There is a consensus among many counselors that each client provides an opportunity, after the session, to look inward, personalize the material, and ask the question "To what extent is this a problem for me?"When a client complains of stagnation in his life, of too many predictable routines and boring people, how can the counselor not examine this pattern in his own life? Fears of growing old, of dying, of loneliness, of failure, of rejection, of loving, of hating, all hit a familiar chord. And the degree to which the counselor has successfully struggled with any of these themes presented in the sessions will determine, to some extent, his or her capacity for understanding the client's fears and resolving them.

A client complains of a bad temper and uncontrolled explosive outbursts. But the counselor *knows,* not just theoretically but personally, the value of a bad temper—how it provides an instant excuse for abusing others: "Sorry. I couldn't help it. I have a bad temper." Beyond such insight, the counselor also knows personally just how to stop himself cold whenever he catches himself acting angry.

Counselors, then, are constantly striving for more mastery in their lives, applying the technology of psychological helping to themselves. At any moment in time the counselor ought to be able to articulate three or four specific personal areas in need of upgrading—and be actively involved in the process

Adopting a Neutral Posture

To be a counselor implies a dedication to helping other people without having a vested interest in the particular directions that they may choose

Based upon his or her particular religious beliefs, lifestyle preferences, and value system, every counselor has a notion about what is generally good for people, whether it be brown rice, plenty of fresh air, a God-fearing home, or an orgasm. Clients, therefore, present the counselor with the dilemma of which way to influence them: in a way that is consistent with the counselor's own beliefs or in quite another direction, one that the client may genuinely prefer

In the social world people are quite liberal in dispensing their opinions on a variety of issues; in the counseling session such casually stated advice can be harmful. Counselors are interested in creating neither disciples nor dependents. They will understand that by answering the client's persistent question "What should I do?" they fall into one of two traps. Either they offer poor advice, which then teaches the client to resent the professional forever and not to take responsibility for the negative outcome, or worse, they offer sound advice, giving the client the clear message that the thing to do with a difficult question is just to run back to the counselor for help.

Yet a counselor always has strong personal opinions on whether clients should join the army or go back to school, get a divorce or have an affair, tell off nosy parents or buy them a present, turn themselves in to the authorities or learn to be more discreet, punt or go for a touchdown. It is first necessary for the counselor to be aware of his or her own values and then, as far as is humanly possible, to block their effects on a client's decisions. Neutrality is the catchword of a therapeutic relationship. While the counselor may feel strongly about choices that clients make, it is also important to accept the consequences of communicating those preferences. This caution does *not* mean that the counselor attempts to hide his or her true feelings from the client, using the mask of professional distance and neutrality. Rather, the counselor works toward conquering the need for an investment in client decisions beyond a professional counseling responsibility to the client.

It is also a necessary survival mechanism for counselors to do everything within their power to be helpful during the session but to refrain from needless worry afterward. The counselor may plan strategy and honestly be concerned with what clients are doing between sessions; however, there is no productive payoff in permitting one's work to interfere with one's personal life. All experienced counselors who have lasted in the field have devised ways to avoid thinking about client problems when they are not in a position to do anything about them

Subjugating Personal Needs

To be a counselor involves subjugating one's own needs, desires, and preferences in favor of the best interests of the client

The principal reason why counseling is such difficult work is that the professional makes a deliberate decision to suspend all distractions—both internal and external—while in session. Whether the phone rings in another room or a siren blares through the streets, the counselor blocks out all stimuli that are extraneous to the task at hand. Even more difficult to banish are internal distractions. To be maximally helpful to the client, to focus all of one's energy therapeutically, it is necessary to immerse oneself totally in the helping role. Attention to a grumbling stomach or an ingrown toenail will reduce one's concentration. To daydream or indulge in fantasy while pretending to listen is obviously counterproductive. And to permit oneself the luxury of liking or disliking clients during a session will only further reduce effectiveness. The counselor, therefore, becomes quite adept in the meditation-type skills of gently pushing aside distracting thoughts, indulgent feelings, and any other internal behavior that reduces concentration, without sacrificing the genuineness of being human

A rationale for the necessity to receive some compensation in exchange for delivering a therapeutic service is that it does require such extraordinary effort to stifle one's natural urges. It is for this reason that counseling is an activity that is far from "natural." It is highly *un*natural to push aside one's urges of attraction, indulgence, and selfishness

Being a Generalist

To be a counselor means learning to use all of one's capabilities, knowledge, and training to help others with their concerns

Unlike the engineer who need only assimilate the theory and mechanics of physics or the surgeon who intensively studies practical medicine, the counselor must study everything related to human behavior It is not enough merely to master the set of generic skills that compose a professional's repertoire without personalizing the knowledge; the counselor must understand why people do the things they do.

The counselor studies mathematics and logic as a foundation for understanding relationships among ideas. Biochemistry, physiology, and psychopharmacology have value for grasping an overall view of body–mind interactions. Sociology and anthropology aid the counselor in understanding interpersonal behavior.

Literature, films, and television illuminate the psychology of characters when faced with conflict. They provide the counselor with metaphors for understanding human processes as well as for conveying ideas to clients. In addition, philosophy, science, and every other discipline help the counselor more fully to appreciate people and their self-inflicted suffering.

In a typical session, the counselor may be expected initially to use a variety of traditional skills, such as rephrasing, summarizing, and questioning. As the process develops, the counselor may employ more sophisticated strategies—role playing or dramatic confrontation. Next, personal devices may be helpful—modeling and self-disclosure about life experiences. The counselor might create intricate metaphors as well as powerful verbal images reflecting experience. In the end, the counselor is willing to try almost anything that could motivate the client to change.

Coping with Discomfort

To be a counselor requires that a person learn to become comfortable when in the presence of others' discomfort.

One goal of counseling is to make people squirm. Until clients become dissatisfied with themselves, disgusted by their self-sabotaging behaviors, they will never change. Counselors often help to intensify this discomfort as a means of encouraging continued flight toward mental health. Confrontation is intended to force the client to face discrepancies, incongruence, and inconsistency. And the counselor must get used to despair. The one place in the world where people feel safe to cry and honestly express their pain is in the counselor's office. Often the feelings of desperation are even exaggerated because the therapeutic environment is so nurturing and accepting. Clients will complain and show rage and hurt. They will cry and scream and stamp their feet. And counselors take the full force of this emotional energy.

It is advantageous to become proficient at facing outbursts calmly. Often it is necessary to reinterpret psychological discomfort as a sign that things are going according to plan rather than as a signal to retreat. Only when clients are uncomfortable may we be certain they are seriously working on themselves. They do not come for a good time.

Teaching through Self-Discovery

To be a counselor involves learning to teach others without their knowing that they have been taught.

I developed the Great Teacher Theory late in my freshman year. It was a cornerstone of the theory that great teachers had great personalities and that the greatest teachers had outrageous personalities. I did not like decorum or rectitude in a classroom; I preferred a highly oxygenated atmosphere, a climate of intemperance, rhetoric, and feverish melodrama. And I wanted my teachers to make me smart. A great teacher is my adversary, my conquerer, commissioned to chastise me. He leaves me tame and grateful for the new language he has purloined from other Kings whose granaries are famous. He tells me that teaching is the art of theft: of knowing what to steal and from whom [Conroy, 1982, p. 271].

Counselors teach through the force of their personalities and the richness of their experiences, focusing the reality of the client so that insights may be gleaned and learnings generated. They do so in subtle ways, recognizing that their job is to stimulate and structure, helping the client to learn through self-discovery. This point is part of the art of counseling because the counselor wants no credit or acknowledgment for his or her contributions, preferring to allow the client to experience fully the sense of accomplishment that accompanies self-learning. Clients need to feel ownership of their learning so they can take the responsibility for both successes and failures.

Dealing with Ambiguity

To be a counselor requires that a person learn to function well with abstract ideas and ambiguous circumstances.

Counselors inhabit a professional world characterized by uncertainty and ambiguity. Clients are often not fully aware of what their real problems are. They report discomfort, vague and abstract, but circle relentlessly when the counselor attempts to help them focus. Very often clients want counseling because they are experiencing a true dilemma wherein no answer or response is truly satisfactory. Consider, for example, the man who has met a woman he deeply loves and wishes to spend his life with. However, she has a child, and he, after some traumatic past experiences, has realized that he is not comfortable in the parenting role. He wants to be with her yet is unable to share her role as a parent. The dilemma is real and no alternative is completely satisfying. He comes for counseling and your job is to help him resolve this thorny issue.

Counselors must develop empathy for clients who seem unfocused, who vacillate daily, and who seem unhappy but don't know why. In a sense, as Tramel (1981) has observed, counselors (and other social scientists) must abandon their search for cause and effect and come to terms with ambiguity and uncertainty, which reflect the reality of the individual. Counselors must relinquish the quest for answers and instead relish the challenge of helping clients with their abstractions and the uncertainty inherent in reality. *To be a counselor means dedicating oneself to the resolution of conflicts that are irreconcilable, solving problems that have no right answers, and mediating disputes among parties who enjoy fighting.*

Being Intentional

⟨To be a counselor means acting by choice but allowing for chance⟩

Intentional behavior that reflects the consideration of options and the selection of choices is a distinguishing characteristic of the therapeutic counselor. A systematic approach to counseling using methods based on scientific inquiry helps counselors to reduce chance effects and to help the clients maximize potential for constructive behavior change (Ivey, 1983). It is also necessary, though, for counselors to be systematic without being too rigid or controlling. They must simultaneously focus on the agenda while capitalizing on the spontaneous.

⟨Counselors must recognize the limits of their technology and the imperfections of their process, retaining flexibility within an intentional matrix⟩ Uncertainty accompanies intentionality, and although counselors must choose interventions, they must also be responsive enough to recognize the variability in persons and environments. Helping clients to know and assimilate both aspects of this reality is to facilitate true adaptability.

Haley (1980) constructed a portrait of the consummately chance-oriented rather than choice-oriented professional: the counselor who is skilled at concealing ignorance and inventing excuses for failure and who, most of the time, lets sessions randomly go where they might, without taking an active role in the direction. Generally, says Haley cynically, when the counselor is in doubt about where to go, he or she can always encourage the client to talk and talk in the hope that it might accidentally make some difference. A second option is never to give too much detail about a case, so that indirection can be masked in esoteric-sounding summaries. "For example, a clinician can say about a woman who has the problem of compulsive counting, 'The Patient was encouraged to explore the origins of the counting compulsion, and the roots of psychopathology were discovered in childhood experiences.' This will sound better than a verbatim transcript, which might read, 'THERAPIST: When you were a child, did you refer to different ways of going to the bathroom as number one and number two?' " (p. 388).

In addition, Haley (1969, 1980) suggests that haphazard, unsystematic, chance-oriented counseling efforts will be encouraged by the following devices:

1. When you don't know what the exact client problem is, then fake it by talking about defenses and theories.
2. Specialize in doing long-term counseling so that the colleagues who referred the cases to you will forget that you didn't help them.
3. Keep the client talking so you can (a) practice "active listening," (b) introduce an air of mystery into the sessions by staying quiet, and (c) not have to risk saying anything stupid.
4. Discuss the past a lot so you don't have to deal with the present problems.
5. Believe that what the client thinks is bothering him or her is only a symptom so you can stall for time while exploring many other problems you know more about.

6. When things go badly in the sessions, blame the client for resisting and not trying hard enough.

‹To be a counselor, then, means resisting the influence of chance effects and professional obfuscation and to strive instead toward developing the wisdom, sensitivity, and integrity necessary to accept the challenge of therapeutic effectiveness›

In the foregoing section we have reviewed some of the more obvious consequences of the choice to be a counselor and have explored them in the context of personal awareness and intentionality. In the next section we will look at intentionality and choice as expressions of the spirit of pragmatism, a philosophy of particular value to therapeutic practitioners.

Intentionality and Pragmatism

Background

‹Galvin and Ivey (1981) introduce the term *intentionality* within the context of pragmatism: "The eventual goal of intentionality is the ability to generate alternative sentences, behaviors, and constructs in any given situation and examine that situation from many different vantage points›(p. 537). Counselors are thus encouraged to assess their interviewing style, identify the underlying constructs that guide their behavior, and analyze the degree to which their skills are, in fact, compatible with their intentions and espoused theory‹Counseling becomes more of a choice- rather than chance-oriented enterprise when the practitioner consistently and specifically measures what is done in the session and then reflects on the results in light of stated goals›

Throughout your counseling career, both as a student and as a clinician, you will be exposed to a staggering variety of seemingly contradictory approaches. One theory may tell you to dig into a client's past for the most minute background information, while another point of view will caution you to remain totally in the present. You will be left in the middle, feeling tugs from different teachers, books, and colleagues to affiliate yourself with one particular school of thought or another.

‹The philosophy presented throughout this book is that *all* theories have something valuable to offer. Everything works—with some clients at some times. A goal for the clinician is to develop a unifying framework or philosophy that allows for the integration of various theories and approaches within a flexible and personal style of operation (see Chapter 7). Pragmatism is just such an option, for it is a philosophy that permits, even encourages, each individual to integrate valuable features of all other existing theories and actions›

‹Pragmatism is the ideal philosophy for counselors because it works toward precision, developing practical, reliable, and useful intervention strategies, and stresses above all else the importance of flexibility> The originators of this uniquely American philosophy, especially William James, Charles Sanders Peirce, and John Dewey, hoped to look at all of human behavior in terms of its likely consequences.〈The pragmatic counselor, then, would choose a particular counseling strategy not because it is convenient, conforms to a favorite theory, or is the most commonly accepted intervention but because it is likely to result in favorable constructive change for a given client in a given situation.>

Contemporary therapeutic systems that combine pragmatic philosophy with an eclectic application of technique to maximize flexibility, practicality, and efficient action include those developed by Haley (1973), Thorne (1967), Brammer and Shostrum (1977), Dyer and Vriend (1977), Carkhuff and Berenson (1977), Dimond, Havens, and Jones (1978), Palmer (1980), Lazarus (1981), Corey (1983), and Kottler (1983). Some assumptions underlying these pragmatic approaches and the basic philosophy of this book are these:

1. Counseling deals with relative rather than absolute concepts—values that change depending on the circumstances and needs of the individual client.
2. Counselors are concerned primarily with useful knowledge, meaningful research, and applied theory that make a difference with a particular case.
3. Counseling relies on functional diagnoses that help to conceptualize a client's behavior in such a way that it can be understood and changed.
4. Counseling combines the best of art and science, humanism and behaviorism, intuition and empiricism.
5. The goal of counseling is to help clients make constructive changes through the use of reliable interventions that have empirical support and a defensible rationale. Prior to any therapeutic action, a counselor should ask several internal questions:
   a. Exactly what appears to be happening?
   b. What do I wish to accomplish?
   c. How will this intervention meet the desired goal?>

If the counselor is unable to answer these questions in a clear and cogent manner, depending instead on intuitive hunches such as "I have a gut feeling that this will work," then it may be necessary to examine personal motives. A detailed analysis of "gut feelings" will aid the counselor to understand more precisely the underlying rationale for intervention choices and will also help to stifle counselor self-indulgence. Before using confrontation, for example, the counselor can ask himself or herself: "Am I confronting this client because he is genuinely disrupting the process or because he is irritating to me?" Beyond eliminating inappropriate verbalizations, defining the rationale for actions helps the counselor to develop for future use a repertoire of strategies that have been found to be effective in similar circumstances.

◁Pragmatism is a useful philosophical stance for counselors because it encourages us to view the profession in a broad interdisciplinary context, thus integrating approaches and techniques from a variety of theoretical perspectives. It also encourages the counselor to avoid an overdependence on a single theoretical construct as heir to truth and facilitates the mechanisms of personal theory building so that relevant principles may be systematically collected from the universe of available knowledge. Perhaps Pablo Picasso best summarized the simplicity of a pragmatic philosophy: "When I haven't any blue, I use red."▷

Reliability and Validity in Counseling

◁Validity and reliability, although technical concepts, are a major part of our everyday lives▷It is impossible to watch TV for more than thirty minutes without using these concepts several times.◁Any commercial challenges our ability to discern the validity of amazing claims made for a variety of products▷Will mouthwash *x* really improve (1) my love life, (2) my professional career, or (3) my social status?▷These claims are made daily and the stakes are enormous. If advertisers can persuade the public that their claims are valid, tremendous success in the marketplace can follow. And so we have all been duped!

Nothing is more frustrating than discovering that the claims made for a product or a service are invalid. We feel angry, ripped off, and taken advantage of, and we resolve to be less gullible in the future. No longer will we accept claims at face value; we will ascertain their validity by scrutinizing the evidence presented.

◁Determining reliability is the other half of the consumer challenge: not only can the product deliver on its claims but do so for longer than 17 seconds?▷Think of the frustration surrounding a product that breaks, disintegrates, or refuses to move on the second use◁More to the point, consider the unreliable automobile: nothing is more useless than two tons of metal that refuses to budge. Products and services must live up to their claims, and further, must consistently do so over their reasonable service life or we will tend to avoid those products and services, seeking replacements or alternatives. Manufacturing and service personnel, if they expect to compete and develop a clientele, must pay particular attention to both the validity and reliability of their products and services, working diligently to achieve a high standard for both▷The same issue confronts therapeutic counselors and their clients.

◁Developing skills, techniques, and procedures that are valid and tend to influence clients to experience constructive change is a primary concern of counselors▷The discussion of validity is thorny. Everyone claims validity for his or her favored approach—and to some extent each is right! Everything *is* valid◁All techniques, approaches, and styles (even the most bizarre) work— with *some* clients at *some* times▷The debate as to whether or not something works can often be better replaced with an exploration of when it works. Kagan (1973) has stated it succinctly: "The most important issue for our field is not if counseling works but rather what methods work consistently" (p. 234).

< We can define <u>reliability</u> as the consistency of valid treatment effects with a wide range of client types. In other words, do your basic counseling/ human relations skills influence most clients with whom you have professional contact to experience constructive change? Consistency of effects is the trademark of the intentional counselor. Achieving reliability in counseling is a function of several factors: selection of valid and appropriate techniques, careful training, and integration of one's personal style into a systematic counseling approach> In a sense, being intentional and reducing the impact of chance effects maximize the potential for delivering valid and reliable counseling services. Such is the essence of professionalism and integrity.

< Achieving reliability in counseling—that is, reducing the impact of chance on counseling relationships—is often related to the counselor's being more consistent. Intentionality refers to the development of a cognitive flexibility integrated into an open and dynamic world view. An intentional person will clarify choices, focus priorities, and implement goals and action> In a sense, an intentional person is an opposite to those who come for assistance or counseling. Often these persons will lack direction in their lives, evidencing an immobility in feeling, acting, and doing that results in their inability to see choices.

< Our goal, naturally, is to help clients create more options, and to do so with methods of demonstrated reliability and validity> This task is a lot more difficult than it seems, for many counselors can feel successful without really being able to prove they have made an impact. This problem has, not surprisingly, received some attention in the literature and is often an unspoken client concern. Personally, we have a responsibility to answer the question for ourselves and to be convinced in our own minds that this thing called counseling actually works, and works consistently.

Outcome Effects in Counseling

Implicit in a discussion of outcome effects in counseling is a challenge to the validity of the process itself. How do we know it works? Counseling can be described as a process that is designed to influence clients toward constructive change> If the process is a valid one—that is, if it does what it claims to do—then we should see evidence of constructive change in clients following counseling, especially as compared with clients not receiving counseling services.

A number of studies (although fewer than one might suspect) have been conducted to explore this question. <u>Eysenck</u> (1952) started a controversy by his conclusions based on a study of 8000 clients in therapy; namely, that they did not improve significantly more than those who received no treatment. As may be expected, these findings generated considerable response. <u>Carkhuff</u> (1969) argued that such challenges to the profession failed to take into account two very basic factors: the effectiveness of the helper and the general availability of nonprofessional helping.

As we have seen earlier, counseling can be for better or worse, and the personal skills of the counselor to a large extent determine the directionality of the helping process. Counselors who function at low levels on basic helping skills can exert a deteriorative impact on clients. Counselors who function at high levels can exert a constructive impact (Carkhuff, 1969). These observations, then, provide one explanation of the puzzling lack of differences in treatment effects. It is possible that within the treatment groups some of the clients (those who had effective counselors) experienced constructive change, while other clients (those who had ineffective counselors) experienced deteriorative change. Thus, when we average the treatment effects for the group receiving counseling, we find that the constructive changes can be counterbalanced by the deteriorative changes, with the result that no *average* differences appeared between clients in the treatment groups and those in the control group. However, individuals may have actually experienced significant positive change. These results suggest that the validity of the counseling process is related to the effectiveness of the counselor who can influence clients in positive or negative directions.

A second factor involved in the lack of difference between treatment and control groups may have to do with the general potential availability of helping relationships. Clients assigned to a treatment group have a counselor and are less likely to seek nonprofessional helping experiences. Clients assigned to control groups will not have counseling and are therefore much more likely to seek nonprofessional help from persons in their environments. If this help is facilitative and action oriented, then it is possible that these persons will also experience constructive change in more informal settings. So it may be that we have constructive client changes occurring in both treatment and control groups because, first, helping is directional, for better or worse, and second, facilitative helping relationships are not the exclusive province of trained counselors and therapists.

Whereas the research by Eysenck (1952), Levitt (1957), Rachman (1971), and others has subsequently been criticized and disputed by other investigators (Bergin, 1971; Smith & Glass, 1977), an interesting and very fruitful dialogue began in which counselors were being asked to demonstrate, to *prove* that their efforts do indeed make a lasting difference in people's lives.

In summarizing the researchers (Truax & Carkhuff, 1967; Bergin, 1971; Strupp & Hadley, 1977; Smith & Glass, 1977; Smith, Glass, & Miller, 1980; Wolpe, 1982) who have been carefully and systematically documenting the known outcome effects of counseling, Osipow, Walsh, and Tosi (1984) draw the following conclusions:

1. Counseling does have a consistently positive outcome effect.
2. All treatment approaches appear to be effective and there is little evidence that one theory is significantly more effective than another.

3. Some treatment approaches and personality styles seem to be more effective with certain kinds of problems and clients.
4. Counseling tends to work best with specific anxieties, fears, or phobias.
5. Counseling is less effective at changing personality traits or improving achievement.
6. Perceived similarity between counselor and client in background, status, and education was a contributing factor to successful outcomes.
7. The longer counseling relationship doesn't necessarily produce better results.
8. Individual and group counseling are equally effective.
9. There is no evidence to indicate that the changes made in counseling will necessarily be permanent.

There are many procedural errors and methodological shortcomings in counseling outcome research that weaken the validity of the results and make accountability difficult (Lambert, Christensen, & DeJulio, 1984). Counselors often complain that they don't have the time or training to conduct well-controlled, meaningful studies. Shertzer and Stone (1980) mention other problems, such as adequately defining and measuring change, developing suitable control groups to compare with those receiving actual treatment, creating accurate assessment instruments, and even conceptualizing which counseling outcomes are actually desirable. No one is exactly certain if counseling ought to help people become better adjusted or more independent, more rational or more emotionally expressive, more risky or more cautious, or if the definition of success ought to depend on the client.

Although we are intuitively certain that counseling works, we can be only reasonably optimistic on the basis of empirical evidence. Our humility is probably constructive in helping us continually to question whether a specific intervention is actually helpful or merely appears to be effective through our biased perceptions.

The Effective Counselor

From the foregoing discussion of the value of pragmatic philosophy, the concepts of reliability and validity, choice versus chance, and the consequences of choosing counseling as a profession, there emerges a portrait of the effective practitioner. The intentional counselor maximizes choice and minimizes chance effects both with clients and in his or her own life.

The intentional counselor embodies the concepts of validity, reliability, and pragmatism in the therapeutic counseling process. The intentional counselor

1. is a *philosopher* in applying pragmatism to the use of theory and technique to help clients experience constructive growth.
2. is a *scientist* gathering data, testing hypotheses, and drawing conclu-

sions about what works with various clients. Strategies and techniques are evaluated in terms of their validity and reliability as the therapeutic counselor strives to develop, within the context of his or her person, a systematic, replicable, and effective helping style.

3. is an *artist* in sculpting clients' insight into problematic behavior and sensitively structuring the opportunities to develop creative awareness and growth in constructive directions. The counselor uses commonly available tools in novel and creative combinations designed to cast the subtle light of insight onto clients' motives and personal dynamics.

4. is a *technologist* who works to apply in a useful and systematic fashion the contributions from basic research and development in the behavioral sciences. The pragmatic integration of learnings from many fields in the form of programs, approaches, and techniques, each designed to help clients experiencing specific problems, is a primary task of the intentional counselor.

5. is a *humanist* who values the essential fabric of the human spirit, is sensitive to issues of human rights, and recognizes the role of values in the process of counseling and living. As humanists, intentional counselors model acceptance, non-defensiveness, and respect within both the therapeutic and the personal context.

6. is a *person,* limited and limitless, who works to maximize self-growth and resist the pettiness and vanity of life. Intentional counselors recognize both their personal limits and assets; they accept themselves as imperfect but strive to minimize areas of low functioning, realizing that the quest never ends. They know both what they can and cannot do and use that awareness to set realistic limits professionally and personally. This portrait of the intentional counselor illustrates and dramatizes the various facets essential to effective therapeutic counseling. Finally, it is important to recognize that counselors are ultimately authentic persons: the qualities described are not layered but integrated and reflect the application of a chosen decision-making process to their own lives and professional development.

Summary

In this chapter we have presented the counselor as an intentional person who is committed to developing a professional style that permits a valid, reliable, and flexible approach to helping clients. We have focused on the need to reduce chance in the helping process and instead replace random effects with intentional intervention. We believe that chance can be decreased as choice is increased when counselors pragmatically, reliably, and deliberately influence client behavior.

Suggested Readings

Bergin, A. E., & Garfield, S. L. (Eds.). (1971). *Handbook of psychotherapy and behavior change* (2nd ed.). New York: Wiley.

Eysenck, H. J. (1978). *The effects of psychotherapy.* New York: Wiley.

Ivey, A. E. (1983). *Intentional interviewing and counseling.* Monterey, Calif.: Brooks/ Cole.

James, W. (1942). *Pragmatism.* New York: New American Library. (Original work published 1907)

Lambert, M. J., Christensen, E. R., & DeJulio, S. S. (1984). *The assessment of psychotherapy outcome.* New York: Wiley.

Smith, M. C., Glass, G. V., & Miller, T. J. (1980). *The benefits of psychotherapy.* Baltimore: Johns Hopkins University Press.

Vriend, J., & Dyer, W. W. (1973). *Counseling for personal mastery* (a tape series). Washington, D. C.: AACD Press.

Chapter 3

The Therapeutic

Relationship

Make a mental list of the important relationships in your life. Include friendships. Add your parents, siblings, and other relatives. Perhaps a few teachers, coworkers, or classmates might also be considered influential in your world. Now, what do your best relationships, all those you have ever known, have in common? What are the characteristics you consider to be most crucial in your past, present, and future interactions with other people?

Important relationships in almost *any* context, except adversarial, have certain desirable elements—trust, for one. Mutual respect, openness, acceptance, and honesty are others. Whether we are examining personal relationships or the unique contact between counselor and client, there will be similarities. For in all kinds of relationships, helping or otherwise, we desire intimacy and intensity. And we might say that the quality we are able to create in these dimensions is directly related to the personal enrichment of our lives. We *might* say the same for helping relationships. We might . . . but we won't.

Qualities of Counseling Relationships

Counseling takes place chiefly within the context of a very special kind of relationship—one that is similar to other successful relationships but one that is also distinctly different. In this chapter we will explore the fundamental aspects of the therapeutic relationship, describe how these qualities are developed, and show how several primary relationship-enhancing skills and interventions may be applied to an initial counseling interview.

⟨In a comparison between personal and helping relationships, the most outstanding distinction would be the inherent *inequality* of the latter⟩ It is clear, from the outset of the first encounter, that the client is in need of some assistance and that the counselor is identified as an expert with specialized talent and skills to provide the desired help. The relationship, therefore, involves a contract in which both parties agree to abide by certain rules: the client to show up on time, to pay bills promptly, and to make an effort to be as open as possible; the counselor to be trustworthy, to protect the welfare of the client, and to do everything possible to help the client reach identified goals in the most efficient period of time. The power between the client and the counselor is thus embodied in a unique structure wherein the client is primarily responsible for the content of the relationship while the counselor has most of the responsibilities for directing its style and structure. Although counselors do make an effort to demonstrate complete sincerity and respect to the client, there nonetheless remains an uneven distribution of status and power. After all, the relationship takes place on the counselor's home turf. There are diplomas and books on the wall. A warm professional atmosphere pervades. Yet the counselor gets the more comfortable chair, and when both speak simultaneously, the counselor usually prevails.

There are many practitioners such as Rogers (1957) and Boy and Pine (1982) who try to minimize the power dimensions of the relationship, believing that equality is crucial to change. There are also others (Haley, 1971; Erikson, 1950; Minuchin, 1974) who make a strong case for the counselor's deliberately and strategically cultivating a powerful position in order to be more influential. In other words, some counselors find downplaying their status to be effective in facilitating change, while others wish to emphasize their capability as powerful models.

The therapeutic relationship is also different from other interactions in that there are relatively specific objectives and stringent time limitations: the relationship exists to seek solutions, and the discussion ends once the minute hand of the clock reaches a previously agreed-upon point. Thus, in addition to many of the characteristics found in other successful human relationships, the counselor–client relationship has several identifying features:

1. There is an explicit goal and purpose to the relationship—to *end* it as soon as therapeutically possible.
2. There is an understanding that one person (the counselor) has more control, responsibility, and expertise in making things go smoothly and helpfully, while the other person (the client) is more important.
3. The relationship is essentially one of interpersonal influence in which the counselor seeks to promote changes in the client through skills, powers, and the force of interacting personalities.
4. The interactions are structured to make the most efficient use of time. Small talk and other meaningless prattle common to personal encounters are not in evidence during counseling, where time is viewed as a valuable commodity.
5. The helping relationship can deal with a variety of human behavior—thoughts, attitudes, and actions—but is often focused on expression and exploration of feelings that are rarely disclosed outside the encounter.
6. To best facilitate learning in any form, Rogers (1969) suggested that the qualities of realness, genuineness, freedom, acceptance, trust, prizing, and empathic understanding must be in evidence within the relationship. He feels it is imperative to value the worth of each individual: "And I am very grateful that I have moved in the direction of being able to take in, without rejecting it, the warmth and the caring of others, because this has so increased my own capacity for giving love, without fear of being trapped and without holding back" (p. 237).

The therapeutic relationship, as the core of all helping encounters, follows a pattern of successive stages. Greenspan and Wieder (1984) use a developmental approach to describe this predictable evolutionary process. *Stability* is initially established through the willingness of the client to cooperate with the structure of counseling. *Attachment* follows as the dimensions of trust, acceptance, and emotional interest are fostered. The final *process* stage includes the more traditional therapeutic work that leads to insight and change.

Historical Perspectives

From whence has come the conception of the therapeutic relationship as we now know it? Rogers is quite open about his feelings on the subject. Many other practitioners also have strong opinions about helping relationships, the ideal form they should take, and how they may best be created. Knowing the evolution of these ideas is helpful in understanding the contemporary status of the counseling relationship.

In modern times, helping relationships began within a religious context: clergy members, exorcists, and other spiritual experts acted as go-betweens in problems between a client and God. The relationship was rigidly defined according to the values of the Middle Ages. At the onset of the Renaissance came Johann Weyer, whom many consider to be the world's first psychiatrist. He condemned the archaic witch-purging practices of religious healers and instead introduced the value of a benevolent, kind, and understanding relationship between doctor and patient. A few centuries later, Sigmund Freud also gave considerable attention to the structure of patient–doctor interactions but stressed a more benign, formalized, and unobtrusive relationship. He was, of course, concerned about such things as "transference" and so warned practitioners of its value and danger.

Historically, the roles within the counseling relationship have not been static. Every theoretical approach has distinct notions about how best to work with clients. Some counselors deliberately encourage dependence in their client relationships, thereby facilitating the transference struggle that Freud (1913) found to be so crucial in overcoming unresolved problems with authority. In this type of therapeutic relationship, the counselor remains aloof, dispassionate, neutral, so as not to fall victim to an erotic involvement that could so naturally proceed from the role of omnipotent love object.

In the therapeutic relationship, according to Carl Rogers and his client-centered school, the counselor becomes the prototype of nurturance, warmth, genuineness, and effective honesty. The relationship is a mutual involvement, a sharing of feelings in an open, accepting atmosphere; the counselor accepts responsibility not only for creating these fertile conditions but for communicating his or her own attitudes and feelings within the session. In his personal equation for creating an ideal relationship in counseling, Rogers (1961) explains his own feelings:

> Here is this other person, my client. I'm a little afraid of him, afraid of the depths in him as I am a little afraid of the depths of myself. Yet as he speaks, I begin to feel a respect for him, to feel my kinship to him. I sense how frightening his world is for him, how tightly he tries to hold it in place. I would like to sense his feelings, and I would like him to know that I stand with him in his tight, constricted little world, and that I can look upon it relatively unafraid. Perhaps I can make it a safer world for him. I would like my feelings in this relationship

with him to be as clear and transparent as possible, so that they are a discernible reality for him to which he can return again and again (pp. 66–67).

A third and quite distinct position is the no-nonsense instructional model of the relationship in cognitive/behavioral counseling. The practitioner creates a businesslike contract with the client to meet certain specific goals, with an action plan for reaching them. In these circumstances, the relationship becomes an encounter between teacher and student.

Recently researchers have been exploring the counseling relationship from another perspective, that of interpersonal influence. Strong and Claiborn (1982), for example, have argued that the interpersonal influence variables of perceived expertness, attractiveness, and trustworthiness all affect the counselor's ability to facilitate change in clients. The relationship is viewed as the vehicle for establishing power and influence.

Regardless of orientation, it is clear that the counseling relationship is a special and necessary aspect of the therapeutic counseling encounter. Indeed, counseling effectiveness has been found to be a function of the quality of the alliance (Parloff, 1956; Truax & Carkhuff, 1967). But although the importance of the relationship is well documented, it is necessary to recognize that a helping relationship in and of itself is not a sufficient condition for behavior change. A therapeutic relationship provides the necessary base from which other techniques and procedures can be applied in an effort to help another person. This base creates the interpersonal context and supportive setting for behavior change: the counselor's facilitative behaviors engender feelings of affection, respect, and trust and conditions of openness, communication, and persuasibility, which then lead to client change (Goldstein, 1980). The progression is shown in Figure 3–1.

Relationship enhancers	Relationship components	Relationship consequences	Outcome
Client structuring Client imitation Client conformity Helper expertness Helper credibility Helper empathy Helper warmth Helper self-disclosure Helper-client matching Helper-client physical closeness and posture	Liking Respect Trust	Communication Openness Persuasibility	Client change

Figure 3–1. Progression from relationship enhancement to client change. SOURCE: Goldstein, A. P. (1980). Relationship-enhancement methods. In F. H. Kanfer & A. P. Goldstein (Eds.), *Helping people change* (p. 20). New York: Pergamon Press.

Counselors as Relationship Specialists

The helping relationship can be defined as a systematic and intentional attempt, using a specified cluster of interpersonal skills, to assist another person to make self-determined improvements in behavior, affect, and/or cognitions. Whereas daily helping encounters such as those between parent and child, teacher and student, supervisor and employee could also be included, it is primarily counselors who are specialists in developing nurturing and productive encounters. May (1983) prefers the use of the term *presence* to describe the counselor's real alliance with a client, who is less an object to be analyzed than a being to be understood. Yalom (1980) considers that the single most important lesson for a beginning counselor to learn is that "it is the relationship that heals" (p. 401). It is the therapeutic involvement with the counselor that symbolically illuminates other relationships in the client's life, as well as providing the opportunity for a real, caring, respectful encounter with someone who is safe. The client feels minimal danger of seduction, manipulation, or betrayal, for the stated bounds of the interaction provide for protection of privacy, confidentiality, trust, and benevolence. It is at once both refreshing and frightening to be involved with a professional who is expert at listening and nonpossessively loving.

The therapeutic relationship helps the client work through feelings of isolation, a condition that the existentialists such as Kaiser (1965) and Yalom (1980) consider the "universal symptom" of humanity. The only cure is communication with someone who is sensitive, receptive, neutral, interested, and psychologically healthy. Imagine the deep pleasure, satisfaction, freedom—the complete and total freedom—to be genuinely open with another person who is doing *everything* within his or her power to subjugate personal needs and focus only on *you*. For one uninterrupted hour you have the absolute attention, full concentration, and vast resources of a specialist in building relationships. This person is caring yet honest, fully capable of perceiving things beyond your awareness and explaining things beyond your understanding. This is a relationship you can truly depend on and use as a model for the kinds of experiences you deserve.

Yalom (1980) further explains that while the therapeutic relationship is only temporary, the experience of intimacy is permanent. The key to developing such a meaningful encounter, irrespective of technique, is through the full engagement with the client in the present moment:

> I listen to a woman patient. She rambles on and on. She seems unattractive in every sense of the word—physically, intellectually, emotionally. She is irritating. She has many off-putting gestures. She is not talking to me; she is talking in front of me. Yet how can she talk to me if I am not here? My thoughts wander. My head groans. What time is it? How much longer to go? I suddenly rebuke myself. I give my mind a shake. Whenever I think of how much time remains in the hour, I

know I am failing my patient. I try then to touch her with my thoughts. I try to understand why I avoid her. What is her world like at this moment? How is she experiencing the hour? How is she experiencing me? I ask her these very questions. I tell her that I have felt distant from her for the last several minutes. Has she felt the same way? We talk about that together and try to figure out why we lost contact with one another. Suddenly we are very close. She is no longer unattractive. I have much compassion for her person, for what she is, for what she might yet be. The clock races; the hour ends too soon (p. 415).

Counselors not only share the attitude implicit in Yalom's moving statement but are quite skilled in their ability to foster helping relationships with a wide diversity of people. From research and experience summarized by Wolberg (1967) and Goldstein (1980) we know there is a specific set of behaviors likely to facilitate a therapeutic relationship, as well as behaviors that will inhibit the alliance.

Facilitative Behaviors	Inhibiting Behaviors
Acceptance	Exclamations of overconcern
Openmindedness	Expressions of overconcern
Reflecting feelings	Moralistic judgments
Open-ended questioning	Punitive responses
Physical closeness	Probing traumatic material
Self-disclosures	Criticism
Sympathetic remarks	Making false promises
Demonstrations of warmth	Threats
Supportive statements	Self-indulgent disclosures
Expertness	Rejection
Consistency	Displays of impatience
Diplomatic honesty	Political/Religious discussions
Structuring	Ridicule/sarcasm
Respect	Belittling client
Patience	Blaming failures
Genuineness	Intolerance
Paraphrasing content	Dogmatic statements
Positive reinforcement	Premature deep interpretations

Counselors must, of course, be consistent in their ability to create constructive relationships with *anyone* who walks in the door. This skill and attitude take practice as well as an openness to new people. This place to start, naturally, is in one's own personal life. To what extent are you, the reader, able to relate to people of all walks of life? It is likely that we all have some more work to do in enhancing our abilities as relationship specialists. A prerequisite to beginning this work is a much clearer notion of the characteristics and dimensions of the helping encounter.

Characteristics of the Helping Relationship

Congruence, Positive Regard, and Empathy

Rogers (1951) followed his early theorizing about the importance of the counseling relationship with a series of research studies during the 1950s and 1960s in which he attempted to develop some empirical evidence for his ideas. The results of these research efforts led him to conclude that there were several major characteristics of the helping relationship (Rogers, 1957).

The first characteristic so identified was congruence: a correspondence between feelings experienced internally and feelings displayed externally. This referred to the ability of the counselor to exhibit a sincere concern for the client. Rogers felt that counselors must not merely use certain techniques and processes but must also *feel* a genuine concern for the client. To pretend to care when the inner feelings are uncaring is to be phony, insincere, incongruent, thereby negatively affecting the development of a therapeutic alliance. Rogers learned that clients need to perceive the counselor as openly and honestly communicating real feelings so that trust can evolve. He believed that congruence is the most important ingredient in the helping relationship and encouraged counselors to work toward developing more of that quality between what they are feeling on the inside and what they are communicating on the outside.

Positive regard, the unqualified acceptance of the client by the counselor, was the second characteristic that Rogers identified. This quality is closely related to warmth and exists independent of the client's behavior, whether positive or negative. It means that the counselor does not evaluate and judge clients' actions or statements; behavior is viewed neutrally, and all people are worthy of respect.

Rogers's research identified empathy as the third characteristic. This denotes the process of attempting to understand, from the client's frame of reference, the thoughts and feelings underlying behavior; that is, the ability to walk around in the client's shoes and know how he or she feels. Empathy communicates to clients that the counselor understands their experience and through this understanding is able to facilitate an increased self-awareness of the client's emotional and cognitive processes. Empathy provides the context in which the counselor can help the client to work toward reintegrating aspects of the personality that have been stressful and problematic.

Attending Skills and Responding Skills

This original research on the counseling relationship was expanded by Charles Truax and Robert Carkhuff (1967) during the latter 1960s. Their work attempted to identify more precisely and behaviorally those central characteristics of the counseling relationship that produce therapeutic change. The most important contribution they made was to conceptualize the characteristics of the counseling relationship as skills rather than as attributes that were a function of personality. Their reconceptualization allowed for further research based on skill-learning models and further identification of relevant subskills important to the counseling relationship. It also makes it possible for most counselor educators to believe genuinely that all students can learn to be more empathic.

Carkhuff (1969) reorganized the basic relationship skills into broad categories of skills and subskills that provided a generic model for the counseling relationship and process. The first two stages of the model—attending skills and reflecting skills—have direct relevance to our discussion of constructive relationships.

Carkhuff identified two important aspects of attending: physical attending and psychological attending. Physical attending refers to the arrangement of the physical surroundings so that they reduce distraction and maximize the potential for interaction. Physical attending also includes variables such as the counselor's body position, posture, and other nonverbal aspects of behavior. It means that we communicate to the client, with all our body and mind, our respect and our readiness to be helpful. Psychological attending, the second component, usually involves the use of reflection of feeling and content to demonstrate to the client full and complete concentration. The skills of empathy, respect, and acceptance are important in psychological attending.

The second general area identified by Carkhuff was the responding skills, which take in the counselor's effort to develop understanding of the client through observation and the development of accurate empathy. This involves reflecting back to the client both his or her feelings and the meaning of the client's communications in such a way that exploration and awareness are facilitated. It shows the client that the counselor understands, from the client's perspective, the issues presented in the interview and adds to the base of respect and regard in the relationship.

Gordon (1975) summarizes the further effects and benefits of the active listening/reflecting mode for relationship building. We include several key points with supporting examples:

1. It indicates to the client that the counselor is intensely interested: "You seem to be saying that you care deeply about what others think, that you feel overwhelmed by their expectations. And that we, you and I, should work together on this concern."
2. It demonstrates that the client has been not only listened to, and heard, but understood: "If I am hearing you clearly, you would like to break out of your shell, but feel so scared that *then* you would be vulnerable."
3. It checks the accuracy of working hypotheses, interpretations, and decoded messages: "You are saying that it's not so much a matter of being able to do the work, it's just that you feel so listless and helpless."
4. It provides an opportunity for ventilation of feelings and catharsis, thus furthering effective flow of communications: "So you're spinning your

wheels, going round and round, feeling more overwhelmed, more frustrated, more out of control."

5. It communicates acceptance of the client: "You feel so misunderstood."

6. It keeps the focus always on the client: "It seems that other people really don't appreciate your efforts . . . and, at times, you're not sure that even *you* appreciate yourself."

7. It moves communication from a superficial to a deeper level: "You want men to acknowledge the total you . . . yet you're concerned that if you demand that, you may end up with nothing—and that really scares you."

8. It promotes insight by trying out new ways of seeing, thinking, and feeling, new understanding and awareness of self: "Even though you say you want close relationships, it sounds like you choose people who won't or can't give this to you. I wonder if you're the one who's afraid of intimacy."

9. It encourages openness and honesty of expression: "Saying you resent your wife's successes is painful, but seems true."

10. It helps the client to solve his or her own problems and accept responsibility for progress: "Even though you feel stuck, you're not willing to share this with your husband. I wonder what kind of relationship you really want to create with him."

The skills of reflecting feeling and active listening thus promote a relationship of warmth and intimacy. A base of trust is created from which all future interventions can be implemented.

Practical Dimensions of the Therapeutic Relationship

The relationship between counselor and client is the primary means by which all therapeutic goals are reached. While it was once thought that the establishment and maintenance of this bond was desirable in and of itself, many practitioners now view the therapeutic relationship as a means rather than an end. Without minimal levels of trust, it is unlikely that *any* productive work may be accomplished.

The client usually comes to counseling with a history of impoverished relationships. With family members, friends, or colleagues there have been some misunderstandings, even conflicts, that lead the client to seek help. The initial suspicions of a client toward new, intense relationships, even a client who feels lonely and isolated, will only be compounded within the strange, artificial boundaries of the counseling encounter.

As we have said, there is an inequality inherent in most professional appointments: the presumed expert controls most of the power in the relationship. Thus, the client begins the relationship at a disadvantage—

unbalanced, overwhelmed, anxious, and confused. Before she or he even has the chance to adjust to the surroundings, check out the environment, and study the counselor, the session usually begins with the question "How can I help you?" Given the difficulties present in the initial encounter, most practitioners agree, on the basis of research, theory, and experience, that the therapeutic relationship must possess certain dimensions to create a favorable climate for change.

Commitment

As in all other meaningful contacts between people, there is an implied, if not explicit, contract in the counseling relationship to act in certain ways and follow certain agreed-upon rules. The commitment to one another is both mutually and flexibly determined but nevertheless specifies the form and texture of the relationship that will develop. The counselor feels bound to this agreement with respect to promises made about what constitutes professional behavior: avoidance of self-indulgence, manipulativeness, and deceit; delivery of specified services; total commitment, in fact, to doing everything possible to aid the client's growth.

The client is also strongly urged to feel a commitment to the relationship, although this personal contract is often difficult to enforce. By modeling honesty, the counselor encourages the client to live under agreed-upon rules: to come on time, give sufficient notice when cancelling appointments, and pay fees as negotiated. Of equal importance is the client's commitment to work with the counselor, to work on himself or herself, and to invest energy and personal risk taking in the relationship. All successful relationships, professional or personal, between client and attorney, mechanic, spouse, friend, or counselor involve a commitment to be fair and just with one another.

Trust

The development of trust in counseling relationships is crucial to productive work. It is the primary responsibility of the counselor to offer interpersonal conditions to the client that are likely to result in trust. But trust is a catch-all word meaning various things and consisting of a number of factors. Several aspects of a trusting relationship are worth repeating: respect for the client's intrinsic right to be his or her own person, warm regard for the client as a unique being, and genuineness, which means being honest and real.

Empathy

Empathy refers to the ability of the counselor to truly understand the client and from a unique perspective. It often involves communicating accurately the feelings and meanings of clients' statements, thereby demonstrating an active understanding of clients' concerns. Egan (1975) distinguishes between two levels of empathy: primary-level and advanced-level accurate empathy. Primary-level empathy refers to the interchangeability between the client's statements and the counselor's responses. At this level of empathic responding, the counselor communicates a basic understanding of the thoughts, feelings, and behavior of the client. Advanced empathy is built upon the primary-level base and emphasizes the counselor's responding in a way that facilitates the deeper exploration of relevant issues. Effective therapeutic counseling relationships are based on the sensitive and timely use of both levels of empathy.

Confidentiality

An essential and unique feature of the counseling relationship (as compared to a personal and informal relationship) is the maintenance of confidentiality to assure safety and privacy. Just as an attorney, priest, or physician must be able to guarantee that whatever is revealed will be considered privileged communication, trust and openness in counseling hinge on a similar promise. It is precisely the knowledge that a counselor's professional and ethical standards protect individual rights that makes it easier for the client to confide personal secrets.

Support

Clients in therapeutic relationships must feel a sense of support from the counselor. This allows them to take risks, to explore painful material, to confront threatening areas, and to work at implementing behavior change. Feeling support ultimately means that the client is not alone in the change process. The client must feel that he or she can *depend* on the presence, availability, and support of the counselor.

Benevolent Power

Interpersonal influence is that dimension of counseling that involves the application of expertise, power, and attractiveness in such a way as to foster self-awareness and constructive change. Lazarus (1981) believes that the most important function of the initial interview in counseling is to inspire hope, to help the client believe in the process and the expertise of the counselor as an influencer. One theorist has even created a whole therapeutic system that capitalizes principally on the placebo effects in counseling, structuring the expectations of the client to maximize favorable results. In this "Placebo Therapy," Fish (1973) recommends using the dimensions of power, expertise, and the aura of omnipotence to increase the counselor's influencing capabilities in the therapeutic relationship in addition to nurturance and acceptance.

Examples include evidence of expertise (for instance, diplomas on the wall), attractiveness (dress, surroundings), and power (managing time in the interview). Each of these social-influence parameters can be used and communicated in a manner likely to develop a constructive relationship and lead to productive change (Bandura, 1977). The use of social influence is a sensitive area because of the danger of manipulation and deceit, which do not enhance therapeutic relationships; thus, interpersonal-influence factors must be communicated openly and within a trusting, warm, and empathic context in order to minimize the potential negative effects of these elements.

We have mentioned several dimensions of the counseling relationship which seem to us to be important. There are many others. However, focusing on developing skill in the sensitive use and targeted application of the characteristics we have described will build a strong base for developing a productive counseling relationship.

Creating a Relationship in the Initial Interview

Some of the theory and research underlying the counseling relationship have been reviewed. The characteristics, components, and skills essential to these relationships can be identified. However, each of these individual aspects must be integrated in the person of the counselor during the interview with the client. The integration process is crucial because the relationship variables will define the context and texture of the interaction that follows. The initial interview provides the opportunity to operationalize relationship skills and provides the first test of the effectiveness of counseling.

Establishing Rules

The relationship between client and counselor is established in their first encounter. Even before the first words are spoken, the two size one another up, assessing the personal competence of each other. The client, usually confused and nervous, will wait for the professional to begin and define the parameters and tone for the sessions. The counselor also bides his or her time, knowing how crucial the first interchange will be to the entire therapeutic process. If ineffective or unsuccessful, the result will be unforgiving: the client will not return for more counseling. Worse yet, the client might return, but with grossly distorted perceptions of what will be involved in the future.

Perhaps the client will view the relationship as unequal, seeing the counselor, an expert, as the authority, the parent, the controller. The client may then adopt behavior appropriate to that situation, showing deference and asking questions; transference, power, and dependence variables will exert themselves optimally as in other unequal relationships, such as those between parent and child, boss and employee, and often, doctor and patient.

The client could also perceive the relationship as mostly equal, especially if the counselor introduces himself or herself on a first-name basis and does not respond with formal detachment. In this case, the client will adapt to the situation and internally define the relationship according to his or her perceptions: "The counselor recognizes that we are equal, that what I have to say is intelligent and important, but we both really understand that *I* need help and I'm here because *he* can offer it."

The initial interview, therefore, serves the function of creating and communicating rules for future interaction that are likely to be beneficial to a productive relationship. In addition to establishing the norms for appropriate conduct and capitalizing on the trust, respect, acceptance, and warmth that are so much a part of the therapeutic encounter, the initial interview also accomplishes several other important goals.

Planting Hope

The client is motivated to make an appointment out of a sense of helplessness. People rarely pay money, risk embarrassment, or inconvenience themselves to hire a professional if there is another way to resolve their concerns. Counseling is usually the last resort, the final step before self-destructive acts are likely to occur.

Clients show up at the first session ambivalent about their behavior and unable to trust their feelings. They want help, they want to change, yet they have also invested themselves in preserving the status quo and will therefore almost always resist, on some level, the interventions of the counselor. They want reassurance, easy solutions to their problems, and simple answers to their complicated questions. But most of all they want to believe that they can learn to trust themselves. Clients want to hope that working for the future is worthwhile. They want to believe in their capacity to make needed changes in their lives. They want hope that, eventually, their pain will diminish and someday be replaced by something better. Clients have hope that we, as professionals, know what we're doing, that we actually can make a difference. Therefore, favorable expectations for treatment, consistent with what can be delivered, must be quickly established in the initial interview.

Assuring Confidentiality

Confidentiality is the verbal contract between two people in which the counselor promises to keep private the communications heard in counseling and the client agrees to believe the promise. Unless such an understanding and basic level of trust can be reached, it is unlikely that the relationship can proceed any further.

For this reason the issue of confidentiality is always discussed early in the initial interview, both to allay fears about how private the sessions will be and to convince the client that the relationship will be safe and sacred, impervious to the questions of a curious parent, spouse, employer, or judge. The therapeutic relationship thus begins with a mutual commitment—that of the counselor to work ethically and competently in the best interest of the client while safeguarding privacy, and that of the client to be as open, truthful, and self-revealing as possible. These commitments will form the temporary bond of the relationship until real respect and intimacy evolve as a function of working together.

Assessing Expectations

Often in conjunction with delivering a statement about confidentiality, the counselor further defines the therapeutic relationship to assure that both parties enter into the verbal contract in ways that will be compatible and satisfying. Clients can come to the first session with fairly outlandish notions about what is possible, probable, or likely to occur. These unrealistic expectations may include any of the following:

- "I talk. You listen. Then you talk. I listen. We take turns until one of us gets too bored."
- "I tell you my problems. Then you tell me yours. Afterwards, I can figure out what I should do by what you have done."
- "I tell you my dreams and then you tell me what they mean."
- "You're like a lie detector. Whenever I don't tell the truth, or exaggerate a little bit, or go through my standard lines, you interrupt me and tell me I'm full of crap."
- "You give me Kleenex and hold my hand and tell me everything will be okay. That's what a helpful person should do."
- "I tell you my problems. You tell me what to do so I can change situations that keep me from getting what I want."

Images of a friend, father-confessor, lover, teacher, coach all emerge in the client's mind as models for what the therapeutic relationship will be like. Many of the misconceptions and distorted expectations can be cleared up after they are discussed in the interview. As the counselor explains what counseling is and how and why it works, the client's images can be modified to reflect a more accurate portrayal. In this process, client and counselor discuss who will do what, in which order, and what is likely to happen as a result of the fulfillment of these expectations.

Collecting Information

Before the counselor can really go to work, some form of data collection usually needs to take place in the first interview. The extent and depth of this activity will depend on the theory to which the practitioner subscribes; a psychoanalytic counselor might spend several entire sessions creating a history, while a behavioral counselor would devote much less time, limiting the focus to specific information about the presenting problem.

Other models for collecting relevant background information about a client's environment are available, most including some preliminary explorations into the client's development, the evolution of the problem, and a description of self-defeating behaviors. In addition, it would be important to know which solutions have already been tried and why the client is seeking help at this particular time.

Most clinicians have a list of favorite questions by which they elicit useful information about how the client characteristically functions. Insightful queries can also create greater intimacy, openness, self-disclosure, and trust in the relationship. The following questions often facilitate the self-examination process and produce valuable data for the counselor. Simultaneously, the client begins to experience the excitement and discomfort of looking inward. Answer these questions for yourself as you review them:

Who are the most important people in your world and how do you spend time winning their approval?

Who else knows that you are having this difficulty and what will you tell them?

What is your favorite part of each day?

When you feel a lot of pressure, what kinds of things do you usually do to calm yourself?

When are the specific times in your daily life in which you feel most uncomfortable and out of control?

Regardless of which questions or data collecting model are selected, the intention in the initial interview is to complete a preliminary inventory of the client's complaints, symptoms, and concerns.

Identifying Problems

The identification of a client's complaints eventually leads to a working diagnosis. Since counselors aren't restricted to a medical model that limits labels to categories of psychopathology, they are able to concentrate on functional diagnoses that describe specific behavior patterns for each client. It is not necessary for the counselor to think in terms of "neurotic," "schizophrenic," or "dependent personality." Instead, efforts are made for the counselor and client to label self-defeating behaviors in specific, operational, and useful ways during the initial interview.

Beginning Intervention

In addition to the traditional uses of the initial interview to begin the therapeutic relationship and collect useful information, Kovacs (1982) feels that other goals take even greater precedence. The counselor must intervene in the very first session on some level "to make at least a small dent in the stasis into which the patient has been locked for some time now" (p. 148). Counseling starts immediately in the first session. It is not enough merely to initiate the relationship, fill out forms, set goals, or create structure. They are but the means of bringing a sense of commitment to the counseling relationship.

First-Session Agenda

The list below summarizes steps that are important in the first session. Each of these components are part of a flexible agenda in which the counselor may simultaneously collect needed information and establish a therapeutic relationship that is equitable, productive, and caring.

Opening. Begin the interview dynamically and enthusiastically sensitizing the client into the excitement of change.

Route. Find out through which avenue the client decided to seek help, how the decision was made, and why this particular choice was made.

Reason. For what reason is the client deciding to get help? Why now?

Experience in counseling. What is the client's previous experience with counseling? Who has she/he seen before and what was it like?

Expectations. What are the client's expectations for treatment? Do they relate to previous counseling experience? What does the client believe will happen?

Definition. Misconceptions and predictably unrealistic expectations can be corrected when the counselor provides a definition of counseling, detailing how the process works and who has responsibility for each part.

Confidentiality. Discussing confidentiality is very important in establishing trust.

Search for content. Identify areas appropriate for counseling content, including presenting problems, self-destructive behavior, and unresolved conflicts.

Important people. Explore the people most important in the client's world, especially those who have a vested interest in the treatment outcome.

Functional level. Assess the functional level of the client across a broad spectrum of behaviors—intelligence, resilience, confidence, exercise, sleeping and eating routines, dexterity, perceptual and cognitive capacities, life skills, and values.

Structure. Determine a structure for the particular client and counseling situation that will make significant progress more likely.

Commitment. Secure a commitment from the client to change and willingness to work towards counseling goals.

Goals. Specifically work with the client to define realistic goals for the counseling that can be reduced to subgoals for and between future sessions.

Summary. Review or, better yet, have the client evaluate what his/her perceptions and feelings are about the first session, the counselor, and their relationship.

Homework. Translate the issues highlighted in the summary into a self-determining homework assignment so that action may continue between sessions.

Closing. Ending the first session, solidifying the relationship, and setting future appointments are relevant details in this final step (Dyer & Vriend, 1974; Vriend & Kottler, 1980).

Summary

Considering the energy, motivation, courage, and desperation required for a client to initiate the first appointment, anxiety during the first encounter is usually quite high. This initial interaction in the counseling relationship is marked by fear—fear of what might happen or what might not happen; fear that there is no cure; fear that there *is* a cure but that it will involve a lot of work; fear the counselor might tell someone else about the session; fear about what friends, family, even the receptionist might think about the fact that the client needs help; fear of revealing deeply guarded secrets; and perhaps most of all, fear of entering into an intense human relationship.

That the counselor is able, often within the first few minutes, to relieve a client's apprehensions is a testimony to the consummate skill of the professional who is experienced at relationship building. Everything in the easy manner, the calm self-confidence of the counselor indicates that this is a person who is comfortable with intimacy. The soft smile, soothing voice, relaxed posture, and interested eyes all communicate an authenticity that helps the client to trust, to open up, to feel prized. Rapport is developed not by accident, nor by magic, but by the deliberate efforts of the well-trained counselor who understands the core conditions of nurturance in human relationships and can create them at will.

Suggested Readings

Avila, D. L., Combs, A. W., & Purkey, W. W. (eds.) (1977). *The helping relationship sourcebook* (2nd ed.). Boston: Allyn & Bacon.

Benjamin, A. (1974). *The helping interview* (2nd ed.). Boston: Houghton Mifflin.

Boy, A., & Pine, G. (1982). *Client-centered counseling: A renewal.* Boston: Allyn & Bacon.

Brammer, L. (1984). *The helping relationship* (3rd ed.). Englewood Cliffs, N. J.: Prentice-Hall.

Carkhuff, R. R., & Berenson, B. G. (1977). *Beyond counseling and therapy* (2nd ed.). New York: Holt, Rinehart & Winston.

Egan, G. (1982). *The skilled helper: A model for systematic helping and interpersonal relating* (2nd ed.). Monterey, Calif.: Brooks/Cole.

Keefe, T., & Maypole, D. E. (1983). *Relationships in social service practice.* Monterey, Calif.: Brooks/Cole.

Lambert, M. J. (1983). *Psychotherapy and patient relationships.* Homewood, Ill.: Dow Jones-Irwin.

Rogers, C. R. (1969). *Freedom to learn.* Columbus, Ohio: Charles E. Merrill.

Chapter 4

Settings for

Therapeutic Counseling

STUDENT: Where can I work after I get my counseling degree?

PROFESSOR: Nowhere and everywhere.

STUDENT: Huh?

PROFESSOR: You're feeling confused and frustrated because the question is more complex than you thought.

STUDENT: Actually I'm angry because you're evading my question with that active listening stuff.

PROFESSOR: What would you like to do with your degree?

STUDENT: See what I mean? There you go again.

PROFESSOR: OK. The reason I answered your question the way I did is that I wanted to be honest with you.

STUDENT: Yes. I appreciate that. But I'm putting all this time and work into my studies. I have a right to know what my degree will qualify me to do.

PROFESSOR: Yes, you have a right to know. In one sense your counseling degree qualifies you to do nothing at all. You will see very few job openings in the paper under the heading "counselor." Very few people—employers, friends, family—will know what a counselor is qualified to do. There aren't many precedents from the courts, the legislature, the media that will prescribe what you are entitled to do and where you are entitled to do it.

STUDENT: This I already know. I looked in the Yellow Pages under "Counselor" and found astrologers, dietitians, palm readers, finance companies, employment agencies, not to mention the usual assortment of mystics, and guidance people. . . .

PROFESSOR: That is true. However, there is also a number of fairly specific slots for counselors to fit in and a virtually unlimited market for creative professionals to develop needed services. That is what I meant when I said that counselors work nowhere and everywhere. Although your degree does not qualify you to do one particular job, there are a hundred different ways that you could put your training to work.

STUDENT: But outside of school counselors and ministers, perhaps a crisis center, college dormitory, or probation department, I've never heard of any other places where counselors can work. I mean, we're not exactly like psychiatrists—everyone *knows* what they do and where they are supposed to work.

PROFESSOR: That's just it. Counselors aren't as limited to working in specific settings, such as hospitals or clinics, or with specific populations like neurotics and psychotics. Counselors work with relatively normal people in almost any place where they hang out—in senior citizen homes or playgrounds.

STUDENT: I know I'm supposed to get better at dealing with ambiguity and abstractions, but couldn't you be a little more specific?

PROFESSOR: Sure. But the possibilities that I name are limited by my own meager imagination. Counselors create jobs for themselves in industry, for example. It is relatively easy to convince corporate executives that profit can be increased if morale is improved among workers. We have had graduates hired to reduce absenteeism, drug abuse, and interpersonal conflicts in companies. Sometimes they also get jobs in public relations or personnel offices. In fact, what training could possibly be better for people management at any level? Counseling teaches you to be sensitive to others' feelings, to respect their rights, to selectively reinforce productive behavior. You learn to confront people nondefensively, to stimulate creativity, to encourage growth at all levels. You tell me where counselors could work.

STUDENT: I just thought about all the creative roles counselors could play in a hospital, for instance. Patients don't exactly feel good about being there. Maybe a counselor-at-large could help prepare people psychologically for their operations.

PROFESSOR: Exactly. Graduates have been hired to do just that, for one thing. Counselors also work as part of teams in other settings. They work with medical personnel in mental health clinics, with teachers, with attorneys, and with administrators. They work everywhere and anywhere that they can persuade people their services are helpful.

STUDENT: Now I'm really confused. How can I possibly decide which direction I should go in?

Several years ago it would have been unheard of to include a chapter such as this one in an introductory text. Historically counselors were prepared for only one setting—schools. But times have changed. School enrollment and funding have decreased. And the demand for counselors in other settings is on the rise.

What Counselors Have in Common

The needs and requirements of a particular environment determine, in part, the adaptations and behavior of organisms in that setting. The Manhattan pigeon, for instance, a mutant bird form that has accommodated to city life, has survived, even flourished, because of its ability to evade taxis, shoppers' feet, and dogs. As Charles Darwin discovered in his travels, there is a staggering variety of species that have successfully adapted to their environments—20,000 different butterflies, 40 kinds of parrots, and 300 species of hummingbird. There is also potentially an endless variety of counselors, each species having successfully adapted to the demands of the work environment. Every client population, geographical area, cultural heritage, institutional policy, physical facility, and psychological climate subtly shapes a new species of counselor. It is even difficult, on the basis of the everyday practice of professionals, to recognize that they are nevertheless members of the same evolutionary family. Even so, there are probably more similarities than differences among therapeutic counselors in various settings. Before we profile the roles of counselors in the places where they work, it is first helpful to understand what they all share in common.

A Unique Identity

All counselors, irrespective of their work settings, identify themselves as part of a shared profession that is distinguished from other helping disciplines. Counseling is *not* the same as social work, psychology, guidance, psychiatry, or education, even though those other professionals often practice counseling in some form. Each field, however similar in its methods and goals, arises out of quite different settings. Psychiatry is a specialty of medicine. Social work came from the streets, psychology from the university, and counseling from the schools. In spite of their recent trends toward convergence, each helping profession is indelibly marked by its birthplace.

Many Different Roles

Osipow et al. (1984) grouped the varied tasks of the counselor into five basic categories, to which we add a few more contemporary roles.

1. *Individual counseling* consists of those one-to-one interactions with clients in which the therapeutic process is applied to resolving personal concerns, career and educational decisions, and problems of human adjustment.

2. *Individual assessment* comprises observation, information seeking, and interpretation of a person's behavior in areas that might include performance, achievement, aptitude, personality, and interests. The results of assessment are valuable for screening, placement, diagnosis, evaluation, and planning treatment approaches.

3. *Group work* structures may be used to accomplish more efficiently the goals of individual counseling. Participants have the added advantages of interaction. Counselors also work in guidance groups in which they serve a more active role, designing educational exploration experiences, providing information, and stimulating personal awareness and growth.

4. *Consultation* activities involve initiating changes on an organizational level, often by working on program development. Counselors consult with the human and organizational components of systems to help the individual parts make a more unified whole. Counselors, as human relations specialists, will intervene to fix or prevent the problems that arise from interpersonal conflict.

5. *Administration* plays a part in many counselors' work: directing the activities of a school, agency, or organization. Public relations, quality control, fund raising, conducting meetings, processing paperwork, and decision making are major components of this kind of work.

6. *Supervision* is a significant role of all experienced practitioners in helping those who are less capable. The counselor may conduct in-service workshops and provide individual or group supervision sessions that may be either emotionally or behaviorally focused. Responsibility for staff training and development may also include attention to improving morale.

7. *Research* is a significant part of determining professional effectiveness. Counselors are frequently required to justify their existence and to demonstrate to funding agencies, regulatory commissions, citizens' advisory groups, and boards of trustees that they are earning their salaries. Research is also crucial in communicating the result of experimentation to other professionals so the field can continue to grow.

A Set of Generic Skills

Regardless of their work settings, theoretical orientation, training program, and client population, counselors all use the same intervention skills:

- self-disclosure—sharing aspects of self to deepen the relationship and facilitate movement;
- confrontation—inviting a person to examine discrepancies in personal behavior and their consequences;
- active listening—attending to all the messages, both verbal and nonverbal, communicated by the client;
- goal setting—assisting the client to set behaviorally measurable courses of action;
- interpretation—attempts to impart meaning to the client by introducing new concepts and/or frames of reference;
- questioning—queries designed by the counselor to elicit further information and/or stimulate further exploration;
- reassurance—the use of psychological or emotional supports during periods of high client anxiety;
- modeling—helping a client to learn new behaviors through vicarious experience and imitation;
- reinforcing—rewarding adaptive behavior through the use of praise or other techniques in an attempt to help a client repeat desired behaviors;
- empathy—the communication of both the feelings and the meanings implied in a client's statements;
- immediacy—helping the client to focus on the here-and-now aspects of counseling, including the counselor–client relationship;
- respect—communicating the counselor's prizing and valuing of the client;
- genuineness—communicating a sense of sincerity, honesty, spontaneity, and openness to the client.

The use of these generic skills is by no means limited to counselors; however, counselors tend to depend on them as a basis for initiating the counseling process and developing an effective counseling relationship. In addition, counselors also use a wide variety of other specialized intervention skills, which depend on theoretical preferences.

A Set of Common Goals

Goals common to counselors and serving to clarify professional identity include:

1. helping clients to work constructively toward life/career planning;
2. helping clients to anticipate, plan, and react constructively to developmental issues and transitions;
3. helping clients to integrate thinking, feeling, and behavior into a congruent expression of self;
4. helping clients to respond productively to stress and reduce its negative impact on their lives;
5. helping clients to develop effective interpersonal skills so that relationships with peers, family, and colleagues can have constructive potential;
6. helping clients to assess strengths and identify weaknesses so that they may develop more personal awareness;
7. helping clients to become aware of the holistic nature of life and to integrate effective principles of living into psychological, physical, and social aspects of their lives;
8. helping clients develop more choices in their lives, with accompanying skills to make constructive decisions;
9. helping clients to become independent of the counseling in the shortest time possible.

Both Developmental and Remedial Orientation

Counselors are interested in and trained for helping individuals to anticipate issues and concerns, develop adaptive life skills, respond constructively to issues and problems, and work toward psychological growth and increased personal mastery. Counselors choose and prize their role because of its orientation toward life-skill development, with an emphasis on improved problem-solving abilities and decision-making skills, as opposed to an orientation that focuses exclusively on diagnosis, evaluation, and remediation.

Although counselors can and do use their knowledge of personality theory, psychopathology, and emotional dysfunctions to work therapeutically, they often focus on prevention of problems before they become more severe. Counselors tend to distinguish themselves as well-trained experts working with those who don't necessarily have neurotic or psychotic symptoms. There are, however, many counselors operating within the mental health system who also do remedial work. The principal advantage of counseling practitioners, in contrast to social workers, psychologists, and psychiatrists, is that they can help people without their being stigmatized or labeling themselves as dysfunctional. One need not be "sick" or "mentally ill" to seek the services of a professional counselor, whereas insurance regulations specifically mandate to the other professions that there must be evidence of a medically defensible diagnosis of mental illness or a significant disturbance of conduct before treatment can be administered.

The role of the counselor is not to instruct but to stimulate the natural growth and potential inherent in human beings. As persons develop, they have the capability to initiate, expand, and maintain psychological growth. In fact, many (Newman & Newman, 1984; Troll, 1975; Neugarten, 1968; Schlossberg, 1984) consider this capacity to be an essential feature of adult development. The crystallization of a client's irreconcilable conflict and the client's resulting discomfort are tools often used by counselors. The client can resolve that anxiety by moving to a more mature developmental stage, which will allow for an integration of the conflict and subsequent reduction in personal discomfort.

Counselors rely heavily on the work of developmental theorists as they attempt to stimulate clients to initiate developmentally relevant growth. Developmental work focuses on client issues and may include psychosexual development (Freud, 1924), cognitive development (Piaget, 1926), psychosocial development (Erikson, 1950), career development (Super, 1957), moral development (Kohlberg, 1969), or ego development (Loevinger, 1976), among many possibilities (see Table 4–1). This core of knowledge may be described as follows:

1. Human development proceeds in a series of stages leading to increasingly complex behaviors.
2. These stages are invariant and sequential.
3. They are genetically determined and adaptive to the culture and environment.
4. The stages alternate between periods of well-adjusted equilibrium and periods of unstable disequilibrium.
5. Growth may be encouraged by stimulating a person to restore equilibrium at a higher stage of development.

It is the work of the counselor to help the client translate immediate issues of concern into a relevant developmental framework so the necessary growth can be identified and initiated. Pragmatically applying developmental theory, the counselor seeks to stimulate client growth toward successive stages of human maturity. During counseling sessions, therefore, conflicts are examined that cannot be resolved at current primitive levels of moral or emotional development. For example, a person operating at Kohlberg's Stage 3 level of moral maturity, wherein the reason for conforming to ethical standards is to avoid others' disapproval, would have great difficulty resolving personal struggles. The counselor would work toward helping the person to develop standards of a more personal nature in order to deal with such questions as these: "Can I lie in order to avoid hurting my brother's feelings?" "Ought I to have an affair?" "Is smoking pot OK even though it's illegal?" "Am I allowed to pursue my own goals selfishly, even at the expense of others' progress?"

Teamwork

It is rare to find a counselor who works alone; most counselors work in institutional or clinical settings as part of a team that is responsible for a

Table 4–1. Developmental Stage Theories

Theorist	Aspect of Development	Age Period			
		Infancy	Childhood	Adulthood	Old Age
Sigmund Freud	psychosexual	oral stage	anal stage, phallic stage, latent stage	genital stage	
Jean Piaget	cognitive	sensorimotor	preoperational, concrete operations	formal thought	
Erik Erikson	Psychosocial	trust versus mistrust	autonomy versus shame and doubt, initiative versus guilt, industry versus inferiority	identity versus role confusion, intimacy versus isolation	generativity versus stagnation, integrity versus despair
Donald Super	career	growth of self-concept	exploration of occupational roles	establishment of career	maintenance of position, decline in power
Lawrence Kohlberg	moral	punishment orientation	individual self-interest, approval seeking, authority maintaining	social contract	universal ethics
Jane Loevinger	ego	presocial	symbiotic, impulsive self-protective	conformist, conscientious	autonomous, integrated

range of activities or services, only one aspect of which is counseling>For example, many counselors work in business and industry settings, helping employees with personal, marriage, career, or substance-abuse problems that can affect their work attitudes and productivity. There, they frequently consult their manager, as well as supervisors, union representatives, personnel department representatives, and others in the work environment. The counselor is a vital member of a team and strives to work in concert with colleagues to advance institutional goals and provide help to individual employees.<Counselors also maintain an active professional liaison with community agencies, mental health clinics, and so on>The same pattern holds true in most other settings, for counselors are specialists in resource identification, consultation and individual counseling.

A Day in the Life

The diversity of counselors' work in various settings can best be illustrated by a typical day at the office. What follows is a realistic glimpse of counselors in each of several traditional and nontraditional roles, including a sampling of the frustrations and problems as well as the excitement and satisfaction.

Private Practice

Through the groggy dream-mist the counselor struggled toward alertness, finally achieving enough to figure out who she was talking to and what the situation was. She calmed the man down and firmly instructed him to take a hot bath, try to relax, and write his feelings down on paper. She scheduled an appointment for him the next day and then tried to go back to sleep.

The counselor has now arrived at her office, which she shares with other professionals in private practice—a few social workers, a psychologist, and a part-time psychiatrist. Her 9:00 client already sits in the waiting room, but first she returns her telephone messages. One call is from a client who wants to cancel her appointment in the middle of the day. The counselor doesn't know whether to feel disappointed because it is too late to fill that spot or relieved because now she has an unanticipated but needed break to catch up on her paperwork. Next she calls a physician whom she has been trying to reach for months, hoping to arrange a lunch meeting and discuss possible referrals. He is out of his office.

The first of six clients for the day then enters her office. She is relatively easy to work with, is highly motivated, pays her bills on time, and will make rapid progress. The counselor struggles with herself during the session because they have just successfuly completed working on the originally stated problem. The client feels great. Her marriage has stabilized. But she wants to continue the sessions. The counselor reinforces the idea that one can never have enough counseling but silently wonders if she is saying that because she means it or because she needs the money. It is such a pain for her to get new referrals.

Yet she feels so proud of her work, her competence, her ability to make a difference in people's lives. In private practice there is the constant pressure to become more skilled at helping; if not, the clients won't return or send their friends. And all over the community she can see the results of her efforts. Her reputation is slowly beginning to build.

Two more clients in the morning. Then lunch. She loves the freedom of answering only to herself and decides to do some shopping and visit with a friend. Back to the office and an hour of paperwork—progress notes, correspondence, forms. A new referral calls but the counselor can't persuade her to come in for an appointment because there are financial difficulties. Maybe she'll call back. A few colleagues are free, so they sip tea together and chat about their day. One colleague in particular is feeling much stress because he has just had a draining session with a client skilled at playing games. Back to work.

The counselor makes a few more calls, including one seeking referrals from a school system and one offering an in-service program for staff on stress management. The company agrees to let her make a presentation. She feels ecstatic: at last, a breakthrough! Then she makes a follow-up call to an ex-client who is still doing quite well and appreciates the counselor's continuing concern.

The clients file in again until early evening. She feels exhausted after so many consecutive sessions. "Is the money worth all the energy it takes?" she wonders as she puts the finishing touches on her case notes. "But it *is* lucrative, and the freedom is wonderful. I like being an important part of so many people's lives and I especially appreciate not having to answer to a boss."

Mental Health Center

The community mental health center is an oasis of support in an isolated rural area. The counselor is still apprehensive about fitting into a culture that is so foreign to his experiences as a city dweller. Yet in a tight economy he felt it a necessary adjustment to go where the work is—in this case, to a large organization of social workers, psychologists, psychiatrists, health educators, and counselors who service a three-county area populated mostly by farmers and factory workers.

The day begins with a planning session for his team. Predictably, the administrator once again reminds everyone to keep up with the paperwork. The counselor groans inwardly as he remembers the stack of progress notes and treatment plans that require his attention. He is then happily distracted by a proposal to do more outreach with the aged. He quickly volunteers to head up a study group to do a needs assessment in the community and prepare materials for several grant proposals. What a coup it would be to direct his own project—especially in such a novel area as counseling older adults. His mind drifts away from the more boring parts of the meeting as he thinks about his own relationship with his grandfather. He resolves to interview the 81-year-old man to see how he thinks counselors could be more helpful to his generation.

Various other staff members present their reports, all jockeying for power and more money to run their individual projects. While the counselor deplores the politics, the personality conflicts, and the interpersonal struggles, he nevertheless jumps in with both feet so he isn't left behind. The clinical director schedules supervision conferences. The medical director reviews the medications of several clients. Finally, one hour late, the administrator closes the meeting with tips on appropriate conduct during the upcoming accreditation audit.

Finally, the real fun starts. The counselor completes two counseling sessions before lunch, the first with a family of six, two of them teenagers whose strivings for independence are hard on all of them. The second session seems calm by comparison: a depressed woman discloses the emptiness in her life and her frustration in trying to find a man.

As the counselor joins several colleagues for lunch he rethinks how to regain more control with the family. The food is lousy, but the conversation is always lively, usually centered on bits of gossip and different perspectives on particular cases. Before he can finish dessert he is sidetracked by the assistant director, who wants to know if she can count on his support for proposed changes in promotion policy. The counselor gives an ambiguous response until he can figure out the political consequences of taking one side or the other during the fight. He decides to be neutral, the safest plan considering his own vulnerable position.

He rushes to a group session he has scheduled with seven teenagers to help them become more vocationally marketable; they are most cooperative, possibly because they get to leave school early for the experience. The counselor absolutely loves his groups—the energy is incredible! This week the kids spend time complaining about their parents' expectations. The counselor structures a successful role-playing activity in which they act like their parents, eventually realizing that complaining can sometimes be an expression of love.

The counselor has a bit of free time before his other appointments. He meets with his supervisor about the uncooperative family, then catches up on his paperwork. All is going well until he gets the day's phone messages. One of his clients decides to discontinue treatment. No explanation. Just a phone call. Now he will have to do a bunch of paperwork and follow-up to close the file. One afternoon appointment talks depressing matters so intensely that the counselor notes that even he is starting to feel depressed: "This poor woman is going to be depressed her whole life and there's probably nothing I can do but hold her hand. That *is* depressing. I've got to put this stuff behind me. My last client is waiting. I'm so glad I thought to include her at the end of the day. She will be her usual entertaining, cheerful self. It feels so fine to know that I'm partially responsible for helping her to feel so good."

Crisis Center

The day begins with a crisis: the coffee is all gone. The crises continue—staff will be short today so the counselor must handle more calls. The first call is from a "regular customer," a gentleman who enjoys waking himself by masturbating over the phone. The counselor giggles, then remembers her training and quickly hangs up.

Next call: a routine referral to Planned Parenthood for abortion counseling. Next: a kid who wants information about the Valium his mother is taking. Then—crisis. A boy calls and says he thinks he just killed himself. He sounds distraught, confused. He took a bunch of pills but he doesn't know what kind. He doesn't care anyway. He just wants to die. He just wanted to say goodbye to someone, anyone; he has no one else. The counselor tries to get his address but to no avail: he hangs up. The counselor starts trembling, but before she can talk her feelings through the boy calls again. This time he's laughing, screams "sucker," and hangs up once again. With all the lambs crying "wolf," how will she ever know for sure when the games and manipulation stop? She feels abused and disgusted.

Someone is asking for her in the lobby. It's an ex-client who just dropped in to say hello and give her a progress report: he is doing fantastically, thanks to her caring work. No time for reveling in the glory or bemoaning the fake calls—she is late for a program at the junior high school, where she is scheduled to give a talk on drugs.

The counselor spends an hour with the kids, giving accurate information, answering questions, discussing her observations about how children are introduced to the drug scene. Afterwards, one teacher solicits her advice about what he can do to help prevent further problems in the school. A few appointments are then set up to meet with any kids who wish more information. She has several valuable encounters—helping one child to work on resisting the pressure of his peers to get high, helping another to realize how dangerous it was for him to be taking pills that he couldn't identify. The counselor next meets with the school counselors to lend assistance and lead an informal workshop on strategies for fighting drug abuse.

She returns to the crisis center, spends two more hours fielding mostly routine calls, then a half hour with her colleagues discussing the frustrating morning. They mutually decide, for their own protection, that it's better to stay more detached and neutral with their clients. The counselor also vows: "I must talk to myself harder so that I don't permit the few bad experiences to overshadow the productive work that I've been doing." The thought is interrupted by the jangling phone—it is a 74-year-old woman, frightened, alone; she just wants to make human contact. The counselor spends a half hour offering reassurance and then decides to leave work a little early so she can meet the woman for coffee.

High School

At 7:25 A.M., when the counselor walks into her office, there are already seven students waiting. Right away she knows why. There was a glitch in the computer yesterday and third-hour English was double loaded. The teacher about blew her fuse but at least she has now settled down. As the counselor finishes rescheduling the last student thirty minutes later she wonders what this activity has to do with counseling.

Not only is scheduling classes boring administrative work but it really eats up time, keeping her from getting to what she wants to be doing—working with kids and their problems. She makes a mental note to mention this concern in the afternoon meeting with the principal, knowing she won't even have the full support of the staff. Some of them actually prefer scheduling to counseling. They consider the work less demanding. The thought is depressing.

On the way to the attendance office to check on a student she suddenly hears shouts and a commotion around the corner. Cringing, she moves toward the disturbance and finds two senior boys wrestling against a locker, each twice her size. Using what she hopes is her most authoritative voice, she pushes between them and manages with the help of another teacher to

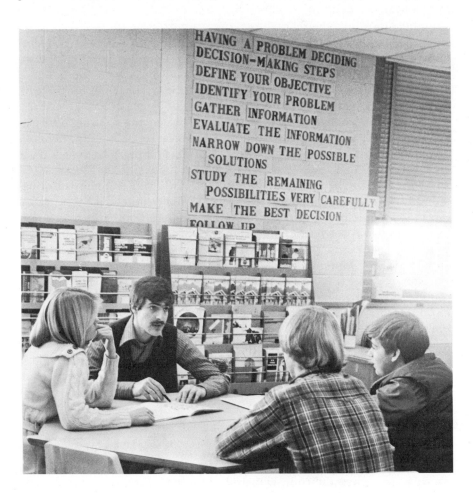

A school counselor helping students make some difficult choices for their futures.

separate them. Her heart sinks when she recognizes one of the offenders as a client for whom she went out on a limb two weeks ago—he was in danger of being suspended for fighting. Now this!

An hour later she feels better. The fighting business has been cleared up and she has just finished a successful interview with a student whose parents have been pushing him toward a military career. It felt good to help him explore what he wants and to become more aware of his tendency to please his parents at all costs. The session seemed to be productive and she felt confident that the student would make some changes.

Her meeting with the principal is grim. Teachers, say he, are complaining because the counseling staff is overloading classes and allowing friends to alter their schedules so they can be together in their mischief. The counselor points out (once again) that class scheduling is administrative work and not the primary responsibility of the counseling department, and further, if teachers are having discipline problems in their classes they should consult with a counselor instead of complaining to the principal.

Lunch provides a needed break. A teacher stops by and suggests that they get together to talk about his frustrations with his job and hassles with the department chairman. The talk with him seems to help. Sometimes the informal sessions over lunch seem to make more difference than all the appointments during the week.

The counselor tries to keep the afternoons open for working with kids. She has two appointments and will finish the day with a group. However, she is worried about the first appointment: a seventeen-year-old senior who is depressed and very worried about smoking too much pot. The session is taxing and she reflects on how difficult it is to work with kids having drug problems. The last individual appointment is a bonus. She has been working with this girl for four months now and can really see the difference. The girl has overcome her shyness, is involved in extracurricular activities, and reports a much improved relationship with her parents. She even has a boyfriend. At the finish of the session, the counselor feels great. As she is leaving for the group, the secretary motions urgently. An irate parent is on the phone demanding an explanation for her son's suspension. She's really hot. The counselor calms her down and makes an appointment to see her after school.

Now for the group. Today's topic is love again. As always, she is amazed at how sensitive the kids are and how they really do confront each other as they interact. They know what honesty means.

Hurrying to meet with the irate parent, the counselor reflects on her day, realizing that the good parts do make up for the bad, but, boy, is it draining and frustrating at times. And there's one more challenge yet to go.

Preschool

The counselor arrives at work to find a three-year-old hiding under a picnic table, surrounded by two teachers and his parents urging him to come out. Instead he screams "Never!" and continues to cry. The counselor reassures the parents, sends them off to work, and disperses the crowd of children and teachers. She then crawls under the table and sits silently for ten minutes, until the child halts his tears long enough to ask why the counselor is acting silly by sitting under a table. Without hesitation the counselor replies simply that she is a little scared today, angry at her parents for dumping her off, and this seems like as good a place as any to hide. The three-year-old understands immediately, nods his head, and tells the counselor that he'll pay extra attention to her today so she won't feel so lonely. He then crawls out and joins the other kids in the sandbox as if this entrance were a natural beginning to a day of school. The counselor too crawls out but makes her way to the morning staff meeting, which she will direct in planning the day's psychological education.

After the play activities for the day have been discussed, the counselor reviews the past week's discipline problems, how they were managed, how they could have been handled differently. She reports on the outcomes of various conferences she conducted with children and their parents, then makes specific recommendations to the teachers about strategies that might be helpful in the future: "When Alice throws a temper tantrum it is best to isolate her calmly in the 'time-out' room." "Pay special attention to Brian— give him lots of hugs today because his father beat him last night." "Don't let Jennifer test you."

As the art classes begin, the counselor works on test evaluations of the children's aptitude strengths and weaknesses, detailing treatment plans for each child. She then spends some time with the director going over administrative chores before an appointment with parents.

The mother and father of a particularly disturbed child show up twenty minutes late and then proceed to pick at one another about whose fault it was. When the counselor tries to intervene, they turn on her and then launch into an abusive tirade against the school, the teachers, and especially the counselor for being responsible for their child's problems. They decide to pull the child out of the school and march up to him while he is occupied on the swings, grab him by the neck, and yell at him all the way to the car. As the child cries for his friends, the parents start arguing again about who is responsible for their having such a screwed-up kid. They spank the child for good measure, throw him into the back seat, and drive off.

Another child sees the counselor fuming, with tears in her eyes, and invites her to play on the slide. They talk about what just happened, and other children ask questions about why parents sometimes get so mad. When the kids resume their play, the counselor excuses herself to break up a fight.

The counselor is exhausted; the children are still literally running circles around her. She mobilizes her energy for the afternoon parent-education class she teaches. Eleven participants attend, almost all of them single parents who have concerns about their effectiveness. She rates the class only "fair" because she feels tired and a few parents are unusually rigid in their beliefs and therefore reluctant to try anything new ("Spankings were good enough for me. Why the hell shouldn't they be good enough for our kids?"). While the counselor patiently explains the negative side effects of punishment, she sees the last of the kids departing. As their cute little legs scurry off, she wonders if she is really preventing any of them from having emotional problems in the future. "I sure would like to see them about twenty years from now," she thinks. "That's an idea! I think I'll talk to the director about organizing some follow-up research."

The Value of a Flexible Specialty

<The days of the counseling generalist are numbered> No longer can the counselor indulge in the luxury of acting like a country doctor who knows a little bit about everything and yet nothing in depth about anything. The technology and knowledge in the field are growing so rapidly that it is impossible to stay current on subjects as diverse as general systems analysis in organizational development, genetic predeterminants of emotionally disturbed children, nutritional imbalances in geriatric senility, indirect hypnotic trance inductions, and unionism among school personnel specialists.

<Most counselors, by design or by circumstances, find themselves a flexible specialty. Because of a need in a particular community for family mediation experts, a counselor may choose to affiliate with a court system to fill the gap. A counselor newly hired by an agency may need to adapt to handling drug-abuse cases, sex counseling, or another area in which the counselor has specialized expertise. Sometimes clientele, by sociometric homeogeneity or geography, will present similar problems of economic hardship, bored marriages, or free-floating anxiety. Again the counselor ends up reading and studying more about those particular concerns and thereby becomes an expert in dealing with future cases>

<While it is probably intelligent to market oneself as a specialist in a few related areas, to increase both one's employability and one's professional mastery, it is not necessary to become so narrow in focus that one typifies Toffler's (1970) victim of "future shock.">Whether one is a financier, physician, or counselor, the consequences of overspecialization can be equally undesirable, resulting in rigidity, obsolescence, and a narrow field of vision.

<It may therefore be advantageous to select a particular field in which to concentrate one's study while continuing efforts to survey the wide educational spectrum. Certain specialties even fit well together, depending on one's interests and skills> A student's career-developmental scenario might run as follows: "As soon as I completed the introductory course I knew immediately the things I *didn't* like, even though I had no idea what I did like. The idea of sitting in an office seemed intolerable to me. I had to find something where I could move around a lot, have variety in my job, try different things all the time. In the class on career information, I took a lot of those tests we're supposed to give to clients, but they only told me what I already knew. So I visited five different agencies, interviewed counselors in

the field as part of a school project, and did two different internships. I tentatively settled on working with small kids for a number of reasons: (1) you can help them before they get into too much trouble, (2) you get to run around a lot while chasing them, so you don't stay cooped up in an office, (3) you get to see their changes in a matter of weeks instead of years, (4) it's a relatively new field, so I should be able to get a job, and (5) if I don't like it I will already be prepared to work with children in any setting I choose." The decision-making process exemplified by this student's reasoning is typical of what ought to go on in every prospective counselor's mind. The marketability of a counseling degree, as illustrated in the dialogue that began this chapter, is dependent almost totally on what the graduate is able to represent effectively to a potential employer. A survey of broad specialty areas that permit career flexibility and the opportunity to develop expertise in the field is offered below.

Selected Specialty Areas in Counseling

Child development and counseling
elementary school counseling
preschool counseling
early childhood education
child counseling in mental
 health agencies
parent education
counseling with battered and
 abused children and their
 families

**Adolescent development and
counseling**
high school counseling
adolescent counseling in
 mental health agencies
career-development specialist
youth probation officer
psychological education
youth work in a residential facility
recreational work

Love relationships
marriage counseling
family counseling
sex counseling
divorce mediation
sex education

Health
nutritional counseling
exercise and health education
bioenergetics
physician's associate
patient education in hospitals
stress management and counseling

Careers
employment counseling
occupational therapy
vocational rehabilitation
career development
career-change counseling

Disabled
counseling with the deaf
counseling with the blind
counseling with the physically
 handicapped

University
student personnel
college administration
college student counseling
adult education
student activities

Drugs
substance abuse counseling
crisis intervention counseling
drug education
alcohol counseling

Behavioral strategies
habit control
weight loss
smoking reduction
enuresis

Consultation
organizational development
industrial psychology
corporate consulting
personnel

Industry
management
public relations
marketing and sales
employee assistance programs
training and development
quality of worklife
employee career development
affirmative action/equal
  opportunity specialist
personnel

Guidelines for Selecting a Counseling Specialty

The student should at least consider concentrating in one or more of the categories in the list. The task of considering them is no less overwhelming than any other career decision and needs to be based on a systematic process of solid self-evaluation and the collection of pertinent information about each subspecialty. Beginning this process early in a graduate program allows maximum opportunity for exploration and can guide a student's class and field work so that the eventual decision on a subspecialty can emerge rather than being forced at the last minute. The choice of some specialties will involve further training beyond the M.A. level, a factor that may be important for some students.

The following guidelines may be helpful in thinking about specialty areas and creating an innovative personal approach to this important task.

1. *Assess personal strengths and weaknesses.* In thinking about your personal strengths and weaknesses, strive to be brutally honest with yourself and assertively seek feedback from trusted friends, peers, colleagues, and professors. Often, a disappointing specialty selection can be traced back to an inaccurate self-assessment. It is important to be scrupulous in all aspects, avoiding any tendency to be overcritical, underplay strengths, or be defensive about weaknesses. Accuracy and honesty are twin hallmarks of an effective self-assessment.

2. *Clarify values related to work.* Personal values exert a substantial impact on work satisfaction and can influence burn-out, career development, and professional effectiveness. It is useful to spend some time early in graduate study confronting personal values and testing them within possible specialty areas. The counseling field is so large and diverse that it provides ample opportunity for individuals to seek or create work settings and specialties that are consistent with personal values. Nothing is more frustrating than choosing a career or specialty that requires considerable investment, only to discover that it doesn't feel right—for instance, that the job requires evening hours and you hate working after dark. You can avoid, or at least minimize, such disappointments and frustrations by paying careful attention to values early in the specialty selection process.

3. *Visit as many different specialty settings as possible.* There is no replacement for reality testing in career selection. Although a specialty might sound interesting and comfortable to you, a visit to a site could provide a completely different perspective on what the job is really like. Many counseling students, for example, believe that they would like to work in a hospital setting. However, upon visiting a site, they may discover that much of their work would be routine and depressing and that counselors are at the bottom of the pecking order. This awareness may cool initial enthusiasm, or it may reinforce a tentative commitment. Regardless of the outcome, decision making will be based more on reality considerations than on fantasy.

4. *Interview as many counselors in the field as possible.* Selecting a specialty depends on awareness of opportunities as well as personal preferences and goals. Interacting with professional counselors allows the student to collect a wealth of valuable information, rooted in day-to-day reality, on work situations and opportunities. A limitation of graduate education is that it is often removed from the experiences of clinicians. You can work to reduce this separation and in the process enrich the base for choosing your specialty.

5. *Maximize internship and practica experiences.* The heart of a professional training program in therapeutic counseling is internship and practica. These dual experiences provide an indispensable source of knowledge and experience for specialty selection. Students should *maximize* internship and practica experiences, seeking as wide a range as possible. This is a time to experiment and to broaden professional experiences. The field portion of your training is, in a sense, the last "free" opportunity to explore professionally. Once you have graduated, it will be much more difficult to avoid making firm commitments.

6. *Develop a "futures" orientation.* Essayists have repeatedly observed that change is the only stable characteristic of the future. In order to prepare for a vital and pertinent specialty area, you will need to develop a professional orientation that looks to the future rather than the past for definition and career opportunity. For example, school systems—historically the largest employer of counselors—are not currently a promising career setting. To insure professional relevance, you will have to anticipate settings and opportunities wherein counseling skills and attitudes will be useful and in demand. Creatively forecasting the future will allow you, as a counselor-in-training, to select specialties carefully and target emerging employment opportunities.

Summary

Selecting a specialty is, in a sense, a subgoal of counselor training. It is useful to begin the process of specialty selection early in your education but to avoid making rigid or premature commitments. Counselors need to be flexible and open to change as they develop as persons and professionals. Specialty selection is really the first step in professional development, which is an ongoing aspect of your work as a therapeutic counselor.

This chapter has provided an overview of the work of professional counselors in a variety of jobs. Each setting for therapeutic counseling is vital, dynamic, and filled with both substantial rewards and grinding frustration. Such is the nature of the profession. Helping people, particularly within an institutional context, is not an easy task but does offer a unique and creative opportunity to make a difference in the world.

Professional counselors work in many settings and perform a variety of tasks. Opportunities for employment in the field are extensive and require a proactive orientation. A major task for students in counselor training programs is to begin to think about their careers and to initiate careful research and planning to ensure maximum opportunity. One aspect of this planning is the tentative selection of a specialty area.

PROFESSOR: So much for our overview of the places where counselors work. Are you any more clear on what you can do with your degree?

STUDENT: You're feeling unsure of yourself and your ability to help me deal with a problem so complex?

PROFESSOR: Yes, it *is* frustrating. All the time I must—ah, yes, I see you *have* learned something. And I know how it feels to be evaded with active listening.

STUDENT: To answer your question: I learned that it is up to me to market myself for the job I really want. The counseling program provides me with a core of basic skills to apply in any setting I choose.

PROFESSOR: Yes, and it is up to me to help you in your choices by providing honest feedback about your assets and limitations concerning possible specialty areas. In addition, I need to stimulate and challenge your thinking about possibilities.

STUDENT: So I guess it's up to me to use the skills and techniques I'm learning in the program and somehow to combine them with my personal strengths and figure out what I'm going to be when I grow up.

PROFESSOR: You bet—and the process doesn't stop. In fact, right now in my own life I've been doing some thinking and evaluating. . . .

Suggested Readings

Blocher, D. H. (1966). *Developmental counseling.* New York: Ronald Press.
Brown, J. A., & Pate, R. H., Jr. (1983). *Being a counselor: Directions and challenges.* Monterey, Calif.: Brooks/Cole.
Havighurst, R. (1953). *Human development and education.* New York: David McKay.

Kagan, N. (Guest Ed.). (1982). Counseling psychology: The next decade [Special issue]. *The Counseling Psychologist, 10*.

Schlossberg, N. K. (1984). *Counseling adults in transition.* New York: Springer.

Whiteley, J. & Fretz, B. R. (1980). *The present and future of counseling psychology.* Washington, D.C.: AACD Press.

PART TWO

COUNSELING

ANTECEDENTS

AND APPROACHES

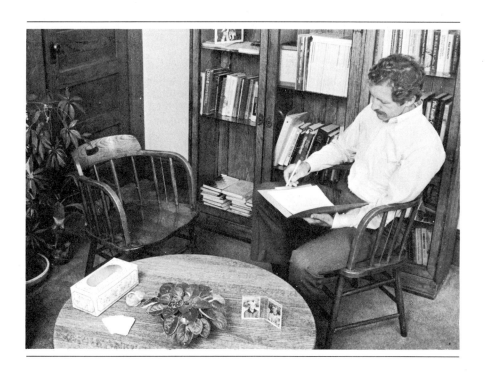

Chapter 5

Insight-Oriented

Counseling Theories

SOCRATES: Come, lie down here.
STREPSIADES: What for?
SOCRATES: Ponder awhile over matters that interest you.
STREPSIADES: Oh, I pray not there.
SOCRATES: Come, on the couch!

...uel fate.
...examine closely, gather your thoughts together, let
...every side of things. If you meet with difficulty,
...me other idea; keep away from sleep [Alexander &
Selesnick, 1966].

Introduction to Theory Construction

Theory has been both a plague and a challenge for students since presocratic times, when philosophers would aggressively query their disciples about the meaning of life. Certainly the contemporary student finds little solace in historical precedent for his or her own struggles to understand the differences among the various theoretical systems that are part of the counseling profession. "What good is theory?" students often ask. "I want to be a counselor, not a philosopher."

Yet confusion abounds within the realm of counseling itself, as the differences of opinion on the structure of the therapeutic relationship (Chapter 3) have shown. Whereas the more insight-oriented counseling approaches focus on creating an authentic human encounter for its intrinsic healing properties, the action-oriented approaches use the relationship as a means to another end. And even within a particular orientation there is much disagreement as to style, form, and content. Carl Rogers, for example, proposed that it is the realness of the encounter that is important, and so he described an insight theory that encourages naturalness, genuineness, and humanness in the relationship. On the other hand, Sigmund Freud's insight theory postulated that the relationship should be as anonymous and formalized as possible so that the client may work through resistance and transference issues.

A theory, therefore, is a blueprint for action. The counselor's choice of interventions, reactions, analysis, and understanding all flow logically from a theoretical model of what people are like, what is good for them, and what conditions are likely to influence them in a self-determined, desirable direction (Geis, 1973). Some students may be surprised to learn that counselors actually have quite complex and well-developed theories of metaphysics (how the world works), ethics (how people should act), logic (cause–effect relationships), ontology (meaning of human existence), and epistemology (how people change) (Kottler, 1983). It is precisely these theories that guide what a counselor does with a particular client at a particular moment.

Theories are valuable in organizing knowledge and information in such a way that they may easily be retrieved. They are no more nor less than models for consistency in action; they permit all practitioners, whether of architecture, medicine, or counseling, to repeat those strategies that have worked previously in similar circumstances (Argyris, 1974). Theories, of course, have other useful functions, such as attempting to simplify the world and developing rules to explain, predict, or guide behavior.

While they are valuable constructs for aiding action, theories are not indelibly inscribed in stone as truth. When you study the various counseling approaches, remember that each is a single attempt to explain the therapeutic process, albeit with emphasis, values, and strengths in some areas and limitations in others. In deciding which ideas have the most personal relevance for you, bear in mind the attributes of good theories set forth by Burks and Stefflre (1979): good theories are clearly and precisely described, as simply expressed as possible, comprehensive in scope, useful in the real world, and valuable in generating new knowledge and research.

In theory construction we are indirectly trying to establish a basis for predicting a client's prognosis, likely consequences of certain interventions, connections among experiences (and nonexperiences) in a client's life, and the impact of our therapeutic efforts. But since no prediction can ever be 100% certain, we also use theory to approximate some degree of consistency. Theories are working hypotheses, subject to change and revision as new information about the world, our clients, and ourselves becomes available. We can not accurately and precisely describe what we see; instead we filter our experiences through slightly focused images, and inadequate language approximates what we think we perceive. Theory is, in a sense, our beliefs about how we explain reality (Burks and Stefflre, 1979).

Gregory Bateson (1979) describes the problem of theory construction in science by listing many of the inherent logical weaknesses in the ways we organize our knowledge:

Problems of Theory - Lesson 9

1. Science can never prove anything, not only because prediction is imperfect and our methods of collecting data are flawed but because *proof* occurs only in the realm of abstraction.

2. In human perception, all experience is subjective and hence is colored by individual perceptions, as well as unconscious motives. We can be certain that the reports of our senses will be slightly distorted as viewed through individual prisms that have been shaped by unique genetic structures and experiences.

3. Explanations are the results of descriptions and these descriptions can be organized in more than one way. Convenience determines how things are classified and, no matter which model is used, some information will be lost or downplayed.

4. For a theory, and hence its predictive power, to be perfect it would have to deal with factors that are 100% controllable. Far from the whimsical, impulsive nature of the human world, even physical laws are minutely capricious.

 5. Theories are constructed from information. Information is not only subject to inadequate description and arbitrary classification but to flawed methods of measurement. Researchers in counseling, for instance, have been debating for decades about whether it can even be reliably demonstrated that therapeutic interventions cure people since we can't agree on definitions of "cure," much less figure out a way to measure the degree to which it occurs.

For the purposes of counseling students, each of the theoretical systems represented in these chapters should be viewed within the aforementioned human context. Each theory is an approximation of truth, one person's or a group's attempt at explaining phenomena that are difficult to understand and virtually impossible to describe fully. These theories, as with all other human structures, are imperfect working hypotheses subject both to random error of the samples of behavior investigated and to the distinctions, limitations, and expectations of the inventors. We advise you to read the following sections openly and critically. Assume that each theory has some merit and value, some practical use and interesting ideas that can help you better to understand the process of counseling.

The theories grouped together in this chapter have one principle in common: it is through the process of self-awareness, self-understanding, self-revelation that true growth occurs. Whether in a gradual clarification of feelings or a brief spurt of insight, whether facilitated through open sharing or in-depth interpretations, whether focused on the present, past, or future, the theories treated in this chapter work through the process of self-discovery. It is their unifying dimension to hold that insight into one's problems, along with a grasp of implications, connections, consequences, and perspectives, is a necessary prerequisite before any real and lasting change can occur.

Client-Centered Counseling

Aliases: Nondirective, Person-Centered, Humanistic, Rogerian, Self Theory

Originator and Revisionists

Before Carl Rogers entered the scene, therapeutic counseling was largely a directive, prescriptive enterprise consisting of advice, diagnoses, interpretations, and authority. With the publication of his books (Rogers, 1942, 1951), the field was irreversibly pushed in the direction of giving clients more autonomy and responsibility for their treatment. Client-centered counseling caught on quickly because of its optimistic philosophy, which emphasized the wonderful potential of humans to learn, grow, and heal themselves when given the opportunity within a nurturing therapeutic relationship. Further,

Carl Rogers (1902) creator of client-centered, nondirective counseling.

nondirective counseling became attractive to North Americans as their first native-born approach, one that stressed positive concepts and relatively simple interventions.

Rogers also strongly influenced two other theorists who were later to refine and adapt his ideas, thus reaching a larger audience. Robert Carkhuff and his colleagues (Truax, Berenson, and Gendlin) ingeniously combined techniques of behavioral analysis into a helping model that presented simplified counselor skills as the essence of constructive intervention. Carkhuff has become the most frequently quoted professional of our time through his systematic research on the dimensions of human nourishment originally identified by Rogers: empathy, respect, genuineness, and concreteness. Carkhuff also helped to convert Rogerian philosophy into a system of action. Thomas Gordon is another adapter of client-centered counseling; he created a popular educational system for training parents (Gordon, 1970) and teachers (Gordon, 1974) by applying the skills of "active listening" to clarify a person's feelings.

Basic Assumptions

Most client-centered counselors are in basic agreement that

1. Human beings are growth oriented and tend toward self-actualization. This natural process of development toward higher stages of

moral, emotional, and behavioral evolution can be facilitated by professional helpers who are able to stimulate the inherent capacity for progress in clients who are temporarily stymied or faltering.

2. The necessary and sufficient condition for change to occur is the therapeutic relationship, which exudes qualities of trust, openness, acceptance, permissiveness, and warmth. The degree to which the counselor is able to create this nurturing atmosphere will influence the client's possibilities for growth.

3. The legitimate focus of counseling content is on affect and thorough exploration of feelings. Both interpersonal relationships and the self-concept may be improved by becoming aware of feelings about oneself and others and by learning to express these emotions in sensitive and self-enhancing ways.

4. The client/student has primary responsibility for the course of treatment/study—what constitutes appropriate content and whether, ultimately, it succeeds. There is thus a goal shared by client and counselor and a mutual understanding of the client's world.

5. Human beings are intrinsically good and trustworthy. They will instinctively move, in a deliberate way, toward goals that are satisfying and socially responsible. Irresponsible or socially undesirable behavior emerges from a defensiveness that alienates human beings from their own nature. As defensiveness declines and persons become more open to their own experiences, they will strive for meaningful and constructive relationships.

Personality Development

Client-centered counseling has not developed an elaborate, well-integrated theory of personality functioning, but rather, has defined a series of formal propositions (Rogers, 1951, 1959). These statements reflect a perspective about human beings that is philosophically phenomenological and has drawn much from self theory:

1. "Every individual exists in a continually changing world of experience of which he is the center" (Rogers, 1951, p. 483). This proposition emphasizes the central importance of the individual and the subjective nature of personal experience. One can never really "know" the full experiences and perceptions of another person.

2. "The organism reacts to the field as it is experienced and perceived. The perceptual field is, for the individual, 'reality' " (Rogers, 1951, p. 484). Reality, for the individual, exists only in subjective terms. Therefore, to work effectively with another, one must enter that person's perceptual field and begin to experience his or her reality.

3. "Behavior is basically the goal-directed attempt of the organism to satisfy its needs as experienced, in the field as perceived" (Rogers, 1951, p. 491). Persons are intentional in their behavior, which is defined by their perceptual field and experienced needs. A lack of awareness of needs or options tends to limit and restrict behavior. Psychological reality for an

individual is based on experienced needs and perceptions, regardless of the objective truth.

4. "The best vantage point for understanding behavior is from the internal frame of reference of the individual himself" (Rogers, 1951, p. 494). To understand another requires concentrating on the reality that exists subjective for that person. Therapeutically, it is necessary to experience people from an empathic, subjective frame of reference while helping them to expand their awareness to include a greater proportion of the external, objective reality.

5. "Most of the ways of behaving adopted by the organism are consistent with the concept of self" (Rogers, 1951, p. 507). Rogers believes that the self-concept is essential to an understanding of the individual. The self-concept is the organized and integrated image that is a compromise between the self as perceived by others and by oneself. It tends to be a relatively stable guide for behavior and changes only when internal dissonance is experienced.

Favorite Techniques

Client-centered counseling is hardly technique-oriented, preferring instead to explore curative variables and refine philosophical assumptions; nevertheless, there are a few standard intervention strategies. The bread-and-butter technique of the client-centered counselor (as well as many others) is reflection of feelings, also referred to as active listening. Communicating from a posture of empathic understanding, the counselor intently attends to a client's verbal and nonverbal messages, interprets the surface and underlying meanings, and then formulates a response that demonstrates a deep-level understanding of the client's feelings. This technique has its advantages:

1. Although it is the most difficult counseling skill to master, it is relatively simple to learn and fosters an open and honest helping relationship.

2. Even if the reflection of feeling is inaccurate and ignores the client's actual messages, it still encourages further self-exploration.

COUNSELOR: You sound so angry at your brother for not writing you to join him.

CLIENT: No. Not really. I'm not so much angry at him as I am frustrated at myself for not telling him it was important that I go.

3. It helps the client to feel reassured that he or she is deeply understood and accepted for his or her feelings.

STUDENT: I really think it's stupid to give us an exam in a class like this that emphasizes skills instead of stuff to memorize.

PROFESSOR: You feel like I don't treat you with enough respect, and you also have some real concerns about how well you are doing in this class.

4. It clarifies a client's feelings so that the situation may be viewed more objectively.

CLIENT: My father always butts into my life when he can't take care of his own.

COUNSELOR: You are really afraid that although you love your father very much, you may follow in his footsteps as a disaster in love relationships.

5. It provides an opportunity for emotional catharsis, bringing relief of pent up tensions and pressure.

CLIENT: I don't know how I feel about it.

COUNSELOR: You are afraid to let yourself feel.

CLIENT: You're damn right I am! I gave that bastard the best years of my life. I don't know whether to cry, scream, fight, or give up. I'm so confused.

6. It encourages the client to move from superficial concerns to deeper, more significant problems.

CLIENT: I don't know. I've just never had good study habits. You have any tricks for doing better on "true–false" exams?

COUNSELOR: You have some real reservations about your ability to discipline yourself. You sometimes feel like you aren't smart enough to hack college and afraid that even if you do study, you'll flunk out anyway.

Encounter groups are another favorite application of the client-centered approach, since they provide additional opportunities for developing a climate of trust, freedom, honest feedback, interpersonal interaction, and improved communications, as well as a reduction of defensiveness, inhibitions, rigidity, and game playing (Rogers, 1970). In the client-centered group format, ground rules are established that encourage participants to be as honest as possible with themselves and others. They are urged to stay in the present, to become aware of their feelings, to express them straightforwardly, and to take risks within the safety of a trusting, cohesive, and intimate group experience.

It is important to mention that client-centered counselors subordinate the use of techniques to the attitudes of the counselor and the relationship created with the client. Those interventions that are emphasized include active listening, reflection of feelings, and clarifications, while directive techniques such as interpretation, questioning, probing, and diagnosis are minimized.

Criticisms of Client-Centered Counseling

Although a valuable and, at the time of its inception, a radical departure from psychoanalysis, client-centered counseling can be criticized on several grounds:

1. ⟨It may give too much responsibility to the client and reduce the role of the counselor as the trained expert.⟩Counselors may merely reflect back what the client has said.
2. ⟨It may be somewhat naive in its view of clients as naturally evolving and lofty in goals that may not be possible.⟩Counselors, for example, may be unable to create "unconditional positive regard" since everything is ultimately conditional.
3. ⟨It does not respond to the difficulties encountered in translating feelings into action.⟩
4. ⟨It is narrow in its focus on affect and tends to ignore thoughts and behavior.⟩
5. It may overemphasize the importance of relationship factors, which may be a necessary but not sufficient condition for therapeutic change.
6. ⟨It is not useful for clients who are in crisis and require directive intervention.⟩
7. ⟨It tends to be more useful for highly verbal clients and less appropriate for those who have difficulty expressing themselves.⟩

Personal Applications

Principles of client-centered counseling can help you to:

1. create greater self-awareness, especially with regard to your feelings, and thereby expand growth and congruence. It helps one to create a growth orientation and encourages an active attitude toward life and personal growth;
2. gain appreciation for the importance of genuineness, unconditional acceptance, and empathy in dealing with other persons;
3. take more responsibility for your own education and life experiences;
4. recognize the importance of exploring your feelings, risking, and sharing them with others;
5. acknowledge the need to suspend your own values and judgments as you encounter other persons so that you may experience their inner reality.

Existential Counseling

Aliases: Humanistic, Phenomenological, Experiential

Originators

Existentialism is a particularly rich and difficult theory because it intersects so many different fields. It had a long and distinguished career as a philosophy long before it was recruited to the more practical dimensions of reality in therapeutic psychology. ⟨Beginning with Socrates and continuing onward into the 20th century, such well-known philosophers as Kierkegaard, Nietzsche, Heidegger, Husserl, Tillich, and Marcel have represented an international search for the ultimate meaning of human existence. These complex philosophies were later absorbed into the world of art (Cezanne, Picasso, Van Gogh, Chagall) and literature (Kafka, Camus, Sartre, Dostoyevsky). Finally, existentialism has been translated into a style of living, a way of being that encourages a person to use and accept anxiety constructively (May, 1983). Fortunately, it is not necessary to comprehend existentialist philosophy in order to make use of its concepts in therapeutic counseling. For our purposes, we will concentrate discussion on its practical applications. Frankl (1962) adapted existential thinking to survival strategies in Nazi concentration camps during World War II. The main determinant, according to Frankl, of an inmate's likelihood of living or giving up and dying was the ability to create a personal meaning to the experience: "If there is a meaning in life at all, then there must be a meaning in suffering. Suffering is an ineradicable part of life, even as fate and death. Without suffering and death human life cannot be complete"(Frankl, 1962, p. 106).

Whether a rationalization or justification of the unjustifiable, Frankl observed the importance of the basic existential hallmarks in the everyday life of anyone who suffers humiliation and pain—in a hospital, death camp, or counselor's office. Freedom, choice, being, responsibility, and meaning are the ideas that helped him to survive and those that help clients to flourish.

> We who lived in concentration camps can remember the men who walked through the huts comforting others, giving away their last piece of bread. They may have been few in number, but they offer sufficient proof that everything can be taken from a man but one thing: the last of the human freedoms—to choose one's attitude in any given set of circumstances, to choose one's own way [Frankl, 1962, p. 104].

May (1958) introduced this previously European philosophy to North American psychotherapists and counselors. The focus of therapeutic intervention is to help the client become responsible for his choices, to manage his freedom and thereby transcend the meaninglessness of his life, moving into a more authentic existence. May has contributed a series of books on love, power, creativity, anxiety, freedom, and various other issues of existential relevance. His goal has been to assist the client to develop insight regarding the life forces that can be mobilized to overcome the existential crises of powerlessness and freedom. "After many a therapeutic hour which I would call successful, the client leaves with more anxiety than he had when he came in; only now the anxiety is conscious rather than unconscious, constructive rather than destructive. The definition of mental health needs to be changed to living without *paralyzing* anxiety, but living with normal anxiety is a stimulant to a vital existence, as a source of energy, and as life enhancing" (May, 1981, p. 19).

If anxiety has its usefulness, so too does the concept of death to the existentialist. Yalom (1980), in his definitive text *Existential Psychotherapy*, writes about the idea of death as the primary savior of man because it motivates an intense appreciation of life's value. By confronting our own vulnerability, the ultimate threat to our existence, we are made aware of people and things that are truly important. Death and the companion existential issues of isolation, meaninglessness, and freedom are seen as the legitimate focus of counseling. Yalom was able to translate much of the confusion, complex language, and abstract ideas of existentialism into a system of helping and an attitude for the helper, complete with methodologies for analyzing and solving human problems.

Existential counseling is richly endowed in its affiliations with Rogers's person-oriented approach, Maslow and Shostrom's self-actualization psychology, and Freud's theory of psychoanalysis. Far from postulating a rigid set of therapeutic procedures, the existentialist offers a way of thinking about clients and their concerns, about humans and their dilemmas, and about life and its puzzles.

Premises of Existential Counseling

The existential approach has been minimally concerned with the techniques and specific interventions of counseling, concentrating instead on philosophical principles that aid the understanding of the client. As an insight-oriented theory, its main goal is to help people to find personal meaning in their actions, their lives, and their suffering. A counselor working from an existential posture would assist people primarily to develop the range of their choices, and hence their freedom to be. The four basic concepts of existential theory are (1) existence, (2) encounter, (3) authenticity, and (4) experiencing.

Clients who present the symptoms of existential anxiety (lack of meaning, fear of death, isolation, avoidance of responsibility) can be helped to become more capable of determining the outcome of their daily life. They become aware of their fears. They understand the significance and personal meaning of their refusal to enjoy freedom. They confront the naked fact that each person, from the moment of birth, stands alone. Yet far from necessarily condemning the self to loneliness, we may choose to take responsibility for our aloneness, our freedom, our choices, and the consequences of what we choose. "The one who realizes in anguish his condition as being thrown into a responsibility which extends to his very abandonment has no longer either remorse or regret or excuse, he is no longer anything but a freedom which perfectly reveals itself and whose being resides in this very revelation" (Sartre, 1957, p. 59).

The existential counselor seeks to enter into the client's world and, remaining in the present, to use the therapeutic alliance—the relationship—as a fulcrum by which to lever more involvement and commitment to living, to being. This process of counseling and change is more than a little ambiguous. The existential approach is a philosophy, an attitude, a way of thinking, analyzing, and experiencing; it is, therefore, difficult to describe specifically how the counselor acts, even though a few techniques reluctantly emerge from the theory.

The basic distinguishing features of an existential approach include

- a focus on issues of freedom;
- a confrontation with fears of death, alienation, and aloneness;
- an emphasis on taking responsibility for one's life;
- a compatibility with other more action-oriented theories;
- a challenge to discover the meanings behind one's choices and actions;
- a search for a personal philosophy to guide daily life

Existentialism is basically an attitude toward living and, as such, emphasizes the role of understanding and insight into the human condition. The counselor works toward knowing the client rather than knowing *about* him. The process of knowing includes the three separate modes of human existence: the client's natural, biological world; the interpersonal world; and the uncharted territory of the solitary individual in relationship to itself. It is the counselor's presence with the client rather than any specific technique that encourages growth to greater freedom and autonomy (May, 1983).

Criticisms of Existential Counseling

Existentialism is often misunderstood by philosophers and can be elusive for those of us who are untrained in this discipline. It has been described as a particularly abstract, ambiguous, mystical theory that is difficult to apply to the circumstances of everyday living. Also, because the philosophy is so intellectually complex, it is not often appropriate for clients who are of low to average intelligence or for people with severe emotional and cognitive disturbances. Needless to say, other individuals who are in the midst of a crisis or who are barely surviving in their basic economic needs are going to be relatively unconcerned with their "existential Angst" or "phenomenological nonbeing" as compared to other, more pressing problems.

The existential approach is also hard to study because it is nonempirical and doesn't lend itself to scientific scrutiny. Further, although practitioners of this theory are extremely versatile and flexible in their willingness to use a variety of techniques, there are relatively few specific interventions available.

Personal Applications

One exception to the criticism of ambiguity in the applications of existential techniques is the work of Viktor Frankl (1978) in the development of one strategy that is remarkably behavioral. Paradoxical intention is a means of reducing anticipatory anxiety for those with inhibiting obsessions/compulsions by breaking the vicious cycle of fearing fear itself. Paradoxically, "the patient is encouraged to do, or to wish to happen the very things he fears" (Frankl, 1978, p. 117).

Frankl describes the case of a 54-year-old woman addicted to sleeping pills. She was ordered to continue her symptoms; if the sleeplessness persisted, she would only be following her doctor's orders (and thus her anxiety would be reduced), and if she disobeyed, as was more likely, she would thereby cure herself of the symptom. The technique works equally well with problems such as anxiety, obsessional neuroses, and vicious cycle syndromes.

Yalom, an expert on group techniques as well as an active proponent of the existential approach, describes several practical strategies that force clients to consider introspectively their phenomenological positions with respect to issues of responsibility, isolation, death, and freedom. One dramatic exercise works well in group sessions and is also constructive for individual reflection. In fact, even in this moment you are reading *about* existential ideas instead of *experiencing* them. The purpose of this exercise is to help participants to experience rather than to understand cognitively. It might be helpful for you to try this experience in your "here and now."

On eight separate slips of paper write answers to the question "Who am I?" (Do that now.)

Next, arrange your answers in order of importance to you. (Go on, do it!)

Taking the cards in order of their personal significance, spend a few minutes with each one, thinking about how your life would be different without that attribute. This journey to the "center of pure self-consciousness" can only be possible after the layers of intellect, emotion, and desire are stripped away.

(Intermission)

The second existential exercise is even simpler (or deceptively so at first glance): on a sheet of paper draw a straight line (or feel free to use the line provided). One end of that line represents your birth; the other end, your death. Draw an intersected line to represent where you are now (Yalom, 1980, p. 174).

Birth ——————————————|———————————————— *Death*

Meditate on your feelings, thoughts, reactions for a few minutes.

Anyone can become more existentially grounded by attempting to live more in the present, to appreciate every waking moment, to use the idea of eventual death as a strong motivation to become more intensely involved in life. We can give meaning to our lives only by directly confronting our motives and values and by choosing our life and world.

Psychoanalytic Counseling

Aliases: Psychoanalysis, Analysis, Freudian Psychotherapy, Psychodynamic Therapy

Originators

The profession of therapeutic counseling can be traced to Sigmund Freud and his early experimentations with hypnosis and the "talking cure," in which he allowed hysterical patients to reveal their innermost unconscious desires. From the late 19th century until his death in exile from his native Austria at the outbreak of World War II, Freud not only revolutionized our conceptions of human psychology but singlehandedly recruited an army of psychoanalytic thinkers to continue his work. Carl Jung, Otto Rank, Alfred Adler, Wilhelm Riech, Karen Horney, Theodore Reik, Franz Alexander, Harry Stack Sullivan, Erik Erikson, Erich Fromm, and Anna Freud form an impressive list of theorists, brilliant in their own right, who were able to expand, revise, and adapt the psychoanalytic approach to their respective settings, situations, and personalities. As a footnote, it is important to realize that even the creators of completely new schools of counseling, such as Fritz Perls, Albert Ellis, Eric Berne, and Rollo May were once practicing psychoanalysts who grew beyond the confines of traditional psychoanalysis.

An additional point of clarification: there *is* a difference between "psychoanalysis," the orthodox application of Freudian theory, and "psychoanalytically oriented approaches," which make use of some Freudian concepts but are more flexible in their application, according to the preferences of the practitioner. Some theorists have successfully abbreviated psychoanalytic methods into a short-term psychodynamic approach that can be more efficient, economical, and appropriate for counseling settings (Malan, 1963; Sifneos, 1967; Davanloo, 1978; Bauer & Kobos, 1984). Our discussion will focus on some of the more universal and practical ideas of psychoanalytic theory, those that are most relevant to the practice of counseling.

Basic Psychoanalytic Concepts

Traditional psychoanalysis is very complex. It requires five years of intensive postdoctoral training, which includes undergoing personal treatment as well as seminars in order to have a working knowledge of the theory. Many terms and words of psychoanalysis have crept into our everyday language—for example, "ego," "catharsis," "unconscious," "oral stage," and "rationalization"—making a basic understanding of some important ideas necessary for any practicing counselor. Even for those who have no intention of ever using this particular style of helping, the conceptual vocabulary of psychoanalysis has become crucial as a mode of communication with other professionals, as one orientation toward analyzing the etiology and development of human

Sigmund Freud (1856-1939), the founder of psychoanalysis and all therapeutic counseling, reviewing a manuscript in his Vienna home.

problems, and as a foundational base for constructing new therapeutic strategies.

Layers of awareness. Freud introduced the concept of different levels of awareness that motivate behavior. He postulated that there are several regions of the mind: the *conscious mind,* which contains those thoughts and feelings that are always accessible; the *preconscious mind,* which holds elements on the edge of awareness that with minimal effort can be made immediately accessible; and the *unconscious mind,* which harbors the secrets of the soul.

Each layer of awareness can be peeled away, gaining deeper access into the human psyche, only by permitting unconscious thoughts to surface. This task may be accomplished through *analysis of dreams, free association* of thoughts, *catharsis* of feelings, and *interpretations* that provide a level of insight sufficient to release unconscious, inhibiting desires and facilitate their continued awareness.

Stages of personality development. As a medically trained physician, Freud had particular interest in neurology and the instinctual basis of behavior. He thus viewed the development of human personality as following a series of biologically determined stages, each an expression of the *pleasure principle*—the child's insatiable urge to reduce tension and maintain psychic equilibrium by self-indulgence in oral, anal, or genital preoccupations. Freud's original conception of psychosexual development is paired with a more recent adaptation by Erikson (1950), which has more contemporary relevance for counselors seeking to understand the orderly progression of human development. Freud was concerned mostly with early childhood development and its impact on later life; Erikson's stages more accurately reflect growth throughout the life cycle, with a particular emphasis on social influences. The two sequences of stages are compared in Table 5–1.

Structure of the psyche. The healthy personality, according to Freud, consists of three separate systems, which function harmoniously and cooperatively to satisfy a person's basic needs and desires. Each of these aspects of personality is less discrete than the structure suggests and should more accurately be considered as an approximate description of processes that influence who one is and how one reacts to the world around one.

The *id* is the source of all energy and instinctual drives. Its sole psychological function is to reduce tension, discomfort, and pain at all costs. The id is impulsive, demanding, and infantile in its wishes, acting without thought or consideration of consequences.

The *ego* is the contact between the id's uncontrolled energy and the world of reality. The ego rationally, intelligently, and logically attempts to harness and moderate blind action. The ego is an integrator, pacifier, negotiator, and compromiser that seeks in socially acceptable and appropriate ways to fulfill a person's needs.

The *superego* is concerned primarily with moral issues. It is the ideal part of oneself, as contrasted with reality or pleasure. Operating as one's conscience, it strives for perfection and virtuousness. In its battle waged against the hedonistic id, the superego often takes home the spoils of "pride" or "guilt," depending on the ego's chosen resolution of the conflict.

Defense mechanisms. The *defense mechanisms* are a major contribution of psychoanalysis to practicing counselors. According to their descriptions, the defenses used by the ego to guard against perceived attack are analogous to the workings of our body's immunological system to maintain a constant equilibrium of fluid temperature, pressure, and content. Change is the enemy. Just as we are unaware of the antibodies in our bloodstream when they are activated to fight foreign protein molecules, our psychological defense mechanisms operate without our conscious awareness in an attempt to reduce anxiety and lower tension. They are ingenious strategies, impressive in their variety and flexibility; but these unconscious mind-directed defenses make the job of counseling and facilitating changes much more difficult. Better we should recognize the opponents that will be resisting our best treatment efforts:

   repression—the selective exclusion of painful experiences of the past from conscious awareness; a form of censorship used to block traumatic episodes;

Table 5–1. Developmental Stages of Personality

Age	0–1	2–3	4–5	6–11	12–18	Early Adulthood	Middle Age	Late Maturity
Freud's stages of psychosexual development	*Oral* Mouth as source of pleasure. Oral deprivation leads to oral fixation. Origins of aggressive impulses. Character of greediness, trust, rejection, insecurity, jealousy, hostility is established.	*Anal* Parental demands require bowel control. Origins of frustration, independence, anger, fastidiousness, stubbornness, control of self and others.	*Phallic* Growth of incestuous desire for parent and birth of repression. Origins of fear, fantasy, unconscious, identification, sexual attitudes, and guilt.	*Latent* Resting reprieve from tension; origins of narcissism in self-perception, socialization process.	*Genital* Need for satisfaction in sex and work. Development of altruism and love relationships. Healthy personality stabilized.			
Erikson's stages of personality development	*Trust versus mistrust* Quality of maternal relationship leads to security, affection, hope, or fear and suspicion. Consistent, dependable care will foster a trusting nature.	*Autonomy versus shame and doubt* Freedom and support of free will and struggle for independence. Origins of fear of failure and doubt develop; shame over rebellious nature.	*Initiative versus guilt* Child can initiate rather than respond—inquisitive and adventurous spirit evolves. Excessive restrictions will foster more guilt over natural urge to explore.	*Industry versus inferiority* Realization of basic competencies, striving to compete and excel; criticism leads to sense of inferiority.	*Identity versus role confusion* Search for sex, age, and career identity—for individuality as a person. Inability to establish stability creates confusion.	*Intimacy versus isolation* Overcoming safety of social distances to love and the fear of losing self in the process.	*Generativity versus stagnation* Issues of productivity and guiding next generation take precedence unless self-absorption and stagnation dominate.	*Integrity versus despair* Realization of wisdom and period of reflection about life or regret over lost opportunity.

projection—the art of putting onto another person those characteristics that are unacceptable to ourselves, such as accusing someone of being angry when we are actually feeling the anger;

denial—distorting reality by pretending that undesirable or unacceptable events are not really happening. In contrast to repression, denial occurs on a preconscious rather than unconscious level;

sublimation—the disguised conversion of forbidden impulses into socially acceptable behaviors. For instance, athletes may unconsciously choose their profession as a way to release aggression. Creative enterprises such as da Vinci's paintings or Shakespeare's sonnets were seen by Freud as sublimated unacceptable sexual desires;

reaction formation—used to counter perceived threats by substituting an opposite reaction for the one that is disturbing. Guilt can be replaced by indignation, hatred by devotion, or resentment by overprotection;

rationalization—intellectually misusing logic to overexplain or justify conflicting messages; for example, "It doesn't matter if I type the paper or not; I'll probably flunk the class anyway."

displacement—rechanneling energy from one object to another, as when an infant sucks a finger or another object in place of the desired breast;

identification—incorporating in exaggerated form the values, attitudes, standards, and characteristics of persons who are anxiety provoking, as when a child punishes herself for being bad;

regression—a retreat to an earlier stage of development because of fear. Any flight from controlled and realistic thinking may constitute a regression;

fixation—the tendency to remain at one level, interrupting the normal plan of psychological development. It is generally a defense against anxiety and results from the fear of taking the next psychological step of development.

In general, defense mechanisms are irrational methods used by the ego to deal with anxiety. They tend to distort, hide, or deny reality and hinder psychological development. They are essential to the infantile ego because of the lack of ego strength; however, they will persist when the ego has not matured sufficiently. One goal of therapeutic counseling, from the perspective of psychoanalytic theory, is to foster the healthy development of the ego.

Criticisms of Psychoanalytic Theory

Traditional psychoanalytic theory has been criticized on a number of grounds, many of which relate to its deterministic philosophy and inflexible closed-system approach:

1. The expense and time involved in psychoanalytic treatment are considerable, requiring lengthy training for the counselor and treatment for the client that could run into years.

2. It is not useful as an approach for treating large numbers of people who require counseling services.

3. There is an overemphasis on the role of insight and very little emphasis on making life changes.

4. The approach is based on experiences with neurotic rather than normal populations and may be skewed in the direction of sickness instead of health.

5. The concepts of psychoanalytic theory are difficult to research and support empirically.

6. Traditional Freudian psychoanalysis places excessive emphasis on basic instinctual desires and forces, ignoring the effects of social and cultural factors.

7. It is not useful for persons in crisis requiring immediate relief of symptoms.

It has become so fashionable to criticize Freud's ideas, especially the rigidity with which some psychoanalysts function, that many valuable therapeutic concepts have been discarded in the backlash. In part to answer their critics and in part to make the treatment more realistic, the core of psychoanalytic thinking has been preserved by some theorists in a new short-term form of therapeutic counseling. More focus is placed on specific problem areas (Bauer & Kobos, 1984). The treatment is more individually designed and the counselor confronts resistance more directly (Bennett, 1984). Efforts are made to establish time limits for both the length of treatment and specific goals (Dasberg & Winoker, 1984). Finally, the clinician plays a more active role in interpreting transference issues and in linking them to previous relationships (Davanloo, 1978).

Personal Applications

One of the distinguishing features of psychoanalytic theory is the strong emphasis placed on applying the concepts and techniques to one's own life. In a revealing letter to a friend, Freud remarked on his own painful struggles with self-analysis, which eventually led to further refinements of his ideas.

15. 10. 97.
IX. Bergasse 19

My dear Wihelm,
    My self-analysis is the most important thing I have in hand, and promises to be of the greatest value to me, when it is finished. When I was in the very midst of it it suddenly broke down for three days, and I had the feeling of inner binding about which my patients complain so much, and I was inconsolable. . . .
    It is no easy matter. Being entirely honest with oneself is a good exercise. Only one idea of general value has occurred to me. I have found love of the mother and jealousy of the father in my own case too, and now believe it to be a general phenomenon of early childhood . . . [Freud, 1954, pp. 221, 223].

The theory and techniques of psychoanalysis naturally lend themselves to personal experimentation; it was that exact method that Freud employed in their invention. Interpreting dreams is an especially fruitful method of understanding our unconscious desires and avoiding resistance, since even our defense mechanisms sleep at night. Other techniques designed to unlock the secrets of the soul include hypnosis and free association. In applying any of these strategies to ourselves it is crucial to follow Freud's imperative that we be entirely honest with ourselves about our desires, wishes, and motives.

Gestalt Counseling

Originators and Basic Concepts

Gestalt counseling has distinguished roots that go back to the very beginning of psychology as a discipline. Scientists interested in the process of learning and perception noted that problem solving is less a gradual phenomenon than it is a critical moment of insight. Kurt Koffka (1935) and Wolfgang Kohler (1929) spent considerable time between the World Wars creating certain laws of behavior that could be used to explain the process of learning. For example, they noted that we tend to perceive things grouped together as clusters, according to their proximity to one another, and that we learn to focus our attention selectively on those events, situations, or stimuli that provide internal psychological equilibrium even though we may thereby distort reality.

The basic goal of Gestalt theory is to describe human existence in terms of awareness. Gestalt counseling has been philosophically influenced by existentialism and psychologically by humanism. Each of these influences has reinforced experience as the central concept upon which awareness is built. Gestalt therapy focuses on the *what* and *how* of behavior and on the central role of unfinished business from the past that interferes with effective functioning in the present. Through helping individuals more fully to experience the present—the "here and now"—Gestalt counselors facilitate greater self-awareness and understanding.

Gestalt counseling is most closely associated with Fritz Perls (1969a), who organized the contemporary Gestalt movement in California and was its central figure until his death in 1970. Gestalt counseling is essentially experiential rather than theoretical and to a large extent is strongly influenced by the character and person of the practitioner. This was certainly true in the case of Perls, who was a charismatic personality.

Gestalt counseling stresses the role of personal responsibility in the development of awareness and experiencing feelings. *Unfinished business* from the past is brought into the present and the impasse it represents is dealt with therapeutically. *Being "stuck"* is a term used to describe the inability to resolve issues and thereby avoid dealing with the "now." _Polariza-tion_ is another key Gestalt concept; it refers to the various parts of the self that are in conflict>In his autobiography Perls interrupts the flow of his narrative to conduct an internal dialogue between his polarized, conflicted selves:

TOPDOG: Stop, Fritz, what are you doing?

UNDERDOG: What do you mean?

TOPDOG: You know very well what I mean. You're drifting from one thing to another . . .

UNDERDOG: I still don't see your objection.

TOPDOG: You don't see my objection? Man, who the hell can get a clear picture of your therapy?

UNDERDOG: You mean I should take a blackboard and make tables and categorize every term, every opposite neatly?

TOPDOG: That's not a bad idea. You could do that . . .

UNDERDOG: So what do you want me to do? Stop letting the river flow? Stop playing my garbage bin game?

TOPDOG: Well, that wouldn't be a bad idea, if you would sit down and discipline yourself . . .

UNDERDOG: Go to hell. You know me better. If I try to do something deliberate and under pressure, I get spiteful and go on strike. All my life I have been a drifter . . . [Perls, 1969b, pp. 117–118].

Techniques of Gestalt Therapy

There are literally hundreds of techniques that have been developed for Gestalt work. A few of the more common ones are described below.

Hot seat. <This technique requires an individual to be the focus of attention and answer all questions with complete honesty and sincerity>The participant is challenged to be the "here-and-now" self at all times, a task that is quite difficult, considering the intensity of questions that could be posed: "What is your most common fantasy?" "What in your life are you most ashamed of?" "Which person in the group are you most attracted to and why?" "What question are you afraid we might ask?"

Resentment expression. <Perls believed that it was essential to express resentments, which, if unexpressed, are converted to guilt>To take an example: make a list of all the things about which you consciously feel guilty. Now change the word guilt to resentment. "I feel guilty because I do not spend enough time with my children" becomes "I resent having to spend time with my children." Exploring and expressing the resentment can help a person become unstuck and work through unfinished business.

Double chairing. This technique is designed to help persons to experience the opposite poles of the self. The counselor explores a problem with a client and identifies the opposing feelings. Two chairs are then set up and the client is instructed to take one and talk to the empty chair from one (specified) pole of the issue. On instruction from the counselor, the client moves to the second chair and talks from the opposite perspective. For example: "I can't stand the way my wife puts me down for everything and I won't take it. I won't spend another minute in that house. I'm going to ask for a divorce and stick with it. Being alone is better than this misery." From the opposite pole: "Even though I feel very dissatisfied and maybe even angry with my wife, I really need to try harder to make this marriage work. We have a lot of years invested, our kids deserve an intact home, and I really don't like the idea of being alone and starting over. Besides, I'm not the easiest guy to live with." The purpose of this technique is to increase the awareness of feelings, resentments, fears, and issues from each pole of the individual's experience.

Owning the projection. In this exercise, the client is encouraged to apply his or her projections to himself or herself to demonstrate how we sometimes avoid our negatively perceived qualities and traits by putting them onto others. For example, a client says to a group member, "I think you are manipulative," then says, "I am manipulative." Or, "I don't think you are trustworthy," then, "I don't think I am trustworthy."

Criticisms of Gestalt Counseling

As is immediately evident from this brief presentation, Gestalt counseling is considerably different from the other insight theories in that little attempt has been made by its creators to explain concepts and more emphasis has been placed on experiential aspects. Consequently, the Gestalt approach is rich in strategies to help the client and counselor stay in the "here and now" and work toward greater integration of the self's polarities.

However, Gestalt counseling has been soundly criticized for its lack of a clearly articulated theory and its limited empirical base. Among other criticisms are these:

1. There is a tendency for counselors to be overly manipulative and controlling.
2. Gestalt counseling is sometimes viewed as antiintellectual because cognitive/thinking factors are greatly deemphasized.
3. Gestalt counseling is sometimes viewed as gimmicky and having a high potential for abuse.
4. It sometimes encourages a "do your own thing" attitude, which can create a sense of irresponsibility.
5. There is very little emphasis on acquiring behaviorally useful life skills.

Honorable Mentions

Because of space limitations and the vast array of theoretical orientations, only a few counseling approaches could be described in any detail. We would, however, like to mention several other insight-focused therapies that have been influential in the field. Our decision not to give them as much space as the ideas discussed above is based solely on our perception that they *currently* exert less influence on the field than those previously mentioned. That is not to say that these theories are not potentially as valuable or useful as the ones we have chosen to present; it is more a matter of our personal opinion about what is most appropriate for beginning students.

Transactional Analysis

Transactional Analysis was developed by Eric Berne (1961), a San Francisco psychiatrist, in the 1950s and 1960s and has grown rapidly since that time. More commonly known as TA, it was developed as one of the first therapies for the lay public and used group treatment as its primary modality. It has enjoyed wide appeal and great popularity, and several TA books have become best sellers: *Games People Play* (Berne, 1964), *I'm OK—You're OK* (Harris, 1969), and *What Do You Say after You Say Hello?* (Berne, 1972).

Transactional Analysis adopts an antideterministic view of human behavior, believes that persons who suffer from emotional problems are intelligent and capable, and believes that all people can remake old decisions that have led to problems. Berne believed that humans are motivated by those basic psychological needs that he termed *stimulus hunger, structure hunger,* and *position hunger.*

Stimulus hunger is the need to be acknowledged or affirmed by others both psychologically and physically. This need is satisfied by strokes, the recognition of other people, which Berne believed were essential to life. Strokes can be either positive (smiles, hugs) or negative (frowns, slaps) and constitute the basic units of human interaction.

Structure hunger refers to the ways in which we use time to maximize the number of strokes received. Berne (1972) identified several options that people have:

1. Withdrawal: escape into the safety of the self to avoid risk. In this mode it is necessary to live on "stored" strokes or to fantasize "artificial" strokes.
2. Rituals and pastimes: interactions based on greetings, pleasantries, and other low-risk, noninvolving social conversations.
3. Activities: time, structured in goals, work, and hobbies, that typically brings strokes from others.
4. Games: interaction based on unwritten rules designed to create a payoff. Games are usually dishonest and covert and generate negative payoffs. They are the most common disturbance in interpersonal behavior.

5. Intimacy: a method of structuring time that, unlike the other four, is designed to bring people together, not keep them apart. It is based on honest, open, and mutual relationships, which carry the highest risks but also offer the greatest rewards of all interactions.

The issues of time structuring in our lives are personalized by James and Jongeward (1971); consider their questions for yourself:

• What did your parents say about time? Did they use phrases such as: "You only live once"; "Enjoy it while you may"; "Don't waste your time"; "What are you going to do, sit around all day? Get going"; or "Relax, honey, there's always another day."?
• Are you fighting time? Killing it? Using it? Enjoying it?
• Now select an average weekday and try to determine what percentage of your time is structured with rituals, pastimes, withdrawing, activities, games, and intimacy [p. 66].

Position hunger is the need to have decisions affirmed; to be told we're OK. It is a reflection of intrinsic self-worth. Early in life one makes basic decisions about the self: either "I'm OK" or "I'm not OK." Once this decision about the self has been made, it provides a script for the ways in which a person structures time and seeks strokes.

Another aspect of Transactional Analysis refers to the three ego states of the personality structure: the Child, the Adult, and the Parent:

> The Child is composed of the feelings and behaviors that were experienced in childhood. It contains spontaneous and natural feelings.
>
> The Parent reflects the incorporation of attitudes, feelings, and behaviors from significant other adults during childhood. The parent ego state can be both nurturing and critical.
>
> The Adult develops over time and reflects the ability to evaluate the reactions of the Child and Parent in an objective and factual manner. The Adult ego state develops throughout the life of the individual, while the Child and Parent remain static after 6 or 7 years of age.

The basic unit of communication in TA is the transaction, which consists of an exchange of strokes. Transactions can be complementary (that is, between equivalent ego states: Parent–Parent, Child–Child, or Adult–Adult) or crossed (that is, between nonequivalent ego states: "What time is it?" [Adult]; "How should I know?" [Child]).

The person in Transactional Analysis analyzes various interactions and attempts to increase personal autonomy and decrease the impact of self-defeating scripts and manipulative game playing. The person is freed from the contaminating and troublesome aspect of Child/Parent in order to experience choices in the present without the limitations of the past.

Individual Psychology

Individual psychology, developed by <u>Alfred Adler</u> (1929) following his break with Freud in 1911 stresses the social rather than the sexual determinants of personality. It views human beings holistically as creative, responsible, "becoming" individuals moving toward their goals. It is essentially a dynamic, pragmatic, and optimistic theory that is flexible and constantly tested by practice.

<u>Rudolf Dreikurs</u> (1950) formulated <u>five basic norms</u> of Adlerian psychology.

1. Socially embedded All problems are basically social problems and emerge from the need to "belong" and find a place in the group. A well-adjusted person is oriented to and behaves in line with the needs of the social situation. A maladjusted person has faulty concepts, feelings of inferiority, and mistaken goals and is overly concerned with what others think of him or her and/or what is in it for him or her.

2. Self-determining and creative Adler believed that life is movement and that individuals have the power to change interactions by what they do. The belief that individuals can change and are active participants in their lives is the basis for such optimism.

3. Goal-directed Behavior, according to Adler, is directed toward goals that are inferred from the consequences of behavior. Looking for "causes" of behavior is unproductive because they are unknowable and, even if known, cannot be changed. Goals, once recognized, can be modified and represent a behavioral choice.

4. Subjective Reality is as we perceive it and is not absolute. Adler further believed that it is not what happens to us that matters, but how we feel about it. As a result, Adler emphasized interactions and movement in all relationships as the unit of analysis.

5. Holistic: Human beings are integrated, whole, and incapable of being reduced to discrete units. One must deal with the entire person.

In Adlerian psychology, feelings of inferiority are the basis of anxiety and destructive to clients. Inferiority feelings are not "feelings" in the usual sense, but are a belief system or a reasoning process about how one should be. One's response to inferiority feelings is the basis for character formation.

Adler (1958) believed that the purpose of counseling is to restore faith in the self to overcome these feelings of inferiority. The process of counseling contains four steps for the individual:

1. Become aware of our own prejudice Recognize that as children we learned that we were not good enough as we were; thus, we were urged to do better.

2. Stop being afraid of making a mistake Overconcern with error encourages more, not fewer, mistakes. Further, it is human to make mistakes; do we expect ourselves to be superhuman? Mistakes reflect an opportunity to learn if they are accepted and we avoid discouragement.

3. Cultivate the courage to be imperfect. Working to resist self-evaluation and to do our best to respond to the needs of a situation is preferable to feeling inadequate because we could improve performance. We don't have to be any better than we are.
4. Enjoy the pleasure in an activity. It is important not to reduce pleasure in life by being overly concerned with success, failure, or prestige. Learning to do one's best and accepting the outcome increases the pleasure in life.

The Adlerian approach is concerned with helping individuals develop a lifestyle that is socially responsible and personally fulfilling, one that allows for growth and a holistic integration. A person who is psychopathological is discouraged and has lost faith in the ability to change.

Character Analysis

Character Analysis was initially developed by Karen Horney (1951) in response to Freud's theory of instincts. She believed that the core of neurosis emerged from cultural conditions and human relations rather than instinctual energy. In character analysis, individuals are seen as one of three types: (1) the compliant type, (2) the detached type, and (3) the aggressive type. A compliant character type tends to move toward people, is somewhat dependent, and has prominent needs for love and approval. A detached character type does not create emotionally close relationships and is distant from self and others. An aggressive type has a strong need for power and control and often moves against people.

Horney believed that basic anxiety comes from the disturbed elements of a parent–child relationship and reflects the child's feeling of isolation and helplessness in a hostile world. Anxiety is produced by anything that disturbs a child's basic security in intimate family relationships. As an adult, the neurotic needs emerge as ways of dealing with anxiety. They include

1. the need for affection and approval;
2. the need for a partner to take over one's life;
3. the need to restrict one's life to narrow borders;
4. the need for power;
5. the need to exploit others;
6. the need for prestige;
7. the need for personal admiration;
8. the need for personal achievement;
9. the need for self-sufficiency and independence;
10. the need for protection.

These needs are classified as neurotic because they are compulsive, reflect instability, and are unrealistic in their nature and expectations. Character Analysis represents an analytic orientation to counseling that substitutes an exploration of social and cultural issues for Freud's analysis of instinctual drives. As an analytic or neo-Freudian approach, it shares both the advantages and limitations of the psychoanalytic model.

Summary

In this chapter, we have presented some of the more prominent insight-oriented theories that influence therapeutic counseling. There are, of course, many we have neglected, such as the other psychodynamic approaches of Jung, Alexander, Bordin, Sullivan, Reich, and Fromm. Part of the task of developing into a mature therapeutic counselor is coming to terms, on a personal and intellectual level, with the many options available.

Each of the insight approaches presented offers the counselor a framework for understanding the client's world and a methodology for promoting greater self-awareness and self-understanding. It is assumed that such exploration and knowledge will lead a client toward making desired life changes. It is also believed that the presence of the counselor and the relationship between counselor and client provide nonspecific curative effects that are helpful in the process of being and becoming.

Suggested Readings

Corey, G. (1982). *Theory and practice of counseling and psychotherapy* (2nd ed.). Monterey, Calif.: Brooks/Cole.

Davanloo, H. (1980). *Short-term dynamic psychotherapy*. New York: Jason Aronson.

Freud, S. (1952). *A general introduction to psychoanalysis*. New York: Washington Square Press.

Jung, C. (1961). *Memories, dreams, reflections*. New York: Vintage Books.

May, R. (1983). *The discovery of being*. New York: Norton.

Patterson, C. H. (1980). *Theories of counseling and psychotherapy* (3rd ed.). New York: Harper and Row.

Perls, F. (1969). *In and out of the garbage pail*. Lafayette, Calif.: Real People Press.

Rogers, C. (1980). *A way of being*. Palo Alto, Calif.: Houghton Mifflin.

Yalom, I. (1980). *Existential psychotherapy*. New York: Basic Books.

Chapter 6

Action-Oriented

Counseling Theories

<The theoretical perspectives presented in Chapter 5 emphasized the importance of self-awareness and understanding in the counseling process. The primary medium used in insight-based approaches is verbal interventions designed to promote the client's exploration of presenting complaints. In this chapter we will examine theories that stress not insight but interventions leading more directly to relief of symptoms. These approaches blend an emphasis on action with verbal processing to accomplish specific therapeutic goals.>

<Action-oriented approaches to counseling are generally characterized by their reliance on behaviorally specific interventions and outcome measures. The counselor in these approaches works actively to structure sessions so that concrete, observable, and measurable goals can be established and accomplished. The role of the counselor tends to be active and directive, working with the client to structure the sessions. Action-oriented counseling gives less attention than insight theories to the therapeutic relationship as well as process, interpretation, and insight. Instead, its proponents emphasize a more objective and scientific approach to counseling that makes use of a variety of techniques and structures.>

Behavioral Counseling

Aliases: Behaviorism, Behavior Modification, Behavior Therapy

Conceptual Perspective

The influence of behaviorism on counseling has come a long way since B. F. Skinner and his rigid prescriptions for human control and manipulation (Skinner, 1938, 1953). Once viewed as a radical counterpoint to the humanism of Carl Rogers and Abraham Maslow, behavioral principles have been assimilated into the mainstream of therapeutic counseling to the extent that even insight-oriented counselors regularly use many of the techniques, for instance, goal setting, assertiveness training, relaxation training, and other methods of skill acquisition.

The term *behavioral counseling* was first introduced by John Krumboltz in 1964.<He suggested that counselors should remind themselves that the purpose of their activity is to foster *behavioral* changes in clients; thus, all counseling is ultimately behavioral>(Krumboltz, 1965). From a behavioristic perspective, counseling can be viewed as the systematic use of procedures to reach mutually established therapeutic goals that will resolve client concerns and conflicts (Thoresen, 1969). The behavioral approach therefore views counseling less as a philosophy of life and more as a set of principles to be used in a targeted and situationally-specific manner.

While there are many variations on the behavioral approach to counseling, most proponents agree that clients' problems are the result of maladaptive learning patterns; treatment thus takes the form of learning new life skills. Concepts central to the work of a behavioral counselor include reinforcement (both operant and classical), social modeling, environmental changes, specific identification of problems and goals, and, especially, objective measurement of changes over time. In many ways behavioral counseling is viewed as an educational process that borrows heavily from learning theory and emphasizes the acquisition of more adaptive ways to act.

The work of Ivan Pavlov, with his salivating dogs and their responses to the ringing of dinner bells, John Watson's discovery that neurosis can be induced by scaring infants, and B. F. Skinner's fascination with teaching pigeons to play ping-pong are important milestones in the development of behaviorism. Those early research efforts were translated into action techniques for promoting systematic client change (Bergin & Garfield, 1971; Kanfer & Goldstein, 1980).

John Dollard and Neil Miller (1950) attempted to combine psychoanalytic insights and practical learning principles into a science of human behavior. Joseph Wolpe (1958, 1969) worked to apply Pavlov's classical conditioning to systematic desensitization. Julian Rotter and Albert Bandura worked independently on a behavioral approach that stressed the impact of social learning and modeling concepts, in which context behavior is shaped by the interactions of an individual personality with significant others. Kanfer and Phillips (1970) used Skinner's operant model as a basis for developing the methods we now know as "behavior modification." Within the counseling literature, significant contributors such as John Krumboltz (1966), Carl Thoresen (1969), and Ray Hosford (1969) have been active in translating learning theory principles into therapeutic practice.

The theory of behavioral counseling is deceptively simple. We are born into the world basically empty-headed, with a few reflexes. All our values, attitudes, preferences, emotional responses, thinking patterns, personality styles, and problems are the result of learned behavior. We are shaped by our environment, reinforced and molded by the world around us. A systematic and scientific approach is used to (1) identify specific behaviors in need of elimination or acquisition, (2) set objectives that are reasonable and desirable, (3) collect data on the client's functioning levels, (4) design and engineer initial change efforts, (5) isolate and diminish client resistance, (6) modify distracting variables, (7) monitor and assess the impact of planned interventions, and (8) make alterations as needed in the treatment plan (Gottman and Lieblum, 1974).

Behavioral Technology

One valuable tool of the researcher in general, and of behaviorists in particular, is the use of time-series charts for graphic portrayal of client change. This method helps the counselor to study a single case intensively, plotting baseline data and the results of therapeutic interventions. It aids in quantitatively and specifically describing the behaviors targeted for changes, as well as noting the effects of any action. In Figure 6–1, the counselor has available at a glance a summary of the client's presenting problems and the results of several attempts to change the behavior.

<A strength of the behavioral approach consists not only in its assessment procedures but in its wide variety of treatment strategies>Its technology of helping is consistently and reliably applied to produce observable client changes, which the behaviorist is skilled at identifying, measuring, and changing. Many behavioral methodologies, succinctly organized by Groden and Cautela (1981), are now part of the repertoire of every therapeutic counselor.

Operant conditioning procedures.   Operant conditioning procedures, including those based on the work of B. F. Skinner (1953) and other researchers are methods in which<the frequency of behavior may be increased or decreased according to the type and timing of stimuli presented>In positive reinforcement strategies the counselor hopes to increase behavior by rewarding the client. Implicitly, the most subtle head nods, "uh huh's," smiles, and twinkling eyes positively reinforce the client's talking, trusting, and opening up. Operationally, this methodology is used in token economics with a variety of normal and maladjusted client populations, often in classroom settings, to spell out and encourage acceptable behavior as it spontaneously or deliberately occurs. Participants receive rewards in the form of points or privileges in exchange for their cooperation and lose points for obstructing progress.

The counselor's task is to (1) identify the specific target behaviors in need of upgrading, (2) discover situation-specific, individually designed rewards that motivate a given client, (3) administer the reinforcement soon after the target behavior is displayed, and (4) slowly wean the client from any dependence on the external motivation in favor of internalized, self-administered reinforcers. These same principles would hold true for any other operant procedure.

Negative reinforcement also produces an increase in desired target behaviors such as assertiveness but does so by removing a stimulus that the client perceives as aversive. Resistant clients, for example, can rid themselves of the inconvenience and discomfort of their counseling sessions only by being more cooperative and working faster to change.

Punishment strategies are used to reduce the frequency of a client's behavior by presenting an aversive stimulus. Unfortunately, many parents and teachers rely too heavily on this strategy because of its seeming convenience, even though it usually produces negative side effects in the child such as withdrawal, aggression, and generalized fears. Another problem with punishment is that its effects are brief and the behavior that is stopped often reappears at a higher level of frequency. Punishment may be used in conjunction with other operant procedures, such as a weight loss program in which the client writes a self-contract.

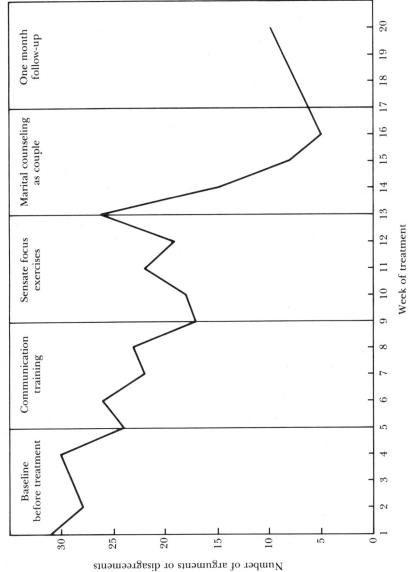

Figure 6–1. Effects of interventions on client's relationship with spouse.

111

Contract

Goals: To lose 15 pounds in 60 days. To change my eating habits to include more fruits and vegetables and less chocolate. To exercise 3 times per week for no less than 20 minutes.

Procedures: I will limit myself to 1500 calories per day and restrict all eating activities to the dinner table. Snacks and in-between meals are strictly forbidden.

Consequences:

Daily reward: For each day I am able to stay within my calorie limit I am permitted to play my tuba for 2 uninterrupted hours.

Daily punishment: For each day I violate my calorie limit I will set my alarm for 3 A.M., wake up, vacuum and clean the house from top to bottom.

Contract reward: If I am successful in losing 15 pounds within 2 months I will treat myself to a 4-day skiing weekend and buy myself a new outfit in a smaller size.

Contract punishment: If I am unsuccessful I will agree to do all housekeeping chores for a month.

Signed _____ Date _____

Witness_____

The behavioral counselor has a variety of other standard techniques that have developed from laboratory research on conditioning processes.

Extinction involves the removal of the reinforcement for a given behavior, such as ignoring a child's temper tantrum. Two factors should be kept in mind when using extinction: (1) during the initial phase, after the reinforcer has been removed, the target behavior increases dramatically; during the second phase, the behavior decreases; and (2) extinction, once implemented, must be applied systematically and consistently.

Covert reinforcement uses mental images that function as reinforcers and can be generated by the client. The client is asked to imagine a situation in which he or she might refrain from an undesirable behavior. The counselor then instructs the client to visualize the reinforcing image.

Contingency contracting is the use of a behavioral contract that defines the necessary contingencies upon which a reinforcer will be presented. Clients decide how often and at which levels they desire the reinforcer, thus shaping their own behavior.

Shaping is a process in which complex terminal behaviors are reinforced in approximate successive stages. The client receives consistent reinforcement in small steps as movement is made toward the ultimate goal.

Classical Conditioning Procedures.   In classical or Pavlovian conditioning, a presented stimulus elicits automatic responses. Systematic desensitization, an example of classical conditioning developed by Joseph Wolpe (1958, 1982), is the most common of these methodologies; clients are taught to substitute relaxation responses for anxiety when confronted by previously frightening situations such as tests or social events. Anxiety is thereafter inhibited. Two basic principles underlie systematic desensitization: (1) one emotion can be used to counteract another, and (2) it is possible to adapt to a perceived threat.

Systematic desensitization initially involves teaching the client how to relax. Next a hierarchy of perceived threat is developed in which the client lists minimally stressful scenes (for example, watching a film of someone receiving an injection) and works toward progressively fearful images (receiving a flu shot in the arm).

The counselor will usually use a hypnotically calm, relaxing voice, even pacing the words...to...the...rise...and...fall...of...the...client's... breathing. The client is instructed to relax each muscle in the body, to imagine all tension draining away, to visualize a floating, drifting scene on the beach, perhaps feeling the warm sun and cool sand, hearing the waves crash against the surf, seeing birds sailing high above. After the client reaches a state of total relaxation, she or he is asked to work through the fear hierarchy, systematically reducing any tension with learned relaxation responses. After a few practice sessions almost anyone can learn to inhibit his or her anxiety.

In flooding, an opposite strategy is employed to erode the stimulus-response sequence. A phobia, fear, or bad habit can be extinguished by bombarding the person with the stimulus until fatigue sets in or until (in the case of a habit) the stimulus loses its pleasurable value. While lecturing on this subject, one of the authors was confronted by a disbelieving student who aggressively asked, "If this stuff works, how could I use it to stop smoking?" The instructor flippantly replied, "Lock yourself in the closet with a pack of Camels and don't come out until you're done smoking them all," never once considering that the student might actually follow the advice.

It was a week later that the student showed up in class again to report his story:

I wasn't sure if you were kidding or not but I decided to try this behavior stuff anyway. I bought a pack of unfiltered cigarettes, went home, told my mother I was doing an experiment for school, and proceeded to lock myself in the bathroom. Since I usually smoke filtered menthols, I was, at first, a little surprised that I actually enjoyed the first two cigarettes. I even thought to myself, not only is this not going to work but now I'm going to be addicted worse. By the fifth cigarette I noticed I was feeling a little dizzy, and by the seventh the smoke was starting to burn my eyes. I finally started to get really sick by the tenth. I guess I must have passed out because the next morning I woke up in a pool of vomit with a cigarette burn on my leg. Not only will I never smoke again but I can't even stand being in the same room with someone else who is.

The lessons to be learned are not only the effectiveness of behavioral strategies but the importance of carefully monitoring their application so that abuse and harm can be avoided. Because the counselor has a more forceful role in behavioral counseling, the client's rights and freedom of choice are jeopardized unless great caution is taken to ensure that the ends justify the means and that the client is fully informed about the implications, dangers, and limitations of a given procedure (Van Hoose and Kottler, 1977).

Criticisms of the Behavioral Approach

Behaviorism has been criticized most often because of its narrow focus on observable human behavior and the lack of attention to feelings and thoughts, which also make up a significant part of a person's functioning. In addition, the behavioral approach works only with the presenting complaint, which could be a symptom of underlying intrapsychic conflicts. Many insight-oriented theorists therefore believe that symptoms thus cured will inevitably be replaced by others, since the internal condition of the client has not been altered.

As an action-oriented approach, behaviorism has also been criticized as mechanistic, manipulative, and impersonal because it downplays the role of the therapeutic relationship and all but ignores the value of self-understanding in the change process. Because it also works toward empiricism (that is, specificity or quantification), prediction, and control, it often sacrifices the values of intuition and artistry in change endeavors.

Rational-Emotive Counseling

Aliases: Rational-Emotive Therapy, RET, Cognitive Behavior Therapy, Rational Behavior Therapy, Cognitive Therapy

Originators

Feeling confined and bored by the rigid structures of traditional psychoanalysis, Albert Ellis (1962) introduced a system of counseling based on principles of logic and rational analysis. During the past several years Ellis has written hundreds of books and articles, even song and coloring books, to further develop and popularize his theory of rational-emotive therapy (RET). Ellis has remained remarkably, perhaps even rigidly, consistent through the years, attempting to live his life as a model of rational functioning. In the past decade he has devoted himself to collaborating with researchers (Ellis & Grieger, 1977; Ellis & Whiteley, 1979) to establish a more solid empirical base for the theory.

There have been many offshoots of RET that put more emphasis on the rational-educational process (Maultsby, 1975) or the cognitive-behavior components (Beck, 1976; Mahoney, 1974; Meichenbaum, 1977). All the proponents of the rational-cognitive-behavioral-emotive approach are in basic agreement that the legitimate focus of counseling ought to be modification of the way people think.

Basic Points of RET

A thunderstorm, missed appointment, critical comment, failing grade, and flat tire are all examples of daily occurrences that can make us feel upset, right? Not so, according to Ellis and company.

Nobody or nothing outside of ourselves can *cause* us to feel anything. There is no "bad temper button" on our foreheads that anyone else can push to make us angry on demand. Granted, there are many things that people do or events that occur that are very conducive to our upsetting ourselves. Nevertheless, it is our choice, due to years of lazy negligence and wallowing in our irrational beliefs, to interpret the world negatively and consequently feel depressed, anxious, guilty, or frustrated.

It is the primary goal of RET to help clients identify their patterns of irrational thinking, those habitual beliefs that lead one to misperceive reality, and subsequently to learn alternative tools of thinking that are, in real-world terms, more logical, consistent, rational, and scientific. According to the ABC theory of emotions (see Figure 6–2), it is evaluative thoughts (B) rather than the traumatic situation itself (A) that will primarily determine the emotional reaction (C). This response will be an extremely negative emotion unless the person vigorously challenges the validity of assumptions, thereby disputing irrational beliefs (D) and making a new, more desirable emotional response (E) more likely.

A	B	C
Activating Experience	*Belief or Interpretation of Experience*	*Emotional Consequence*
Reading chapters on counseling approaches that present a dozen complex theories	"I feel so stupid that I can't understand all of this stuff."	confusion
	"This is terrible. I'll *never* be a good counselor since I already feel lost."	frustration
		anxiety
	"I *should* be able to pick this stuff up faster."	anger

	D	E
	Disputing Irrational Beliefs	*Emotional Effect*
	"Of course I feel overwhelmed—that is what an introductory student is *supposed* to feel when presented with an overview of the field in but a few weeks."	relief
		mild tension
		mild annoyance
	"Just because I don't understand everything about these theories doesn't make me a stupid person—just a person who will have to work a little harder and have more patience."	excitement
	"This isn't a terrible situation, it's only difficult and slightly uncomfortable."	

Figure 6–2.   ABC theory of emotions

Thoughts or behaviors are viewed as irrational if they create significant emotional conflicts with others, block constructive goals, do not adhere to objective reality, or needlessly threaten life. Originally Ellis proposed 11 separate irrational beliefs (Ellis & Harper, 1975), which he later simplified to four basic ideas (Ellis, 1977).

Awfulizing.   "Awfulizing" is the habitual exaggeration of reality by "disasterizing" about the future, focusing on the worst possible outcome:

- "OK, I'll study to take the dumb test again, but I'll probably never pass it."
- "It's just *terrible* that we have to live through this divorce."
- "I can't believe this *catastrophe:* can you just imagine my shame when I found out he was already *married?*"
- "Yeah, sure, my speech went well, but what a *total flop* when those people in the back left early."

Since it can never be proved that anything is totally bad and since things can always turn out worse than they actually did, awfulizing makes a major emotional tailspin out of a minor disappointment. By keeping expectations to a minimum and countering exaggerations with more appropriate, realistic interpretations of life's unexpected events, such irrational beliefs can be neutralized.

"I can't stand it."   As a corollary and companion to the irrational belief represented by awfulizing, this belief also distorts the relative significance of things when they don't go our own way. For those people with a low tolerance for frustration, life's normal setbacks take on gargantuan proportions of pain.

In reality, we can stand everything but death—up to and including having to go to the bathroom desperately with no facility around. Indeed we grit our teeth, cross our legs (unless walking quickly), and bear the pain until we can find release. This metaphor is typical of those a counselor might use humorously to illustrate the childish foot-stomping we resort to when confronted with disappointment.

Musterbating.   A close relative of masturbation in its potential for self-abuse, the use of "musts," "shoulds," and "oughts" are, Ellis believes, the cornerstones of all emotional disturbances. The use of these words, and the underlying thoughts they represent, imply that a person expects special treatment and that the forces of the universe have to cooperate to provide what is demanded:

- "I *must* do well in all situations and circumstances, and when I don't, it's *awful.*"
- "I *must* be loved and approved of by everyone to feel worthwhile."
- "They *ought* to have given me the job. I deserved it. It just isn't fair."

There is nothing inherently fair and equitable about the world we live in. In spite of our expectations and demands that we get what we want and feel we deserve, rarely does the world cooperate. To expect it do so is irrational.

Self-judgments.   Evaluating oneself or others in absolute terms of good, bad, right, or wrong, and therefore condemning less-than-desirable performance, represents the fourth kind of irrational belief.

- "I completely blew the whole interview; I'm a horrible counselor."
- "I'm just not comfortable at parties because I make such a fool of myself."
- "You're not a very good mother to let your kids have so much freedom."
- "He's a real idiot and can't do anything right. If *I* were in his place. . . ."

It is irrational to expect perfection of oneself or others, on any level, since such a goal is impossible. Treatment of this irrational belief is approached by teaching clients to rate their behavior rather than personhood and not to permit themselves to dislike other people but only to disapprove of things they might do (or not do).

According to the tenets of RET, all human beings have each of the irrational beliefs in varying quantities, although their effects, intensity, and destructive potential will depend on the individual. Essentially, the counseling strategy involves defining, discriminating, debating, and disputing the client's irrational thinking patterns while substituting alternative thoughts that are more appropriate and logical. So the reasoning goes: if we can change how we think, we can change how we feel, and therefore how we behave.

Therapeutic Techniques

Since RET is action-oriented in its application of insight, there is a rich variety of techniques available to the practitioner in his or her quest to confront irrational thinking.

Disputing irrational beliefs.   The counselor, in a role that is active, directive, and confrontive, probes the client's unique irrational beliefs by acting as a logical springboard of ideas. The focus is usually in the present, and client and counselor verbalizations normally have about equal shares of time. The content is, of course, cognitive in nature, concentrating on how the client characteristically thinks. The following are examples of interventions:

- "*Where is the evidence* that you are a loser just because this one relationship has ended?"
- "Who said the world was fair? Oh, *you* did. Well, it's *your* rule?"
- "What are you telling yourself to make yourself feel upset?"
- "Is it really *terrible* that things aren't working out the way you would like, or perhaps only a little inconvenient?"

Rational-emotive imagery.   As an action-oriented modality, RET provides opportunities for safe rehearsal of new ways of thinking. This mental practice creates more positive habits, which lead to greater internal control of emotions. An imagery exercise might take the following form:

> Just relax and lean back. Let all your muscles go loose and your mind feel free. Now imagine that situation you so dread. You are walking down the street and you meet your ex-wife. How do you feel right this moment? scared? angry? and depressed too? OK, now practice what we have been discussing. Change the fear to mild apprehension, the anger to mild irritation, and the depression to sadness. Signal when you've done that—OK, now, what did you tell yourself to change your feelings? Which thoughts did you change?

The client is thus helped to practice a new, more constructive way of thinking, both in the sessions and as systematic homework between counseling meetings.

Psychological homework.   As do other behavioral methods, RET relies on regular assignments between sessions to reinforce new ideas and provide opportunities to test skills in the outside world. Homework may be individually designed and may include reading assignments and specific risk-taking activities, or it may be of a more general nature that requires the client to practice new skills by rehearsing the ABC theory of emotions in real-life situations.

Self-talk.   A client is taught to think differently by talking differently to himself or herself. This strategy involves closely monitoring the choice of words such as "should", "must," "ought," and "can't" and substituting other words more consistent with rational thinking. The counselor listens carefully to the language patterns used by the client, confronting irrational self-statements and helping the client to rephrase. Increasing client awareness of the insidious reinforcing nature of irrational thinking is an objective of this technique. Clients often spend time monitoring television, radio, and the conversations of others, as well as their own speech patterns, to improve their proficiency in recognizing irrational statements.

Criticisms of RET

1. Human beings are multifaceted, with feelings as well as thoughts. Critics suggest that RET puts undue emphasis on thought process to the exclusion of many legitimate feelings, thereby contributing to repression and denial of feelings.
2. RET is probably less effective with some kinds of clients—those who already have problems with overintellectualizing or who don't have the capacity to reason logically (young children, schizophrenics, some clients with character disorders, or clients with minimal intelligence).
3. Many RET counselors complain of boredom and burn-out from continuously repeating the same arguments and processes with all clients.

4. RET is difficult for some professionals to practice if they are not outgoing and combative and don't enjoy vigorous debate and confrontation.

5. Because the counselor's role is so verbal, active, and directive, the client may feel overpowered, dominated, and without much responsibility for the outcome.

Personal Applications

Among counseling approaches, RET lends itself particularly well to personal adoption by the professional. Ellis has said repeatedly that by talking our clients out of their crazy beliefs, we cannot help changing our own in the process. Other RET practitioners report that they have noticed themselves becoming more psychologically healthy as they become more experienced clinicians.

Personally useful ideas from RET include

1. The idea that because we create our own emotional misery through distorted thinking we can potentially change these negative feelings by changing the way we think about our situations. A flat tire, highway accident, critical comment, and missed appointment can all be viewed as inconveniences or disasters, depending on our point of view.

2. The technique of carefully monitoring our language for words such as "should," "must," and "ought" that imply irrational beliefs. As we become more aware of illogical language, we start to hear faulty phrases in others and ourselves: "She makes me so angry" (how can anyone make you feel anything without your consent?); "This weather is so depressing" (rain is just rain—it's *your* interpretation that makes it seem depressing; "It just frustrates me so much" (don't you mean, "I frustrate myself over what I perceive is happening"?).

3. The structure of mentally rehearsing difficult tasks for the future or painful events of the past to relieve anxiety and work through unsolved irrational beliefs. These imagery techniques are helpful, for instance, in allaying fears for an upcoming interview in which penetrating questions can be asked: "What's the worst that could happen? Even if I mess up the interview and perform less than perfectly, does that mean I'm not a good counselor and will *never* be competent? And even if *that* were so, what does that have to do with my 'goodness' as a human being?"

Strategic Counseling

Aliases: Strategic Family Therapy, Structural Family Therapy, Neurolinguistic Programming, Ericksonian Therapy, Problem Solving Therapy, Brief Therapy, Tactical Therapy, Ordeal Therapy

Origins

Perhaps the most exciting change in the direction of therapeutic counseling to occur in many years, strategic counseling combines the methods and theory from a number of disciplines into a dramatic action-oriented helping model that often requires but a few sessions to rid clients permanently of their presenting complaints. Milton Erickson—psychiatrist, hypnotist, wizard—grew up physically handicapped. He discovered ways of getting other people to do things for themselves or for him without having to ask. As a professional adult, Erickson developed new ways of helping people through the uses of metaphor, paradoxical instructions, hypnotic suggestions, and other elaborate and sophisticated communication devices (Haley, 1973).

Richard Bandler and John Grinder systematized what Erickson did intuitively by creating a communication model of counseling that diagnoses a client's personal style and then matches the helper's mode to ensure greater rapport and influence. The efforts of a Gestalt therapist and a linguistics professor were thus merged to create neurolinguistic programming, a system of eyewatching and language patterning that allows counselors to pursuade clients to change on conscious and unconscious levels (Bandler and Grinder, 1979).

Jay Haley and Cloe Madanes were also strongly influenced by Erickson but moved in another direction, one that emphasized symptoms in the context of family systems. In collaboration with the "Palo Alto group," Haley, his mentor Gregory Bateson, and a host of skilled researchers, theoreticians, and clinicians in sociology, education, medicine, anthropology, and psychology, combined forces to revolutionize strategic counseling with families.

Haley and his associates sought to examine individual problems as metaphors for patterns that exist in the family. A child who develops problems in school has found a way to distract the parents from their own troubles. As long as they focus on the child's delinquent activities, they function as a cohesive team. Once the child recovers, the parents begin their bickering anew. Haley (1976) sought to break the destructive chain by analyzing and changing the patterns of communication between family members. He was later to refine his theory into a form of "ordeal therapy" in which the goal is to present a therapeutic problem more difficult than the client's presenting concerns (Haley, 1984).

While Haley and other family therapists such as Virginia Satir and Salvador Minuchin were laboring on the East Coast, the Palo Alto group continued to flourish, culminating in the publication of two works that describe the art and science of doing counseling briefly and strategically. In *Change: Principles of Problem Formation and Problem Resolution* (1974), Watzlawick, Weakland, and Fisch described a new way of looking at problems: seeing them as a vicious-cycle process in which the client's attempted solutions only maintain the problem. In *The Tactics of Change*, Fisch, Weakland, and Segal (1982) give an example: "The husband withdraws 'because my wife nags' while the wife nags 'because my husband withdraws' " (p. 13). The authors argue that the only efficient way for a therapist to intervene in such a system is to assume a "maneuverable" position having maximum flexibilities while limiting the client's avenues of escape. They provide specific descriptions of various tactics that effectively change the ways a client can respond, thereby forcing the client to choose other, more self-enhancing responses.

Strategic Interventions

The strategic practitioner follows an orderly sequence of steps: understanding the dynamics of the client's relationships, identifying the sources of conflict, and planning a strategy for change (Madanes, 1984). The principal strength of this approach, however, lies not with its innovations in theory but rather with its creative, often radical prescriptions for change. The great majority of the contributors to strategic counseling would agree on the basic assumptions that (1) the counselor's role is highly active and directive, (2) counseling need not take a lot of time to be effective, (3) analyzing family and individual communication patterns is crucial to understanding the client's problems, (4) intervention efforts are action oriented, with insight largely ignored, (5) strategies are all individually designed to match the client's personal style and situation, and (6) if one strategy doesn't work, try something else.

Bandler and Grinder (1979) eloquently summarize the important issue of flexibility in counseling:

> One of the operating procedures of most disciplines that allows a field to grow and to continue to develop at a rapid rate is a rule that if what you do doesn't work, do *something else*. If you are an engineer and you get the rocket all set up, and you push the button and it doesn't lift up, you alter your behavior to find out what you need to do to make certain changes to overcome gravity.
>
> However, in the field of psychotherapy, if you encounter a situation where the rocket doesn't go off, it has a special name; it's called having a "resistant client" [p. 13].

Strategic methods are controversial. They tell us to do everything that just a few years ago we learned not to do: be active, directive, controlling, and mysterious. The counselor, as an expert, accepts responsibility for designing treatment methods that are effective. The task of getting clients to respond differently to their life situations requires artistry and skill in persuasion, motivation, and influence, as well as a sense of humor and the absurd (Haley, 1984; Madanes, 1984). Here is a sampling of some flexible, unusual, and ingenious strategies.

Pretending is a strategy that Madanes (1984) prefers when working with children who have disruptive symptoms irritating to their parents. After the child has been deliberately directed to engage in the symptoms, they lose their controlling power. Other forms of directive intervention involve shifting the power in a family, changing the family members' style of interaction, and posing paradoxical tasks: the client is given instructions that the counselor hopes she or he will disobey. With clients who wished to lose weight, for example, Milton Erickson was fond of ordering them to gain five pounds before the next session. If they complied, they demonstrated the potential control they had over their weight—the ability to increase (and, by implication, decrease) it at will. More likely, however, they would think Erickson crazy, deliberately disobey the order, and lose weight, thereby following the road to recovery.

Many of the other strategic interventions, such as metaphorical directives, power shifts, and reframing, will be described in the chapter on marital and family counseling. The action orientation of the strategic approach is already evident: counselors seek to influence behavior dramatically by disrupting existing life patterns. Since much of strategic counseling is intuitive and creative, *it requires a solid base of clinical experience and supervision before it can be safely and effectively used.* This approach to helping tends to work best with complex family systems and with individuals who have strong commitments to maladaptive behavior.

Criticisms of Strategic Counseling

1. The client is not given primary responsibility for the content or focus of the session; it is clear that the counselor is the authority in charge.
2. The process is deliberately mysterious, so the client never understands what has happened or why.
3. Insight is unnecessarily downgraded or totally ignored as a distracting variable, even though self-understanding is an important goal of many clients.
4. Ethical problems are potentially associated with such explicit influence and control. There is some danger if directives are misinterpreted or used irresponsibly.
5. Many of the strategies are intuitively constructed and are therefore difficult to learn and apply reliably.
6. The influence of the counselor is crucial to the success of these techniques and may therefore minimize the curative effects of the therapeutic relationship.
7. There is a limited empirical base for these approaches, and by their nature they prove difficult to research.

Multi-Modal Counseling

Aliases: Eclectic, Pragmatic

Originators

Arnold Lazarus is one of several action-oriented practitioners who have sought to combine features from several theories into a flexible system for analyzing and treating clients' problems. Originally a behaviorist, Lazarus was influenced by the behavioral therapy of Joseph Wolpe and, later, by the cognitive therapy of Albert Ellis. He has endeavored to create an approach to counseling that is behavioral in its systematic analysis, comprehensive in its scope of exploring the total person, and pragmatic in its selection of techniques.

Other attempts to integrate existing theories into a multidimensional model include Thorne's (1967) "Eclectic System," Brammer and Shostrom's "Emerging Eclecticism," Carkhuff and Berenson's "Helping System," Dyer and Vriend's "Personal Mastery Counseling" (1980), Bordin's "Psychological Counseling," Kottler's (1983) pragmatic group approach, the tactical approach of Watzlawick, Weakland, Fisch, and Segal, and Blocher's (1966) "Developmental Counseling."

Basic Concepts

This theory is called "multi-modal" because it seeks to understand and intervene at the levels of all seven modalities of the human personality. People are capable of experiencing sensations, feelings, thoughts, images, observable behavior, interpersonal responses, and biochemical and neurophysiological reactions. These human components are conveniently organized into the acronym BASIC ID, in which each letter represents a different modality that can be used to explore and change behavior. In Table 6–1, each component is accompanied by examples of client symptoms and counselor interventions at a compatible level. Multi-modal assessment thus permits the practitioner to understand at a glance how the client characteristically functions, how, where, and why the presenting problem manifests itself, and how specifically to use the profile as a blueprint for promoting change.

Premises of the Multi-Modal Approach

Each of the following principles represents an attempt to integrate several action-oriented theories into an eclectic, flexible position. Even for those without a multi-modal orientation, many of the concepts are valid and useful.

1. Avoid formal diagnostic labels because of their poor reliability and validity in favor of the BASIC ID profile for describing clients' problems.
2. Eliminate psychological jargon from the descriptions of theory and technique, relying instead on a precise everyday vocabulary. The language of the system includes only basic terms such as *nonconscious process* (in lieu of the more complex "unconscious" and "defense mechanisms"), *defensive reactions, private events,* and *vicarious processes.*
3. Focus on resolving the presented problem, the symptoms that the client wishes to change, rather than some underlying conflict.

Table 6–1. Sample Structural Profile of BASIC ID in Multi-Modal Assessment

	Modality	Client Symptoms	Counselor Interventions
B	Behavior	inability to work, sexual impotence, pouting and withdrawal	role-play job interviews; sex therapy; assertiveness training
A	Affect	helplessness, depression, uselessness and apathy, anger	share feelings about control; awareness of anger; release of frustrations
S	Sensation	tension, tiredness, laziness	relaxation training
I	Imagery	fantasies of being a famous artist, image of dying young, revenge fantasies to get former employer	positive imagery
C	Cognition	"I deserve a good job," "They all think I'm strange," "I'm a loser," "I'll never make it"	bibliotherapy; systematic self-talk to dispute irrational thoughts
I	Interpersonal	rejecting and indifferent to his wife, lonely and isolated from his friends, bad temper with child, superficially cooperative during sessions	marital counseling to improve communications; paradoxical strategies
D	Drugs	sleeps a lot, lacks appetite, does not exercise, uses marijuana daily	begin exercise routine to stimulate energy and appetite; consider vitamin supplements; refer to physician for physical exam

4. Shape the human personality by classical and operant conditioning (behavioral theory), social learning (modeling theory), irrational ideas (rational-emotive theory), nonconscious processes (psychoanalytic theory), and biological factors (neurophysiological theory).

5. Design individualized treatment strategies for each client and BASIC ID modality profile. Match language and approaches to the particular circumstances.

6. Track interactive effects between the various modalities to establish the client's sequential firing order. For example, one person will feel sick (sensation), imagine that he is dying (imagery), tell himself that he will never see his children again (cognition), feel anxious and scared (affect), scream at a sales clerk (interpersonal), hurriedly leave the store (behavior), and finally take five milligrams of Valium to calm the panic (drug). Firing order: S I C A I B D. The treatment strategy would therefore be matched to attack the sensations (body awareness exercises),

images (emotive imagery techniques), and cognitions (disputing irrational beliefs).

7. Use follow-up questionnaires as an integral part of treatment to monitor client progress years after sessions have ended.
8. The choices of techniques available are virtually unlimited and may be borrowed from *any* approach.

Some Multi-Modal Techniques

Fantasy exercise.   Use your imagination and creativity to picture yourself on a deserted island, where you will spend six uninterrupted months. Survival will not be a problem, for there are plenty of provisions. While you are gone the rest of the world will remain frozen in time waiting for your return.

Before you leave, you have the choice of going alone or with someone. Which would you prefer?

OK. You have now arrived. There is shelter and shade, a beach, food, and water. Your companion (if you choose one) welcomes you. She or he is attractive and friendly.

How will you spend your time?

What happens and how does it develop?

Imagery.   A client visualizes a scene or an experience for therapeutic benefit. To be effective, (1) imagery should be concrete and specific in detail, with evidence of sight, sound, touch, and smell, (2) the client should be a participant in the scene, not an observer, (3) the client should be able to switch the scene off, and (4) the client should be able to maintain the scene without drifting.

Behavior rehearsal.   The term refers to the technique of practicing or rehearsing new behaviors either in a group or in individual session. The purpose is to increase comfort with the new behavior and to receive feedback on performance.

Self-monitoring.   Clients observe and record specific things about themselves. The purposes of self-monitoring are (1) to develop a base line for behavior change, (2) to gather information so as to improve and clarify problem definition, (3) to increase the client's self-awareness and sensitivity to problem situations, and (4) to identify antecedents and consequences of problem behavior.

Problem solving.   Problem solving is the systematic process of responding to personal decision making about problematic situations. The elements of problem solving include problem definition, brainstorming, determining courses of action, analysis of alternatives, selection of preferred options, and implementation. Problem solving is useful in multi-modal approaches because it provides a rational and cognitive context in which to state concerns.

Criticisms of the Multi-Modal and Other Eclectic Approaches

1. The multi-modal approach could be considered to be *too* routine and systematic. All clients are assessed according to their BASIC ID profiles, and then the counselor operates as a glorified technician, selecting interventions from the "fix-it manual."
2. It is difficult enough for counselors to master the theory and techniques of one system without trying to learn the technology of all systems. The result of such an effort could be mediocrity: the work of an inept generalist who can do a little of everything—and none of it very well.
3. The technician's approach may cause the counselor to see clients as problems rather than as persons. An excessively clinical approach can neutralize relationship aspects and may create an overly structured relationship.
4. There may be a tendency to use a shotgun approach and to become unduly concerned with symptom alleviation at the expense of helping the client to resolve underlying problem areas.

Honorable Mentions

Here we present briefly several other action-oriented theories to familiarize you with some of their basic concepts and unique contributions.

Reality Therapy

William Glasser (1965) is credited as the founder of reality therapy, which reflected his dissatisfaction with contemporary psychoanalytic theory. It is an essentially didactic approach that stresses problem solving, personal responsibility, and the need to cope with the demands of a person's "reality." Reality theory is based on the assumption that all individuals need to develop an identity, which can be either a "success identity" or a "failure identity."

The counselor's job is to become highly involved with the client and to encourage motivation toward a plan of responsible action that will lead to constructive behavior change and a "success identity." The reality-therapy approach is active, directive, and cognitive, with a strong behavioral emphasis that makes use of contingency contracting. The counselor assumes simultaneous supportive and confrontative roles with clients.

Reality therapy is a short-term treatment that has been widely used in schools, institutions, and correctional settings. It is a fairly simple therapeutic approach and can be mastered without lengthy training and supervision. The disadvantages of reality therapy include its tendency to reward conforming behavior, the danger of the therapist's imposing personal values of reality, and its tendency to treat symptoms rather than possible underlying causes.

Trait-Factor Counseling

Trait-factor counseling rests heavily on the work of E. G. Williamson (1939, 1950). The major assumption of trait-factor theorists is that human behavior can be ordered and measured in terms of defined traits or factors. They emphasize a rational and largely objective procedure for counseling and believe that it is a more effective substitute for the intuitive and impressionistic approaches implicit in other theories. Needless to say, trait-factor counseling relies on measurement and on factor analysis in particular.

Trait-factor counseling emphasizes the use of information to evaluate the client's characteristics and thereby to help the client improve decision-making skills. The counselor's job is to present a variety of data, ranging from test scores to social data and the results of self-evaluation, and then to assist the client to organize self-appraisal and actuarial data in a manner likely to maximize effective decision making.

Williamson and Biggs (1979) describe the steps through which trait-factor counselors help clients develop effective decision-making skills:

1. Counselors assist clients to describe their characteristics more fully and more accurately by providing them with both information and a variety of normative reference points.
2. Counselors assist clients to clarify their decision-making patterns and assess the role of values, attitudes, and risk-taking tendencies that affect their decisions.
3. Counselors assist clients to gather comparative information on the distinctive characteristics of individuals involved in the clients' own areas of educational and vocational interest.
4. Counselors assist clients to determine the probabilities of success with various alternatives. Clients assess these data and use the information to clarify and refine their personal decision making.

Advantages of the trait-factor approach include a focus on the individual and a recognition of the impact of individual differences on decision making. This approach also allows the client to collect and integrate a variety of data and to make decisions that include an objective and empirical component. Among its disadvantages are a tendency to view the individual as a function of traits and factors rather than as a whole person and a tendency to pay relatively less attention to feelings and affective states as they affect decision making.

Expressive Therapies

Expressive therapies include a variety of therapeutic approaches that, although loosely integrated, rest on the assumption that primarily nonverbal media are effective in the release and resolution of clients' problems. Expressive therapies tend not to rely on language and thus are able to by-pass much resistance and to intensively explore underlying conflictive and dysfunctional issues. Frequently, the use of expressive therapy is not theoretically isolated but occurs as an adjunct to other theoretical modalities. We offer several examples of these alternative approaches to balance the more traditional modalities that we have previously explored.

Art therapy. Art therapy has long been a form of treatment for children, helping them to express feelings actively as well as to talk through images represented in their drawings. The *Journal of Art Therapy* contains suggestions for using materials to promote better cooperation in children, for diagnostic data-gathering, and especially for helping people become more creative and emotionally expressive. Practitioners resort to alternative therapeutic media such as musical instruments, games, sculpture, drawing, writing, puppetry, and drama when verbal strategies are ineffective. Resistances and emotional blocks can therefore be bypassed through treatment strategies that are primarily nonverbal.

Biofeedback. Another action method that can be used to improve client control, biofeedback gives clients accurate information about their psychophysiological responses. Readings can be taken of bodily functions such as brain activity, heart rate, muscle movement, blood pressure, and skin responses to improve muscular and neurological control. Katkin and Goldband (1980) suggest that biofeedback may be applied to teach relaxation skills and thereby to reduce general tension, to control migraine headaches, to modify vascular disorders such as hypertension, to better tolerate chronic pain, to relieve sexual dysfunctions, to control seizure disorders, or to prevent stress-related problems.

Exercise. Other more natural forms of handling stress have evolved through the work of running gurus like James Fixx and exercise educators like Jane Fonda. The running movement is an example of a popular trend that eventually led to a form of self-therapy. Other exercise regimens such as swimming, biking, aerobic dancing, and weight lifting have provided symptom relief for a significant part of the population.

It is only recently that mental health and medical experts have begun to recognize the potential benefits of exercises such as running to improve creativity, confidence, self-control and well-being, as well as to reduce negative addictions, boredom, anxiety, and depression (Sachs and Buffone, 1984). Running and similar activities have thus become integrated into many therapeutic programs as adjuncts to treatment, as transitional support systems after counseling has ended, or even as a sole means of psychological and spiritual rejuvenation. Some therapists such as Glasser (1976) recognized awhile ago that positive addictions like running can combat self-destructive patterns and be a form of self-medication for stress.

Summary

The past two chapters have reviewed most of the major therapeutic systems, moving from the formal insight-oriented theories to the precise action-oriented approaches that include more emphasis on the technique and technology of change. At this juncture, your state of confusion is probably unavoidable, if not desirable. It *is* overwhelming to study so many different explanations of how best to do counseling, especially when each system appears to have attractive components.

On an unconscious if not deliberate level, your mind is already sifting through the vast array of new ideas and making decisions about what to reserve for further study and what to throw out because of apparent clashes with your values, personality, skills, and interests. In the next chapter you can carry on with the task of building a tentative personal theory of counseling; this is a process that will continue throughout the balance of your life. We urge you to keep an open mind.

Suggested Readings

Bandler, R., & Grinder, J. (1975). *The structure of magic* (Vol. 1). Palo Alto: Science and Behavior Books.

Bergin, A. E., & Garfield, S. L. (Eds). (1971). *Handbook of psychotherapy and behavior change* (2nd ed.). New York: Wiley.

Corey, G. (1982). *Case approach to counseling and psychotherapy*. Monterey, Calif.: Brooks/Cole.

Cormier, W. H., & Cormier, L. S. (1979). *Interviewing strategies for helpers: A guide to assessment, treatment, and evaluation*, Monterey, Calif.: Brooks/Cole.

Ellis, A., & Grieger, R. (Eds.). (1977) *Handbook of rational emotive therapy*. New York: Springer.

Ellis, A., & Whiteley, J. M. (Eds.) (1979). *Theoretical and empirical foundations of rational-emotive therapy*. Monterey, Calif.: Brooks/Cole.

Fisch, R., Weakland, J. H., & Segal, L. (1982). *The tactics of change*. San Francisco: Jossey-Bass.

Glasser, W. (1976). *Positive addiction*. New York: Harper & Row.

Gottman, J. M., & Lieblum, S. R. (1974). *How to do psychotherapy and how to evaluate it*. New York: Holt, Rinehart & Winston.

Haley, J. (1984). *Ordeal therapy: Unusual ways to change behavior*. San Francisco: Jossey-Bass.

Kanfer, F. H., & Goldstein, A. P. (Eds.). (1980). *Helping people change* (2nd ed.). New York: Pergamon Press.

Lazarus, A. A. (1981). *The practice of multi-modal therapy*. New York: McGraw-Hill.

Chapter 7

Developing a

Personal Style

After a brief (or even prolonged) study of the various counseling theories, a reasonable reaction is to be both impressed and confused. Each theory seems to be useful in understanding people and behavior and appears helpful in promoting lasting change. Yet the theorists seem to contradict one another, and each stands on propositions that directly refute what another holds as sacred. How is it possible for Rogers to help people when he is actively listening, while Ellis is aggressively disputing, Freud is wisely interpreting, Perls is integrating, Lazarus is defining, and the rest are analyzing, diagnosing, clarifying, and counseling in their own unique ways? It is clearly difficult for the practitioner to make any sense of the conflicting opinions and the passionate dogma presented by the various theorists.

A Personal Journey

A sketch of the authors' own professional development illustrates the process of acquiring a personal counseling style. Our first introduction to counseling theory occurred with our exposure as undergraduates to the idea that there were different theories that attempted to explain the human condition. It was comforting to learn that we were experiencing developmental growth and that our confusion was to be expected. Erik Erikson reminded us that crisis and the resolution of opposing polarities are central to personal and social development. It appears that this principle is no less true for the development of a personal theory of counseling than it is for life-span development.

In our next phase of professional development, we became personally involved as clients in counseling. The counselor we selected was sensitive, helpful, and a Freudian. Naturally, Freud's became the next theory to explore. Freud was wonderful! He wrote so well. The analytical model offered many interesting possibilities. A Freudian analyst can be detached, knowledgeable, mysterious, and best of all, omnipotent. Joining the Freudian theory group was like being part of a club, or maybe even a religion. People were zealous in their belief of Freud, his theory, and his teachings. At that early point in professional development, however, it seemed to us too confining to choose such an encompassing theoretical model.

In graduate school, we found Rogers's theory a refreshing change. As Rogerian counselors, we were instructed to be kind, smile, and develop an accepting environment for clients. Reflecting feelings was effective but the way we were working felt stale and restrictive. Perhaps our own inner voices were urging us to not become satisfied with what had become easy.

Impatient with some of the limitations of dealing only with feelings, we next sought out skilled professionals to teach us other alternatives. We imitated them until we recognized that we were ready to add more to our professional skills. We practiced rational-emotive techniques and found them extremely useful. Moving on to existential theory, we added some new

As each person finds his or her own form of self-expression, each counselor constructs a personal theory of practice.

understanding and searching techniques to our repertoire but they also aided our tendency to intellectualize. We therefore welcomed the relief of Gestalt theory's apparent simplicity, but then realized that it was a lot more complex than we had patience for.

To develop our skills further, we attended many workshops, discovering strategic counseling, family counseling, group counseling, and other approaches. By that time we had begun to integrate meaningful parts of the various theories and refine our own techniques through our work with clients. Then we began to teach counseling theory and help students to work toward integration. In the struggle to develop our own opinions, we had to sort through everyone else's, saving what seemed useful and fit each of our unique styles. It is at this stage that you are now encountering us. We are still exploring new ideas and developing models to help our clients. And we are sometimes still confused.

This autobiographical case study typifies the progression of professional development for many counselors as they develop a personal theory. Initially, it is easy to imitate and follow specific rules; later, it is important to integrate these techniques into a style that is personally congruent.

Grabbing Truth by the Tail

The past century in psychology, since the days in Wilhelm Wundt's laboratory, William James's classrooms, and Sigmund Freud's consultation chambers, might well be called the "Hundred Years' War." There is no doubt that the proliferation of significant research, the advances in theory, the development of technology, and the growth of therapeutic counseling as a profession have been spectacular during modern times. The scholarly debates, round-table discussions, and controversial dialogues in the literature are in fact necessary for the continued progress of any field. Only through dispassionate analysis of conflicting points of view may we ever hope to improve the quality of our theories in explaining complex phenomena and the effectiveness of our interventions in promoting constructive change. However, in many ways, the history of counseling theory is a spotted record of petty skirmishes, insignificant fights, and self-serving platforms.

Professional counselors who, above all else, stand for the values of flexibility, openness, genuineness, sensitivity, and aggressive truth seeking, have often been guilty of levels of rigidity and resistance to change that would even make our clients blush in embarrassment. The field of counseling, which is, after all, the perfect marriage of philosophy and science, has actually evolved into forms of tribalism, denominationalism, parochialism. We have different sects under the guise of scholarly theories. Each therapeutic approach, whether psychoanalytic, behaviorist, Gestalt, rational-emotive, nondirective, existential, strategic, or whatever, has developed a passionate following of disciples. Each theory claims to be the heir to "truth" and has an impressive body of evidence to support that belief.

Unfortunately, the main attribute of tribalism, in the wilds of Africa or Academia, is a single-minded determination to preserve the status quo and repel outside agitation. With all his wisdom and far-sighted perspectives, Freud set this precedent by ostracizing those of his disciples who were troublemakers—independent thinkers—expelling the apostles who dared question the sacred word of the master. Thus Jung, Rank, and Stekel to name but a few, left the camp in exile, only to begin their own tribes.

It was Freud's notion to set up a brilliant psychological defense mechanism to protect his ideas—his children—from mutilation. To legitimately criticize his theory, Freud felt that one first had to undergo psychoanalysis. If, after completing the treatment, the critic still persisted in attacks, obviously the psychoanalysis was unsuccessful and further work was indicated. Our intent here is not to criticize Freud, who unfortunately has been the scapegoat for a century of attacks, but rather to point out the precedent he established as the protective creator of ideas he did not wish to see deviate from his intent or control.

The history of counseling, which is the applied study of personality, is, itself, a chronicle of the influences of a number of formidable personalities. New schools of counseling are generally not discovered in the laboratory, nor are they usually the result of formal experimentation; they are, rather, the insights and conclusions of a single clinician, or a small group of practitioners, who has found a particular set of assumptions and techniques to be reliably helpful with clients. In each case the theory is the result of a life's unique experience and a personality's individual expression. It can be no coincidence that traditionally trained former psychoanalysts such as Albert Ellis, Eric Berne, and Fritz Perls branched off to create new approaches that reflect their unique attributes and values. Carl Rogers, the embodiment of a congruent, genuine, warm human being, constructed a theory that is an extension of his personality. Similarly, Albert Ellis, a logician, a clear thinker, a convincing debater, developed an approach branded with his unique assets. Can we do less for our clients, who are *our* responsibility and respond to *our* unique personalities, than to construct a personal theory of action that has been pragmatically designed for our particular situation?

As Ivan Turgenev explained to Leo Tolstoy in 1856, "The people who bind themselves to systems are those who are unable to encompass the whole truth and try to catch it by the tail; a system is like the tail of truth, but truth is like a lizard; it leaves its tail in your fingers and runs away knowing full well that it will grow a new one in a twinkling" (Boorstein, 1983, p. 81).

A Personal Theory

Criteria of Effectiveness

In exploring why a particular counseling theory may or may not produce desirable results, Boy and Pine (1982) identified several influential factors. The effectiveness of any counseling theory, personalized or otherwise, will depend on

1. the quality of the therapeutic relationship. Any theory is functionally impotent without the cooperation, trust, and motivation of the client—circumstances that can be created and maintained only by a supportive, nurturing relationship.

2. the perception of shared power. Without approximate equality of responsibility between counselor and client, the encounter is likely to be devoid of commitment, freedom, and independence. Milton Erickson has

been credited with this definition of counseling: two people sitting down and trying to figure out what one of them wants. Sometimes there is the illusion of equality, since both counselor and client understand their respective roles—one to cooperate, the other to imitate.

✓   **3.** the counselor's understanding of theory. Before one can use an idea effectively, one must understand its subtle complexities. Far beyond imitating one's professors, mentors, supervisors, or colleagues, the counselor should explore the body of knowledge, research, and skills associated with the chosen theory—its history, influences, antecedents, process, goals, outcomes, strengths, and weaknesses.

✓   **4.** intellectual and attitudinal commitment. Credibility and enthusiastic application depend, to a large part, on the counselor's personal commitment to the theory. This loyalty depends on more than either an emotional allegiance of one's beliefs (as in a religious system) or an alignment of one's intellect. A balance is necessary between the two so that the counselor may believe in the power and value of a theory, but as a passionate scholar rather than a zealot.

✓   **5.** flexible integration with institutional requirements. Boy and Pine's final criterion for effective theory application brings in an important aspect of reality—counselors do not work in a vacuum. There are powerful pressures from administrators and colleagues, diluted roles, and institutional policies that often make pure application of one's theory impossible. A theory should look good not only on the drawing board or when a counselor is functioning in a pure, unencumbered way but also when the counselor is conflicted, distracted, hurried, and pressured. The theory should be useful in reality.

Guidelines for Usefulness

The criteria just listed are optimally useful when adapting an existing theoretical structure for personal use. For those who are motivated (by growth, curiosity, or the desire to be more flexible and effective) to construct their own theory from the abundance of diverse ideas, there are many other guiding concepts to consider. For instance, one helpful approach is to identify potentially valuable ideas in existing theories. The key to progress is to improve on what has already been done rather than starting over and over again. The impetus to create a new theory comes from the rebellious internal drive to wear one's *own* clothes instead of hand-me-downs from an older sibling. The critical attitude of doing it oneself can lead one to overreact to the limitations of the status quo and thereby reject everything, instead of just those parts that are inhibiting. Freud, Adler, Rogers, Perls, Ellis and all the rest had something valuable to say, some idea that is salvageable for a new theory, some concept or technique that could still be useful in a slightly altered form.

Often the complaint of the counseling student is that theories tend to be needlessly complex, with jargon and language that are abstract, ambiguous, and incomprehensible. Considering for a moment how difficult it is to explain and understand a phenomenon as complex as the human organism in its process of psychological change, one can see that a simplistic theory is unlikely to suffice. Nevertheless, that is not to say that in your own theory-building you cannot work toward clarity, precision, and simplicity of language without sacrificing utility.

Patterson (1980), in his classic book on counseling theory, reviews more formal criteria that might be considered in evaluating or creating a theory. A theory should be (1) important, in the sense that it is relevant, applicable to a variety of circumstances, as well as (2) comprehensive in its attempt to include all known information. It should be both (3) parsimonious and (4) precise, including the fewest possible assumptions and the clearest possible hypotheses and predictions. It should also be (5) operational, with its concepts specifically stated so as to be testable and (6) empirically verifiable. It ought to be (7) practical as well as fruitful; a useful theory leads to predictions, which lead in turn to experimentation and thus to further knowledge and other theories.

Stages in Developing a Personal Theory

The process of developing a personal theory of counseling can seem overwhelming, especially to the beginning student, but it is more manageable when broken down into steps. Each of the stages describes a plateau on the road to developing a personal theory and represents a series of questions that can be answered on a personal level and from which generalizations must emerge. A personal theory evolves ultimately from two major sources of knowledge: the techniques and theories of counseling and the richness and realities of life itself. Minuchin and Fishman (1981), two leading family therapists, admonish the beginner to "disengage from the techniques of therapy and engage with the difficulties of life" (p. 10). Developing a valid and useful personal theory of counseling depends on knowing yourself well and participating in the experience of life.

The stages you will encounter en route to your own theory are laid out in Figure 7–1.

Entry

The counseling student begins the task of theory building by learning an overview of theories. Even those students with substantial practical experience choose a formal counselor education program to legitimate their status as well as to refine skills and acquire additional knowledge. The course of study normally begins with an introduction course, using a text similar to the one you are reading.

The first stage of professional theory development is usually confusing. Within a short period of time the beginning student is exposed to a variety of

Decision to enter program

Critical incident, career change

Formal course work

Soak in overview and follow progression

Eclecticism

Practicum/internship experience leads one
to abandon formal theory temporarily to get
through the experience

Theory hopping

Interaction with colleagues leads to greater
flexibility and experimentation

Figure 7-1. Stages of personal theory building

approaches to counseling. Their conflicting points of view can be disorienting enough, but the student is also learning about relevant theories in other courses. Just when the names and terms of basic theories are beginning to make sense, additional input from these other courses renews the confusion. Learning about the history of counseling includes the study of various theories of education, philosophy, and psychology. To the list of names such as Ellis, Perls, Freud, and Rogers is added influential philosophers like William James, John Locke, Jean-Paul Sartre, and Jean Jacques Rousseau, as well as important educators like Robert Gagne and Jerome Bruner.

The introduction to human development includes the theories of Erikson, Piaget, Maslow, and Havighurst; theories of learning include those of Skinner, Pavlov, Watson, Guthrie, Thorndike, Lewin, and Mowrer. A study of personality theories such as those of Sullivan, Allport, Kelly, Cattell, Hilgard, and Eysenck is included to help the student better understand people. It is no wonder, then, that the first stage in a beginning counselor's attempts to construct a personal blueprint for guiding behavior is marked by swings from enlightenment to frustration.

Eventually most new students, out of a sense of self-preservation, decide to suspend judgment temporarily and try to understand all the theories, deferring evaluation until later. It is difficult, if not impossible, to organize information at this point because all the information is so new that it is hard to know what questions to ask.

The slightly stressful job of the learner is occasionally interrupted by an inevitable question that will push the student onward to the next stage of theory building. The query is "What are you?" Students' responses reveal the first of their many alliances to a particular theory.

Mentorhood

When you attempt to answer that deceptively simple question, consider the consequences of declaring your primary theoretical affiliation. Since "I don't know," "What do you mean?" and similar responses may make you appear nonstudious or less mature than your classmates, you will probably prefer to name a particular theory that sounds good and that you understand to some degree. Now you have catapulted yourself into the second stage of theory construction and will experience added pressure to find a label to describe the way you think (even though you are not yet certain about your choice).

During this phase a student is sometimes impressionable and susceptible to hero worship. Professors or supervisors who are good at their work and skilled at helping others learn are good candidates for this role. These mentors and modeling influences are particularly important to later development, for they provide guidance and a behavioral model. It becomes relatively easy to affiliate yourself with the point of view of a model whom you admire and even to convince yourself that this is the model that will work best for you.

You now have reason to study one theory thoroughly and intensively. An unfortunate side effect of concentrated interest can be a mental block to examination of other theories that increase cognitive dissonance. Some practitioners never progress beyond their allegiance to one counseling approach. Many of them become extraordinarily knowledgeable and skilled at applying its concepts; they can devote time and energy toward improving themselves as specialists in a particular style. With such a commitment comes an increased acceptance of one's mentor and of the support system of other like-minded practitioners. There are special books, journals, meetings, and conventions, all intended to help counselors grow in their chosen affiliation. The result can be immunization against others from outside the "club" who could lead a confused sheep astray.

For many students, participation in the practicum or internship helps to shatter the illusion that only one theory works. The temporary sanctuary of mentorhood is left behind as the student continues on to the next stage.

Eclecticism

Held (1984) distinguishes between technical and prescriptive eclecticism. In the former, the counselor is a technician, a skilled master of technique who may be successful on a practical level without a well-articulated guiding philosophy. Prescriptive eclecticism rests more firmly on a solid theoretical base and places more emphasis on prediction and explanation of phenomena. Flexibility is the hallmark of both eclectic approaches, in which professionals subscribe to parts of many different theories.

Renewed flexibility is the logical result of your first actual experience as a counselor. You soon realize that imitating a mentor is hollow without developing an integrated understanding of the theory. You may have temporarily abandoned organized theory in your attempts to get through the practicum experience, experimenting with a variety of ideas to alleviate personal anxiety while helping a client. Adventurous students will even try out a few of their own ideas, but such behavior may be risky unless it is successful. You are wise to be conservative and cautious in trying out the range of theories as you have personally interpreted and integrated them. When in doubt, you can always fall back on the ideas of your mentors—who, after all, have spent decades developing and practicing the techniques—or revert back to a previous theory of your own. When not under pressure, you can find another favorite to study. Ever so slowly your own personality and preferences begin to demonstrate a unique style.

Experimentation

School is over. The counselor, as an employed professional, has the opportunity to test the theories and techniques that were presented in the classroom. Refinement of theory is encouraged by colleagues and supervisors, who have firm ideas of their own regarding the best ways to help clients. The fundamental concepts favored in the textbooks and classroom are sometimes downplayed by the seasoned professionals, who warn: "Forget relying on theory. Around here we do things our own way." Of course, the supervisors are really presenting theories of their own choice.

This particular stage of professional development is often marked by experimental theory-hopping, trying out attractive concepts, listening to more experienced peers, and remembering the wise words of mentors. Books play an influential role as the ex-student revels in new freedom while anxious for the excitement of new ideas. Because there is so little time and structure to reinforce learning, reading classic books becomes the mainstay of further theory development.

Pragmatism

Not all counselors reach the stage of pragmatic flexibility, nor do they want to. Many practitioners remain satisfied and quite effective at applying the concepts of their favorite theory. Those who are successful as counselors work hard at avoiding the boredom and restlessness that could accompany single-theory allegiance. The principal advantage is a sense of comfort and familiarity with a theory and its accompanying techniques. The counselor becomes increasingly more experienced and eloquent at personalizing and adapting the preferred theory in his or her work with clients.

For others, single-theory allegiance feels conforming, limiting, and routine. Some choose to move beyond mere eclecticism, or a stance of technical proficiency in many techniques, to a philosophy of pragmatism.

As originally conceived by the first psychologist, William James: "Pragmatism unstiffens all our theories, limbers them up, and sets each one at work" (James, 1907, p. 46). The pragmatic counselor is concerned with integrating the body of knowledge from all relevant disciplines into a personalized and pluralistic philosophy that is empirically based and can be practically applied to specific situations.

Summary

Theory is not the enemy. It should not constrict one's freedom and movement. In the words of Leona Tyler, one of our profession's most eminent theoreticians, "If by theory one means a tightly organized set of postulates from which rigorous inferences can be drawn, I certainly do not have one. Furthermore, I do not even want one . . . If by theory, however, one means simply the organized set of concepts by means of which one attempts to fit experience into a meaningful pattern, then I may call myself a theorist" (Tyler, 1970, p. 298–299). To Tyler, theory is no more and no less than the search for personal meaning, the organization of ideas, a way of thinking about a part of the world.

The preceding chapters on theory have given you a foundational base to understand the variety of approaches to counseling. It is advisable to study the concepts exposed to you in class and in texts, to practice new skills you see demonstrated, and to learn the techniques described in the various theoretical orientations. However, only after you have mastered, summarized, and mimicked these approaches should you then strive to personalize them. Store away your books, lecture notes, and images of how your professors do counseling. Only then can you *become* a therapeutic counselor, an effective agent of change.

The teaching of skills, knowledge, and techniques are the tasks of good teachers; integrating them is the task of the student. To be a true man or woman of knowledge, the student should follow the wisdom of Castaneda's (1971) Don Juan: To choose a path with the heart and to follow it, to look, rejoice, laugh, see, to *see,* and finally to know.

Suggested Readings

Argyris, C., & Schon, D. (1974). *Theory in practice: Increasing professional effectiveness.* San Francisco: Jossey-Bass.

Beutler, L. E. (1983). *Eclectic psychotherapy: A systematic approach.* New York: Pergamon Press.

Boorstein, D. (1983). *The discoverers.* New York: Random House.

Corsini, R. J. (1984). *Current psychotherapies* (3rd ed.). Itasca, Ill.: F. E. Peacock.

Garfield, S. L. (1980). *Psychotherapy: An eclectic approach.* New York: Wiley.

James, W. (1907). *Pragmatism.* New York: New American Library.

Patterson, C. H. (1980). *Theories of counseling and psychotherapy* (3rd ed.). New York: Harper & Row.

Stefflre, B., & Matheny, K. (1968). *The function of counseling theory.* Boston: Houghton Mifflin.

Van Hoose, W. H., and Pietrofesa, J. J. (Eds.). (1970). *Counseling and guidance in the twentieth century: Reflections and reformulations.* Boston: Houghton Mifflin.

Chapter 8

Research and

Counseling Skills

We have discussed many of the theories relevant to the counseling process and highlighted some of their strengths and weaknesses. Each individual counselor must determine which of these theories to use and how best to present them in sessions and, given his or her own counseling style, must also evaluate how well they work for various clients. This is a complex task that requires an understanding of the counseling process, a mastery of the basic therapeutic skills, and a functional knowledge of research methodologies.

The Marriage between Research and Practice

In this chapter we present a unique approach to research for the therapeutic counselor that integrates the methodologies of science with the skills of clinical practice. As Eldridge (1982) has noted, the roles of the counselor as researcher and as practitioner fit hand in hand. The process of counseling involves not only *doing* but *assessing* the impact of various behaviors on client change. We wish to know precisely the effects of any given theory, attitude, or action so that we may reliably duplicate the intervention in the future. We want to know which counseling skills are most likely to produce desirable results. And we would like to standardize certain therapeutic rituals in order to predict consistently how the client will respond to almost any action we might take. We know, for example, after years of investigation, that the skill of reflecting feelings has certain predictable outcomes: (1) the focus of the session stays with present-oriented affect, (2) communication continues with the client taking the lead, (3) the client feels that his or her messages were understood and processed, (4) emotional catharsis is encouraged, (5) conditions of trust and respect are generated, and (6) exploration is facilitated (Rogers and Truax, 1967; Truax and Carkhuff, 1967). This counseling skill is therefore valuable when it is desirable to reach these particular goals.

There are many things that influence what a counselor does in a session with a client. Certainly many of the previously presented theories on the practitioner's personal philosophy and style of practice play a significant role. The counselor's personality or mood on any given day and the client's concerns and goals might also influence the choice of interventions. Nevertheless, there is also a core of fairly specific skills that most counselors use on a regular basis and a fairly solid research base exists to support their effectiveness.

This chapter not only will introduce you to a group of pivotal skills that describe what counselors do during much of their time but will also present the part research plays in our field to identify discrete behaviors, to test their effectiveness in a variety of situations, to help make decisions about which interventions to use with various clients, concerns, and settings, and generally to help the clinician to function as a practical scientist. You will, therefore, become familiar with the terminology and methodology of the research process and its relationship to the process of therapeutic counseling. Both activities follow a consistent pattern:

1. awareness of a problem in need of a solution,
2. systematic study of the context and background of the problem,
3. summary of what is known about the problem and what has been tried before to solve it,
4. functional definition of the problem in such a way that it may be solved,
5. generalization from the study of particular instances to a similar class of events,
6. prediction of outcome and selection of actions with their probability of success,
7. testing of hypotheses in a plan of action,
8. evaluation of results,
9. inferences drawn and generalizations made to other situations.

Both the researcher and the counselor are systematic in their efforts to understand the world, how it works, and how changes can be most effectively implemented. Consider, for example, the scientific method outlined above as it is applied to a particular case in counseling.

1. *Awareness of problem:* A young woman seeks professional help because of anxiety, an inability to sleep, and panic attacks that leave her feeling dizzy and wobbly.

2. *Relevant background:* The woman is employed as a medical assistant and works in the same office as her husband and father, who are both physicians. Prior to the onset of her symptoms she has been a person in remarkable control of her body, her mind, her life. She is generally happy but discusses some career dissatisfaction. Exploration of her past reveals that she feels much resentment toward her parents for showing favoritism to a younger, rebellious sister and for forcing her into a medical career she never liked.

3. *Prior attempts at resolution:* Antianxiety medication, psychoanalytic therapy, and a variety of neurological tests have produced no further insight into the problem and no alleviation of the symptoms.

4. *Functional definition:* Her symptoms are defined by the counselor as her body's attempt to break through her overcontrolled exterior and let her know she is not living her own life. Further, the symptoms give her an excuse to quit her job, put distance between herself and her parents, and at the same time create more intimacy with her husband without the added work strain. The problem is defined as career-induced anxiety that is exaggerated by irrational thinking processes, repressed feelings, and a tendency toward overcontrol.

5. *Generalizations:* A series of counseling skills, including restatement of content, reflection of feeling, advanced-level accurate empathy, interpretations, open-ended questioning, probing, self-disclosure, and confrontations were used to explore the connections between her specific symptoms and

her life history. It is discovered that it has always been difficult for her to ask for help or initiate life changes; generally some dramatic event precipitates action in such a way that she doesn't have to make decisions. Insights into her relationships with family members were also generated and she was helped to explore her feelings.

6. *Predictions:* It is predicted that if she would quit her job, reduce the unnecessary pressures in her life, begin an exercise regime, confront her parents with denied feelings, and work toward being her own person within the nurturing environment of the counseling relationship, her symptoms would significantly diminish.

7. *Hypothesis testing:* The prediction was tested as a hypothesis by implementing the plan of action within the context of the supportive counseling relationship.

8. *Evaluation:* Within days after she quit her job, the woman's symptoms reduced in frequency and intensity. However, as weeks progressed and the woman was forced to deal with issues of boredom, structuring her time, and confronting her family members, the anxiety returned. As successive parts of the treatment program continued and she dealt more constructively with her need for control, the anxious and panicky feelings as well as psychosomatic complaints eventually diminished. A 90-day follow-up visit indicated that although her symptoms occasionally returned she was able to deal successfully with them by applying rehearsed cognitive self-talk strategies.

9. *Inferences:* The client was able to generalize the work she did on these few aspects of her life to other components. She learned to relinquish complete control in other relationships and situations and to live a more spontaneous and flexible existence. The counselor was able to draw inferences from this case to other therapeutic situations. His own theory of counseling was sufficiently refined to include the new wisdom gleaned from this experience. It is thus likely that future therapeutic efforts will be even more effective as the practitioner incorporates the lessons of this case into his counseling approach.

This case study illustrates the research process in action as the counselor systematically identifies and defines the underlying complaints, intervenes, and assesses the impact of treatment. As you become more comfortable with the language and strategies involved in interpreting research literature as well as conducting meaningful evaluation projects, it will become easier to apply the skills of helping in a more intentional and consistent manner.

Research for the Counselor

There are three aspects of research that are important for students of therapeutic counseling to learn. First is the terminology and language of the field, by which communication is possible with other professionals. Many of the terms we use in everyday practice, such as "hypothesis," "variable," and "variance," are an integral part of the research process. Second is knowledge of the classic studies of the field and their implications for clinical work (see Table 8-1). Third is the means to conduct one's own systematic studies of topics that have personal interest.

Most counseling students (and many practitioners) approach discussions of research with great trepidation, much ambivalence, and a healthy degree of skepticism. But the value of developing research expertise is undeniable, as Remer (1981) enumerates:

1. As consumers of research, counselors must be capable of critical analysis of the various methodologies, statistical procedures, arguments, and conclusions of their professional literature.

2. Knowledge of research helps counselors to put new findings to work in clinical practice.

3. It is more expedient to interpret summaries and syntheses of the research literature than to wade through all the studies in a particular area. Research skills save time and energy.

4. Research permits the practitioner to generate new knowledge and share the results of creative enterprises, experimentation, or systematic study with others who are encountering similar difficulties.

5. Exposure to research trains the counselor to think analytically, intentionally, and systematically about problems.

6. Most important of all, according to Remer, research serves an important function in building new models of behavior. It helps counselors to sort out and organize the great mass of information to which they are exposed.

7. Counselors have an ethical responsibility to know the effects and limitations of the methods they use.

Table 8-2 reviews the types of research design most common in therapeutic counseling.

You will be expected, before graduation, to have a good working knowledge of basic research skills in addition to your counseling skills. Barkley (1982) suggests that the student should be able, at the very minimum, to pose good research questions, to use clear definitions of terms, to understand sources of confusion and ambiguity and how they may be controlled, to be aware of problems associated with observation and measurement, to understand the value of documentation in the literature, and above all to be knowledgeable about the process of research and be motivated to learn more about it throughout his or her professional life.

Research on Therapeutic Attributes

The research process, in almost any form, seeks to answer questions, to satisfy curiosity, and to accumulate useful knowledge. In the field of counseling the task of converting a largely mysterious enterprise into a

Table 8-1. A Sampling of Classic Research in Therapeutic Counseling

Date	Author	Title	Contribution
1920	Watson & Rayner	"Conditioned Emotional Reactions"	Demonstrated that emotional reactions to stimuli can be conditioned or learned.
1938	Skinner	The Behavior of Organisms	Demonstrated the principles of instrumental conditioning.
1950	Dollard and Miller	Personality and Psychotherapy	Applied learning theory to the psychotherapy process.
1950	Fiedler	"A Comparison of Therapeutic Relationships in Psychoanalytic, Nondirective, and Adlerian Therapy"	Suggested that personal variables other than therapist's theoretical orientation determine the effectiveness of the therapeutic relationship.
1952	Eysenck	"The Effects of Psychotherapy: An Evaluation"	Suggested that persons receiving psychotherapy did not improve more than persons not receiving psychotherapy.
1954	Super	"Career Patterns as a Basis for Vocational Counseling"	Demonstrated the relationship between self-concept and occupational choice.
1954	Whitehorn & Betz	"A Study of Psychotherapeutic Relationships between Physicians and Schizophrenic Patients"	Suggested that patient improvement was tied to the personality of the physician.
1956	Bateson, Jackson, Haley, and Weakland	"Toward a Theory of Schizophrenia"	Brought emphatic attention to the influence of family on psychological conditions.
1957	Rogers	"The Necessary and Sufficient Conditions of Therapeutic Personality Change"	Clarified the core conditions necessary to facilitate therapeutic change.
1958	Wolpe	Psychotherapy by Reciprocal Inhibition	Developed desensitization as a therapeutic technique.
1963	Truax	"Effective Ingredients in Psychotherapy: An Approach to Unraveling the Patient–Therapist Interaction"	Suggested that therapist-offered conditions would result in either improvement or deterioration in patients.

(continued)

Table 8-1. A SAMPLING OF CLASSIC RESEARCH IN THERAPEUTIC COUNSELING

DATE	AUTHOR	TITLE	CONTRIBUTION
1966	Holland	The Psychology of Vocational Choice	Presented the hexagonal model to describe the relationship between personality and occupational interests.
1968	Strong	"Counseling: An Interpersonal Influence Process"	Suggested that counselors effect change through a social rather than a therapeutic process.
1969	Bandura	Principles of Behavior Modification	Clarified the effects and empirical base of behavior modification.
1969	Carkhuff	Helping and Human Relations	Summarized research on "core" conditions of counseling and developed rating scales to measure counselor effectiveness.
1971	Bergin	"The Evaluation of Therapeutic Outcomes"	Suggested that psychotherapy is not much more effective than absence of treatment.
1971	Ivey	Microcounseling: Innovations in Interviewing Training	Presented a training system for interviewers based on microanalysis of skills and feedback.
1974	Meichenbaum	Cognitive Behavior Modification	Presented the research base to support the use of cognitive intervention in behavior modification.
1977	Smith and Glass	"Meta-Analysis of Psychotherapy Outcome Studies"	Used meta-analysis techniques to describe effectiveness of psychotherapy.

comprehensible model of helping with discrete, sequential, and behaviorally specific components is a particularly useful function of the research process for beginning students. Thanks to historical analyses, case studies, and developmental, experimental, and descriptive research, we can now accurately define and teach the core skills that most effective clinicians use.

For example, one aspect of the therapeutic encounter that has been extensively researched is the role of the counselor's interpersonal influence on client change (Heppner & Dixon, 1981). Strong (1968) originally concep-

Table 8-2. A Taxonomy of Research Methodologies in Counseling

Type	Goals	Methods	Limitations	Clinical Examples
Historical	Develop perspective on future based on analysis of past; especially concerned with trends, causes, and effects	Collection and criticism of source materials; examination of evidence and investigation of chronological events	Reliability, objectivity; complete data is not available for analysis	A meta-analysis of counseling outcome studies to determine the effect of therapeutic interventions
Descriptive	Describe relationships among variables in the present; intensively investigate a case or program over a period of time; collect data within a conceptual framework	Surveys, case studies, comparative studies, longitudinal studies, developmental studies	Prone to experimental biases; expensive and labor intensive; liable to sampling errors	An analysis of stage theory as it applies to adult developmental tasks
Experimental	Hold some variables constant and manipulate others to predict results in controlled conditions	Laboratory studies, hypothesis testing, well-controlled experimental designs	Group rather than individual focus, difficulty in control, reductionist orientation, possible lack of external validity—oversimplifies interactions among phenomena	An analysis of the effect of counselor-offered facilitative conditions on depth of self-disclosure in initial interviews
Evaluative	Gather information to make judgments on the merit or performance of various programs or procedures, to improve decisions about competing programs or treatments	Experimental, case study, cost-benefit analysis, impact analysis	Objectivity, availability of relevant data, resistance by sponsoring organization	The effect of group counseling on the self-concept and school behavior of low-achieving adolescents

tualized those dimensions of influence, those attributes of power, that make counselors effective. After two decades of systematically exploring his compelling hypothesis—that there are specific variables in a counselor's presence that affect the client's perceptions and capacity for change—three main characteristics emerged. Perceived expertness was found to be an influential factor: stature, titles, diplomas, credentials, and status all have their impact

(Strong & Dixon, 1971; Siegel & Sell, 1978; Atkinson & Carskadden, 1975; Strong & Schmidt, 1970). Yet here we see an aspect of research that the student might as well get used to: often there are later studies that fail to replicate the original results. In this case seven other investigators, among them Claiborn and Schmidt (1977), did not find that perceived expertness was especially crucial.

The second dimension of perceived attractiveness was also considered important. Counselors who are better looking were considered to be more intelligent, friendly, and helpful (Cash, Begley, McCown, & Weise, 1975; Carter, 1978; Fretz, Corn, Tuemmler, & Bellet, 1979). But there are measures of attractiveness other than physical characteristics. Nonverbal behaviors such as smiling and responsive attending favorably influence the client's opinion (LaCrosse, 1975; Claiborn, 1979), as do certain types of self-disclosure (Merluzzi, Banikiotes, & Missbach, 1978; Hoffman-Graff, 1977).

Finally, interpersonal influence is, in part, affected by the counselor's perceived trustworthiness, especially as it is communicated nonverbally (Kaul & Schmidt, 1971; Claiborn, 1979). Whereas it is likely that current and future research efforts will continue to alter Strong's conceptual model of interpersonal influence, this example gives us a realistic glimpse of how investigators approach the problem of identifying those counselor attributes, behaviors, and skills that make the most difference. Observations are made about the nature of reality (in this case, therapeutic counseling). The effects of specific components of a complex process are isolated, defined, and tested. Finally, results are replicated and applied to related situations. Often there are as many new questions generated as there are answers supplied.

The Generic Skills of Counseling

There are a number of counseling skills that can be considered generic; that is, they provide a technical base for the counseling process that can be used in a variety of theoretical approaches. In a broad sense, these skills can be seen as essential ingredients of the counseling process, those components of counseling that are necessary but not sufficient for effective therapeutic counseling.

In an article on the competencies that professors value in counseling students, White (1980) found several factors to be significant. Naturally, teachers of varying theoretical orientations differed on the characteristics of the ideal student, the behaviorists preferring students who are efficient, the client-centered professors appreciating those students who work on personal development, and the eclectic teachers, of course, desiring flexibility in their students. There were also differences among professors according to their academic ranks. Assistant professors liked students who are competent in counseling strategies and who work on their personal development; associate professors held similar values but also prize efficiency. Full professors felt quite differently; they wanted students who are active in research and professional activities.

Obviously, it is important for the student to master all these competencies. In addition to these student skills and the research skills already presented, there is a set of core therapeutic skills that have been described by Carkhuff (1969), Egan (1982), and Cormier and Cormier (1979), as well as others. Therapeutic counseling is a skilled process that requires the deliberate and systematic application of these specific helping skills. It is important to emphasize that helping can work for good or ill. That is, persons receiving help (whether clients, patients, or friends) can either suffer or improve as a result of helping efforts. Helpers with low-level skills have been shown to have either neutral or detrimental effects on clients; helpers with high-level skills have been shown to have constructive impact (Carkhuff, 1971; Carkhuff & Berenson, 1967; Truax & Carkhuff, 1965).

Before discussing specific steps and skills involved in the helping process, let's review the goals of helping. The overall goal of therapeutic counseling is the development of new behavior that is more adaptive, self-enhancing, and personally fulfilling. Self-exploration is the first goal of helping, and subsequent steps follow a pattern that employs the skills of attending, responding, initiating, and communication, eventually leading to constructive action.

The process of exploration, understanding, and action is continuously recycled in the helping process. Action provokes feedback, which provides a stimulus for further self-exploration, which, in turn, facilitates increased and more accurate self-understanding. Real understanding is often the result of learning that follows action. Finally, action is further modified in accordance with a more accurate understanding of self.

Significance of Attending Skills

Perhaps the basis for all therapeutic interventions is the physical and psychological attending to persons in need of help (Ivey & Authier, 1978; Claiborn, 1979; Carkhuff & Anthony, 1979). It is through posture, body position, head nods, facial expressions, eye contact, gestures, and verbal encouragements that the counselor communicates intense interest in everything a client says and feels. And it is through such active attending that the counselor can also observe the nonverbal cues evident in the client's behavior. A quivering lip, clenched hand, or furrowed brow provides evidence that is helpful in understanding what the client is experiencing.

Effective listening, the core of attending skills, involves the following elements:

1. *Have a reason for listening.* Know what to listen for and how it will be important to the client's exploration, understanding, and action.
2. *Be nonjudgmental.* To listen effectively, you must suspend temporarily the things you say to yourself. Let the client's message sink in without making decisions about it.
3. *Resist distractions.* Resist both internal and external distractions so that your attention and listening focus will not be disturbed.
4. *Wait to respond.* Give yourself time to respond fully and deeply to the client's statements, avoiding hasty and possibly superficial responses.
5. *Reflect content.* Reflecting back to the client what you hear him or her saying both communicates understanding and provides an opportunity to check out the accuracy of your perceptions.
6. *Look for themes.* Be selective with all the stimuli presented and attend to only the content that is relevant and meaningful. Identifying themes will help you to understand where the client is "coming from" and how the client perceives his or her relationship to the world.

Naturally, counseling involves considerably more than attending and listening skills. Instead of describing therapeutic skills further, let's look at their use. Until now, we have focused on how counselors think. We will now introduce what counselors *do* in their sessions—the specific interventions that are often used to facilitate client self-exploration, self-understanding, and desired changes in behavior, feelings, and thoughts.

Skills that Facilitate Client Change

Listening Skills

Cormier and Cormier (1979) distinguish among several response options that tend to promote verbal expression and convey interest:

1. passive listening—the use of verbal encouragement and nonverbal attending to acknowledge messages communicated by the client
Examples:
  "I see."
  "Uh huh."
  "Go on."
  "Yes."
2. parroting—repetition of the client's words to indicate interest, demonstrate accuracy of listening, or stall for time until a more elegant response can be formulated
Example:
  CLIENT: "Boy, am I upset!"
  COUNSELOR: "You're really upset!"

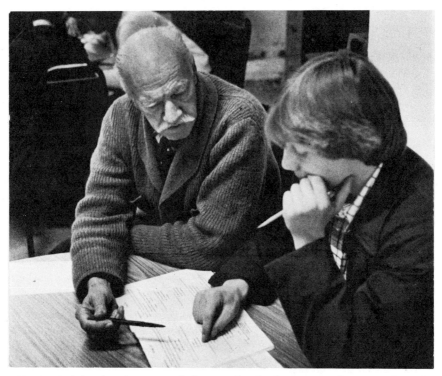

Effective helping involves a nonjudgmental attitude, an attentive posture, and a willingness to resist internal and external distractions in order to focus on the client's concerns.

3. paraphrasing—restatement of a message's content for clarification or to focus the client's attention
Example:

> CLIENT: "My life feels useless. My job is a dead end. I don't have any friends. And my parents are always on my case."
> COUNSELOR: "You are isolated, trapped, badgered, and don't see a way out."

4. clarification—confirmation of a message's accuracy or encouragement of further elaboration of an idea
Example:

> COUNSELOR: "Are you saying that this issue of feeling vulnerable and getting hurt when you trust others has been a lifelong theme?"

5. reflection of feeling—focusing on affect to promote catharsis and self-expression
Example:

> CLIENT: "I don't know. Maybe this marriage isn't worth holding together any longer. We've already tried just about every option."
> COUNSELOR: "You feel so frustrated and overwhelmed trying to resolve your conflicts without help from your wife. It's as if she had

already given up on your relationship and now you are feeling hopeless and helpless."

6. summation—linking several ideas together in a condensed way to promote insight, cut off rambling, identify significant themes, or draw closure

Example:

> COUNSELOR: "So far you have talked a lot about the ways you keep people at a distance. You tend to hang back whenever you feel a potential for a friendship, and those who approach you are quickly discouraged by your reluctance. You have also mentioned that you might have learned your aloofness from your parents, who never seemed to have much time for you."

Exploration Skills

Dyer and Vriend (1980) term the following counselor behaviors helpful in drawing out client concerns, facilitating insight, and exploring thoughts and feelings. Most client-centered counselors use these skills as the staple of their therapeutic efforts:

1. probe—open-ended questioning to gather relevant data or to encourage self-examination

Example:

> "What are the things you've tried to do throughout your life when you have faced similar struggles?"

2. immediacy—attempting to bring the focus to the present, to comment on the style of interaction in the session, or to give feedback

Example:

> "Right this very moment you are deferring to me in just the same way you back down from your boss."

3. self-disclosure—sharing of personal anecdotes from the counselor's life to build trust, model personal effectiveness, or capitalize on identification processes

Example:

> "I can recall the time in my life, at about your age, when I would see someone I liked. I finally swallowed hard and started taking risks. Although I felt rejected a lot, eventually I started meeting new people."

4. interpretation—promoting insight by pointing out the underlying meaning of a behavior or pattern

Example:

> "So to compensate for the lack of attention you got from your father, you have constantly searched out relationships with men who are nurturing and dependent."

5. confrontation—diplomatically identifying discrepancies between (a) what a client has said in the past and is saying now, (b) what a client says versus what she or he does, or (c) what a client describes about herself or himself and what you actually observe

Example:

> "Whereas you have repeatedly called yourself shy, withdrawn, boring, and a loser, I notice that in our sessions you are usually quite animated, outgoing, and assertive in getting what you want."

Action Skills

Behavioral counselors rely on several action responses to move the client beyond self-understanding to constructive life changes:

1. information giving—concise, accurate, factual information, provided to dispel myths, pique client interest, or create structure

Example:

> "One of the reasons why you may be having difficulty initiating sex with your girlfriend is that you are not beginning a series of pleasurable activities called 'foreplay' that slowly lead to lovemaking. Instead, you just rip off your clothes and jump into bed."

2. advice giving—interventions designed to provide practical suggestions or motivate the client to action

Example:

> "Perhaps the next time you go out on a job interview you might want to give more attention to your appearance and the impression you give."

3. goal setting—structuring a direction, planning for the future, providing a basis for measuring progress, and obtaining the client's commitment to make needed changes

Example:

> "You are saying, then, that in the next week you would like to concentrate on being more open with your friends and that, on at least three occasions, you will tell people something that they don't already know about you."

4. reinforcement—giving support and encouragement to increase the likelihood that desirable behaviors will continue

Example:

> "The more risks you take, the more courageous and confident you feel. After the great week you have had, I can hardly believe you are the same person."

5. directives—instructions designed to change the structural patterns of interaction or communication by specific means

Example:

> "Since you aren't having much success by urging your husband to come in for counseling, I think it would be best if you tried a different approach and let him know you'd prefer he didn't come in."

Summary

In this chapter, we have described the use of counseling skills and techniques within the context of the research process. It is imperative that counselors work systematically to identify useful techniques, test their effectiveness, and enlarge their repertoire of effective responses. Research has demonstrated the value and efficacy of a solid base of skills; however, this evaluative process must continue within the context of each interview. Counselors should critically and empirically evaluate their use of skills and techniques from the perspective of developing effective action programs for the clients they serve. The research process provides the tools for developing, describing, and reporting new ideas and skills for working with clients. It also allows us to assess the impact of what we do and make adjustments as needed with particular clients and therapeutic situations.

Suggested Readings

Benjamin, A. (1981). *The helping interview* (3rd ed.). Boston: Houghton Mifflin.

Carkhuff, R. R., & Anthony, W. A. (1979). *The skills of helping: An introduction to counseling.* Amherst, Mass.: Human Resources Development Press.

Cormier, W. H., & Cormier, L. S. (1979). *Interviewing strategies for helpers: A guide to assessment, treatment, and evaluation.* Monterey, Calif.: Brooks/Cole.

Egan, G. (1982). *The skilled helper: A model for systematic helping and interpersonal relating* (2nd ed.). Monterey, Calif.: Brooks/Cole.

Garfield, S., & Bergin, A. (Eds.) (1978). *Handbook of psychotherapy and behavior change: An empirical analysis.* New York: Wiley.

Goldman, L. (Ed.). (1978). *Research methods for counselors: Practical approaches in field settings.* New York: Wiley.

Chapter 9

Assessment and Testing

You have now begun, perhaps with some reluctance, to read the one chapter in this book that you believe you can live without. We hope to present to you a convincing rationale not only for why a systematic study of the assessment process is important but for how and why counselors use both standardized and nonstandardized instruments in their work. Considering that we have so few technological aids, mechanical devices, or other equipment to assist us in diagnosing problems and gathering relevant information about our clients, we would be well advised to develop our knowledge and skills in the one sort of measurement in which there is some expertise.

A Brief History

At the beginning of this century, James Cattell, one of the first experimental psychologists, coined the term "mental test" to describe his attempts to measure the intellectual ability of students. Building on the work of Sir Francis Galton and his development of rating scales, questionnaires, and statistical methods, Cattell began the science and industry of testing, along with researchers in Europe—Kraepelin, who made assessments of the mentally ill, and Binet, whose scales measured children's mental abilities. Although Binet's and later Terman's intelligence tests for screening school children were the first widely accepted tests, it was World War I that gave the real impetus to psychological and educational testing as we know it today. The Army Alpha and Beta were the first group intelligence tests designed to screen those who might be unfit to serve. The experience with these tests and the extensive data collected from their use provided the base for a significant expansion of testing in the 1920s.

The second major acceleration in the development and use of testing occurred in the years around World War II, again for many of the same reasons. Tests such as the WAIS (Wechsler Adult Intelligence Scale) and the MMPI (Minnesota Multiphasic Personality Inventory) were first developed and extensively used during that time. In recent years, though, testing has come under increased criticism, primarily because of concerns that intelligence tests, in particular, are culturally and ethnically biased. These problems have led to the placing of a number of restrictions on the use of tests and to some professionals' disenchantment with them.

Nevertheless, testing and the use of tests to make predictions about people have continued to expand. Computers have greatly simplified the process of test development, scoring, and interpretation. The current explosion in the availability of microcomputers is likely to increase the use of tests further still. These recent developments and innovations renew concerns about bias, privacy, and confidentiality.

The Value of Testing

Perhaps a useful way to begin a study of testing and assessment is to explore why it is important in the first place. The process of counseling involves decision making at many levels to help the client resolve concerns, effect change, and plan for contingencies and opportunities. For decision making to be maximally effective, it must be based on self-understanding, awareness of various options and alternatives, and a fund of relevant information. We have already described a number of widely accepted techniques used in therapeutic counseling to provide information for decision making. Verbal and nonverbal techniques, in particular, have been presented as basic counselor-offered conditions that facilitate counseling and help the client integrate a variety of information about self and relevant counseling issues. Testing, as part of an appraisal process, is an additional source of useful information about clients that can affect the decision-making process. In fact, tests offer a type of information not readily available through nontest methods: they gather information that highlights the ways in which clients are alike and different. The results of a test or series of tests can provide clients with information about themselves and illustrate how they compare with others who are similar to them. This information can help clients understand themselves and can be an asset in exploring alternatives during decision making. It also helps counselors to describe people and predict their behavior (Wiener and Stewart, 1984).

The information provided by testing is not always consistent, and therefore it is essential that the counselor be skilled in appraisal technology so the discrepancies in test data can be resolved in an exploration of the information. In order to help clients have the broadest possible source of information about self, the counselor must be knowledgeable about the selection, use, and interpretation of tests. To be uninformed about testing and assessment is to arbitrarily delete a potentially valuable source of data that could improve the quality of decisions about change of lifestyle, work, or behavior patterns.

Testing and assessment depend to a large extent on quantitative methodology and statistical analysis, features that are often troublesome to students and can present a barrier to developing skill and expertise in the process. Many students who enter the field of counseling have limited backgrounds in mathematics, quantitative processes, and systematic analysis. Their reactions often range from anxiety to overt hostility when they are confronted with the need to master subjects utilizing those techniques. Remer (1981) has reviewed the resistance of students to analytical courses and has attempted to point out why it is necessary to engage in quantitative study:

1. analytical courses help students to create a balance between the experiential and cognitive aspects of counseling;

2. analytical courses help students to expand themselves and become aware of new alternatives and perspectives;

3. analytical courses help students to learn the language of research and thus to have the necessary skill to understand and use research in the field;

4. analytical courses help students to be more disciplined, to organize information more rigorously, and to generate hypotheses more fully and creatively;

5. analytical courses help counselors to discharge their ethical responsibility to be aware of the limits of their techniques and practices;

6. analytical courses help counselors to develop the necessary skills so they can use and interpret tests accurately, fully, and ethically;

7. analytical courses help students and counselors to become familiar with research so they can make informal judgments about various counseling techniques, theories, and practices.

It may be that it is necessary to confront personal biases against analytic methodology and to challenge oneself to grow beyond personal resistance. To do so requires an openness to experience and the identification of a support system such as testing and assessment to aid in the process. This knowledge is not only crucial to collecting meaningful information from the client, but is helpful in formulating a diagnosis with which to begin therapeutic efforts.

Formal and Functional Diagnosis

As the client enters the office, furtively glances around for a place to sit, briefly locks eyes with the counselor, and finally, with an inward sigh, burrows deeply into the couch, the mutual assessment process has already begun. While the client nervously checks out the furniture, books, and framed diplomas, and wonders what sort of image she or he is projecting, the counselor casually yet systematically makes careful observations. The client's dress, posture, and bearing are noted, and where and how she or he has chosen to sit. Facial expressions, gestures, body language, and other nonverbal behavior also give valuable cues regarding the client's style.

The interview progresses. Information about the presenting complaint, the solutions that have already been tried, and the current life situation are identified. The counselor is searching for a summary statement of the client's problem, a formal diagnosis to describe the general pattern of behavior, and a behavioral label to describe meaningfully and individually what the client is doing, feeling, and thinking. Making these distinctions is important. In the assessment process, diagnoses are significant because they have implications for selecting a treatment strategy and because they are often required by the system. For example, the diagnosis of "cyclothymic personality disorder" might imply a condition involving dramatic mood swings that have been chronic throughout the client's life and may be biochemically triggered, thus suggesting the importance of medical consultations on the case. The diagnosis, however, gives us very little meaningful information about what the client is like as a person. Although useful in the general understanding of a behavioral syndrome, in formulating goals, predictions, and prognoses for the case, and in creating a few working hypotheses for designing a treatment strategy, a diagnosis itself is not enough to begin work.

Psychiatric Diagnosis

It is currently expected of therapeutic counselors in community agency settings to have a working knowledge of the diagnostic system developed by the American Psychiatric Association. The *Diagnostic and Statistical Manual of Mental Disorders* (DSM-III) (American Psychiatric Association, 1980) is the Bible of the mental health professions, containing authoritative information and "official opinions" about the range of mental problems. Counselors rely on the DSM-III (1) as a source of standardized terminology in which to communicate with other mental health specialists, (2) to satisfy the record-keeping requirements of insurance companies or credentialing agencies like the Joint Commission on Accreditation of Hospitals, (3) for classifying clientele in statistical categories, as is necessary for research and accountability, (4) to predict the course of a disorder and the progress of treatment based on available evidence, and (5) to construct a treatment plan that will guide interventions (Seligman, 1983).

The actual process of differential diagnosis with the DSM-III is complex, and mastery of the system requires considerable study. Basically, each discrete disorder is listed with information about its essential features, common symptoms, frequency of occurrence, predisposing factors, and suggestions of other disorders with similar behaviors. The clinician can therefore follow a "decision tree," a series of questions to narrow down the possible diagnoses:

> Are there known organic causes?
> Are there psychotic features?
> Is there impairment of intellectual functioning?
> Are symptoms under voluntary control?
> Is this an isolated case or a recurrent pattern?
> Is there a disruption of daily routines?
> Did the onset of symptoms occur in childhood?
> Is there a thought disorder?

Each successive question helps the diagnostician to formulate progressively more specific ideas into a five-digit numerical representation of the differential diagnosis. Each of the five axes provides a shorthand code of the particular disturbance. For example, Spitzer, Skodol, Gibbon, & Williams

(1981) analyzed Freud's most famous case, that of "Little Hans," to determine a multiaxial diagnosis as it would be constructed by a modern-day clinician. The little boy Hans was sent to Freud because of his fear of horses and because of debilitating nightmares when away from his mother. His symptomatology would be coded as follows in one DSM-III multiaxial diagnosis:

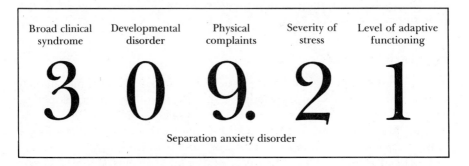

Broad clinical syndrome	Developmental disorder	Physical complaints	Severity of stress	Level of adaptive functioning
3	0	9.	2	1

Separation anxiety disorder

The various diagnostic choices are divided into several broad categories, such as childhood disorders, organic mental disorders, personality disorders, psychotic states, substance abuse disorders, affective disorders, and adjustment reactions. Each of these general syndromes then contains descriptive labels leading to more precise, specific categories—for example, anxiety disorder ——————→ phobic disorder ——————→ agoraphobia. The therapeutic counselor is thus equipped with a system for recognizing, identifying, analyzing, and understanding those client complaints that are classified as mental disorders.

Ethical Concerns

Diagnosis, in and of itself, creates its own ethical problems, not through its use but through its abuse and imperfections. First of all, it has less-than-perfect reliability: when several clinicians view the same client in action they may be unable to agree on the proper category. Diagnoses are often inconsistently applied and err in the direction of pathology instead of health. Counselors often find this last point to be particularly restricting, since much of our orientation views client symptomatology from a developmental rather than psychopathological perspective; that is, rather than trying exclusively to find out what is wrong with clients, we attempt to focus on their internal strengths, capacity for self-healing, and resources for resolving normal life crises.

Other sources of error that affect the accuracy and validity of a psychiatric diagnosis include the counselor's expectations, theoretical orientation, and observational skills, as well as the client's inconsistent behavior, attitudes toward treatment, similarity to the counselor in basic values, and socioeconomic background (Stuart, 1970). Poor people are more often diagnosed as crazy, while rich people are labeled eccentric.

Application of the medical model to therapeutic counseling has been eloquently and passionately denounced as morally unacceptable by such influential writers as Thomas Szasz, R. D. Laing, Erving Goffman, Theodore Sarbin, and even Chief Justice Warren Burger (Edwards, 1982). Critics warn that the diagnostic scheme developed from the medical model is not useful for therapeutic practice because its concepts are descriptive rather than normative, exhibit physical symptoms instead of behaviors, rely on known physical causes, use physical treatment interventions, and define the client as "sick" or "diseased."

Moreover, diagnoses can be dehumanizing in that they pigeon-hole human beings into slots that will be difficult to escape. Some clinicians are especially concerned with the overuse of terms like "minimal brain dysfunction," "hyperkinetic," and "retarded" to describe children who are disruptive, active, or easily distracted. Although in some cases these labels denoting disturbances of conduct or organic problems may be justified, there are other instances in which the child's behavior is the logical response to a teacher's or parent's confusing messages. Meanwhile, the labels remain forever imprinted in the minds of others and in the records that follow the child wherever he or she may go.

Behavioral Diagnosis

For many of the reasons just mentioned, functional behavioral labeling is an alternative assessment strategy. In this process, a client's specific behaviors are described in meaningful, illustrative, individualized language, not only to help the counselor to understand exactly which concerns are to be addressed but to aid the client's understanding of how, when, where, and with whom the self-defeating patterns are exhibited. There are thus therapeutic advantages to functional behavioral labeling:

1. Clients learn the methods of identifying and describing complex, abstract, ambiguous processes in specific, useful terms.
Before:
> "Ah, I don't know exactly, I just can't seem to concentrate any more."

After:
> "I have difficulty structuring my study time on the weekends I spend at home, particularly when I allow the distractions of my brother and girlfriend to interfere."

2. Clients understand that they are unique individuals with their own characteristic concerns.
Before:
> "I've been told that I'm a drug addict."

After:
> "I'm a person who tends to overindulge in cocaine and marijuana when I feel school pressures building up."

3. Clients describe their behavior in such a way that it can be changed. Whereas a *personality* characteristic is stable, invariant, and permanent, a *behavior* can be changed.

Before:

"I'm shy. That's the way I've always been."

After:

"I sometimes *act* shy when I meet a new guy I find attractive."

4. Clients label their behavior in the specific situations in which they have difficulty.

Before:

"I'm depressed."

After:

"I feel depressed in situations like my job and marriage, in which I feel powerless to do anything to change."

5. Clients accept responsibility for their destructive behaviors rather than blaming them on something beyond their control, like bad genes.

Before:

"I'm passive. Everyone is my family is. What do you expect?"

After:

"I act passively in some novel situations because I have learned to let others take charge. Yet in other situations in which I feel more comfortable, I don't act passively at all."

Within the context of the assessment process are several methodologies that may be used to collect valuable data, formulate workable diagnoses, and create specific behavioral assessments. In Chapter 3 we discussed the initial interview as an important structure for eliciting information as well as enhancing the therapeutic relationship. Several other structures and tools are also quite useful in the process of assessment.

What Is Assessment?

Assessment is a multifaceted process that involves a variety of functions such as testing and evaluation in an effort to determine an individual's characteristics, aptitudes, achievements, and personal qualities. Assessment can be viewed as an integrative process that combines a variety of information into a meaningful pattern reflecting relevant aspects of an individual. Assessment never depends on a single measure, nor does it emphasize one dimension at the expense of another. For an assessment profile to be meaningful and useful, it must provide a means of understanding the individual from as broad and integrative a perspective as possible.

The major obstacle to true knowledge about people, laments anthropologist Konner, is not a dearth of information but rather too much disorganized data. For information about a culture, or individual client, to be useful, it must be systematically collected and meaningfully organized. "So there are two tasks, really: first, the assessment of what we know, the assembly of the pieces; second, the discernment of a human face" (Konner, 1982, p. xiii).

Only with maximum accurate information can an assessment be appropriately used in counseling. An assessment of a candidate's suitability for entrance into a graduate counseling program might include a standardized test score, a measure of past academic performance, a review of related experiences and accomplishments, recommendations from knowledgeable observers, and a self-statement of goals and objectives. Each of these segments would provide information from which to construct an integrated portrait. Assessment attempts thus to build a comprehensive composite of an individual's characteristics, qualities, or aptitudes from as broad a vantage as possible, sampling all pertinent sources of information.

To conduct an assessment requires that a wide range of information be gathered to illuminate as many relevant aspects of the person as possible. Information sources can be divided into two general categories. Standardized measures include tests that have been designed to ensure uniformity of administration and scoring and for which norms are generally available. Nonstandardized measures, which do not ensure uniformity of measurement and tend to be subjective, take a more general and diverse approach and do not provide normative data. Each of these approaches will be discussed separately.

Standardized Measures

A test is nothing more or less mysterious than an attempt to measure a sample of behavior objectively and consistently (Anastasi, 1982). Whether the issue is a client's career preferences, mathematical skill, verbal reasoning ability, personality characteristics, or potential for success, tests are a convenient basis for judging the strength, utility, or desirability of various human qualities.

Tests are used to match the most capable and well-suited individuals with a particular program, position, or job. They have value as predictive devices for hypothesizing about a person's future performance or action. And certainly tests help counselors in their overwhelming task of understanding clients, how they characteristically act, their strengths, deficiencies, values, aptitudes, mastered skills, and, most important, their potential and capacity for growth.

Despite their value as standardized tools that have been scientifically designed to be fair, objective, reliable, and appropriate, testing procedures have many problems. They are not unbiased instruments; indeed, they reflect the values of the authors and their socioeconomic and racial backgrounds. Shertzer and Linden (1979) review several other criticisms and cautionary factors involved in testing procedures:

1. Tests create classificatory categories that are potentially harmful to clients. Application of labels such as "retarded," "mentally ill," "under-

achieving," and "passive-dependent" often follows test interpretations. And even though sticks and stones will break your bones, names will *also* hurt you.

    2. Test construction is an imperfect science leading to results not necessarily accurate or useful. Test validity and reliability statistics are not impressive. For instance, when a mother brags that her son has an "IQ" of 116, she is certainly exaggerating appropriate levels of confidence in that magical number. To be honest, she would actually have to state the result in a considerably more cautious way: "There is a 68.4% probability that my son's *real* IQ falls somewhere between 110 and 122."

    3. Charges of sexual and racial bias have been directed against many standardized instruments because the questions and norming procedures reflect the language and customs of the white middle-class majority.

    4. Testing is often used as an excuse to guide clients in specific directions, often limiting their future vision and potential. A fifth-grader who shows early promise as a math wizard may never have the opportunity to develop latent artistic and writing talents.

    5. Tests often reveal hidden and disguised information (one of their functions) and therefore may be construed as an invasion of privacy. They reveal aspects of the self a client may not wish others to know.

    Their limitations and ethical problems notwithstanding, standardized tests have several useful functions that cannot be duplicated by alternative assessment strategies such as the clinical interview and other nonstandardized procedures. First of all, the fact that tests are standardized means that attempts are made to ensure uniformity of administration and evaluation for all clients. No matter where the test is being administered, at what time, by whomever, to whomever, subjective factors will tend to be minimized. The concept of standardization also refers to the common practice of providing "norms," or measures of normal performance, so that any individual's sample behavior may be compared with that of a large group of others.

    Standardized assessment procedures provide a data base for making predictions about a client's future behavior. In making clinical judgments about whether a client is a likely candidate for suicide, a good prospect for a particular job opening, or potentially responsive to counseling, the interpretation of results from tests is invaluable. Tests can also be used to evaluate the effects of various counseling methods to determine if supplemental interventions are necessary. They are often used as selection and classification tools as well, helping in the complex process of matching the right jobs with the best people. Finally, tests are simply an additional source of information for clinicians, a concise summary of the client's typical behavior.

    Whether administered in groups for the sake of efficiency and economy or given individually, tests come in every conceivable size, shape, and purpose. There are instruments for measuring ability, aptitude, achievement, personality, and interests.

Tests of Ability

We are not altogether certain how to define intelligence (it has often been facetiously described as that which intelligence tests measure). Nevertheless, there are a number of instruments that attempt to assess an individual's general mental ability or stable intellectual capacity to reason, generalize, adapt, and apply skills and knowledge. They are also said to measure "native intelligence," though they may actually reflect a person's scholastic/academic potential rather than any functional "street smarts." Most of the tests of general ability include a set of tasks that require a client to demonstrate memory, pattern recognition, abstract thinking, decision making, verbal and analytic skills, general knowledge, and ability to manipulate the environment. The two most popular such tests are the Stanford-Binet, which is considered to be more accurate as a measure of verbal intelligence, and the Wechsler Scales (WAIS, Wechsler Adult Intelligence Scale; WISC-R, Wechsler Intelligence Scale for Children; WPPSI, Wechsler Preschool and Primary Scale of Intelligence), which are designed for each of several age groups and thus have better diagnostic utility. The Wechsler and Stanford-Binet are examples of individually administered intelligence tests that attempt to measure IQ as a general underlying composite of intelligence, often with an emphasis on verbal and nonverbal problem solving. Administering these tests requires special training and often a state license. Group tests of intelligence, such as the Otis-Lennon Mental Ability Test, tend to measure IQ as scholastic aptitude and are more dependent on postlearning experiences and opportunities. These tests do not have the same administration requirements as the individual tests and are often used by counselors.

Tests of Aptitude

Aptitude tests are concerned primarily with prediction of a person's performance in the future. All of us have, at one time or another, run the gauntlet of tests to determine if we are good candidates for an available slot. It is likely that you have had experience with the Scholastic Aptitude Tests (SAT) for admission to college or the Graduate Record Exam (GRE) for entrance to your counseling program.

The Law School Admission Test (LSAT) is another example of a test used to predict success in programs of advanced study. At the level of state employment agencies, aptitude tests such as the General Aptitude Test Battery (GATB) are used for job placement, and school systems rely on instruments like the Differential Aptitude Test (DAT) for assessing academic aptitude and for identifying children with special talent.

Tests of Achievement

Often called proficiency tests, achievement tests are used to measure learning, acquired capabilities, or developed skills. They are widely used and can be adapted to almost any type of task from measuring course content (a typical exam) to administering the road test for a driver's license. Results can be used as diagnostic tools, to demonstrate accountability, and, since past performance is the best measure of future performance, as predictors. Commonly used tests in this category are the California Achievement Tests and the Academic Competency Test (ACT).

Tests of Typical Performance

Tests designed to measure an individual's day-to-day behavior or performance are interested not in what a person *can* do (ability) but in what a person *does*. Although motivation is important in this type of test, it is less so than in ability testing. Two common categories of typical-performance testing are personality and interest inventories.

Personality inventories.   These tests are designed to gather information on an individual's preferences, attitudes, personality patterns, or problems. Results are expressed by comparison with a specific reference group. A concern with personality inventories is the possibility of faking responses, but most instruments of this type have a scale to detect a tendency to present an overly favorable profile (see Table 9–1). Examples of personality inventories include the Edwards Personal Preference Schedule (EPPS), the Personal Orientation Inventory (POI), and the Minnesota Multiphasic Personality Inventory (MMPI). Another type of personality measure is the projective type, which does not use a pencil and paper format but is individually administered. This type of test requires a client to respond to unstructured stimuli such as an inkblot or an incomplete sentence. A qualified examiner then interprets these responses as reflective of personality organization and structure. Examples include the Rorschach and the Thematic Apperception Test (TAT).

Interest inventories.   Interest inventories attempt to develop a profile of an individual's career-interest areas through a series of questions about preferences, jobs, hobbies, and other activities. The pattern of responses is then compared to the responses of persons successfully engaged in a variety of occupational areas. Profiles are constructed by matching high and low scores in occupational clusters. A limitation of these inventories is that interest does not reflect ability and it is possible for a person to dislike a career area in which he or she has earned a high score. Commonly used interest inventories are the Strong-Campbell Interest Inventory (SCII) and the Kuder Preference Record.

Selecting Tests

One of a counselor's important responsibilities is to select tests from the myriad of choices available. The selection of a test is complex because a number of competing factors must be analyzed and evaluated. Among the resources frequently consulted in the effort to evaluate and select tests, here are three important ones:

Table 9–1. MMPI Scales and Simulated Items

Validity (or Test-Taking Attitude) Scales

? (Cannot Say)   Number of items left unanswered.

L (Lie)   Fifteen items of overly good self-report, such as, "I smile at everyone I meet" (answered true).

F (Frequency or Infrequency)   Sixty-four items answered in the scored direction by 10 percent or less of normals, such as, "There is an international plot against me" (true).

K (Correction)   Thirty items reflecting defensiveness in admitting to problems, such as, "I feel bad when others criticize me" (false).

Clinical Scales

1 or Hs (Hypochondriasis)   Thirty-three items derived from patients showing abnormal concern with bodily functions, such as, "I have chest pains several times a week" (true).

2 or D (Depression)   Sixty items derived from patients showing extreme pessimism, feelings of hopelessness, and slowing of thought and action, such as, "I usually feel that life is interesting and worthwhile" (false).

3 or Hy (Conversion Hysteria)   Sixty items from neurotic patients using physical or mental symptoms as a way of unconsciously avoiding difficult conflicts and responsibilities, such as, "My heart frequently pounds so hard I can feel it" (true).

4 or Pd (Psychopathic Deviate)   Fifty items from patients who show a repeated and flagrant disregard for social customs, an emotional shallowness, and an inability to learn from punishing experiences, such as, "My activities and interests are often criticized by others" (true).

5 or Mf (Masculinity–Femininity)   Sixty items from patients showing homoeroticism and items differentiating between men and women, such as, "I like to arrange flowers" (true, scored for femininity).

6 or Pa (Paranoia)   Forty items from patients showing abnormal suspiciousness and delusions of grandeur or persecution, such as, "There are evil people trying to influence my mind" (true).

7 or Pt (Psychasthenia)   Forty-eight items based on neurotic patients showing obsessions, compulsions, abnormal fears, and guilt and indecisiveness, such as, "I save nearly everything I buy, even after I have no use for it" (true).

8 or Sc (Schizophrenia)   Seventy-eight items from patients showing bizarre or unusual thoughts or behavior, who are often withdrawn and experiencing delusions and hallucinations, such as, "Things around me do not seem real" (true), and "It makes me uncomfortable to have people close to me" (true).

9 or Ma (Hypomania)   Forty-six items from patients characterized by emotional excitement, overactivity, and flight of ideas, such as, "At times I feel very high or very low for no apparent reason" (true).

0 or Si (Social Introversion)   Seventy items from persons showing shyness, little interest in people, and insecurity, such as, "I have the time of my life at parties" (false).

1. *Buros Mental Measurements Yearbook* (Buros, 1978) contains reviews of major tests by experts in the field, who evaluate them critically, emphasizing shortcomings and strengths. It is a reasonably objective source of information about tests and should be consulted in the process of making selections.

2. Test manuals accompanying published tests compile relevant data on theoretical base, development, standardization, validity, reliability, and other technical features. This information can assist the potential test user to evaluate its suitability for a target population.

3. Test reviews often appear in professional journals, which also publish articles reporting technical data.

Each of these sources can provide useful information to the counselor, who must then relate these data to the characteristics of the population to be tested. Ideally there should be a high degree of correspondence between the test objectives, the standardization sample, and the population to be served. In collecting test-evaluation data, the counselor should consider a number of factors:

1. Validity, the most important single factor in test selection, refers to the extent to which the test measures what it claims to measure. Evidence supporting validity claims of tests must be carefully analyzed to determine if the test is appropriate for the ways in which it will be used.

2. Reliability refers to the consistency of scores and freedom from error of measurement. Evidence supporting reliability should be carefully evaluated for relevance to the target population.

3. Usability takes in factors such as convenience, cost, and ease of interpretation, which need to be carefully considered, along with things like reading level, suitability of content, design of the booklet, ease of administration, scoring procedures, examiners' qualifications and required training, and reviewers' comments.

In selecting tests it is helpful to remember that no one test will be ideal for a given task; there are trade-offs. It is the counselor's responsibility to select tests that have the highest possible relevance for the purposes at hand, recognizing their limitations and imperfections.

Nonstandardized Measures

Nonstandard assessment measures are widely used to gather information about clients. They represent a "nontest" approach and are especially useful in gathering data that does not lend itself to numerical reduction. Combining the results of standardized and nonstandardized measures often creates an optimal base for developing a truly multifaceted assessment process. Some of the more common types of nonstandardized measures are described below.

Observational Assessment

Observational measures are commonly used to gather information that is often unavailable through other means. Observational procedures can be classified by type, setting, and method, as shown in Table 9–2 (Shertzer and Linden, 1979).

Table 9–2. Classification of Observational Procedures

Type	Setting	Method	Example
systematic	natural	direct observation by time or event sampling of behavior	noting the number of times a client averts eyes when an emotional topic is introduced in counseling
controlled	contrived	the interview; situational test	observing responses to standard questions in a mental status exam or intake interview
informal	natural	anecdotal observation; developmental; unobtrusive measures; sociometric methods	observing nonverbal behavior in group room prior to the group counseling experience; case notes and records

The interview is the most commonly used observational technique in counseling; however, other methods are used. Anecdotal data, for example, often form the basis for progress notes, and role-playing structures might be seen as situational tests. It is important to emphasize that observational methods lack the normative data available from well-defined populations, a characteristic of standardized assessment tools, and are therefore more susceptible to biases. They have also been criticized because subjects can change their behavior if they know they are being observed, and the relatively limited range of situations available for observation may not produce an adequate sample of behavior.

Rating Scales

Rating systems provide a common basis for collecting certain types of observational data. They differ from observation in that observation is only the recording of behavior, while rating involves both recording behavior and simultaneously making an evaluation of specified characteristics, which are usually tabulated on a scale. The value of ratings depends primarily on the care taken in the development of the rating form and the appropriateness with which it is employed.

Self-Assessment

Self-assessment is a valuable nonstandardized assessment tool that is often underutilized in appraisal programs. Self-assessment reinforces self-determination and recognizes that the individual is truly the "expert" on himself or herself. It further enhances the participatory aspect of assessment. There are a number of self-assessment devices, many of which are based on the logic of the Self-Directed Search (Holland, 1972) and Goal Attainment Scaling (Paritzky & Magoon, 1982), available for use in assessment programs.

Using Assessment in Counseling

Ideally, in conducting an assessment, a counselor would choose options among both standardized and nonstandardized measures to ensure the broadest possible base of information on which to plan intervention techniques. Although it is not always possible to develop a comprehensive base for each client assessment, counselors should strive for the fullest range of information and acknowledge the limitations of overrelying on a single measure.

Test Interpretation

There has been much criticism of assessment, and especially of testing, in counseling (Goldman, 1972); however, if properly interpreted, tests and assessment results can be very useful in stimulating exploration and helping clients to plan, develop self-understanding, improve decision making, and set appropriate goals.

A prerequisite of effective interpretation of tests and other assessment results is a thorough understanding of their technical aspects, including limitations of the assessment data. Further, the ability to integrate information into meaningful patterns, as in the case study method, is a crucial skill. Undergirding these skills, however, is the necessity of applying counseling methods in both individual and group interpretations. The development and availability of microcomputer technology is likely to serve as an aid to the counseling in the process (Sampson, 1983), but it is unlikely to replace the need for trained counselors to work in face-to-face situations with clients exploring assessment results.

The interpretation of assessment data should fully engage the client in thinking about the implications of the assessment results for his or her own problem solving and self-awareness (Biggs and Keller, 1982). Clients should not have interpretations done *to* them, but must be directly involved in the process. The following factors should be considered in interpreting test results to clients (Miller, 1982):

1. Engage the client in a discussion of feelings about the test experience.
2. Review the purpose of the testing procedures and discuss how the results will be presented. Ensure that the client understands concepts such as norms, percentiles, stanine, ranks, and other relevant measures, including the use of profiles.

3. Present the test scores and examine the actual test. Discuss what the scores actually mean to the client.
4. Integrate the test results with the client's other self-knowledge, helping the client to see the relationship between the scores and the self.
5. Assist the client to develop a plan for operationalizing the results of the testing experience, using the test scores and other self-knowledge.

Summary of Assessment Principles

1. Never use an assessment device without having a specific purpose and use for the results.
2. The results belong to the test taker, who has a right to have them explained in understandable terms.
3. The test user is responsible for preparing clients to take the test under optimal conditions (pretest orientation).
4. No set of numerical test results captures the essence of a human being.
   a. It's possible and desirable to describe things nonnumerically.
   b. Numbers have no meaning in themselves; only *people* experience meaning. Thus there is no such thing as objectivity.
   c. Numbers as labels imply static beings. Humans are dynamic.
5. Things that can be measured precisely tend to be relatively unimportant.
6. Assessment must be carried out with techniques that
   a. are suitable for the test taker;
   b. are of high validity and reliability;
   c. engage the participation of the assessed person as much as possible;
   d. are supported by multiple observations.
7. Interpretation should focus on strengths, on what is possible, and on remedying weaknesses. Healthy optimism is a key to helpful interpretation.

Summary

In this chapter we have presented a brief overview of the major themes involved in testing and assessment. The field is broad, the focus controversial, and the need for technical expertise and cogent thinking great. Assessment cannot ethically be avoided by counselors; it's their job to observe, evaluate, diagnose, and intervene. It is our contention, and we hope your growing awareness, that using as broad a range as possible of relevant assessment devices, including standardized instruments, provides to both the client and counselor the maximum amount of potentially useful information. Assessment will be done: the only question is, will it rest upon a defensible base?

Suggested Readings

Aiken, L. R. (1982). *Psychological testing and assessment.* Boston: Allyn & Bacon.

American Psychiatric Association. (1980). *Diagnostic and statistical manual of mental disorders* (3rd ed.). Washington, D.C.: Author.

Anastasi, A. (1982). *Psychological testing* (5th ed.). New York: Macmillan.

Buros, O. (Ed.). (1978). *Mental measurements yearbook* (8th ed.). Lincoln, Neb.: University of Nebraska Press.

Goldman, L. (1970). *Using tests in counseling* (2nd ed.). Englewood Cliffs, N.J.: Prentice-Hall.

Lyman, H. B. (1971). *Test scores and what they mean* (2nd ed.). Englewood Cliffs, N.J.: Prentice-Hall.

Wiener, E. A., & Stewart, B. J. (1984). *Assessing individuals.* Boston: Little, Brown.

PART THREE
APPLICATIONS OF
COUNSELING

Chapter 10

Group Counseling

In some ways group counseling is not unlike the therapeutic experience of individual sessions. In both settings a systematic helping procedure is used to further the work of individual clients toward improving their personal functioning: identifying specific behaviors clients wish to change, understanding the underlying causes of problems, and designing strategies for making constructive changes. Although individual and group counseling modalities share similar theoretical heritages, basic strategies, and desired outcomes, there are indeed some fundamental differences between them that warrant closer inspection. There is no doubt that counseling in groups is more complex, requires more leader training, and has potential to do more good or harm than similar helping efforts in individual counseling. It is for these reasons that students are given additional training in group modalities, as well as being cautioned in their judicious use.

Survey of Groups

We live in a world of groups: social groups, family groups, ethnic groups, athletic groups, fraternities and sororities, neighborhood groups, professional groups, religious groups. The only time we are ever really alone is when in the car or the bathroom, and even then we are often invaded.

The composition of any group, whether for social, business, or therapeutic purposes, involves a collection of persons gathered together for compatible goals. While they may (and usually do) have personal motives and objectives that they wish to satisfy as a result of their participation, group members agree on a set of basic governing principles to guide their collective behavior. These norms and roles implicitly or explicitly specify leader actions as well as appropriate member behaviors (Baird & Weinberg, 1981).

Encounter Groups

Groups have many different terms and labels that have been somewhat arbitrarily used, leaving the public as well as some professionals a bit confused. The most ambiguous category includes names such as Human Relations Group, Human Potential Group, T Group, Training Group, Encounter Group, and Growth Group, all of which developed from the early work of the National Training Laboratory (NTL), Esalen Institute, and the writings of Carl Rogers and Kurt Lewin.

While there are substantial differences in the quality and execution of these experiential-type groups, depending on the leader's training and experience, they all have a free-flowing flavor within an educational model. They are designed for relatively normal persons and usually have a fairly loose structure, and the leader is viewed primarily as a facilitator-participant rather than an expert (Rogers, 1970).

An Encounter Group in Action

The silence has lasted four minutes by the clock, but it feels like an hour. Everyone looks to the leader, who merely smiles and waits. Finally, one woman, in exasperation, screams out, "I'm tired of this crap! When are we going to *do* something?"

The leader meets her eyes squarely and responds softly, "This is *your* group. What do *you* intend to do?"

Another participant chimes in, then another, all voicing their frustration at the aimless direction in which they have been moving: "What are we supposed to be doing here?"

The leader answers, "I feel frustrated too, but isn't this a bit like our lives? It is up to us to create structure. Maybe a good place to start would be for us to tell each other how we feel about one another. For instance, Martha, in the beginning I thought, I mean I *felt,* that you were real tight and inhibited, until you were the first to speak up. I wonder if anyone has any feelings about me?"

Guidance Groups

In contrast, guidance groups, although sharing an educational emphasis, tend to be didactic and instructional rather than experiential and focused on feelings. They often have planned, structured activities and fairly definite goals that are identified by the leader, who operates in an instructor-facilitator role. Guidance groups are often found in school settings, where counselors attempt to provide relevant information on careers, sex, job possibilities, colleges, and other topics that might be of interest. Generally, they focus on preventing problems in the future by encouraging developmental growth, aiding the decision-making process, teaching valuable life skills, and providing useful information. Guidance groups are particularly well suited for many structured interpretations that facilitate self-awareness and values clarification.

A Guidance Group in Action

"You have all had time to study various careers, visit job sites directly, and hear some interesting talks by representatives of various professions. Still, many of you are confused as to which direction to move in and are even more uncertain as to what you are uniquely suited to do. Although just beginning your lives, you already are aware of things you like and dislike as well as those things you can easily do or not do. Perhaps it might be helpful for you to get some honest feedback from your friends in this group who know you so well. Tina, you had mentioned earlier that you could never be in a medical profession because you can't stand sick people. Based on what the rest of you know about her, what careers do *you* think she'd be good at?"

Counseling Groups

Group counseling is the modality most appropriate for the students of this text. The techniques and strategies are all designed to help resolve interpersonal conflict, promote greater self-awareness and insight, and help individual members work to eliminate their self-defeating behaviors. Most often, the clientele have few manifestations of psychopathology, but rather, as in all the realm of counseling, wish to work on personal concerns in daily living (Ohlsen, 1977).

Group counseling is usually focused in the present rather than dwelling on the past. It is relatively short-term, spanning a period of weeks or months, and stresses relationship support factors to resolve stated conflicts. The leader is always a trained expert who is prepared to protect individual clients' rights while stimulating constructive interpersonal action. Clients are usually helped to work toward individually designed goals, although there is a common interest in becoming more intimate, trusting, accepting, empathic, and interpersonally effective.

A Counseling Group in Action

COUNSELOR: Who wants to use group time today? We've cleared up some loose ends from last week and got progress reports on what has happened during the week, so let's move on.

KILE: Well, if nobody else wants. . . .

SARAH: Damn it, Kile. You talk too much. Why don't you give someone else a chance?

KILE: But I was only. . . .

COUNSELOR: Sarah, you seem unusually frisky today. I don't think you're as angry at Kile as at yourself for letting things slide so long. But there's plenty of time for both of you. And I remember that you, Nicolas, had a concern you wanted to work on as well. Let's budget our time accordingly.

KILE: Sarah, I know you're not angry at me and I'm glad you finally want to work on something. I only need about ten minutes anyway. Two weeks ago you guys helped me a lot—and things are much better with my girlfriend. The only thing is that I'm having second thoughts about getting married. I just wanted to get some feedback from the rest of you as to how *you* felt before you got married and how you feel about your situations now.

Therapy Groups

In practice there is often very little difference between group counseling and group therapy, while in theory the goals and purposes are miles apart. Psychotherapy in groups most often takes place in hospital, medical, or clinic settings with patients who are diagnosed as having some form of psychoneurosis, personality disorder, or psychosis. These severe disorders require longer treatment, intensive analysis, and structural personality changes.

The content of most counseling programs does not adequately prepare students to deliver group psychotherapy services. Often counseling practitioners may find themselves, by choice or circumstances, functioning as group psychotherapists and so often seek to supplement their training with further study in psychodynamic methodologies, psychopathologic process, psychodiagnosis, psychophysiology, and psychopharmacology.

A Therapy Group in Action

The therapy group has been meeting weekly for two years. The support has been crucial for many of the participants, who include an alcoholic, a spouse abuser, a man with severe depressive episodes, a woman with an eating disorder who indulges in periodic binges, another woman fearful of crossing bridges, a man with chronic anxiety and insomnia, and a man who won't admit he has any problems, although his behavior is passive-aggressive. There are two leaders: a psychiatrist who monitors medication and a psychologist who works with them in testing. Both have a psychoanalytic perspective and have been working to help each patient minimize his or her symptoms, understand past actions, and function more normally in their worlds. The sessions are usually quite emotionally charged, requiring all the skills and training of the two leaders to reduce manipulation, resistance, and game-playing and avoid casualties. The group has acted as a buffer, a transitional step between the members' intensive individual therapy sessions and a gradual tapering off of treatment that will eventually lead to a monthly check-up and support system.

Some Considerations in the Use of Group Modalities

There has been considerable debate in the literature about whether group counseling is essentially safe and successful as a treatment modality or whether it produces too many casualties and is a waste of time. Some proponents (Bergin & Garfield, 1971; Ohlsen, 1977) claim that therapeutic groups hold the future of our field because of their tremendous influencing power and efficiency. Critics (Corazzini & Anderson, 1980; Lieberman, Yalom, & Miles, 1973) believe that group therapies are faddish and possibly detrimental.

It may, therefore, be helpful to review some considerations in the use of groups so that you, as a student, may realistically assess the potential and dangers of this helping procedure. If you choose to work in groups, as a leader of a counseling group, as an administrator conducting meetings, as an instructor in the classroom, as a public figure in the media, or as a consultant in the field, you would be well advised to study the contraindications of group methods carefully so that you may adequately prepare needed safeguards as well as face your critics. Similarly, you can best capitalize on the therapeutic variables that operate in groups only if you are well aware of what can and cannot be effectively accomplished.

The history of group work is checkered with the contributions of many distinguished professionals as well as the practices of charlatans and witch doctors. Recall that throughout human history, group hysteria has accounted for more havoc and death than all contagious diseases. After all, what is war but an organized form of group work, in which one team, led by leaders who are masters of group dynamics, attempt to obliterate the other team in the name of abstractions like territorial boundaries? In our recent history, we have witnessed the dramatic influencing capabilities of self-serving group leaders who could induce murder or suicide with their persuasive tongues and intricate knowledge of the power of group forces. Adolf Hitler, Charles Manson, and Reverend Jim Jones are but a few of the more skilled group tacticians of this century who could warp group dynamics to suit their own needs.

It is no wonder that therapeutic groups are often viewed with suspicion by the public and by some clinicians. Only in the past few years have standards for acceptable practice been developed and systematic training programs implemented (Patterson, 1972). For these reasons, new graduates sometimes experience frustration when trying to begin group work in their schools or agencies. They get opposition from their clients, who resent the increased pressure to participate in an uncomfortable setting and resist the coercion. Further, clients are often more inhibited in groups, less willing to disclose because of fears—some of which are justified. How, after all, can confidentiality ever be enforced and guaranteed in a group? Who can promise never to let a secret slip inadvertently or deliberately talk about private things outside the group? And who would believe such promises?

There are also complaints from parents and spouses: "What's this? I heard that you stuck my son in one of those touchy-feely groups? I'll not have a child of mine in one of your orgies." Or, "I notice my wife is different since she's been hanging around with those dingbats in that group. How dare you people interfere in my life!"

There is also resistance to implementing group strategies from some senior colleagues in administration or counseling who never received group training. Many counselor/therapist education programs added their first course in the techniques of group work during the past ten years. And the majority of group counseling classes currently focus as much on theory as on any practical considerations for how to organize, market, begin, run, and end a therapeutic group.

In group work, clients receive less time than they would in individual sessions and have less privacy. Groups require more sophisticated training on the part of leaders and are generally not suited for people who are easily intimidated or manipulative or who talk incessantly.

Why then would we ever choose to work in group settings? Why indeed?

Counteracting Potential Limitations

It has been our own experience as counselor educators and practitioners, as well as specialists in group work (and therefore a little biased), that several of the distinct disadvantages such as those just mentioned can be controlled or minimized through sufficient caution and training. Lieberman et al. (1973), for example, have reviewed the issue of client casualties in encounter groups and offer the following guidelines to group leaders:

1. Evaluate the normative structure of the group and assess members' expectations about the forms and structures the group will assume. This is most effectively done in a pregroup interview.

2. Evaluate the psychosocial relations in the group and pay particular attention to members with minimal interaction.

3. Recognize the importance of cognitive factors on positive group outcome.

4. Organize the group experience around a theoretical framework and plan activities and interventions accordingly. The choice of an intellectual posture is less important than the consistent use thereof.

5. Monitor carefully the ratio of confrontation to support and avoid overstimulating the group members. Too much stimulation, especially confrontation, can lead to casualties, while too little can result in apathy and high group dropout.

6. Be aware of the leader's impact on the group members through the transference process and temper interactions with timing and patience. Avoid the temptation to use transference to force member "breakthroughs."

7. Accept responsibility for the constructive emotional climate of the group.

8. Allow members to "exit" an experience without censure if the focus or experience becomes uncomfortable or too intense for the participant. Follow up on dropouts to resolve any lingering negative effects.

9. Understand the dynamics of the change process and help members to create more adaptive structures for implementing change beyond the group experience.

Issues such as the suitability of certain personality types (passive-dependent, sociopathic), appropriateness of the group for individual problems, and level of psychological functioning (borderline personality, psychotic) can be handled through screening procedures that would permit participation only of those who are reasonably respectful of others' rights and who seem to be good candidates for groups (however that may be operationally defined).

There are other issues that may not be so readily dismissed. Confidentiality can not be strictly guaranteed, and it is true that clients receive less attention than in private counseling. With these limitations in mind, the leader must take extra care to ensure that time is spent equitably and that adequate safeguards are planned to prevent anticipated problems. Taking these conditions as givens, we can more realistically survey some of the powerful advantages implicit in therapeutic groups.

Advantages of Group Work

Cost Efficiency

It would take a counselor two full working days to see a dozen clients in individual sessions; the same number could meet in a single group session for two hours. The counselor is thereby able to reach more prospective clients in a considerably shorter period of time, and at significant savings to the institution and clientele. Most counselors and agencies are already so overburdened with work demands that group modalities allow for the most cost-efficient means to help the largest needy population.

Spectator Effects

While one person is receiving help in a therapeutic group—struggling, confronting, exploring, growing—a dozen other clients are carefully observing the process. They are internalizing the therapeutic messages, personalizing and adapting the content to their own lives. As one client complains about conflicts with a roommate, all others in the group (and those who are now reading these words) must ask themselves: How am I getting along with my spouse/friend/roommate? What things in this relationship am I willing to fight for and which freedoms am I prepared to sacrifice? How do I enjoy my privacy? Do I want to live alone? How could we better settle our arguments?

Group work has the distinct advantage of permitting others to learn by observation. Clients are able to monitor the leader's behavior, imitating the behaviors that they wish for themselves: how to speak with confidence, how to create metaphoric language, how to take risks. The clients also scrutinize one another. When one member experiences success, the rest will live it vicariously. When a member is censured for monopolizing too much time, the others note the lesson as well.

The learning effects become contagious as an active participant is silently or not-so-silently cheered by the enthusiastic spectators, urging him or her forward and also tasting the thrill of victory or defeat. Each time a client opens up, takes a risk, or tries out a new behavior and *doesn't* die as a consequence, the other clients will feel more ready to test themselves.

Stimulation Value

It is no surprise that the quantity and quality of ideas generated through group interaction are significantly more enriched than the results of solo brainstorming (Meadow, Parnes, & Reese, 1959; Brilhart & Jochem, 1964). Discovery of this fact revolutionized industrial product design: experts from compatible fields learned to pool their problem-solving efforts.

The atmosphere of a therapeutic group is a virtual utopia of emotional and cognitive stimulation, with its emphasis on freedom of expression, honest feedback, interchange of novel ideas, acceptance of individual differ-

Counseling groups provide opportunities for feedback, lively interaction, support, belongingness, and supervised practice of new behaviors..

ences, prizing of creativity and spontaneity, emphasis on experimentation without a fear of failure, and focus on risk taking, sharing, and giving. In such an environment it is impossible to be bored or to repeat an experience in exactly the same way.

Group sessions are exciting and fertile atmospheres for change because of the collective energy available. The sum is greater than its parts. Giggles quickly become contagious. As new ideas are passed around they grow with each input, contribution, refinement. You can feel the hearts beating in a group. You can smell the sweat and sense the nervous shuffling. You can hear the pounding in your brain as it tries so hard to understand. And the sights are a visual Disneyland—nonverbal behavior to monitor, facial expressions, gestures of defiance, respect, or affection, territorial imperatives, positionings and status hierarchies, insight in action. A group is alive with ideas and emotion and change. It is stimulation itself. It is a dozen people struggling to understand themselves and each other.

Not only do therapeutic groups prevent burn-out in the counselor, who must constantly stay on top of things, but the clients are energized by the lively interactions, spontaneous humor, and abundance of stimulation. Many practitioners with hectic schedules often deliberately plan group sessions to help not only their clientele but also themselves. The groups are often so professionally rewarding that the leader, although carefully monitoring his or her own behavior to avoid self-indulgence or meeting his or her own needs in the session, nevertheless, cannot help growing.

Opportunities for Feedback

Where can you go for truth? Ask your mother or your best friend for an opinion on your new shoes or what you should change about yourself. They will lie, or at least hedge, to water down an unpleasant truth. Where can you go to find out what people really think of you?

A counseling group provides the opportunity for participants to receive straightforward, honest, and constructive reactions to their behaviors, both attractive and ineffective. After role playing or risk taking, a client gains feedback from astute observers that helps in making needed adjustments, identifying areas in the life and personality of the client that could be upgraded, as well as providing reinforcement by acknowledging progress. When feedback is diplomatically confrontive, honest without being destructive, expressive but devoid of clichés, sensitive but not overly evasive, concise by boiling down the essence of a person's behavior into a memorable image, it becomes one of the most powerful of therapeutic devices for promoting change.

In one introductory exercise used to open groups, for example, the leader wishes to encourage an exchange of first impressions among participants. Early in the therapeutic experience, the exercise helps them to give one another the gift of honest reactions. After members are instructed about the purposes of such an exercise—to encounter one another in a personal way, to collect information on possible areas of needed growth, to hear (perhaps for the first time) of the effect they have on others—they are then educated in the requirements of effective feedback. They are reminded to avoid stereotypes and clichés, to be concise rather than long-winded, and to be honest, helpful, and constructive by including both attractive and ineffective behaviors. To give the exercise structure and direction, which are often necessary in initial sessions until members learn rules and roles, they are asked to write down the name of the animal that each person in the group brings to mind. Using their observations of each person's gestures and appearances, their own intuition, and any other data available, trying to be creative in their thinking, clients send feedback to one another by disclosing the animals of which they are most reminded and the reasons why.

Angela, a shy, withdrawn girl learns that some of the others see her as a turtle because "she loves to swim beneath the surface where no one can see" or a golden retriever "because she appears loyal, affectionate, and maternal" or an opaline gourami (the speaker is a fish expert) "because she's cautious when people are around, but prances when alone; she has a beautiful display of colors and grace yet she hides behind the plants even if she sees a tasty morsel to eat; she prefers to wait for things to come to her."

Other members learn from the feedback on first impressions that they may resemble a Colorado River mule because they are survivors, are self-sufficient, and have a flexible diet, or a Hobbit because of their playfulness, innocence, perceptiveness, and love of adventure, or a Queen Bee because they are good organizers but manipulative and overdemanding.

Any and all feedback in a group is aimed at providing experiences that are rarely available in the "outside world"—direct, honest, and sensitive statements about how exactly one person feels and thinks about another.

Support

The tarpon, among the world's greatest sport fishes, will fight for hours longer against the hook and line when accompanied by others of his school. It is as if he couldn't give in with his peers watching, urging, goading him to fight a little longer. There is also a human need to give and receive support in groups. Our ancestors huddled together in their caves for security and division of labor. In the evolutionary scheme of things, the PTA, fraternity, and neighborhood club have inherited many of the social-protective functions of the bonds we originally formed as hunter-gatherers. Groups supply the nurturing elements of intimacy and psychological bonding—the cohesion that results from close proximity over time. A therapeutic group can develop into a surrogate family, without the rigid, authoritarian hierarchies of some natural families. Such an experience can even be sampled within the relative artificiality of your classroom. Although the physical environment, seating arrangement, competition, professional authority, and threat of grading are something less than ideal circumstances for promoting a sense of true cohesion, there is nevertheless a feeling of belongingness that develops among classmates. Students can draw support from one another, pool their emotional and cognitive energies to get through the hard times, and savor the enlightening experiences.

Structured Practice

Within a group, a person can not only receive feedback but also experience the support and encouragement necessary to practice new behaviors. Often individuals undergo stress and frustration in their daily lives because they lack needed skills. Shyness prevents them from initiating new relationships, or frustration keeps them hostile and defensive, or low self-esteem triggers procrastination; each of these limitations can be viewed as a skill deficit, and the group becomes a place to develop and refine useful life skills. A man who is passive with his wife, for instance, can practice assertive skills. Group members provide feedback and help him to monitor the development of those skills. Laboratory experiences such as these help group members to put insights to use and to rehearse new behaviors in a nonthreatening setting.

The group, as a learning laboratory, can also be used for reality testing. Fears, anxieties, and inhibitions can be examined and explored, permitting the member to test out the validity of those feelings. Commonly a person will hold feelings in to avoid "hurting" someone else. This concern can be tested in the group by checking out others' reactions and practicing giving both constructive and critical feedback to determine the recipient's reaction. Often the person will learn that being protective and withholding honesty is more "hurtful" than disclosing it and can then work toward a personal awareness of what "hurting" means.

Basic Assumptions about Groups

One human life is so complex in its origins, history, functioning, and consciousness as to defy complete understanding by all the social and physical scientists in the universe. Yet when this solitary life is combined with a group of other lives, the network of ideas and interactions that could be generated is staggering. A single action by an individual group member—rearranging his position on the chair, for example—could signify restlessness, agitation, back pain, hemorrhoids, a desire for attention, postural difficulties, a need for increased blood flow, or an itch. If that same person were to communicate with another in the group, with his eyes or gestures, not to mention the possible variations of his voice, the effects would ripple like waves through the minds of all those present. Each person would seek a personal interpretation of the action and would respond to the stimulus both internally and externally. And it is the leader's task to sift through the confusing assortment of often conflicting stimuli, to attend to those that have relevance to the present situation and goals, to make sense of and give meaning to the behavior, to predict likely consequences, and finally, to act therapeutically in the best interests of those who are present.

The group leader not only must have mastered basic counseling technology but must understand dynamics and assumptions as they are applied to group behavior. Initially, each client comes to the group with different expectations, interests, and goals. The most basic assumption about groups, therefore, is that there are often discrepancies among the participants' hopes and expectations and even between the leader's and the members'. Coalitions are formed on the basis of these common interests and backgrounds and often on the basis of perceived similarities in attitudes, abilities, or attractiveness. The leader may be viewed as the "outsider," as a function of his or her expert role, or possibly as the only "insider," since the counselor alone really knows what is going on during the beginning sessions.

Assuming a diversity of expectations helps the group leader to plan for and permit the realization of individual goals that are compatible with the flexible structure. Individual members are thus helped to clarify their reasons for attending the group and encouraged to set specific goals that may be realistically attained during the time allotted.

LEADER: Before I discuss some ideas regarding what options are available for you in this group and how we can spend our time, let's hear from some of you as to why you decided to come.

ELKA: I didn't *decide* to come. My parents threatened to ground me for the semester unless I agreed to try this a few times. They think I'm too young to get married; I don't.

NANDO: I heard this was a good place to meet girls. I could always use some new ladies in my life.

BETH: I've got some problems at work. I don't know what to do. I was hoping to get some advice.

FRED: Too much dope. I get high too much. Every day. I want to stop. Maybe you guys can help me.

Another assumption about therapeutic groups to which most (but not all) practitioners would subscribe is that the leader is not a participant of the group but a trained expert. Efforts are thus devoted to keeping the focus on the members, avoiding self-indulgent excesses, and generally staying in the role of paid professional who does not deliberately use group time for self-serving purposes.

CASSANDRA: O wise one, you always sit here so omnipotent—like you know everything about anything. You are leading us, helping us. What are some of *your* problems? Why don't we help you?

LEADER: I do have lots of things I could work on in this group—my impatience, my overdriving ambition—and I know that you are all skilled enough to help me; but I don't feel comfortable using *your* time to work on *my* concerns. I'm being paid to help you. I can go to another group (and I do occasionally) where I get help. Thanks for your concern, Cassandra. But did I hear you resenting the control you feel I have? Is that something you would like to work on, since your lack of control has been an issue before?

For group work to be successful, or even to get off the ground, there must be an atmosphere of trust. Even more so than in individual sessions, the issue of confidentiality must be directly addressed so that it is clearly understood that all communication within the group is to be private and secure. Actually, there is no way confidentiality can ever be guaranteed or enforced in a group setting, for members are not legally bound to comply with any particular codes. Inadvertent breaches of trust can also occur, destroying the hard-won confidence. It is for these reasons that the leader openly, forcefully, and explicitly discusses the issue:

HECTOR: Why should I ever spill my guts here? I don't know you people. How can I believe anyone is trustworthy if I don't know them?

LEADER: Your point is a good one. There is a risk involved in being open, in this group or anywhere else. You should therefore pace yourself so that you disclose only what you feel ready to share. You will have to trust your own instincts on this. But remember, the degree to which you risk is related to how much you grow. Let's work on some situations that could test your confidential oath and discuss how they might be handled. What would you say, for instance, if your best friend asked what's going on in your group? OK, what are you permitted to talk about outside the group? And what are some of your fears about what would occur if someone in here did tell others what you said?

In counseling groups, perhaps even more than in individual sessions, client discomfort is associated with change. The very structure of a group environment, with its active audience, stimulates approval seeking, fears of failure, peer pressure, and other forces that do little to help the client feel at ease. This phenomenon isn't necessarily undesirable. A "healthy" amount of discomfort can motivate a person to get off dead center, to reduce dissonance, to make changes, and to restore equilibrium. As risk taking in a group accelerates, with members sharing their feelings, admitting inadequacies, and confronting themselves and one another, there are direct pressures from other members (which are usually held in check by the leader to protect individual rights) and subtle pressures from within to conform to the risky norm. Some begin to squirm as they watch others grow, leaving them behind. The more they hang back and remain passive, the more dissatisfied they become with their present ineffective functioning. The only way to reduce their discomfort is to leave the group (which sometimes happens if the leader doesn't carefully monitor readiness levels of each participant) or to make needed changes in themselves.

MONICA: This is the eighth session and I know I haven't said much, but I'm just not all that good at talking in front of groups.

STEPHEN: As long as you believe that crap you don't have to do anything else. Just sit there and watch us sweat. I'm tired of you getting a free ride.

LEADER: [Interrupting Monica before she can defend herself] Back off, Steve. Your point is well taken even if you put it so harshly. Monica, before you answer him, what's going on inside your head?

MONICA: Just that maybe he's right. I wish I could get involved but I'm too scared. And yet I hate coming here because I can't open up. I tried to stay home. But I can't do that either. Then I'd really feel like a chicken. I'm so confused; I just don't know what to do.

LEADER: How did you feel about what Steve said?

MONICA: I think he—

LEADER: Talk to him.

MONICA: Ah. I don't know . . . OK. Steve, I think you're a bastard and you tried to hurt me. You didn't have to be so cruel about it. I heard what you said but I didn't like the way you said it.

LEADER: Now we're off and running.

Much of the growth in groups occurs through observation, identification, modeling, imitation, and other social learning processes that are often not found in individual sessions. There are opportunities to watch the leader in action, presumably an expert in social-interactive skills, a model of the fully functioning person. The leader disperses wisdom or settles disputes with Solomon-like grace. The leader articulates metaphors and speeches worthy of a Shakespearean soliloquy. The leader orchestrates behavior, structures situations, organizes, takes charge. The leader radiates warmth and kindness and enthusiasm. And all the while, the others watch carefully, nodding to themselves when they see something they like, consciously selecting behaviors for their own repertoire, captive to the power and force of the leader's personality.

A client also learns while watching peers struggle with their concerns. Every presented problem is internalized by the attentive audience, adapted to their particular lives. Clients learn not only from one another's mistakes but from each other's failures.

ORLANDO: Last week, Gianina, when you were talking about how bored you were being a housewife, I was, at first, bored listening to you. I mean, what could I get out of your situation? My problem is that I'm too busy. I have too much work to do. Then I realized that although our styles are different we are both hiding from the same thing.

GIANINA: I don't understand. Your life is far from boring. I stayed a housewife, until last week anyway, because I was afraid to venture out.

ORLANDO: Exactly. And I keep myself so occupied so I don't have to deal with myself and confront how boring I feel I really am.

LEADER: Were there others as well who identified with Gianina's concerns last week?

Groups provide many opportunities for realistic rehearsal of new behaviors. Much of what constitutes the permanent acquisition of new learning involves not only the observation of desired behaviors but the opportunity to practice skills under supervision. Clients spend a good portion of their time applying what they have learned in the laboratory. They can experiment and refine interaction skills and social behaviors. They can take risks or confront others, and afterwards, receive constructive feedback. Before they venture out into the world to wrestle with a problem, they can first use other group members to help rehearse before the big performance.

LEADER: OK, Jerry, who in the group most reminds you of your family members? Let's role-play the disaster you expect to occur when you get home tonight. Maybe we can even give you some ideas on how to handle it.

JERRY: Well, Brenda for sure reminds me of my mother. No, Brenda—I mean you both are so calm and relaxed.

LEADER: Don't apologize—just choose your characters.

JERRY: OK. I guess Joe would be good to play my Dad. But act real gruff. Grunt a lot and don't look at me when you talk. That's right. Also fidget more. Perfect. Patty, you can be my older sister. But you have to act confident but aloof. And Louis, you're crazy enough to be my older brother. I guess that's it. Unless someone wants to be my dog?

LEADER: All right, now set the stage and program everyone the way they would normally act. Then you enter the scene and we'll see what happens. We will periodically stop the action, analyze what you did or didn't do, and give you some helpful suggestions. Perhaps we should even add a helper: Nancy will be your alter ego, and every time you are evasive or wishy-washy or back down she will say aloud what you really want to say. Ready? Lights—camera—action.

The structure and ambience of therapeutic groups are well suited to working on interpersonal conflicts. The arrangement of chairs in a circle encourages direct communication among all as equals. If particular members make eye contact only with the leader while talking, that behavior is quickly extinguished. *Constructive* confrontations are stressed by encouraging the open and honest expression of feelings toward one another. Members are also helped to communicate and offer feedback sensitively and empathically while they are taught to hear and interpret personal messages nondefensively.

Cues for Intervention

Although a group leader's behavior involves mainly intuition, artistry, and feeling for the situation, there are some fairly specific instances in which therapeutic intervention is almost always necessary. In individual sessions, the counselor, while relying heavily on "gut wisdom," also knows that when a client becomes self-deprecating or self-deceptive or drifts from reality, an intervention is called for. In group situations there is a virtual overload of stimuli to attend to. The most difficult task, therefore, is to describe not just how and when to intervene but with whom. A leader's behavior can be at best distracting, or at worst destructive, if ill timed or inappropriately directed. For these reasons, even the beginning student ought to become familiar with the minimally prescribed instances that signal therapeutic action.

Abusive Behavior

Without exception or qualification, in the event that it can be determined that the physical safety or emotional welfare of any participant is in danger, the leader must intervene. Much of the research on casualties in group work supports the idea that the leader should take responsibility for protecting client safety (Lieberman et al., 1973). This can be done only by carefully monitoring each member for cues of internal distress, as well as keeping a close eye on group interactions to ensure that verbal abuse is minimized.

Usually, interactions that are hostile in their intent are quickly dissipated, or at least brought into the open to be dealt with in a relatively controlled manner. When a member is unaware of or insensitive to the negative effects generated by a comment or outburst, the leader also steps in to repair any damage. However, the vast majority of therapeutic efforts are directed toward heading off potential abuse *before* it occurs. With some experience, a leader can detect the signs of imminent explosive behavior and can therefore intervene before a fight or screaming match breaks out, in much the way that a skilled classroom teacher always knows when trouble is about to erupt.

Rambling and Digressions

For any number of reasons—to avoid meaningful dialogue, to resist treatment, to play games—or oftentimes simply because a client is verbally disorganized, the flow of conversation will stray from anything of therapeutic value. Perhaps someone will tell a long-winded story with no direct relevance. Or another might interrupt proceedings to prove some obscure point. Or there is a client, as inevitably there has been in every group we have ever known, who is just scatter brained, "off the wall," or in a different hemisphere. His or her interjections can be maddening, interrupting a meaningful silence, badgering the leader with questions intended to win approval, or breaking into every interaction with the preface, "That reminds me of the time. . . ."

Whether the group's ramblings are mildly inconvenient or downright pathological, the leader will usually establish some norm for appropriate input. Initially, interventions are used subtly to play down digressive comments and reinforce those that are on target. Sometimes the interventions must be more direct. For Cindy, a client who is particularly prone to digressions, the leader may finally cue feedback to indicate when comments aren't appropriate: "Jacob, how was it helpful to hear what Cindy just said when she interrupted you? Oh, it wasn't? You wished she would wait until you were through?" and then, "Cindy, what feedback did you just hear?"

Withdrawal and Passivity

Often the effects of verbal abuse, needless rambling, or other factors internal to the client will result in withdrawal in one or more members. Withdrawal is particularly difficult to deal with: the leader wants to safeguard the right to privacy, yet does not want clients to slip into complete passivity. Furthermore, withdrawal is not obvious; it is recognized only by an absence of behavior. The leader must identify individual patterns for each client in order to read signs of withdrawal in averted eyes, scooting back the chair, answering in monosyllables, or acting in some other uncharacteristic manner. The counselor may decide to draw the person into the group directly ("You're not saying much today. What's going on inside your head?") or consult with the person after the group in a private conference, or even choose to wait and let other members bring up the issue.

Lethargy and Boredom

One function of the group leader is to spice up the learning experience to maintain participants' interest. After only a few sessions, a routine sets in that can become predictable or boring. The leader uses humor, spontaneous actions, dramatic gestures, and a playful spirit to keep things stimulating. Whenever yawning becomes prevalent, or monotonous voices, or behavior in which clients only appear to be going through the motions (which happens frequently), the leader intervenes.

> "It is up to each one of you to accept responsibility for your own growth in this group. Usually when you are confronted with a repetitive episode or when you feel lazy, you are content to daydream or doodle, biding your time until the ordeal is over. However, when you feel your mind drifting away in here, as many of you were doing just now, you are cheating yourself of a potentially valuable experience. It is too easy to write off the times you aren't intensely involved in what is happening. You are in this group because you wish to learn to be more focused in the present, to enjoy each moment to its fullest. Why not begin now? Throughout the rest of this session, and those thereafter, when you catch yourself feeling restless or bored, force yourself to focus on what is going on. There is *always* so much to attend to even if you find a particular discussion uninteresting. Watch the reactions of the others, how they are responding nonverbally to what they are hearing. Notice what I am doing or not doing and what my rationale might be. And closely scrutinize your own internal behavior. When you drift away, what are you hiding from? There is never a legitimate excuse for feeling bored in this group."

Semantic Errors

Depending on theoretical preferences and linguistic sensitivity, every counselor has a list of favorite semantic errors to pounce on. Language is the principal evidence we have of a client's thought patterns; how a person speaks aloud and expresses ideas, the choice and arrangement of words, accurately indicate how that person thinks and feels about his or her situation. Group leaders will intervene when clients distort reality, exaggerate, or use illogical communications. A facilitator versed in the client-centered approach may correct participants by asking them to change "I think" to "I feel." Rational-emotive counselors would interrupt members when they express themselves with "I must" or "I should," asking them instead to substitute more accurate verbalizations such as "I may" or "I could." And a follower of neurolinguistic programming techniques would correct variations that are incomplete in their surface structure; "*They* made me do *it*" is converted from a statement having ambiguous referents to a complete communication: "Several of my elementary school teachers (they) made me play without making any kind of a mess (it)."

The leader of a group has the responsibility to understand, to relate, to facilitate, and to structure the interaction of the group members in a way that maximizes the therapeutic potential of the experience for all participants.

This is a challenging and, at times, overwhelming task that demands the total energy and concentration of the group leader, who must be trained and skilled in individual and group-focused counseling skills.

The foregoing list of intervention cues is far from complete. Dyer and Vriend (1977) mention others, such as when a group member speaks for others, seeks approval, or acts inconsistently. Kottler (1983) includes many common critical incidents that require intervention, such as unequal participation, superficiality, collective silence, power struggles, and patterns of resistance. Corey and Corey (1982) identify other such instances, including monopolistic behavior, advice giving, "band-aiding," intellectualizing, or becoming seductive, superior, or dependent. The counselor must rely on acquired skills and experience to deal with these situations efficiently and effectively.

Specialized Skills of Group Work

Working with groups requires the use of numerous techniques in addition to those used in individual counseling. Some practitioners are reluctant to lead counseling groups because of their anxiety over the responsibilities and techniques needed to function effectively. To some extent, inadequate preparation is the result of limited training in group leadership, and counselor educators have expressed concern over the teaching of group counseling skills and abilities (Dye, 1980).

A number of attempts have been made to identify the specific skills of group leadership (Ivey, 1971; Lieberman et al., 1973; Dyer & Vriend, 1977; Ohlsen, 1977; Harvill, Masson, & Jacobs, 1983). Four of them are compared in Table 10–1. However, there is little empirical evidence that these particular skills are unique to group counseling. Gill and Barry (1982) have attempted to fill the gap by proposing a three-stage classification system (Table 10–2) for group-focused counseling skills. The criteria they selected for building this model of group counseling skills included the following qualities:

1. *appropriate*—the behavior can reasonably be attributed to the role and function of a group counselor;
2. *definable*—the behavior can be described in terms of human performance;
3. *observable*—experienced as well as inexperienced observers can identify the behavior when it occurs; the behavior can be repeated in like form by different people in different settings;
4. *measurable*—objective recording of both the frequency and quality of the behavior can occur with a high degree of agreement among observers;

Table 10–1. Group Counseling Skill Classification Systems

Ivey (1971)	Lieberman, Yalom, and Miles (1973)	Dyer and Vriend (1977)	Ohlsen (1977)

1. minimal encouragers
2. open questions
3. closed questions
4. paraphrase
5. reflection of feeling
6. summary
7. directions
8. expression of content
9. expression of feelings
10. cognitive restructure
 	
1. group focus
2. individual focus
3. self focus
4. topic focus
	1. emotional stimulation
	  a. revealing feelings, beliefs
	  b. confrontation
	  c. stylistically emoting
	  d. risk taking
	2. caring
	  a. friendship
	  b. love, affection
	  c. acceptance, support, praise
	  d. invitation to seek feedback
	3. meaning attribution
	  a. explaining
	  b. cognitizing behavior
	  c. interpreting of reality
	  d. labeling behaviors
	4. executive function
	  a. limit setting
	  b. rules, norms setting
	  c. goal setting
	  d. group management
		1. identifying, labeling, clarifying, and reflecting feeling
		2. identifying, labeling, clarifying and reflecting behavioral data
		3. identifying, labeling, clarifying and reflecting cognitive data
		4. questioning, drawing out, and evoking material appropriate for counseling focus
		5. confronting
		6. summarizing and reviewing important material
		7. interpreting
		8. restating
		9. establishing connections
		10. information giving
		11. initiating
		12. reassuring, encouraging, and supporting
		13. intervening
		14. dealing with silence
		15. recognizing and explaining nonverbal behavior
		16. using clear, concise, meaningful communications
		17. focusing
		18. restraining, subduing, and avoiding potentially explosive and divisive kinds of group happenings
		19. goal setting
		20. facilitating closure
			1. developing readiness
			2. relationship building
			3. relationship maintaining
			4. problem identification
			5. definition of counseling
			6. definition of criteria to appraise client's growth
			7. resistance
			8. countertransference
			9. feedback
			10. termination

(Gill & Barry, 1982, p. 303)

Table 10–2. Classification System for Group-Focused Counseling Skills

Stage I	*Stage II*	*Stage III*
Group Formation: Facilitating Cooperation Toward Common Goals Through Development of Group Identity	*Group Awareness:* Facilitating a Shared Understanding of the Group's Behavior	*Group Action:* Facilitating Cooperative Decision-Making and Problem-Solving
1. *Norming* stating explicitly the expected group behavior	1. *Labeling group behavior* identifying and describing group feelings and performance	1. *Identifying group needs* asking questions and making statements that clarify the wants and needs of the group
2. *Eliciting group responses* inquiries or invitations to members that encourage comments, questions, or observations	2. *Implicit norming* describing behavior that has become typical of the group through common practice	2. *Identifying group goals* asking questions and making statements that clarify group objectives
3. *Eliciting sympathic reactions* inquiries or invitations to members that encourage disclosure of experiences or feelings similar to those being expressed	3. *Eliciting group observations* inquiries or invitations to members that encourage observations about group process	3. *Attributing meaning* providing concepts for understanding group thought, feelings, and behavior
4. *Identifying commonalities and differences* describing comparative characteristics of participants	4. *Eliciting mutual feedback* inquiries or invitations to members that encourage sharing of perceptions about each other's behavior	4. *Eliciting alternatives* providing descriptions of possible courses of action and inviting members to contribute alternatives
5. *Eliciting empathic reactions* inquiries or invitations to members which encourage reflection of one member's expressed content or feeling	5. *Identifying conflict* labeling discordant elements of communication among members	5. *Exploring consequences* inquiries or invitations to the group that evaluate actions and potential outcomes
6. *Task focusing* redirecting conversation to immediate objectives; restating themes being expressed by more than one member	6. *Identifying nonverbal behavior* labeling unspoken communications among members (facial expression, posture, hand gestures, voice tone and intensity, etc.)	6. *Consensus testing* requesting group agreement on a decision or course of action
	7. *Validating* requesting group confirmation of the accuracy of leader's or members' perceptions	
	8. *Transitioning* changing the group's focus on content or feelings being expressed	
	9. *Connecting* relating material from group events at a particular time or session to what is happening currently	
	10. *Extinguishing* ignoring, cutting-off, or diverting inappropriate talk or actions of members	

(Gill & Barry, 1982, p. 304)

5. *developmental*—the behavior can be placed within the context of a progressive relationship with other skills, all contributing to movement of the group toward its goals; the effectiveness of the behaviors at one stage in the counseling process is dependent on the effectiveness of the skills used at earlier stages;

6. *group-focused*—the target of the behavior is the group, or more than one participant; the behavior is often related to an interaction between two or more participants; the terms *group, we,* and *us* may be used; the purpose of the behavior is to facilitate multiple interactions among participants, to encourage shared responsibility for helping to promote participation, or to invite cooperative problem solving and decision making (Gill & Barry, 1982).

The classification system consists of a three-stage developmental framework. In Stage I, which occurs early in the life of the group, the counselor uses skills that relate to the development of group identity, cohesion and norms, and clarifies the nature and function of group interaction.

In Stage II, the necessary skills allow group members to explore and understand their behavior and to examine the effects individuals have on the group. Stage II also requires the use of group maintenance skills (validating, transitioning, connecting, and extinguishing).

An action orientation emerges in Stage III group leadership skills. The counselor and clients begin to plan strategies designed to help each individual. The counselor must be adept at directing the decision-making process, as well as relying on basic intervention skills: cutting off extraneous statements, drawing out those who have been passive, holding and shifting the focus, and tying things together (Harvill, Masson, and Jacobs, 1983). Closure to a group, or even this chapter on groups, also involves summarizing statements of important content and urging participants to continue further learnings after the formal growth process has ended.

Summary

Counseling in groups represents a powerful and economical strategy for counselors to deliver services in a variety of settings. Group work is especially effective because it more closely simulates social interactions and interpersonal communication patterns than does individual counseling. At the same time, group work is more demanding on the therapeutic counselor, who has a much more complex task in both structuring the effective development of the group and accepting the responsibility for the growth of multiple clients. Specialized training and supervision are essential so that counselors can learn to use group-focused skills effectively and include group work as a part of their professional activities.

Suggested Readings

Benjamin, A. (1978). *Behavior in small groups*. Boston: Houghton Mifflin.

Corey, G. (1981). *The theory and practice of group counseling*. Monterey, Calif.: Brooks/ Cole.

Corey, G., & Corey, M. S. (1982). *Groups: Process and practice* (2nd ed.). Monterey, Calif.: Brooks/Cole.

Dyer, W. W., & Vriend, J. (1980). *Group counseling for personal mastery*. New York: Sovereign.

Gazda, G. M. (Ed.). (1982). *Basic approaches to group psychotherapy and group counseling*. Springfield, Ill.: Charles C Thomas.

Hansen, J. C., Warner, R. W., & Smith, E. J. (1980). *Group counseling: Theory and process*. Chicago: Rand McNally.

Kottler, J. A. (1983). *Pragmatic group leadership*. Monterey, Calif.: Brooks/Cole.

Shaw, M. E. (1981). *Group dynamics*. (3rd ed.). New York: McGraw-Hill.

Yalom, I. (1975). *The theory and practice of group psychotherapy*. New York: Basic Books.

Chapter 11

Career Counseling

Historically, career or vocational counseling has been the principal domain of counselors. It is through the process and techniques of vocational guidance that the counseling profession was introduced and implemented in numerous settings. In recent years, however, there has been a gradual yet perceptible shift in emphasis from vocational/career issues to personal/emotional issues. Among the diverse reasons for this shift, several merit close examination, especially from the perspective of the novice in the field.

One reason, suggested by Whiteley (1980), involves the complexities of the transactions that are an integral part of career counseling. Many counselors prefer to focus on the interpersonal development of the individual, a process that is more manageable. Another reason for the seeming deemphasis on vocational counseling has to do with the contention that career preferences and choices are actually reflections of personality. This view supports an emphasis, then, on personal/emotional factors rather than vocational/career issues.

Another reason for the shift away from career counseling is the limitations of many of the theories and practices of this specialty. Theories of vocational choice tend to be microcosmic in their view of human experience and are somewhat outdated, reflecting a period of American culture in which a person training for a stable life career was the norm, manufacturing and industry were primary employers, and discrimination against women and minorities was accepted. Times have changed and these theories may be much less useful now. Another aspect of this problem is the lack of clear empirical evidence on the effectiveness of career interventions (Fretz, 1981).

A final limitation involves the myth that "real" counseling is personal/emotional and that vocational/career counseling is somehow a second-class cousin that requires fewer skills and is more "routine." This attitude is not only false but dangerous. As we will see in this chapter, much of one's self-esteem and many of one's needs are met by career activities. To achieve a modicum of personal fulfillment, one must participate in effective life/career planning. Individuals who experience vocational chaos (such as unemployment, underemployment, and job dissatisfaction) report high stress, relationship difficulties, and low self-esteem. Perhaps some of you have experienced these situations and can recall the anxiety, fear, and loss of confidence. Economic dislocations and the impact of rapidly changing technology exacerbate the need for trained and effective career counselors. Few persons will not, at some point during their work life, require such counseling services.

The Functions of Work

"Rich man, poor man, beggar man, thief. Doctor, lawyer, Indian chief." Home from our first day at school, we first became eligible for that eternal question from well-meaning relatives—that question that still plagues (and will *always* plague) us: "What do you want to be when you grow up?" . . . As if we had to grow up to *be* something . . . or as if we wanted to be something we are not . . . or as if we had to grow up. But even Peter Pan lost *that* fight.

Work is supposedly what we have prepared, educated, and trained ourselves to do. Long ago we shed our existence as hunter-gatherers whose only job was to find enough to eat. Now we are specialized. Everyone, and we mean *everyone*, is engaged in some purposeful, productive activity. Some receive financial remuneration for their efforts—they sell their time and talent; others work for internal rewards, or receive other forms of compensation by way of a cooperative division of labor. But labor we all do. Even the children are working—mastering new skills, taking in new knowledge. Even though they sometimes work in places called playgrounds, we are not for a moment deceived that these little people are not laboring away at their age-related developmental tasks. They are working their bodies, testing their minds, learning about cooperation, competition, and a million other lessons they will later find useful after they "grow up" and work in a "real" job.

Work is more than a source of income. For most people, vocation is very much tied into sense of identity, self-image, and sense of worth. Jobs are a measure of status, a major object of devotion of one's time and energy. They are a testing ground for skills and information that have been accumulated over a lifetime. They are the source of many friendships.

People who are satisfied in their work are those who are probably most content with their lives. Lonely, depressed, anxious, problem-ridden people—those who seek a counselor's help—are often those who are not content with their life's work, whether that role is one of homemaker, student, or corporate executive. Career frustration, job stress, and discontent with one's decisions and current vocational development are thus major preoccupations for many people and therefore a significant part of a counselor's work.

Roles of Counseling

If work is what you *have* to do and play is what you *want* to do, then a major goal of counseling is to teach people never to work a day in their lives. Some people are able to adopt an attitude that helps them to enjoy their jobs, to have fun, and to feel fulfilled. When the alarm clock rings, they jump out of bed eager to begin their day. Yet others, working in an exactly equivalent position, feel only dread, boredom, and disgust with what they do for a living. Take the case of the Pickens brothers described by Terkel (1972) in his book *Working*. Both boys have paper routes. They both get up at the same time and basically do the same things. Yet note how the difference in their attitudes about their jobs affects their perceptions. One boy plays, the other works.

CLIFF: It's fun throwing papers. Sometimes you get it on the roof. But I never did that. You throw the paper off your bicycle and it lands someplace in the bushes. It'll hit part of the wall and it'll go booooongg! That's pretty fun, because I like to see it go boooongg!

TERRY: It's supposed to be such a great deal. The guy, when he came over and asked me if I wanted a route, he made it sound so great. Seven dollars a week for hardly any work at all. And then you find out the guy told you a bunch of bull . . . I don't see where people get all this bull about the kid who's gonna be President and being a newsboy made a President out of him. It taught him how to handle his money and this bull. You know what it did? It taught him how to hate the people in his route. And the printers. And dogs [Terkel, 1972, p. 16].

Counselors spend a lot of their time helping people: children who are searching for careers, adults who want to make job changes to think and feel differently about what they are doing. Attitude is all-important in any activity, and certainly in one that can become as routine as going to work. The ultimate goal of almost every person, and therefore every counselor who is giving assistance, is to wake up with energy and excitement, with enthusiasm and anticipation for the day's events that lie ahead.

Therapeutic counselors help people with career indecision on a number of fronts outlined by Fuqua and Hartman (1983). Developmental problems such as career immaturity are resolved by exploring the client's interests and career alternatives and applying decision-making strategies. Situational problems such as job stress are worked on within the context of a supportive, problem-solving relationship to develop alternative responses. And chronic problems such as psychological dysfunctions are resolved in longer-term counseling to initiate more extensive personality changes. In each case, counselors strive to develop more positive attitudes, as well as to accomplish the objectives described below.

Facilitating Self-Awareness

The first step is to help clients discover what they really want and need—to become aware of what they value most. An exercise designed to clarify precisely these issues might ask the person to rank-order the following work values according to personal preference:

_____ long vacations	_____ variety of tasks
_____ flexible hours	_____ minimum of pressure
_____ power	_____ friendly coworkers
_____ responsibility	_____ creative opportunities
_____ big money	_____ being physically active
_____ status	_____ helping people
_____ security	_____ benevolent boss
_____ independence	_____ opportunities for advancement

The self-awareness process includes much more than clarifying one's values. Attention is also given to an honest appraisal of one's strengths and weaknesses in aptitudes, skills, and potential.

Becoming Familiar with the World of Work

Whatever structure is used—a Career Day, guest speaker, reading and research, experimentation—the stated task is to help people become more aware not only of themselves but of the career options that are possible. A person might ask, "Given the parameters of a profession that allows me to work with people, use my verbal fluency, and structure my own time, what jobs are likely candidates?" or, "Which careers would involve being outside, using my creative energies, and moving around a lot?"

There are more than 30,000 different occupations, each divided into one of nine categories in the *Dictionary of Occupational Titles,* such as service, technical, processing, and clerical professions. Often entire families of careers can be explored, depending on a client's interest. A few may be examined in greater detail, eventually narrowing down the choices to realistic possibilities.

Teaching Decision-Making Skills

Since vocational development is an ongoing life process, it is hardly functional to focus only on finding a first job for a client. "All over the country, a generation of professionals is career hopping—switching occupations so promiscuously it's a wonder they don't collide with each other coming and going" (Gelman, 1984). People make decisions to try different careers for a number of reasons; for instance, early retirement, boredom, desire for growth, new opportunities, or new interests. People must learn to make quality decisions about when and how they should initiate career changes. And as people get older, more established and secure, taking new risks becomes more and more difficult.

The counselor can help by teaching people how to make intelligent decisions. "The process often involves learning to collect and assess useful information, generating alternative courses of action and predicting their probable consequences, narrowing the field to a plan of action, taking risks, and dealing with the aftershocks of change. The counselor performs a directive role in organizing the process, but also takes a nondirective position on the individual's actual choice and its outcome" (Hazler & Roberts, 1984, p. 409).

Teaching Employability Skills

There are other even more practical skills that can help people find and maintain satisfaction in their careers. Clients are helped to develop personal marketing strategies to sell themselves and their potential during interviews.

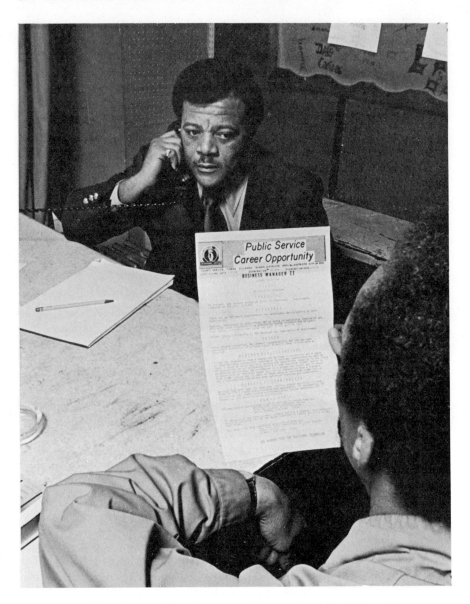

Career counseling often teaches decision-making and employability skills.

They are also encouraged to work on overcoming inertia, resisting procrastination, relieving job-related stress, building an interpersonal support system, and avoiding feelings of frustration and failure (Brown & Kottler, 1979).

In other words, the goal of all career-counseling efforts ought to be directed toward providing life skills for making and implementing decisions. How these decisions ought to be made and, in fact, how people even develop vocationally are topics of considerable debate.

Theories of Career Development

Just as there is a collection of theories that attempt to explain learning processes, personality styles, cognitive development, abnormal behavior, social functioning, and models of motivation and change, so too are there varied approaches to vocational development with which counselors are required to familiarize themselves. Pertinent questions come immediately to mind, many of them reviewed by Whiteley and Resnikoff (1978):

> How do people make career choices?
> Which facts are most influential in making career decisions?
> What parts do genetics, the environment, and cognitive and emotional responses play in career development?
> What are the characteristics of people most likely to be vocationally dissatisfied?
> What roles ought counseling to play in the shaping of career development?
> Ought counselors to be providing guidance or giving advice, teaching specific skills or facilitating awareness in these helping efforts?
> How and why do people change occupational directions in midstream?
> Which theory best explains the reality of vocational development?

Clearly these questions need answering—if not for our own peace of mind, then to better enable us to help clients select fulfilling occupations and learn the skills for remaining satisfied and productive. As we review each of the major theories of career development, try to approach the subject with the same critical eye that is helpful in salvaging useful concepts from counseling models. Look for concepts that make sense and help explain this complex process of development. The theories of Caplow, Super, Holland, Roe, Hoppock, and Krumboltz will be briefly described. Note the value and applicability of their ideas to your own career choices and confusions.

Theodore Caplow's Theory

The first theory, and certainly the simplest, for our attention is one based on the notion that career choices are the results of random events, accidents, errors of being at the right/wrong place at the right/wrong time. While not exactly using an astrological model, the sociologist Caplow (1954) believed that birth order and the accidents of inheritance (parentage, race, nationality, and background) strongly influence one's chosen occupation.

When many people are asked how they ended up in their current profession, their responses are often muddled. Answers such as these are not uncommon:

> "I don't remember. I always wanted to be an electrician. My dad is one. And his father was too."

"My cousin got me this job and it seemed kind of easy to stay with it."
"I didn't really intend to go into psychology, but there were no girls in business administration. So, at orientation, I walked out the door and psychology happened to be across the hall."
"I didn't have much choice. In our town there were only two options for a girl—waitressing and working in the mill."
"I was just walking down the street when I saw this sign that said 'Help Wanted'."

Many of our life's decisions are affected by quirks of fate and the "throw of the die." However, if we were to subscribe to a theory of random movement, there wouldn't be much point in having counselors to provide guidance and encourage self-responsibility.

Donald Super's Theory

For Super (1957), a person's self-concept is all-important in determining vocational development, a process that he views as ongoing and orderly through successive stages. An occupation is the individual expression of one's interests and abilities at a particular time. As a person's preferences and skills evolve, so does his or her career, reflecting the changing self-concept.

Super introduced his theory in a series of ten propositions (1953) about the nature of developing career identities:

1. People differ in their abilities, interests, and personalities.

2. They are qualified, by virtue of these circumstances, for a number of occupations.

3. Each of these occupations requires a characteristic pattern of abilities, interests, and personality traits, with tolerances wide enough to allow both variety of occupations for each individual and variety of individuals in each occupation.

4. Vocational preferences, competencies, situations, and self-concepts change with time and experience, making choice and adjustment a continuous process.

5. This process may be summed up in a series of life stages, characterized as those of growth, exploration, establishment, maintenance, and decline, and these stages may in turn be subdivided into (a) fantasy, tentative and realistic phases of the exploratory stage, and (b) the trial and stable phases of the establishment stage.

6. The nature of the career pattern (that is, the occupational level attained and the sequence, frequency, and duration of trial and stable jobs) is determined by the individual's parental socioeconomic level, mental ability, and personality characteristics, and by the opportunities to which he is exposed.

7. Development through the life stages can be guided partly by facilitating the process of maturation of abilities and interests and partly by aiding in reality testing and in the development of the self-concept.

8. The process of vocational development is essentially that of developing and implementing a self-concept; it is a compromise process in which the self-concept is a product of the interaction of inherited aptitudes, neural and endocrine make-up, opportunity to play various roles, and evaluation of the extent to which the results of role playing meet with approval of superiors and peers.

9. The process of compromise between individual and social factors, between self-concept and reality, is one of role playing, whether the role is played in fantasy, in the counseling interview, or in real-life activities such as school classes, clubs, part-time work, and entry jobs.

10. Work satisfaction and life satisfaction depend upon the extent to which the individual finds adequate outlets for abilities, interests, personality traits, and values; they depend upon establishment in a work situation and a way of life which is satisfying.

Super recognized how people differ in their personalities and unique strengths and therefore choose occupations that will permit them to use their competencies. The pattern of development begins during adolescence with the *exploratory stage,* in which a person uses fantasy, play, and role experimentation to help clarify the emerging self-concept, and moves tentatively onward in the early twenties to a first job. The *establishment stage,* through experimentation and trying out various options, helps the person to discover an occupation well suited to satisfy personal needs. The self-concept adjusts to fit the stabilized career choice. Stability may or may not last into the *maintenance stage;* during the 1950s, when Super was writing, there were far more opportunities and less mobility and economic pressures, and it was more the norm to continue evolving a single career. In today's times of high unemployment, greater flexibility, and changing situations, the maintenance phase may involve a return to earlier developmental tasks in the search for personal and professional satisfaction. The *decline stage* is characterized, naturally, by dealing with reduced energy and trying to maintain one's position until retirement.

Super sees counselors as aiding an individual's progressive development, facilitating maturation of ability, improving the self-concept, encouraging reality testing, expanding interest, and negotiating a compromise between fantasy and reality.

John Holland's Theory

Whereas Super focuses on self-concept, Holland (1973) believes that career choices are expressions of the total personality. Satisfaction thus depends on the compatibility of a person's work situation and personality style.

Holland rested his theory on four major assumptions:

1. Individuals can be categorized into six different personality types—realistic, investigative, artistic, social, enterprising, or conventional—depending on interest, preferences, and skills.

2. Environment can also be classified into the same six types and tends to be dominated by compatible personalities.

3. People search for environments in which their personality type can be comfortably expressed; artistic people search for artistic environments, whereas social people look for social environments. They wish to exercise their skills and abilities, express their attitudes and values, and participate in agreeable problems and roles.

4. The behavior of an individual is determined by the interaction between personality type and environmental characteristics. If personality type and work environment are known, then Holland believes that the outcomes of vocational choice, achievement, and job changes can be predicted.

Holland's personality types can be arranged into a hexagon (see Figure 11–1) that clarifies relationships among personality types. Adjacent types are most closely related; those opposite each other have the least in common. *Social*, for example, is most similar to *artistic* and *enterprising* and most unlike *realistic*. Certainly these personality types do not describe everyone, but they do provide a structure (for those of us who think "conventionally") for understanding why people choose their careers. Each type is described below.

Figure 11–1. Holland's personality types

1. *Realistic:* This person is logical, objective, and forthright. Preference is given to dimensions such as physical prowess, aggression, and domination. A realistic type prefers activities in which to manipulate objects, tools, machines, and other tangible things. This person is likely to be emotionally stable but less sociable and inclined to select technical, agricultural, or trade occupations. He or she is practical and tends to have underdeveloped verbal and social skills but highly developed motor skills. The realistic person chooses careers such as laborer, farmer, carpenter, engineer, or machine operator. The realistic environment allows realistic people to perform preferred activities and be rewarded for technical abilities.

2. *Investigative:* By relying on intelligence and cognitive skills, this personality type is a problem solver. Socially aloof and introverted, the inves-

tigative individual prefers intellectual tasks that require academic proficiencies. He or she also tends to be analytical, critical, intellectual, methodical, precise, rational, and reserved. This person exhibits traits of creativity, independence, and self-confidence but is often not realistic nor practical. Career choices for this type include scientist, scholar, research worker, and theoretician.

3. *Artistic:* This is a sensitive, impulsive, creative, emotional, independent, and nonconforming individual who values cultural activities and esthetic qualities. This person may develop competencies in art, drama, music, writing, and language and avoid structured situations. Not surprisingly, a creative type chooses careers such as actor, writer, musician, and artist.

4. *Social:* This person is highly skilled at dealing with other people. She or he is usually accepting, responsible, cheerful, nurturing, and caring. If you have noticed a similarity between this type and yourself or your classmates, it is because this category is most often descriptive of those who choose helping professions. Take note, however, because this type often evades intellectual or physical tasks, preferring to use strengths in interpersonal manipulations.

5. *Enterprising:* This person uses highly refined verbal skills for leadership and sales professions such as marketing, business, and politics. He or she is enthusiastic, energetic, dominating, persuasive, extroverted, and aggressive. Much concern is devoted to attaining status, power, and leadership roles. Some examples of enterprising vocations are business executives, sales, politics, and promotional work.

6. *Conventional:* This type of person prefers activities that are routine, structured, and practical. A conventional type is self-controlled, orderly, inhibited, and efficient. Examples of conventional vocations include bankers, bookkeepers, office workers, and clerks.

To a large extent, Holland believes that there is a real relationship between personality and educational/vocational decision making. He further believes that interest inventories (such as the Strong-Campbell Interest Inventory) are really personality measures. Members of a vocational group have similar personalities, and each vocation tends to attract and retain people with similar personalities.

Because people in a vocational group have similar personalities, they respond to situations in like ways and therefore tend to create characteristic environments. Vocational satisfaction, stability, and achievement depend on the congruence between an individual's personality and the environment in which he or she works.

Robert Hoppock's Theory

Hoppock (1976) stressed the function of the job in satisfying personal needs, but his theory has attained wide popularity also because of his efforts to integrate ideas from a number of other theories. Vocational development begins with the first awareness that a job can help meet one's needs and continues as the person is better able to anticipate how potentially satisfying a particular career could be as compared with others. Once a person becomes aware of other jobs that could satisfy personal needs, then occupational choices are subject to change. The degree of job satisfaction can be determined by assessing the difference between what a person wants from a job (emotionally, financially, and so forth) and what she or he actually has attained.

Hoppock (1976) describes his composite theory in ten basic postulates:

1. Everyone has needs: basic physical needs and higher-order psychological needs such as self-esteem, respect, and self-actualization. People vary in the pattern of their need structures, and the individual reaction to needs influences occupational choice.

2. People tend to gravitate toward occupations that serve their perceived needs. A person who has a strong need for power and status will be influenced to seek occupations that have them. Few people are controlled by a single need; most have a variety of needs that act in concert to influence occupational choice.

3. It is not essential that a person have a clear intellectual awareness of needs for them to affect choices. Individuals with self-understanding and insight may understand the forces that influence them, and others may simply experience pleasure or satisfaction in certain occupational areas.

4. Hoppock believes that life experiences help to develop a pattern of individual occupational preference and, as such, suggest a developmental perspective on vocational choice. Contact with occupations occurs both experientially and vicariously, supporting the need for both work or occupational experiences *and* occupational information, especially during the years of formative development.

5. Given the great diversity of occupational choices, it is necessary for the individual to develop effective decision-making skills based on solid self-awareness and a rich informational base. A trial-and-error process of occupational experimentation is usually not appropriate. The number of occupations and the extensive training many of them require preclude that approach.

6. Self-understanding is the basis on which occupational choice rests, and as such is a primary goal for career counseling.

7. Understanding the self is only one half of the occupational choice process; one must also have accurate and thorough information about available occupations. A person cannot choose a career without the knowledge that it exists. Likewise, accurate information dispels stereotypes and myths about the activities involved in various types of work.

8. When a person's needs are met by a job, then the person experiences job satisfaction. It is important to emphasize that money is not the only need satisfied by a job; other higher-order needs are just as crucial to satisfaction as basic security needs. For a worker to perform effectively and with the motivation to deliver quality, the ratio must be positive. Industrial and assembly workers are often good examples of this principle; although well paid, many do not have higher-order needs satisfied, and as a result their performance on the job is low, the quality erratic, and absenteeism a problem.

9. Individuals can delay need satisfaction if they perceive their job as having the potential to satisfy their needs in the future. Opportunities for advancement and career mobility are, therefore, important if a firm wishes to maximize satisfaction.

10. If the balance between needs and satisfaction is unfavorable, then a worker will change jobs if another position appears to offer the potential to meet needs more fully.

In using Hoppock's theory of occupational choice, the counselor's role is to (1) stimulate the client's self-awareness of interests and needs, including the clarification of values, (2) promote insight into that which gives life personal meaning, (3) provide accurate and complete occupational information, and (4) help match the client's perceived strengths and weaknesses with occupations likely to provide maximum need satisfaction. Hoppock's theory has a number of implications for counselors:

The counselor should always remember that the needs of the client may differ from the needs of the counselor.

The counselor should operate within the framework of the client's needs.

The counselor should provide every possible opportunity for the client to identify and to express his or her own needs.

The counselor should be alert to notice and to remember the needs that the client reveals.

The counselor should help the client gather information about occupations that may meet his or her needs.

The counselor should help the client to anticipate how well any contemplated occupation will meet the client's needs.

The counselor should stay with the client through the process of placement in order to provide the further counseling that will be needed if the desired job is not available.

The counselor should follow up the client some months after placement in order to see how well the job is meeting the needs that the client thought it would meet [Hoppock, 1976].

Anne Roe's Theory

On the basis of her intensive investigations of scientists' early childhoods, Roe (1957) created a theory that emphasizes need satisfaction in career choices. Persons from child-centered, rejecting, or accepting homes are predisposed to compensate for (or duplicate) in their jobs experiences they missed (or enjoyed) in their childhood homes.

Roe suggested that the emotional climate of the home is one of three types: (1) emotional concentration on the child, (2) avoidance of the child, or (3) acceptance of the child. Emotional concentration on the child has two extremes: overprotecting and overdemanding. Overprotecting parents limit exploration by the child and encourage dependency. Overdemanding parents set very high standards for the child and rigidly enforce conformity.

The avoidance type is divided into those ranging from rejecting to neglecting. A rejecting parent resents the child, expresses a cold and indifferent attitude, and works to keep the child from intruding into his or her life. A neglecting parent is less hostile toward the child but provides no affection or attention and only the bare minimum of physical care.

An accepting pattern is divided into casual acceptance and loving acceptance. Casually accepting parents are affectionate and loving but in a mild way and only if they are not occupied in other ways. They tend to be easygoing. Loving accepting parents provide much warmth, affection, praise, and attention. They encourage the child and help in an appropriate way. These six subdivisions produce, according to Roe, two types of vocational behavior. The categories of loving, overprotective, and overdemanding tend to produce a major vocational orientation toward persons. The remaining categories—casual, neglecting, and rejecting—produce a major vocational orientation away from persons.

This theory has generated considerable research, which has, overall, failed to bear it out. However, Isaacson (1971) suggests that four limiting factors may account for that result:

1. an accurate evaluation would necessitate a long-term longitudinal study ranging from early childhood through maturity;
2. many of Roe's statements are generalizations and are thus vague and ambiguous;
3. parental behavior is inconsistent;
4. the home environment is only one influence on the child.

Roe's position has been criticized for its excessive focus on early determinants of vocational choice, yet Roe has been influential in helping counselors to understand the value of careers in satisfying a person's needs for belongingness, respect, self-esteem, independence, and self-actualization, in addition to Abraham Maslow's lower-level drives to provide economic security, safety, and fulfillment of physiological needs.

John Krumboltz's Theory

You may be more familiar with the name of Krumboltz as a practitioner of behavioral counseling than as a theoretician of career development. Nevertheless, Krumboltz has developed a social-learning theory that attempts to synthesize the factors that influence career decision making. First, Krumboltz acknowledges the impact of genetic endowment—how race, sex, physical characteristics, native intelligence, and abilities limit some choices and expand others. Not everyone can *choose* to be a professional basketball player, brain surgeon, or ballet dancer, regardless of motivation or interest.

Second, environmental factors play a part in career development. The economic climate, occupational opportunities available, labor laws, union rules, technological developments, family resources, educational systems, and other variables outside the individual's control, influence occupational decision making.

Third, previous learning experiences (in behavioristic terminology, conditioned stimuli and reinforcers) shape the person's attitudes and interest toward various professions. Some children are reinforced by their parents for reading, others for their physical or mechanical powers.

A final factor to be considered, according to Krumboltz, is a person's "task approach skills," which are his or her performance standards, work habits, unique perceptions, and abilities to alter problem-solving strategies flexibly according to the demands of the situation.

As examples, Krumboltz (1978) traces the career development of several individuals identifying how successive steps in the process are affected by genetic, environmental, modeling, learning, and skill factors. The case of "Barbara" (Figure 11–2) illustrates Krumboltz's various propositions in action. He summarizes the responsibilities of a counselor in the career development process as follows: "(a) to help the client learn a rational sequence of career decision-making skills, (b) to help the client arrange an appropriate sequence of career-relevant exploration/learning experiences, and (c) to teach the client how to evaluate the personal consequences of these learning experiences" (Krumboltz, 1978, p. 127).

Other Theories

There are other theories, of course, besides those already mentioned. Eli Ginzberg (1972), for example, described career development as a continual, life-long process of decision making in which the person is trying to reconcile goals and preparations with the reality of limited opportunity. Like Super and Ginzberg, Tiedeman and O'Hara (1963) are developmentalists who suggest that career development is a process of identifying with work through the interaction between personality and society. They suggest the importance of decision making in the process of defining the relationship between personality and career. They have, however, been more precise in plotting the changes people experience in their evolving sense of identity.

Career Education

Career education, career development, and vocational assistance are lifelong processes that often require supportive services at various developmental levels. Career education can be defined as "a process that occurs over an extended period to help the individual learn about work alternatives and make a career choice leading to a satisfying, productive vocational life" (Hansen, Stevic, & Warner, 1982).

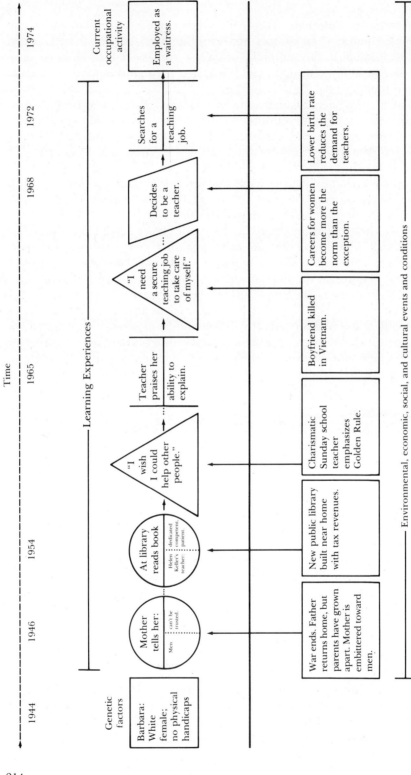

Figure 11–2. Illustrative excerpt of factors affecting "Barbara's" occupation selec-tion (Krumboltz, 1978, p. 115)

214

Career education is an important ongoing process that has crucial significance in elementary, secondary, and postsecondary schools. There are five basic components of career education as defined by Hoyt, Evans, Mackin, & Mangum (1972):

1. *There are career implications in every learning experience.* All school-related experiences have career implications that knowledgeable professionals can help students to understand. It is important that career education be accepted as an institutional responsibility rather than a function of the counseling and guidance staff.
2. *Skill training is necessary for entry into an occupation.* Educational experiences should have a work-related skill component attached to them. Counselors should be ready to work with clients and other professionals to structure appropriate skill-related activities.
3. *Cognitive and experiential ways must be provided for students to understand work-oriented values.* The counselor must help the student to gain self-understanding, knowledge of alternatives, awareness of values, and decision-making skills in both cognitive and experiential ways.
4. *Opportunities must be provided for observing work, work environments, and ultimately, work experience.* Individuals must have the opportunity to develop experiences and knowledge about work, occupations, and work environments. Counselors can work with students, employers, and educational institutions to create these opportunities.
5. *The interrelationships among home, family, community, and societal values should be identified.* The impact of these values on career decisions and preferences needs to be clarified.

Each of these general components, which are not necessarily sequential, requires the assistance of professional counselors who provide information as needed, consult with other involved personnel, and structure activities and experiences designed to facilitate career awareness, self-understanding, and occupational information. Career development, as a lifelong learning experience, must be stressed, and the factors involved in career development need understanding by counselors and clients. Abilities, interests, and values are the factors.

Abilities

Individuals must have an understanding of their abilities in order to identify potential areas for job exploration and career development. Persons must recognize the need to develop basic academic skills and to maximize potential abilities to participate fully in the career development process. In an era of rapidly changing technology and job obsolescence, the task of identifying abilities will extend well into the adult years. It has been estimated that most adults will confront periods of unemployment in their lives (Herr & Watts, 1981). A thorough understanding of abilities, including needs for remediation, will be helpful to both students and adults as they participate in the career development process.

Interests

A knowledge of interests (and the personality tendencies they suggest) will be helpful to individuals as they attempt to match aptitudes with available occupations. Interests are often the key to occupational satisfaction; persons whose interests are not represented in their occupational choice can suffer much unrest and dissatisfaction. It is also important for the counselor to emphasize that abilities and interests are not always neatly related and that interest alone is not a sufficient condition for job satisfaction in positions requiring abilities other than those of the client.

Values

Values are an important factor affecting career development. Occupations that reflect values similar to those held by clients can lead to greater job satisfaction, especially with regard to motivation and job performance. The ill-defined or poorly defined values of many clients can interfere with effective decision making. Counselors must work with clients, helping them to clarify their values and relate them to abilities and interests. Clients who are aware of the relationship among values, interests, and aptitudes can be described as vocationally mature and more likely than others to experience job satisfaction and career advancement.

Decision-Making Skills

In some ways, career development—and certainly career choices—can be viewed as a decision-making process. Clients who are unable to integrate knowledge about the self with occupational information will make little progress in career choice. Helping clients to develop refined decision-making skills is an essential dimension of occupational assistance.

Some clients will come to career counseling aware of the skills involved in decision making. For others, knowledge may be absent or fragmentary, requiring the counselor to assess the client's level of decision-making skills and provide appropriate information. Decision-making models contain several specific steps (Horan, 1979):

1. *Defining the problem.* The counselor helps the client define the problem, exploring various aspects and identifying a stated vocational issue. Specific counseling skills are used to elicit information, establish priorities, and crystallize salient issues. It is essential that sufficient time be spent on this step since it will set the tone for future steps. Problem identification may need to be done at several stages in the process.

2. *Finding and using information.* Once the vocationally related problem is identified, then the counselor assists the client to gather useful informa-

tion. Sources might include testing, occupational, vocational, and educational information, and computer-assisted job search. The counselor must also help the client to use the information in an appropriate manner by interpreting tests, clarifying misunderstandings, and generating conclusions.

3. *Creating alternatives.* In this step the counselor and client combine forces to identify as many alternatives as possible. Those that are clearly inappropriate are excluded and the remaining alternatives are examined in light of information on aptitudes, interests, values, and availability.

4. *Developing plans.* In this stage plans that may be either tentative or firm, depending on the client's needs, are developed. The planning stage should be detailed, sequenced, and have contingencies built into it. This is a crucial step in decision making because it translates the information into action oriented steps.

5. *Implementing plans.* Implementing and following through on plans is primarily the responsibility of the client, although the counselor should be available for consultation and support. Sometimes clients experience difficulty at this stage, and the counselor should intervene to determine if there are flaws in the plan and if personal counseling is needed.

6. *Evaluation.* Evaluation helps the client to determine the effectiveness of the decision-making process and to feed results into a new problem formulation. It is important to emphasize to clients that they are ultimately implementing a process as much as a specific decision. Vocational decision making is a lifelong undertaking that requires continual refinement and development.

The process of career education and vocational choice is highly complex. Counselors can help clients to perform this crucial life work in a systematic and objective fashion, providing information and assistance at critical points. The ultimate goal of career education is to assist individuals to optimize their resources and to make vocational choices that are likely to lead to job satisfaction and career development.

Trends and Issues in Career Counseling

The world of work is rapidly changing and evolving, requiring major adjustments on the part of the labor force and vocational counselors. There is little doubt that the fundamental nature of our society has changed from an industrial base to an information base. We are living in the information age, with the impact of technology felt in every sector of the world of work, simultaneously creating labor shortages (in the case of computer specialists) and surpluses (in the case of assembly and manufacturing workers). Given recent developments in microcomputers and the shift from industrial to service, professional, and technical work, there seem to be emerging two classes of workers: skilled and specialized service, professional, and technical workers who form an elite and highly employable class, and an underclass of workers without employable skills (Cianni-Surridge, 1983). These forces are likely to create technical problems and labor shortages in addition to the human problems created by dislocations. Vocational counselors must be ready to respond to these issues, particularly those involving retraining and the use of technologically dense systems.

Retooling Workers

As the pace of change accelerates, many workers are likely to experience unemployment and job elimination. Choate and Epstein (1982) estimate that 90 percent of the labor force in the 1990s are those working today. Career guidance professionals will have major responsibility for helping workers who have become occupationally obsolete to cope with the stress of transition and dislocation in addition to developing marketable skills through retraining and retooling.

Work and Leisure

As productivity increases through the application of technology to work, efficiency is likely to increase, meaning that people will work less. In fact, productive work may become a relatively scarce resource. To compensate for decreased demands of work, individuals must increase their skills and abilities to use leisure in a manner that will be personally fulfilling.

Work and leisure must not be seen as antithetical but as psychologically related aspects of a career (Blocher & Siegal, 1981). Career counselors must recognize the importance of leisure as they assist clients to engage in life/career planning that will include creative and fulfilling ways in which to use their time. Leisure can be used effectively once the misperception of leisure as nonproductive is eliminated. Some of the productive uses of leisure might include alternative ways of seeking fulfillment, techniques for managing discretionary time, and resources for reducing stress and maximizing consciousness (Cianni-Surridge, 1983; McDowell, 1981). Leisure, then, must be seen by the vocational counselor as a companion concern to work.

Using Technology

Technology is likely to affect career and vocational counseling more than any other specialty within the counseling and guidance field. At present, there has been an increase in the use of computer-based interactive career guidance systems (such as DISCOVER and SIGI), which allow users to integrate occupational and educational information with interests and values in order to improve career decision making. These systems are likely to continue to be used with such refinements as video discs that depict information more realistically. The availability of this technology requires that the career counselor be technologically literate and computer "smart" to assist clients effectively in career decision-making activities.

As microcomputers become more widely used, simulation is likely to emerge as an important career development strategy. Simulated work experiences will allow clients to gain concrete experience and to develop relevant career skills optimally in a "no-lose" environment. With computer networking, increasingly sophisticated software, and video disc simulations, clients will be able to sample interactively an ever greater and more diverse range of jobs, activities, and career guidance resources. These future technological developments will require a career counselor who has the skill and ability to use them in career education and vocational guidance.

Summary

In this chapter we have provided an overview of the importance and diversity of career counseling. The importance of this specialty will increase with the impact of technology on our society. The counselor's role in a "high-tech" society is to help individuals assimilate the effects of technology, thereby allowing people to develop to their fullest potential.

Suggested Readings

Crites, J. O. (1981). *Career counseling.* New York: McGraw-Hill.

Healy, C. (1982). *Career development counseling through the life stages.* Boston: Allyn & Bacon.

Isaacson, L. E. (1977). *Career information in counseling and teaching.* Boston: Allyn & Bacon.

Michelozzi, B. N. (1980). *Coming alive from nine to five: The career search handbook.* Palo Alto, Calif.: Mayfield Publishing.

Terkel, S. (1972). *Working.* New York: Avon.

U.S. Department of Labor. *Dictionary of occupational titles* (latest ed.). Washington, D.C.: Author.

U.S. Department of Labor. *Occupational outlook handbook* (latest ed.). Washington, D.C.: Author.

Whiteley, J., & Resnikoff, A. (Eds.) (1978). *Career counseling.* Monterey, Calif.: Brooks/Cole.

Chapter 12

Marital, Family,

and Sex Counseling

It has been said that all counseling is, in fact, family counseling, since working with one person to change behavior cannot help affecting the feelings, attitudes, and behavior of others with whom the person lives. Whether the other family members are actually in attendance or not, they will most certainly be influenced by what happens in counseling sessions. It is for this reason that working with family members together is considered by many clinicians to be more humane, efficient, responsible, and realistic than individual counseling (Framo, 1981).

What was once an obscure specialty for radical social workers has recently become mainstream counseling for practitioners of all disciplines who seek to initiate changes through the involvement of those persons who wield a significant influence in the client's life. Since psychiatrists, psychologists, educators, counselors, and social workers have joined forces under the American Association for Marriage and Family Therapy (AAMFT), an influential and relatively cohesive movement of practice has developed.

Family counseling is significantly different from individual counseling because the practitioner must be more active, directive, and involved in the family's communication pattern. Rarely can the clinician afford the luxury of operating from single-theory allegiance because strategies for working with a family tend to be extremely flexible and pragmatic. In addition to being knowledgeable about theory, research, and skills that are required for individual treatment modalities, the family counselor has expertise in several other areas.

For example, there are organizational structures and natural developmental processes that are part of all family systems. Each family is composed of a number of smaller coalitions and subsystems. Minuchin and Fishman (1981) label such groupings "holons"—those individual parts of the whole that make a couple, family, or community. Coalitions or holons are formed by spouses, parents, or siblings, each contributing to the ways in which the family functions. In viewing the family as an interdependent system of individuals governed by rules, Amatea and Fabrick (1981) have described several properties that are held in common. One pattern is circular, a cycle of repetitive, interrelated parts in which each family member responds to cues elicited by another; Figure 12–1 is an example. This structural analysis, originally proposed by Minuchin (1974), depicts the family unit as a delicately balanced, homeostatic mechanism that, similar to the body, resists and adapts to outside intrusions.

There are also developmental models that describe the natural evolution of families as they grow over time. The counselor needs to be familiar with the various developmental crises and tasks required of a family, such as those of adjusting to a newborn infant, launching a half-grown adolescent, or adapting to the "empty nest syndrome."

The family counselor should consider family interactions and the impact they have on children's behavior. The research of Gregory Bateson and his associates on family interaction suggests that each family has unique

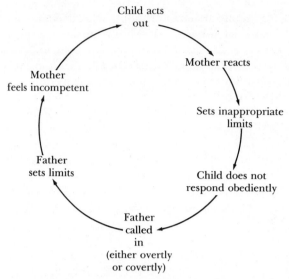

Figure 12–1. Viewing family interaction as a circular causal chain (Amatea & Fabrick, 1981, p. 226)

patterns of functioning, some of which can predispose its members to confusion, even schizophrenia (Bateson et al., 1956). In their now-famous theory of the "double bind," Bateson and company described the "logical" process by which paradoxical messages are communicated simultaneously on different levels. In certain dysfunctional families, communications often take the bizarre form of "go away—come close" messages. A child may be overtly invited to be more intimate and loving with her parents while at the same time she is being subtly rejected for her affections: "Please leave us alone." In such a case, schizophrenia may be the *only* way of escape for a child.

Family Counseling Theories

Okun and Rappaport (1980) have organized the various approaches to family counseling according to their emphasis on the systems and components of family behavior. The communication theorists, which include Don Jackson, Virginia Satir, and Jay Haley, stress specific interventions with the interactions within a family. They believe that understanding human communication—verbal and nonverbal, sequences and hierarchy, direct and indirect, patterns and rules, content and messages—is the key to helping family members change their destructive behaviors.

Whereas the communication theorists are concerned primarily with the style of interactions among family members, the structuralists such as Salva-

A family counseling session in action, showing the alliances, coalitions, and boundaries as evidenced by the seating arrangements.

dor Minuchin place more emphasis on the family's organizational dynamics. A new glossary of terms is added to the counselor's repertoire to describe the various ways in which a family functions (Umbarger, 1983). Words like *system, coalition, boundary, hierarchy, alliance, structure,* and *subunit* are used by the structuralists to "map" the family power and dynamics, "track" the content of sessions, and plan a treatment that involves all family members.

It is not necessary for the counselor to choose between the structural and strategic approaches, for they hold ideas in common and complement each other with their respective focuses. These two family therapies agree on certain principles (Stanton, 1981):

1. People affect and are affected by their family contexts.
2. Families have predictable developmental stages and crises that are helpful in diagnosis.
3. A client's presented symptoms are maintained by (and, in turn, maintain) the family system.
4. When an individual changes, the family system changes; or, when the context changes, the individual changes.
5. Techniques from a variety of theories are useful.
6. Emphasis in counseling is placed on the present rather than the past.
7. Work should be centered primarily on resolving the presented symptoms.
8. The family counselor accepts responsibility for facilitating change.
9. Interpretations are used more for labeling and diagnosis than for promoting insight.

10. Behavioral tasks and homework are assigned to the family members.
11. Counseling is usually brief, often lasting less than six months.

Fraser (1982) is another who suggests that all theorists view the family as being governed by rules designed to maintain the status quo. The system is dysfunctional when rigid, repetitive patterns have become so established that needed actions are not taken or that actions are taken when they are not appropriate.

Despite their similarities, each approach has distinctive features that permit the counselor to switch from one to the other according to the requirements of the situation. Stanton (1981) recommends that counselors begin structurally to diagnose, analyze, and test boundaries and rules, since this approach is more direct and comprehensible. They can move to strategic intervention once they have encountered resistance, defensiveness, or confusion. Then it may be effective to revert back to structural theory to pull together any loose ends. In this methodology, therefore, it is possible to *think* structurally and *work* strategically. By thinking structurally, the counselor is aware of various predictable patterns and styles that will commonly arise.

Patterns of Communication

Virginia Satir (1972) described four types of dysfunctional, defensive patterns of communication between family members. *Placating* occurs when a person becomes helpless, apologetic, or deferential to avoid conflict with others. *Blaming* puts the focus on others so that a person can avoid responsibility for problems and also exercise power. The *computer* is analytic, detached, ultrareasonable to avoid feelings of vulnerability, and the *distractor* hides within dizzy irrelevancies to keep things on a superficial level. One can imagine witnessing all these styles as family members joust with one another: mother accusing father of culpability for son's delinquency, father apologizing for his incompetence in a pitiful voice and then resorting to a computer posture to comment on circumstances, and, all the while, son moaning on the couch with a stomach ache, attempting to distract everyone from the subject.

Power in Relationships

Relationships among family members can be symmetrical or complementary. In the former, according to Haley (1976), there is much competition; in the latter there is an emphasis on exchange as people manuever for position and power. Minuchin introduces the notion of *boundaries* to describe how the various coalitions in family relationships tend to intersect. Sometimes, for example, the boundaries between parents and children are clearly defined, and at other times an alignment may develop between mother and son, with a disengaged boundary between them and father. Matters become considerably more complicated as the counselor joins the family system, creates different boundaries by manipulating the various coalitions, and finally restructures the system so that more constructive lines of affiliation develop.

Power within the family must also be carefully understood and balanced. Each family has a regimented hierarchy, within which each person has a specified amount of control and responsibility. Counseling often takes the form of reestablishing a single hierarchical organization in which the boundaries are more clearly delineated so that the parents are in charge and the children have less power.

Madanes (1983) records the case of a depressed man whose symptom was treated by resolving the hierarchical incongruity in his marriage. The husband had previously been dominant in the relationship, but as the wife developed outside interests and a career as a therapist, his own life and business began to fail. The husband's depression became a source of power in the marriage because the wife, as a professional helper, could do nothing to bring relief. The counselor's interventions focused on restoring a more balanced power hierarchy by reorganizing the way the couple dealt with one another. No longer useful as a form of one-upmanship, the symptom vanished.

Balance of power between spouses can be viewed as a metaphor for other communications in the marriage. Consider a case in which the husband has all the power—in career, in decision making, in spending money. The wife develops symptoms of depression. Husband tries to help, but fails repeatedly. Husband becomes restricted in his own life by catering to wife. Wife indirectly controls husband and situation is reciprocal: husband tells wife what to do about her life, then complains because she doesn't comply. Wife complains that husband is insensitive and can't or won't solve the problem. Both use power and helplessness, metaphors for submissiveness and rebellion. Another example of the power struggles within a family is illustrated below. The counselor initially plots the family organization, then identifies the problems of each member, and finally develops a series of interventions.

Family Structure

Mother is overinvolved with grandmother and daughter.
Grandmother and daughter have a friendly alliance.
Father and son have a weak and peripheral affiliation.
Father and mother are minimally involved.
Father and son are both isolated from power in family.
Daughter and son are actively engaged in conflict.
Complete circle represents a closed boundary separating family from influences of outside world.

Structural map of a family organization

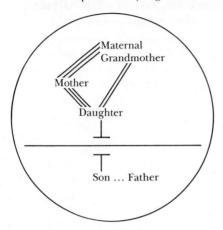

Family Symptomology
Son is the identified client, who brought family to counseling because of fighting at school and home.
Father is passive, withdrawn, uncommunicative, and depressed.
Mother is domineering, controlling, manipulative, and anxious.
Father and mother have marital problems; only son's acting out keeps them together.
Grandmother is lonely, isolated, and dependent on mother.
Daughter spends more time with mother and grandmother than with age mates; provokes her brother.
Initial Therapeutic Interventions
Solicit cooperation of mother, who is in control.
Rearrange coalitions with mother and father together against distracting influences of children and grandmother.
Invite father to take more power and control.
Strengthen bonds between mother and son, father and daughter, to equalize involvement.
Help grandmother to expand her social world.
Help son to stop rescuing parents.
Open boundary isolating family from outside world.

A child will often develop problems as a way to protect the parents from having to face their own difficulties (Madanes, 1984). For example, a child in the family described above may begin to act out and become a common focus for the parents. In responding to the child's misbehavior, the parents are allowed to ignore their problem interaction pattern and the child feels powerful because she is keeping the family together. While this intervention by the child will keep the parents "together" in their interaction, it will result in a serious family breakdown. As a counselor, you will often see families like this who present a "problem" child and view themselves as concerned parents who have no problems of their own.

Symptoms as Solutions

Family systems analysis provides a larger context within which to view the problems of the identified client. Rather than approaching treatment with the usual intention of promoting individual insight and then helping the client to make specific changes, the family counselor often looks at the behavior of the disruptive family member as helpful or constructive in some regard. The disruptive behavior continues because it is unconsciously supported and maintained by others within the family system.

Haley (1980) suggests that counselors, particularly when working with severely disturbed adolescents, view the child's disruptive behavior as stabilizing the family structure. The child's behavior protects the parents from one another, forcing them to find solace in sharing their frustrations over their inability to control the unruly behavior. *All* family members, therefore, must be seen together to clarify the power and hierarchy structures. The family counselor's role is to help the parents regain control over themselves and the adolescent.

Haley finds it helpful when working with disruptive children to assume the following: (1) the client's symptoms are serving a protective function, (2) the client has the capacity to assume responsibility for disruptive behavior (and is not a victim of external forces), (3) the power hierarchy of the family is confused such that the "little" people are controlling the "bigger" people, (4) the *real* problem is the family communication pattern, not the young person, and (5) once power is once again restored to parents and the child is no longer permitted self-indulgence and failure, once the confusions, inconsistencies, and conflicts in family communications are cleared up, then the child can act more normally and responsibly without destabilizing the other family members.

Therapist Salvador Minuchin, for example, is fond of using a simple procedure to restore the natural balance and power to a family with a rebellious adolescent. If the mother feels that she can no longer control her spirited child, and the boy, too, seems to be begging for limit-setting by his attention-seeking ploys, both family members may be asked to stand. Minuchin will then put them back to back, the son's head reaching his mother's shoulder, and thoughtfully consider the picture, finally asking, "Who is taller and bigger?" After getting a confused response, he may ask them to arm wrestle, proving once again who is the stronger, bigger parent and who is the weaker child. He hopes to reestablish appropriate control and power by reminding the family members who is really in charge.

When the child's destructive acting-out behavior is diagnosed as the solution to another, more important problem within the family, then interventions can be directed toward helping the parents to resolve their conflicts. Once the child's "help" is no longer needed, the child can then revert to more appropriate behavior to deal with his or her own internal conflicts.

Case Example of Family Counseling in Action

The diagnosis and analysis of the interdynamics within a family or even a couple's relationship are often extremely complex. A 45-year-old salesman and his 40-year-old lover enter counseling to attempt to resolve a long-standing and increasingly frustrating problem between them. While George can quite easily become erect during sexual foreplay, once he attempts to initiate intercourse with Joanne he quickly loses penile rigidity. The questions that come immediately to the mind of the counselor operating strategically within a family diagnostic structure are: "How is this particular problem of erectile dysfunction helping this couple? What solutions to another problem is the symptom offering?"

Naturally, some data collection and exploration are in order. The counselor learns in due course that George had nursed his cancer-ridden wife for a period of 15 years, until her recent death, and suffers some residual guilt. Joanne, too, has had some life concerns. Her own romantic history is speckled by three failed marriages. Both Joanne and George are genuinely trying to create a loving, respecting relationship, and they care deeply for one another. Yet they are unable to proceed beyond their current impasse as long as their lovemaking is doomed to mutual frustration. Interestingly, however, George's "failure" occurs *only* with Joanne. In several attempts to test himself with prostitutes, he has found, to his relief, that he was easily able to consummate the sexual act.

What, then, do we know about this couple?

1. George's erectile problem is *not* organically caused, as evidenced by his awakening with morning erections and the problem's occurring only with Joanne.

2. George, as a salesman, has a high need for continual success to feel complete as a man. His area of greatest vulnerability is repeated failure at something—making a sale, for one thing, and certainly satisfying the woman he loves.

3. George still feels incredibly guilty about his failure to be a perfect nurse and husband to his dying wife. During the last three years of his wife's illness he had a few sexual relationships, but only for physical relief.

4. The most difficult thing for Joanne to handle is the idea that she may not be attractive or sexy enough for George. Her anger and frustration are building as she realizes that an unknown prostitute can illicit sustained sexual arousal in George and she, his intimate friend, cannot do the same.

5. In their adult lives neither George nor Joanne has ever been able to sustain an intimate romantic involvement. Joanne forces relationships by pushing things too quickly; George has a desperate fear of losing control in relationships in which he would feel vulnerable.

Now the counselor can begin to put pieces of the puzzle together. What would be the likely consequences of solving this problem? Answer: marriage.

Marriage is the one thing that both fear most. George still has unresolved guilt and feels the unconscious need to punish himself by not performing as he is capable. Joanne is desperately afraid that once the relationship moves on to the next stage it will certainly fall apart as have all her other relationships. Yet as long as they remain at this current stage, admittedly locked in a frustrating dance, they can at least stay together. Their fears are temporarily displaced by focusing on the sexual problem.

Most of the traditional sex counseling techniques, of course, prove useless in eliminating a symptom that both partners unconsciously wish to continue. To remove much of the performance anxiety, the counselor tells them to do what they already can do, play in bed during foreplay, and not worry about intercourse. They comply and the inexplicable occurs: George can no longer become erect at all.

"It's as if this were the smartest penis in the world," the counselor explains to the couple. "It is so smart that in spite of our best efforts to resolve this problem, your penis persists in figuring out ways to continue its stubborn unwillingness to cooperate. The lack of complete sexual fulfillment is actually helping both of you in the *only* way that could ever save your relationship in the long run. You are forced to slow down the pace of your relationship. Since you can't relate sexually, you *have* to relate emotionally. You are spending hours together holding hands, hugging, talking. You are really developing intimacy before you can ruin the relationship by removing the sexual mystery.

"But that's not all. It is also permitting you, George, to pay for your guilt, or at least give you time to work through your feelings. Yes, the problem provides you both with time to adjust to one another emotionally by restricting your sexual options."

George feels as if he had been saved! So he isn't a failure after all. While he certainly doesn't believe his penis has made decisions, he begins to recognize that he has, indeed, needed time to explore and develop a truly intimate relationship. He recognizes that subconsciously limiting his sexual activity is a way to force himself truly to know Joanne. Joanne, too, feels relieved. Maybe it isn't her fault after all. She does agree that she feels closer to George than she has to any other man in her life. The reason is that the absence of sex has allowed them to become more alluring to one another. They feel more nurturing and caring than they could have with a normal sex life because both have had so many other issues interfering with the development of intimacy along with active sex.

The counselor next instructs them to appreciate each other by talking about all they have gained from each other. Now they can finally relax and enjoy one another without worrying about their inadequacies. The counselor then sends the clients away from the session with a reminder: "This problem will be resolved when both of you are ready. Meanwhile, just enjoy each other and continue to work together to achieve complete intimacy."

With the pressure lifted, they are able to appreciate each other and their relationship in spite of the sexual dysfunction, which persists for a few more weeks. The following sessions deal with the issues of guilt, sense of failure, and intimacy, until they are able to experience sexual intimacy without fear.

As of this writing George and Joanne are happily married and able to appreciate each other sexually, emotionally, and intellectually.

Interpreting Symptoms as Metaphors

Most communication has messages on two levels: digital and analogic. One part of communication is literal and content oriented, while another, deeper communication expresses messages of a more subtle kind. For example, when a person says to her spouse at the dinner table, "You eat so fast I don't know how you even can taste or enjoy your food," she is, in fact, making a literal comment about her husband's table manners. However, in addition to this digital statement, she may also be communicating metaphorically about another aspect of their relationship that is rushed without enjoyment: their sex life.

Now, the counselor has the choice of interpreting the disguised meaning of the communication or responding on a likewise symbolic level. Haley (1973), in writing about Milton Erickson's preferred strategy, relates that "whatever the patient says in metaphoric form, Erickson responds in kind. By parables, by interpersonal action, and by directives, he works within the metaphor to bring about change. He seems to feel that the depth and swiftness of that change can be prevented if the person suffers a translation of the communication" (p. 28). The couple in this example may be requested to go out and have a slow, drawn-out, leisurely meal. This message, and its subsequent action, permits the partners to practice their foreplay in an indirect, minimally threatening situation.

Since people communicate on these different levels, the family counselor must learn to recognize the ways in which children and adults express different issues through their behavior. Presenting complaints or identified symptoms are thus often interpreted as something quite different from their surface messages. This theoretical construct is common to many individual therapeutic approaches, such as psychoanalysis and Gestalt counseling. The only difference may be that the strategic family counselor is less interested in explaining or interpreting the metaphor and instead prefers to operate on the same level as the family members.

Diagnostic Questions

To aid in the diagnosis of family problems and to sort out the confusing connections among symptoms, metaphors, power hierarchies, and other relevant variables, there are some specific questions that will facilitate data collection:

What is the problem?
When does the problem occur?
Where does the problem occur?
Where are various family members when the problem occurs?
What is each member of the family doing when the problem occurs?
What are the effects on each family member?
What are the benefits to the client? (other family members?)
Who in the family has had a similar problem?
Where is the power (money, decisions, time)?
Who is being protected?

Reframing

Two types of diagnosis are useful in family counseling. The first variety includes applying those labels that help the counselor to grasp the processes and problems involved. We have already mentioned diagnosing client position, family hierarchy, communication style, and symptoms as solutions and metaphors in this context. However, there is a second kind of diagnosis, the one communicated to the client. It is therefore the counselor's initial task to define or reframe the present problem to the client or clients in such a way that it may be resolved.

Clients come into counseling sessions with preconceived notions of what is wrong with them and why:

> "My marriage is on the rocks because my wife wants to go back to school and start a career rather than taking care of the family."
> "My boy is having trouble in school because his teachers are too strict and don't appreciate his uniqueness."
> "I've never been able to hold a job because everyone in my family has always been lazy."

In the process of reframing, the counselor redefines the presenting complaint for the family, using both ingenuity and creativity to think on concrete and metaphorical levels. In the resulting working diagnosis, the counselor identifies issues that can, in fact, be responsive to change, so that the family will be more willing to work on them. There isn't much that can be done to help a client who is complaining about another person's behavior, unless, of course, the other person will come in for counseling and willingly change what the accuser dislikes. In initiating counseling for clients with the complaints quoted above, the most important task would be to reframe the client's perceived difficulties. The husband who wants compliance from his wife would be helped to view the problem more as a lack of communication: he hasn't conveyed his desires in such a way that his wife could understand (and accept) them. The problem of the boy having trouble in school would be reframed to say that although he is clearly a talented comic, he is performing for the wrong audience. The person without a job would be helped to redefine his problem as a lack of skills and/or motivation rather than a lack of employable genes.

The value of reframing is exemplified in the case of a 35-year-old client who arrived for his session, huffing and puffing, his face flushed, and his hand wrapped in a towel that was quickly turning red with blood. The flustered counselor, a tiny woman of 90 pounds, looked up at the 230-pound mechanic and responded, "Oh, I see you had some trouble. What happened?"

Still standing in the foyer, the man smiled with a glazed, stunned look and answered, "I locked my damn keys in the car and I got mad. And when I get mad I like to hit things. Anything. I can't help it. Boy, am I mad. Now, what's all this shit about you wanting to see me about my kid?"

The counselor went to her supervisor immediately following the session. She calmed down, at least enough to hear the more experienced clinician reframe the man's behavior: "What do you think about this guy? Blustering his way in to a first session with his hand all bloody. *This* is funny. *This* is hysterical. This guy is no bully, this guy is a clown. Next time he comes in, treat him like a clown and see what happens. And, just in case you need me, I'll be close by."

During the next session the man responded with a burst of anger to the counselor's accurate confrontation about how he had been neglecting his son. He stamped the ground and rose with a menacing stare. The counselor, of course, was startled, but then regained her composure and looked at the humor in his behavior. She smiled, seemingly unaffected by his threatening behavior, thinking, "This guy really is funny."

The man anxiously demanded some explanation of the counselor's calm appearance. He was used to having people feel afraid of him. She told him compassionately how silly he really looked stamping around like a child; then, as an afterthought, she moved back a little and waited.

Yes, he agreed, he probably did look funny, but he does get what he wants by intimidating other people. He eventually admitted, though, that he hated himself for behaving so badly and appreciated the counselor's seeing through the mask and allowing him to discuss his vulnerable feeling.

While this was a risky strategy, it nevertheless demonstrated the power of reframing behavior, casting it in a different light. Not only is the client able to view his behavior as more manageable but the counselor is also able to see the behavior in compassionate rather than threatening terms.

Directives

The idea of deliberately telling clients what they should do goes against the grain of almost all counseling systems. Counselors are, after all, supposed to be neutral, objective, detached, and not prone to giving advice. A rationale for the violation of this golden rule is that such interventions are often successful. Furthermore, family counselors, by the very nature of their work, are more active, structuring, and directive than they would ever consider being when working with individual clients. Put all members of a family together in a room, particularly those who are so conflicted they had to ask for help, and the situation often turns chaotic. Unless the counselor is prepared to jump in and take the initiative, the family counseling session could make matters considerably worse.

A number of directive options are available to the family counselor. They may be designed to be either obeyed or disobeyed, depending on which is more likely to work. They can be simply and straightforwardly presented or explained in such a complicated and confusing way that the client will rebelliously do the opposite. The best directives are those that involve everyone in the family, are precisely described, provide sufficient motivation to encourage completion of the task, and are simple enough that they can be reasonably accomplished (Madanes, 1983).

In using directives, the counselor seeks to initiate changes in the family structure by getting people to act differently. The goal is to realign the hierarchy of power along more desirable paths; for instance, with the parents in charge rather than the children or grandparents, or with both spouses on an equal footing. The process of initiating all directives usually involves (1) redefining the problem in a less threatening form and describe it in a way that allows resolution, (2) motivating and preparing the client to follow (or not follow) the directive, and (3) presenting the directive clearly, simply, and realistically, ensuring that all participants understand what they are to do or not do.

According to Fisch, Weakland, and Segal (1982), all directives, and for that matter all therapeutic interventions, are designed to interrupt the current attempted solution to a family problem; that is, the symptoms of the identified client. They further offer the following tactical maneuvers that require active counselor direction:

Forcing the Spontaneous

Many psychosomatic complaints, performance problems, and thought disturbances occur spontaneously, in spite of a client's attempts to control them. Trying too hard to fall asleep, reach orgasm, or stop a tic only makes things worse. It is not reasonable to ask the client to cease behavior not within conscious control. Instead, the client can be directed to continue the behavior at will. A person who can't sleep may be told to stay up or to get up after fifteen minutes and to work on an important but nonstimulating task. The client is then able to make the first step toward resolution of the problem: if she or he can exhibit some control of the uncontrollable problem by exercising some choices around its occurrence, then the problem seems less ominous and not as wayward as the client originally believed. A paradoxical directive of this type allows the counselor to be successful, and the client perceives himself or herself as making progress. The client who complies with the suggestion is exhibiting control, and the client who doesn't abide by the directive to fail is then cured of the problem. This type of directive is safe for both the counselor and the client because it provides ample opportunity for positive outcome.

Opposition through Compliance

In the physical world, when we attempt without success to solve a problem by a certain action, we will try something else—usually the opposite action. If we try to open a door by pushing it, and it won't budge, we may try pulling it. If we attempt to loosen a screw by forcing it to the left, and it doesn't move, we will try turning it to the right. Yet when an attempted strategy doesn't work in emotional family struggles, with participants locked into no-win battles, a person will often try the *same thing* harder. If a wife fights for her independence in the marriage by repeatedly resisting her husband's orders, and then discovers she is worse off, she will nevertheless struggle harder. If parents have attempted on numerous occasions to get their rebellious adolescent to comply to house rules and they have found that the youngster is only getting worse, the parents will demand even more compliant behavior.

This second category of directives takes the form of suggesting to those without power that the only way they will ever get any control is to back down. By deliberately taking a "weak position" and "giving in," they finally break the vicious, repetitive cycle. Thus, benevolent sabotage begins to defuse the conflict: "I'm sorry I burned your toast. I don't know what's getting into me." The powerless client is able to feel more dignity and control since she/he backs down by choice. The key to using compliant tactics effectively is to avoid sarcasm or overt game playing. The client must attempt a "one-down" instead of the "one-up" position that didn't work. Once the opposition ceases, the cycle is often broken, and the other family member(s) no longer derive satisfaction from their positions. It's no fun to dominate if the other person won't fight back. And it's no fun to rebel if the others won't force compliance.

Pretending

A favorite ploy of Madanes in working with children is to direct the parents to encourage the symptom deliberately and to ask the child to *pretend* to have it. Much of the tension associated with the symptom is thereafter dissipated since everyone is "only pretending." Consider the case of a "28-year-old adolescent" who was still so dependent on his father that he carried around a paging device, a beeper, so that his father could reach him at any time, usually to scream at him for some mistake he had made in the family business. The young man was constantly late, missed appointments, and botched orders, and each time his father would furiously bawl him out. Neither man much enjoyed the pattern, but each felt powerless to stop it.

The counselor directed the son to bungle something deliberately, a minimum of three times per day. He was to pretend to make mistakes so that his father could no longer determine when the young man was truly irresponsible and when he was only faking. The son, too, improved after discovering that since he could control when he made mistakes, and pretend to do so, he could certainly refrain from such errors whenever he chose.

A way to involve other family members is to encourage them to criticize the person's "performance." Another pattern is thus broken, since instead of trying to deter the symptoms they are now trying to help the person do them even better. With the introduction of directives to pretend, the metaphorical symptoms are no longer allowed to be part of reality. The problem diminishes because it is no longer taken seriously.

Slowing Down

Whenever anyone tries too hard to do something, the task becomes more difficult. The directive to slow down is often most effective during initial interviews, when clients are apprehensive about being asked to do something they won't be able to do. If the presenting problem is resolved too quickly, before the clients have had the opportunity to make new adjustments or discover other ways of relating to one another, it is possible that the family structure will break down.

During the first session with a woman complaining of a marriage that is falling apart, the counselor specifically directs her to stop trying to fix things: "Leave things just the way they are for now. This way, your husband too will have the chance to get involved in solving the problem. I know, now he says that he won't come in for counseling. That is certainly the case as long as you keep nagging him, but let's see how things change once you slow down. The marriage isn't comfortable anyway, so by backing off you can hardly make things worse."

The therapeutic circumstances are now programmed for success no matter what the outcome. The client immediately feels released from her sole responsibility for fixing the marriage. She can loosen up and take a deep breath. She also focuses on herself rather than trying to change her husband. And if things don't immediately improve, the client will be more patient and willing to keep working.

Sex Counseling

Sex counseling is the single most successful result of integrating many diverse theoretical structures into a unified technology of helping. With reported success rates of well into the 80 to 95 percent range for a variety of sexual dysfunctions, such as impotence, premature ejaculation, and orgasmic dysfunctions, in the absence of physical causes, sex counseling is one of the most well-developed therapeutic specialties. First, the treatment is successful because it attacks sexual problems using insight methods as well as structured homework. Second, the treatment is relatively short term (usually 3 to 10 sessions). And third, the nature of the counseling strategy requires the practitioner to be flexible and pragmatic enough to try a variety of interventions.

Helen Singer Kaplan (1974), in her classic book on the theory and techniques of sex therapy, readily admits that treating clients with sexual problems by insight methods alone is probably unethical because the technology does exist to help people relatively quickly by more behavioral interventions. The sex counselor, therefore, not only uses much of the family counseling theory already discussed but also combines psychoanalytic and other insight theories with solid applications of behavior modification. Such techniques as relaxation training, sensate focus exercises, and cognitive restructuring are frequently used in counseling couples with sexual problems.

Sex counseling is a specialized application emphasizing behavioral treatment to reduce specific symptoms. It is often a part of marital and family counseling, begun once basic communication problems are resolved. For sex counseling to be effective, the couple's commitment to the relationship and willingness to experience the therapy are essential prerequisites. The basic treatment plan usually takes a six-step form.

1. Clinical Assessment Interview

With both partners present, or in separate intake interviews, the sex counselor does a detailed data-gathering interview to learn about family history, sexual attitudes in the childhood home, religious influences, how sex education was presented, first sexual experiences, and current attitudes toward various sexual practices. The assessment includes consideration of previous sexual difficulties, as well as a detailed description of current problems and attempts to solve them.

Once a working relationship has been established, the counselor feels free to ask direct questions: "What do you think about during sex?" "When one of you wants to make love, how do you initiate?" "What would you like to do that you are not doing?"

2. Physical Exam and Medical History

It is extremely important with sexual difficulties (as well as with any other psychological problem having a possible organic origin) that any physical causes be ruled out before attempting psychological interventions. It would be important to know about any drugs that the clients are taking; certain medications for high blood pressure, for instance, will affect sexual responsiveness. Chronic alcoholism also presents special problems, as do diseases such as diabetes. Hormone levels can be assessed to detect estrogen or testosterone deficiencies in the blood. A thorough medical history and exam are also valuable to rule out certain physical processes that can affect sexual performance.

3. Exploration of Relationship

If organic causes are eliminated, the next place to look for the sources of sexual problems is in the relationship between the couple. Sexual behavior is one way in which partners communicate with one another. Time is generally spent (at least a few sessions) working to improve the communication between partners, helping them to build trust and commitment for the work that lies ahead. In the open, accepting therapeutic atmosphere, clients are helped to dispel their fears of failure, always a contributing factor to sexual problems. They are asked to share their likes, dislikes, and fantasies with one another, all the while becoming more sexually intimate in a nonthreatening, verbal manner.

4. Sensate Focus Exercises

The counselor will next introduce the behavioral sequence in the treatment, essentially a prescribed series of progressive exercises that the couples will do at home. Initially, all pressure is removed by specifically prohibiting the couple from any further attempts at intercourse. They are absolutely forbidden to try, thereby removing the threat of failure. The sensate focus exercises involve selfishly, yet sensitively and nondemandingly, giving and receiving nongenital pleasure through touching. Very gradually the couple add to their repertoire by (1) giving backrubs for one week, (2) nongenital touching and mutual pleasuring in other areas of the body, (3) light genital stimulation without orgasm, (4) genital touching to orgasm, (5) intercourse without orgasm (or erection), and (6) intercourse to orgasm.

The couple is able to progress slowly through these steps, doing no more than they are comfortable doing. Success is virtually guaranteed if the couple will follow the structure and resist the temptation to jump ahead to fulfilling the sexual act.

5. Specialized Techniques

The sex counselor will use a variety of educational and therapeutic options to facilitate better communication, awareness, and sexual responsiveness. Films and books may be used for demonstration purposes. Vibrators are often recommended for inorgasmic women. There are also several specific procedures, such as the "squeeze technique" used for premature ejaculation. Certain sexual positions are often suggested for various problems, and focused fantasy exercises help combat distracting thoughts.

6. Evaluation

All throughout the duration of treatment, the counselor works with the couple to combat the usual resistances. Recognizing that when the symptoms go away the couple will have to find another way to communicate is a problem that should be addressed early in the therapy. Once sexual functioning is restored, the counselor helps the spouses to integrate what they have learned and continue their marital growth and enrichment.

Summary

In this chapter we have presented an overview of the basic theory and techniques of marital, family, and sex counseling. Most counselors are faced with many clients who experience adjustment reactions and problems in these areas. Professionals who work with children and adolescents in particular need knowledge and expertise in family counseling. The major focus of these techniques is to clarify the system of relationships that occur in marital and family interactions and to identify opportunities to interrupt dysfunctional patterns. In working with family systems, counselors attempt to help clients restructure relationships toward developmentally healthy goals and to reduce the impact of destructive systems of relationships. Counselors must skillfully blend specific marital, family, and sex techniques within the framework of individual and group counseling skills.

Suggested Readings

Framo, J. L. (1982). *Exploration in marital and family therapy*. New York: Springer.

Glick, I. D., & Kessler, D. R. (1980). *Marital and family therapy* (2nd ed.). New York: Grune & Stratton.

Humphrey, F. (1983). *Marital therapy*. Englewood Cliffs, N.J.: Prentice-Hall.

Kaplan, H. S. (1974). *The new sex therapy*. New York: Brunner/Mazel.

Madanes, C. (1983). *Strategic family therapy*. San Francisco: Jossey-Bass.

Minuchin, S., & Fishman, C. (1981). *Family therapy techniques*. Cambridge: Harvard University Press.

Okun, B. F., & Rappaport, L. J. (1980). *Working with families*. North Scituate, Mass.: Duxbury Press.

Satir, V., & Baldwin, M. (1983). *Satir step by step: A guide to creating change in families*. Palo Alto, Calif.: Science and Behavior Books.

Umbarger, C. C. (1983). *Structural family therapy*. New York: Grune & Stratton.

Chapter 13

Drug and

Alcohol Counseling

Drug Use and Drug Abuse

Everyone without a drug habit, raise your hand. Now, let those who are smugly confident that they hold nothing in common with your basic drug addict (and so are holding their hands quite high) consider the following:

1. A drug can be *any* substance ingested into the body that produces an altered state of consciousness or change in body chemistry.
2. Andrew Weil (1972), a noted pharmacologist, has a theory that all humans have an innate drive to alter their consciousness. From spinning in circles as children to eating spicy foods as adults, the goal is to experience sensory overload.
3. Drug use not only is common among human beings but is found among other creatures. When animals in Africa are subjected to crowding, poaching, and other stressful conditions, they resort to intoxicants. Elephants will munch fermented fruit. Grasshoppers will literally get high (given their jumping prowess) after eating marijuana. Peruvian llamas are fond of cocoa leaves. Rats, when given choices between plain water and alcohol, prefer the booze, especially at bedtime.
4. The difference between drug use and drug abuse is a matter of degree (see Figure 13–1). Once a need for drugs has been established in order to maintain effective functioning, addiction and physiological dependence prevail. The most widely used (and probably abused) drugs are those that happen to be legal. Coffee, cigarettes, chocolate, and cola beverages all contain sufficient quantities of amphetamines to create full-fledged addictions.
5. Almost every person alive has some oral addiction, and the world is filled with regional choices. Whereas alcohol has permeated every known culture (except that of the Eskimos, who live in a climate too cold to grow anything), more exotic drugs are found in every region. Cocaine originated in the Andes of Peru and Bolivia, coffee and hashish in Southern Arabia, peyote in Mexico, opium in India and Mesopotamia, and, of course, tea in China.

It may now be evident that most people ingest drugs in some form, whether as a food additive, beverage, medication, or intoxicant. There are many factors that determine whether a person can safely and responsibly use drugs (such as an occasional cup of coffee or glass of beer) or will abuse addictive substances (heroin, for example) or become psychologically dependent (as is common with marijuana).

Counselors are often required to work with these various forms of drug use and to make a determination with the client as to which behaviors are self-destructive and out of control.

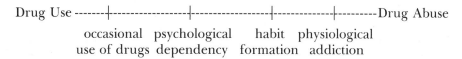

Figure 13–1. Continuum of drug behavior

The subject of drug use and abuse merits its own chapter in an introductory counseling text for a number of reasons. First, most people, and especially clients who tend to be externally controlled, regularly use drugs in some form. Often alcohol, marijuana, coffee, or tobacco is a troubled person's effort at self-medication for distressing symptoms. The externally oriented drug abuser denies responsibility for problems, blames others for experienced misery and feels that since someone else has created the emotional pain, an externally available substance will fix things. The unfortunate part is that such a person is perfectly correct. Drugs *do* provide immediate relief. They dull pain and are great distracters. While using drugs at moderately abusive levels (whatever that means), people can still function through their day in a purple but painless haze.

The second reason for studying a speciality such as drug counseling is that traditional therapeutic interventions tend not to work. Insight into the reasons underlying self-destructive behavior in the form of drug and alcohol abuse is not sufficient to alter the behavior. Clients with drug and alcohol problems are so immune and resistant to change that sometimes very dramatic and creative interventions must be found.

Finally, clients have the same expectations for their counseling sessions as they have for their drugs: instant, magical relief. The addictive personality, found in many clients, belongs to an individual who is insecure, impatient, and impulsive, refuses to postpone gratification, and uses the treatment hour as he or she uses drugs in an attempt to provide a temporary lift in spirits (Burnett, 1979).

Many people engage in mood-altering behavior to create a sense of euphoria or well-being or to block out unpleasant events. It is important to recognize that drug taking is a behavior and follows patterns that can be understood and modified to the same extent as any other. The behavior will persist if it minimizes discomfort or maximizes pleasure and satisfaction. Nothing will decrease the hold of drugs unless there is an adequate substitute for the feelings drugs provide (Oakley, 1983). It is necessary for counselors to assess and observe a client's behavior to determine whether the client is displaying symptoms of abuse and reliance on mood-altering substances.

America as a Drug Culture

People are constantly encouraged to purchase drugs in order to feel better and to buy products that help with weight loss. The implicit, if not explicit, message is that comfort and ease are of maximum importance. There is little glorification for the hard work or discipline involved in maintaining a healthy body. Advertising has clearly had some impact on drug use in our society (Cornacchia, Smith, & Bentel, 1978). Advertisements on television and in other media promise to make one feel happier, younger, sexier, more attractive, and less tense. They persuade people to buy over-the-counter drugs as a means of relief from suffering and to create a desirable personal image. Advertisements clearly imply not only that the use of these drugs will create wonderful results but that the drugs are also harmless.

The government has taken many steps to protect the consumer. In 1906 the Pure Food and Drug Act was passed to prohibit interstate commerce of adulterated or misbranded foods and drugs. The Harrison Act of 1914 required dealers and dispensers of narcotics to register annually with the Treasury Department's Bureau of Internal Revenue. The Narcotics Manufacturing Act passed in 1960 required all manufacturers of medical narcotic drugs to be licensed and made it illegal to manufacture or to attempt to manufacture narcotic drugs without a license. In addition, annual quotas were established for the purchase and manufacture of narcotic drugs. In 1965 Congress passed the Drug Abuse Control Amendment in order to provide better control over the manufacture and distribution of certain legal and illegal compounds.

The Controlled Substance Act of 1970 replaced or updated all previous laws concerned with both narcotics and dangerous drugs. Under the law, the Food and Drug Administration (FDA) considers the state of current scientific knowledge of various drugs, the risk to public health, the psychosocial dependence liability, and whether the substance is an immediate precursor of a substance already controlled under this title. This law established five schedules of drugs that must be continually updated.

Although legislators try to keep current in providing protection for the consumer, our society continues to approve and even encourage use of substances such as caffeine, tobacco, and alcohol. It is important to recognize that the acceptance of alcohol as an appropriate drug by all citizens over a certain arbitrary age encourages the development of a milieu in which drug use is considered normal.

Almost all drugs are available to adolescents, not only "on the street" but also on the school grounds. It is not uncommon to find adolescents sniffing glue, gasoline, or lighter fluid, using heroin, or taking barbiturates or amphetamines during school hours. Marijuana is so commonly smoked by many adolescents that it is considered normal by school officials. There is also frequent use of PCP, an anesthetic employed in veterinary medicine that, when used in excess, produces a toxic psychosis often associated with violent and self-destructive behavior.

What Counselors Should Know about Drugs

Marijuana

Marijuana is one of several popular choices for most drug-using adolescents and young adults. Pharmacologically, marijuana *(Cannabis sativa)* is not a narcotic and does not produce physical dependence. Among the middle class, the drug is used because limited doses produce mild euphoria and act as a pleasant relaxer. The abuse potential of marijuana is controversial. It is often argued that marijuana is a "healthy" drug; it does not suppress the appetite and it does not lead to true addiction, although frequent use may result in psychological dependence. In recent years, more and more states have moved to decriminalizing personal possession of marijuana, creating confusing messages for children who learn that pot is okay to use in some areas but not in others. Yet many, many clients experience problems related to a *relatively* harmless drug (at least compared with narcotics, depressants, and amphetamines) such as marijuana. Whereas there may be no actual physiologically addictive potential, the side effects, such as withdrawal symptoms and increased tolerance, make marijuana easily habit forming. It is also relatively inexpensive and produces its exhilarating effects within minutes. The problems lie in the accompanying circumstances: daily users cannot seem to function without pot as a crutch. It is common for some people to smoke their first joint before brushing their teeth in the morning and to continue smoking up to ten marijuana cigarettes as boosters throughout the day. While all the evidence is not yet in regarding the long-term health effects of Cannabis use, it is clear that a sizeable part of the younger population does experience negative *psychological* effects such as lethargy, impaired judgment, and decreased internal control.

Depressants

If a relatively innocuous drug such as marijuana can create psychological problems for the user, then more powerful substances can lead to even greater difficulties. Drugs are usually classified according to the ways they affect the central nervous system. Depressants, of which alcohol is the most commonly used, slow down and sedate the nervous system. While the depressant effect is often desired, by a physician prescribing barbiturates or by a user who is self-medicating for a calm, tranquilized state, the risk of overdose is great. Depressants are more easily addictive even than heroin and are widely abused as a "middle-class" drug in the form of sleeping pills and tranquilizers such as Valium and Xanex.

In addition to the dangers of addiction and potential for overdose, tranquilizers create problems for the counselor trying to work with clients who have come to depend on artificial means to reduce their anxieties. Such clients are often reluctant to learn new coping strategies when easy relief is just a swallow away. It is much more difficult to learn internal control of their emotions and how to take charge of their life than it is to pop a few pills or down a few cocktails, particularly when the alternative is a very uncomfortable and painful withdrawal from the drug's grip.

Table 13–1. Commonly Used Depressants

Barbiturates	Major Tranquilizers	Minor Tranquilizers
(sleep medications)	(psychotic medications)	(sedative medications)
Amytal	Thorazine	Alcohol
Seconal	Compazine	Valium
Tuinal	Taractan	Librium
Nembutal	Prolixin	Equanil

Stimulants

Stimulants are a class of drugs that speed up the central nervous system, increasing heart rate, depressing appetite, stifling fatigue, and producing feelings of euphoria. Amphetamines are commonly prescribed as diet pills; mild forms of "speed," such as nicotine or caffeine, also suppress the appetite. "Uppers" are often abused by those who want extra energy or alertness, as well as by those who want a recreational high in social situations. Cocaine is probably the most common "social" stimulant used today and presents some very special treatment difficulties for the practitioner.

Many practitioners require that a client use a therapeutic support system in addition to regular counseling sessions. Alcoholics Anonymous, Narcotics Anonymous, or any other good group experience is often used to help people to feel more accountable. We can recall only one case (out of perhaps two dozen) in which counseling alone was successful in helping a cocaine abuser. The treatment required only one session and took the following form:

> "I wish I could help you. I really do. You seem like a nice guy and you have a lot going for you. But counseling just doesn't work too well with cocaine addicts. Actually nothing works. I know I sound discouraging, but I'm trying to be honest: there is no known cure for your particular problem. My best advice is that you continue exactly what you're doing because ultimately that is what might save you. After you have spent all your money, used up all your credit, lost your job, your friends, your wife, your kids, and all your worldly possessions, perhaps then you can start over. You will have no other choice. Certainly you won't be able to beg, borrow, or steal more cocaine. I'm sorry, but there is nothing I can do to help you."

The gentleman left more than a little shaken. He called back a month later to report that he had, in fact, been so frightened that he had not touched the stuff since our one and only meeting.

Table 13–2. Commonly Used Stimulants

Amphetamines: as stimulants	Preludin: for weight reduction	Ritalin: for adults as anti-depressant; for hyperactive children	Cocaine: for recreational use

Narcotics

Narcotics are painkillers. They deaden everything—hunger, sex, appetite, physical complaints, depression, anxiety—and do so effectively enough that they can seduce a user into addiction very quickly. Within a week of daily use, a user will develop a tolerance, requiring higher dosage of the drug to get the same effect.

Counseling a person into and out of withdrawal is highly unlikely. More often, therapeutic sessions are used as adjuncts to medically supervised treatment programs that usually use other drugs as a bridge.

Table 13–3. Commonly Used Narcotics

Morphine: as a pain suppressant	Heroin: for recreational use	Codeine: as a cough suppressant	Demerol: as a muscle relaxant

Hallucinogens

Hallucinogens, as a class of drugs, are used exclusively for their mind-altering properties and for recreational purposes. In all their varieties, psychedelic drugs alter perceptions, sensations, moods, and thought patterns. Some claim the drugs have educational value (those of the Timothy Leary school) or therapeutic value (those of the Carlos Castaneda school). According to Andrew Weil (1972), most of the dangers associated with psychedelic drugs occur when they are not used in ritualized ways. In those societies that have strict rules for who may use psychedelic drugs, under what specific conditions, and at what intervals, problems of drug abuse are rare. Similarly, in our society those who restrict themselves to a nightcap or to a drink during the cocktail hour usually don't experience problems of alcohol abuse.

Table 13–4. Commonly Used Hallucinogens

Marijuana (hemp plant)	LSD (synthetic)	PCP (synthetic)	Mescaline (cactus)	Peyote (cactus)	Psilocybin (mushrooms)

Effects of Drug Abuse

Milby (1981) has listed many of the negative physical effects that result from drug abuse. These symptoms are in addition to the relationship casualties that usually occur as the abuser alienates friends, family members, and coworkers.

1. Death has to be at the top of the list. Reports of drug overdoses occur in the newspapers so routinely that they are no longer news. Suicide is certainly a distinct possibility for a person in an altered state of consciousness, and it is not unknown for people to die from convulsions while withdrawing from barbiturates.

2. Through neglect, disinterest, and distraction, the diet of a drug abuser often suffers. Many drugs tend to stifle the appetite; other drugs (narcotics, alcohol) lead the user toward malnourishment.

3. Disturbances of sleep are common results of introducing artificial stimulants or depressants into the bloodstream. Certainly anyone who has had a few cups of coffee before bedtime or who has fallen asleep while still feeling the effects of alcohol knows that the quality of sleep is impaired. The loss or disruption of sleep presents added dangers for the drug abuser, whose perceptions and reactions are already less than optimal.

4. Many other physical symptoms can develop as a result of long-term drug use. Naturally, after foreign substances are ingested, the body reacts. Some problems are the result of the ways in which the drugs are introduced into the body. For example, nasal damage results from repeated snorting of cocaine, lung damage has been reported in marijuana smokers, and skin disorders occur in those who inject heroin. A variety of musculoskeletal, respiratory, gastrointestinal, and central nervous system disorders are also possible, even likely, after long-term drug or alcohol abuse.

Why People Use Drugs	Why People Abuse Drugs
euphoria	biochemical predisposition
availability	physical addiction
cultural exposure	maintaining intoxication
pain suppressant	external control
boredom	habituation
rebellion	social reinforcement
entertainment and curiosity	poor self-image
enhancement of reality	addictive personality
peer pressure	escape
stress reduction	impulsivity
social lubricant	instant gratification
self-medication	

Adolescent Drug Use

Many counselors interpret the drug abuser's behavior within the context of family dynamics. Haber (1983) summarizes much of the theory and research on this point of view and suggests many ways in which the client expresses anger, dependence, aggression, and independence through drug problems. The family is stabilized in its distraction by and attention toward the abuser's behavior. The family has its scapegoat. And the abuser has feelings of control. Everyone continues helplessly along, unable to break the destructive patterns that bind the family members together.

While noting the alarming number of adolescents involved in drug and alcohol use and abuse, we must also recognize that the age of onset is decreasing. It is almost a puberty rite to have experimented with drugs by the time one is 13. Schlaadt and Shannon (1982) state that "in 1965, the average age of a child's first encounter with alcohol was 13.6 years; in 1975, the age dropped to 12.9" (p. 128). The significance of such early use of drugs relates to the development of crucial social and personal skills between ages 10 and 15. This is a difficult time and drugs are an available way to ease pain and discomfort. Unfortunately, they also increase antisocial behavior and may lead to the development of a deviant lifestyle.

Several studies report that the earlier drug use starts, the longer it persists and the more intense it becomes (Oakley, 1983). Research shows, for example, that the sooner a youngster begins experimenting with alcohol, the greater his or her chances of becoming an alcoholic (Alibrandi, 1978). Biddle, Bank, & Marlin (1980) found that parents exert more influence through normative standards and peers exert more influence through behavior modeling. They also found that parental influence declines in the mid-teen years and rises again as the adolescent finishes high school. North and Orange (1980), on the other hand, strongly suggest that peer pressure is more influential and see adolescent drinking as stemming from a desire to conform. When there is disparity between parental and peer pressure, there will clearly be dissonance for the adolescent. The resolution of this dissonance will depend on the resources, both internal and external, available to the adolescent in making decisions about drug use.

The frequency and intensity of adolescent drug use are of concern to the counselor. Early identification, treatment, and support are crucial to reducing the negative effects of drug and alcohol use in the next generation. Working with adolescents on drug abuse problems is sensitive and should often include family treatment, for abusive behavior of this variety often has its roots in family dysfunction. Murphy (1984) recommends that family counseling efforts focus on reducing current levels of denial, shame, resentment, guilt, anger, and insecurity.

Abuse in Special Populations

There is a tendency to ignore or accept the abuse of drugs and alcohol by people whose lives are perceived as having diminished quality. We are going to introduce you to two such populations that you are likely to encounter as a counselor: elderly and handicapped people. Further counseling issues are covered in Chapter 14.

The major similarity among most special population groups with regard to drug and alcohol abuse is the willingness of society to overlook or accept the behavior. This tendency results in part from sympathy and denial. Since the lives of special populations are often viewed as lower in quality, it is reasonable to view any form of pleasure as acceptable. Recognizing the serious problems of special populations means having to work with them to improve the quality of life; denial of problems reduces the responsibility to work toward change. The attitude of society and even of immediate family members is an important factor in treatment because it means that there will often be little support for behavior change.

The Elderly

Drug abuse by the elderly may be intentional but often is not; most of the time it results from using prescribed medications. Older patients frequently visit several different doctors, each of whom prescribes a variety of medications. The elderly therefore form the largest group of consumers of legal drugs (Task Force on Prescription Drugs, 1968). Furthermore, the elderly have a decreased ability to metabolize medications and are more susceptible to their actions, interactions, and side effects (Pascarelli, 1981).

Although both prescription and nonprescription drugs are abused by the elderly, alcohol is by far the most serious drug problem for this population. About one-third of elderly alcoholics have developed an alcohol problem later in life, usually as a reaction to stress. The remaining two-thirds of elderly alcoholics appear to be long-standing alcohol abusers who drank heavily into old age. Since both types of elderly alcoholics tend to drink in response to stress, favorable responses to treatment, especially in the company of contemporaries, have been reported (Pascarelli, 1981).

In the elderly, a number of characteristics have been identified that tend to trigger drug and alcohol abuse. Depression and its effects increase substantially with aging. Persons over 65 years of age account for twenty-five percent of all suicides. The health habits of elderly abusers are often poor; they do not eat regularly or properly, and their sleep is frequently disturbed. They tend to rely on medication for a sense of well-being. Behaviorally, they tend to stay at home, feel lonely and abandoned, focus on the past, and have little interest in activities, remaining isolated and uninvolved. Drinking helps to pass the time.

Developmentally, elderly abusers are needy, lonely adults who are angry and feel a sense of despair about their lives and selves. They are depressed and often feel powerless and unwanted, a state of mind that is temporarily blunted by drugs and alcohol. They sense, rightly at times, an attitude of indifference toward them because they are old and worthless. Professionals and lay people tend not to place a priority on counseling services for this population because they are old and set in their ways and are going to die soon anyway. As a result, much professional care of the elderly abuser focuses on management and custodial issues. Little emphasis is placed on identification, treatment, and rehabilitation.

The Handicapped

Thirty-six million people in the United States are physically or mentally disabled, a population particularly vulnerable to alcoholism, drug abuse, and related problems. Although the magnitude of the problem has not been clearly established, estimates range to as high as 60 percent for patients with spinal cord injury (Anderson, 1981). The National Institute of Alcohol Abuse and Alcoholism estimates a similarly high rate of alcohol problems for the handicapped.

There is a high risk of alcohol and drug abuse in the disabled population in several respects:

1. There is easy access to prescription medication, especially for pain and severe spasms. Physicians often prescribe drugs on account of their own feelings of pity and guilt and a notion that this is the least they can do, given the tragedy of the situation.

2. The drug abuse path is taken as the result of the frustration and anxiety of being disabled and being thrust into a nonproductive and dependent role.

3. The disabled are an oppressed minority in our society; therefore, the lure of a substance that produces highs and numbness is an attractive alternative. According to initial findings of a study of the Center for Independent Living (CIL), 25 percent of the clients are abusing substances that cause social, mental, or physical dysfunction.

4. Abuse is often the result of medical intervention and the rehabilitation process. Of the disabled at CIL, 41 percent receive drugs prescribed unnecessarily and often take them in combination with alcohol (Hepner, Kershbaum, & Landes, 1980).

A major problem in treating drug abuse and alcoholism in disabled populations relates to diagnosis. Counselors are often unaware of the problem and treatment is often delayed until the symptoms become chronic (Vash, 1981). A growing advocacy movement has focused attention on the multidisabled alcoholic and encouraged programmatic responses at the community level. Although awareness of the problems of this population is improving, there is still a need for increased attention to the treatment of the handicapped drug and alcohol user. Many people are unacquainted with the symptoms of alcoholism and drug abuse and unfamiliar with the treatability of the problems, and some administrators and clinicians are reluctant to become involved (Lowenthal & Anderson, 1980).

Alcohol and polydrug use is widespread among the handicapped due to lack of access to prevention and treatment services, architectural barriers, lack of training and sensitivity to the specific problems and needs of the disabled, and attitudinal barriers that negate the desired effect of these services by reinforcing the client's poor self-image. Substance abuse is an easy way to avoid the difficult and painful work necessary to develop social skills and overcome social isolation (Hepner et al., 1980).

To varying degrees, the blind, deaf, paralyzed, and orthopedically impaired communities have reacted similarly in that they discourage the identification and treatment of alcohol or drug problems. They live in close association with each other and share a common identity and fear of being labeled by what a few deviant members might do. They already have shared the burden of the stigma of their disability. People who are constantly reminded of their disability rather than their ability find the addition of an alcohol or drug abuse problem an unwanted burden. Treatment for this population is therefore difficult and dependent upon early identification, support, and reduction of the threat of stigma.

Principles for Counseling the Chemically Dependent

Medical Model

Pietrofesa et al. (1984) summarize the various treatment models that are used in alcohol and drug counseling. In the medical model favored by many hospital, mental health, and clinic settings, substance abuse and alcoholism are classified as diseases similar to diabetes or cancer. It is presumed that the patient has some genetic predisposition to chemical abuse that may be exacerbated by family conflicts or other life pressures. The abuser is helped through a detoxification program on an inpatient or outpatient basis that may include forced abstinence, intensive psychotherapy, family support groups, and possibly medications to help with withdrawal symptoms. Antabuse, for example, is a prescribed drug that helps alcoholics stay sober by causing nausea at the first taste of an alcoholic beverage. Because the medical model approach absolves the client of responsibility for his or her condition, the counselor works intensively on issues related to self-control and compliance to the prescribed program.

AA/NA Model

The Alcoholics Anonymous/Narcotics Anonymous (AA/NA) model is somewhat compatible with the medical approach in that the abuser is labeled as helplessly addicted forever unless complete withdrawal is initiated.

Through powerful peer support groups the client is helped to make radical lifestyle changes, to abstain from all drugs and alcohol, and to admit that as an addict the only salvation is by rigorous adherence to the AA or NA program. As long as the abuser attends regular meetings (often several per week) and follows the prescribed steps, continued recovery is possible.

One problem associated with AA and NA programs is the emphasis placed on external control—often a conflict with the values of therapeutic counseling. Participants may learn to substitute one form of dependency for another: whereas they may no longer abuse drugs or alcohol, they nevertheless *must* go to meetings in order to maintain the cure. It is for this reason that individual counseling can be even more helpful in conjunction with AA and NA programs, giving focus to issues of autonomy, independence, and self-control.

Therapeutic Model

In the therapeutic model the various approaches to counseling are applied to the specific problems of substance abuse. Whereas there isn't much evidence to support the effectiveness of traditional therapies with alcohol and drug problems, there are practitioners who nevertheless attempt such strategies with mixed results. According to the various theories, the counselor may work on delving into repressed conflicts underlying the drug symptoms or perhaps concentrate on issues related to self-control. Any of the theoretical models presented in Chapters 5 and 6 could conceivably be applied to substance abuse programs. However, regardless of the therapeutic model, several suggestions have been made for working with alcohol/drug abusers:

1. Recovery from drug or alcohol addictions is unlikely without some support system as an adjunct to counseling (Armor, Polick, & Stambul, 1978).

2. Group counseling modalities are often helpful in providing support, positive modeling, motivation, intimacy, and constructive confrontation for substance abusers (Fuhrmann & Washington, 1984).

3. Family counseling strategies help the counselor to recruit more power and support, to collect more information about the problem, and to resolve conflicts that are sabotaging recovery (Murphy, 1984).

4. Since most drug abusers are, by definition, externally controlled, the counselor should spend time confronting the excuses for failure and the denial of responsibility for the problems (Dyer & Vriend, 1977).

5. Alcohol and drug abuse are often forms of self-medication in which the client attempts to cope with debilitating depression or anxiety. Attempts should be made to identify and treat the underlying pain that is being anesthetized.

6. Physical exercise programs that involve daily structured commitments are often helpful in creating more positive addictions. Activities such as biking, running, swimming, and aerobics have been found to reduce tension, increase productivity, improve confidence, and provide an alternative to drugs (Sachs & Buffone, 1984).

7. Watch for manipulation, deceit, and lying, which are not uncommon among those who are used to saying anything to get what they want. Developing trust is a major issue in the counseling.

8. Rules and limit setting are often needed to structure acceptable and inappropriate behavior within the sessions. For example, the counselor may refuse to work with the client unless she or he can agree to maintain sobriety for at least eight hours prior to any session.

9. Because drug and alcohol abuse are often associated with low self-esteem, considerable work should be spent helping the client to improve confidence and self-worth (Capuzzi & Lecoq, 1983).

10. Varieties of adventure and risk taking other than the drug-induced kind should be substituted (Capuzzi & Lecoq, 1983). As the person finds more fulfillment in a career, course of study, hobby, intimate relationship, social network, travel experiences, or any passionate project, the need to use drugs for excitement or boredom decreases.

Summary

Drug and alcohol abuse presents some special challenges for the counselor because (1) the problems are so widespread, (2) the effects of the drugs are intrinsically rewarding and resistant to extinction, (3) the support system of an abuser repels efforts to disrupt the status of any member, (4) the abuser tends to be externally controlled and thus unresponsive to efforts toward self-control, (5) abusers tend toward irresponsibility—they may miss or break appointments—and so may be uncooperative clients, (6) physiological addictive effects complicate change efforts made on a psychological level, (7) abusers are ambivalent in their motivation since the drugs *do* work, in spite of side effects, to temporarily reduce symptoms of boredom, anxiety, or depression, (8) there is some evidence that genetic factors may predispose some people to abuse in spite of their best intentions, and (9) drug and alcohol abusers have learned, as a matter of survival, to be manipulative, deceitful con artists, qualities not generally considered optimal for a productive therapeutic encounter.

Because of these many factors contributing to an abuser's situation, the counselor should develop a multifaceted treatment program to combat resistance on physiological, psychological, family, and cultural levels. Traditional insight-oriented counseling interventions are largely useless without taking additional therapeutic measures. Even with the best resources available, prognoses for chronic drug and alcohol abusers are guarded.

In general, when working with any kind of alcohol/drug abuser, the counselor would be well advised to use every possible resource available in the client's world and in the repertoire of therapeutic options. Particular attention should be paid to factors such as family influences, peer pressures, underlying internal conflicts, and tendencies toward escapism and immediate gratification of needs. It is normally necessary for the counselor to spend more time than usual on trust dimensions of the therapeutic relationship and to define clearly what constitutes responsible behavior, both within and outside the counseling sessions.

Suggested Readings

Aubrey, R. F. (1973). *The counselor and drug abuse programs.* Boston: Houghton Mifflin.

Forrest, G. G. (1978). *The diagnosis and treatment of alcoholism.* Springfield, Ill.: Charles C Thomas.

Lowinson, J. H., & Ruiz, P. (Eds.) (1981). *Substance abuse: Clinical problems and perspectives.* Baltimore: Williams & Wilkins.

Milby, J. B. (1981). *Addictive behavior and its treatment.* New York: Springer.

Oakley, R. (1983). *Drugs, society, and human behavior.* St. Louis: C. V. Mosby.

Weil, A. (1972). *The natural mind.* Boston: Houghton Mifflin.

Zimberg, S. (1978). *Practical approaches to alcoholism psychotherapy.* New York: Plenum.

Chapter 14

Counseling

Special Populations

Working with special populations requires the skills needed for all therapeutic counseling, plus knowledge about and sensitivity to the needs of particular groups. The same counseling skills are used with women and with men; the same theories of change apply to the physically handicapped as well as the athlete. Depression or anxiety does not feel qualitatively different to a Chicano, Black, or Caucasian. Group dynamics operate in similar ways in groups of children, middle-aged adults, and older adults. Homosexuals feel loneliness, frustration, or anger just as do heterosexuals. The delinquent, disabled, or drug-addicted clients all respond to empathy, confrontation, and other therapeutic strategies, depending on the counselor's finesse and appropriate use of interventions.

Influence of Biases

Finesse *does* make a difference. Working successfully with special populations requires special knowledge and special applications of therapeutic skills. It is necessary to understand the language, customs, and culture of a variety of ethnic groups. In addition, an awareness of your own biases and how they affect your perceptions and behavior is important. Even if you do not believe that you perceive the deaf, the elderly, the minorities, the disadvantaged, or the handicapped as different from other people, *they* often perceive others as unaware of and unresponsive to their needs. So, although your desire to treat all people as equals is laudable, it might cause you to appear insensitive. Members of special populations know they have some unique issues, and a counselor who fails to acknowledge them will likely be perceived as ineffective.

Biases and prejudices work both ways. As a counselor, you must be prepared to examine how your beliefs might interfere with counseling. But that is only half the problem. Clients also have prejudices, which affect their reactions to the counselor and interfere with the development of a therapeutic relationship. A client may perceive you as too young, too straight, or too inexperienced, for example, and those perceptions may alter how the client responds to you.

Biases and prejudices are caused by a lack of tolerance for individual differences. People who deviate too far from accepted standards are socially restricted or locked into mental institutions or prisons. Many people feel uncomfortable or threatened by people who have different views, skin color, dress codes, sexual preferences, or patterns of social interaction. Some fears are caused by lack of exposure. Some result from the awareness that "bad" things can happen to all of us; the discomfort people experience at seeing a handicapped or mentally ill person is often related to our own fears. Rigidity of thinking, fear of the unknown, avoidance of risks, and many other self-defeating behaviors likewise contribute to an individual's inflexibility.

There is also a danger that teachers and counselors who work with large numbers of students or clients will class them in groups rather than seeing them as individuals. Their generalizations are likely to be misconceptions.It is improbable that all persons in any group possess the same characteristics, but a certain mind-set can lead us to judge a whole group by some few individuals in the group. Thus biases are formed.

In assuming that prejudices are bad, inappropriate, self-defeating, and ineffective, we as authors are demonstrating our bias about counselors. By postulating a list of guidelines to eliminate bias and prejudices, we can be accused of prescribing our own beliefs as appropriate and effective behavior for all human beings and especially important for counselors. We urge each practitioner to assess his or her own thoughts, feelings, and behaviors and identify those biases that might interfere with effective counseling.

To change a belief system with which you have operated with for many years requires learning new information, working hard at new behaviors, and establishing new ways of thinking. Biases are not changed simply because one wants to be different or because one believes one *should* be different. Biases are changed by hard work and self-examination. The first and perhaps the most difficult step is to acknowledge our biases and then to admit that those biases have an impact on our behavior and our interaction with others. It is not uncommon for people to believe or even to say that although they are prejudiced against a certain group of people, they never let that prejudice interfere with their work. It is unlikely that anyone who has strong biases and/or prejudices is completely able to conceal those feelings from others. In counseling, for example, diagnostic biases abound. There are excellent examples that demonstrate the greater frequency of certain diagnoses among specific groups. Diagnosticians are often seen to have a bias against lower-class patients. A severe psychotic diagnosis is more likely to be bestowed upon a lower-class patient than a middle-class patient, given similar manifestations of pathological symptoms.

Counselors, irrespective of their sex, rated female clients with deviate career goals as being more in need of counseling than those with conforming career goals (Thomas & Stewart, 1971). This finding raises an important issue: bias is not necessarily directed toward someone who is different from us—the opposite sex, in this case—but can also be directed toward people who are like us. The societal expectations, norms, and socialization processes operate systematically to define appropriate roles for women, Blacks, senior citizens, and disabled persons. Prejudices and biases can be and are formed against any conceivable definable group of people: veterans, WASPS, Ku Klux Klansmen, homosexuals, hunters, blue-collar workers, executives, long-haired hippies, middle-class suburban housewives, and Cadillac owners are all groups of people for whom certain stereotypes have been established in our society. There are, of course, many more.

Beliefs and Attitudes

A person's beliefs and attitudes are founded in four human activities: thinking, feeling, behaving, and interacting. Firmly anchored attitudes are resistant; even repeated contradictions of stereotypes fail to change attitudes because the contradictions are treated as exceptions (Benn, 1970). Festinger (1957) suggests in his theory of cognitive dissonance that if an individual engages in behavior that is inconsistent with his beliefs, he will be sufficiently motivated to resolve the conflict by changing his beliefs to coincide with his behavior. That is to say that if an individual were compelled by either peer pressure, legal mandates, or professional requirements to behave in a less biased way toward a particular population, he would, in order to restore a state of equilibrium, alter his beliefs to be congruent with the new behavior. Following public compliance, private opinion will change (Festinger, 1964; Bandura, Blanchare, & Ritter, 1969). If behavior change does produce a change in attitudes, then the legal mandate against racial or sexual biases in hiring practices may indeed have an impact on attitudes.

Another theory of behavior change is the self-perception theory, which views behavior as the observable manifestation of inner states. How one acts is an indication of inner feelings. According to this theoretical position, it is possible by observing a person's overt behavior in specific situations to infer what the person's beliefs are about that situation. Likewise, changing our biased behavior in counseling can effect a change in our biased beliefs (Bandura, 1971).

The point of view proposed by Ellis (1962) is that changing one's beliefs and attitudes will result in a change of behavior. According to rational-emotive theory, it is the way one thinks about experiences that governs behavior, rather than the other way about. Still other theories see the process as circular in nature, each part influencing the other. It is probably difficult to determine whether biased and prejudiced behavior is a result of attitudes or beliefs or whether the behavior itself causes the attitudes and beliefs. Maybe you as a beginning counselor ought to examine what the process is like for you: are your behaviors the result of what you think and believe, or do you see your beliefs as stemming from your behavior? Understanding how this process works may help you to determine which method you can use to attack your own biases. It is important, of course, that you not generalize from yourself in working with clients and assume that they will be influenced exactly as you are, but you will also have to help them ascertain their own best methods for attacking any biases that they may want to change.

Preferred Client Types

In a classic study of professional biases, psychiatrists, social workers, and clinical psychologists were surveyed to find out their preferred client types. What emerged was the YAVIS profile (Schofield, 1964). The YAVIS client is young, attractive, verbal, intelligent, and successful. All groups of clinicians in the survey preferred female clients between the ages of 20 and 40. Social workers and psychiatrists preferred married females, whereas psychologists did not differentiate. Psychologists and psychiatrists had rigid levels of acceptable education and preferred high school graduates with some college experience, but not "too much" education. For example, graduate school experience was considered to create a difficult client. Non-preferred clients included the very young (under 15) and those over 50, widowed or divorced clients, uneducated people, and those in agriculture, fishery, forestry, and semiskilled or unskilled types of jobs. Although the evidence indicates that counselors and other professionals have definite preferences, the YAVIS population represents but a small portion of the types of clients that most of you will work with in counseling settings. Part of the reason for preferring particular clients is that those clients make us, as professionals, feel more successful about our work. Clients who improve quickly allow counselors to feel more powerful and competent.

It is important in counseling to use your distinctiveness and individuality to help others without imposing your morality or beliefs on them. The following is a list of suggestions originally designed for counselors who work with minority populations (Ho & Shipley, 1974) that can be adapted for counseling with a client group of any target population:

1. Do not deny cultural or physical differences. Your client is aware and will be made uncomfortable by your denial.
2. Feelings of warmth and genuineness transcend all ethnic, religious, cultural, and physical barriers.
3. Treat each client as an individual rather than as a member of a group.
4. Avoid projection, but use your own life experiences effectively to help others.
5. Share your own personal involvement and discoveries in ways that will benefit your client without imposing your views.

Counseling Women

The majority of counseling clients are women. Although they are not members of a minority group, they are a special population that is often a victim of biases. With a few notable exceptions (Melanie Klein, Anna Freud), men created most of the foundational theories of this field, some showing biases regarding the roles women should play. Certainly Freud's portrayal of the "weaker sex" as dependent, hysterical, inferior people established a precedent. Most of the theories that followed continued to reinforce conventional stereotypes of women as sex objects who need counseling for their boredom.

Hare-Mustin (1983) reviews several psychological problems that have a high incidence in women but that have been neglected by counselors. Because women are often limited to stereotypical roles in the family, they may experience frustration associated with blocked goals and routine lifestyles. Their husbands may complain about how hard they are working to make money, yet when they are recruited as temporary babysitters while the mother takes a "breather," they often develop a new respect for the strain of managing a household. Even when women work the same number of hours as their husbands, an inequitable division of labor in household chores is common. The woman, after working an eight-hour day, must then complete the majority of tasks related to cooking, cleaning, and raising children. Although this arrangement is not true of all couples, it remains the predominant model in our society. Members of the younger generation do not demonstrate marked changes in attitude toward women as the primary homemaker. A great number of female clients report feeling misunderstood, unappreciated, and underutilized because of their responsibilities in the home.

Women also experience problems with their changing body images and their reproductive functions. There are stresses associated with pregnancy (or its avoidance) and breastfeeding. The menstrual cycle may present special difficulties, as when mood swings precede the onset of the monthly period. New research on women who have severe reactions or PMS (premenstrual syndrome) has brought attention to these bodily changes (Turkington, 1984).

Women are much more likely than men to become depressed and to stay depressed longer (Weissman & Klerman, 1977). The books of Sylvia Plath, Doris Lessing, Alice Walker, and other writers document the depressive episodes all too familiar to women who feel powerless, ignored, abused, and neglected in their lives.

Kaplan (1983) claims that one reason more women than men are labeled and treated as mentally ill is that the current diagnostic system is founded on inherently masculine-biased assumptions. The American Psychiatric Association's DSM-III overemphasizes disorders that are caricatures of traditional female roles—that is, diagnoses that describe women who are overconforming in their efforts to satisfy sex-role stereotypes. Thus, favorite labels include terms like "hysterical," "passive-dependent," and "anorexic," which all describe the symptoms of a woman trying too hard to be subordinate, emotional, dependent, and skinny. Although critics (Williams & Spitzer, 1983; Kass, Spitzer, & Williams, 1983) argue that there is no empirical evidence to support the validity of Kaplan's claims, counselors nevertheless ought to be aware of the danger of creating additional problems for female clients by labeling overconforming behavior as pathological.

Eating disorders are a particularly dramatic example of the attempts of women to live up to the ideal standards of body image created by our culture. All models are tall and thin. While striving for this narrow conception of beauty as slimness, some women lose control of their original goal to become thinner and perceive losing weight as a contest. One problem that is gaining in prevalence is anorexia nervosa, or drastic weight loss to the point of starvation. This disorder almost always has its onset in adolescent girls who are overdependent, perfectionistic, and self-critical. Bulimia, or compulsive food gorging, is another way women destroy their bodies through abusive eating habits, often the consequence of rejection and a poor self-concept. Until recent efforts by Salvador Minuchin (Minuchin, Rosman, & Baker, 1978) and others to treat eating disorders in a family counseling context, the prognosis for these female-oriented problems was not positive. Now, counselors are experiencing successful outcomes by intervening on a structural level within the family unit.

Schlossberg and Kent (1979) present a model for working with women and their special problems that includes an emphasis on developmental transitions. The counselor's role, after becoming aware of transitional crises such as the birth of a child, is to educate the client about universal problems and then to make needed adjustments. A developmental model is often difficult to put into practice, particularly since the traditional theories of Erikson, Freud, Kohlberg and others are so sex-biased. Schlossberg (1984) has attempted to downplay the traditional roles of women as caretakers in an effort to equalize the developmental life cycle for both sexes.

Doherty (1978) also raises serious questions about the validity of our counseling interventions with women on the grounds that the personality theories from which they derive are authored by men and focused primarily on male concerns. Concepts such as "penis envy," "oedipal complex," and stereotypical portrayals of women as emotional and nurturing make it more difficult for them to attain the autonomy and independence so prized by most psychological theories.

Counseling Minorities

Hall and Maloney (1983) ascribe much of the failure and ineffectiveness of mental health programs to the lack of recognition given to the needs of minority groups. In their review of the literature pertaining to treatment of minority populations they conclude the following:

1. Minority clients are diagnosed as having more severe disturbances and pathological conditions than White persons—a not surprising finding, considering that most tests of mental illness are culturally biased and most diagnosticians are not members of minority groups.

2. Minority clients will tend to use mental health services only in cases of emergency or severe psychopathology, again skewing the perceptions of clinicians, who may be used to working with normal or neurotic Whites but very disturbed minorities. It is a cultural norm, for instance, among South American populations to handle most psychological problems through the resources of the family and church, relying on counselors or therapists only in extreme cases.

3. Minority clients more often drop out of treatment prematurely, usually within the first six sessions (Sue, 1977). Whether this tendency is a function of poor motivation or a difference in how they are treated is not clear.

4. In inpatient settings, evidence does indicate that Black clients are treated differently from Whites, more often receiving stronger medication, seclusion, restraints, and other punitive "therapies" and less often receiving recreational or occupational therapy (Flaherty & Meagher, 1980).

5. The minority group attitudes toward psychological disturbances are markedly different from those of Whites, more often stressing the roles of organic factors. Hispanics have more faith in the power of prayer than in psychotherapy for healing what they believe are inherited illnesses (Edgerton & Karno, 1971). The expectations of minority clients are thus not conducive to success, since so often the faith and hope that are so important are not operating at high levels.

6. Many people feel more comfortable and prefer working with others whom they perceive as similar (particularly with regard to race or ethnic background). Yet there are relatively few trained minority counselors who are available to serve this need.

7. With minority clients, and particularly with those of the lower class, it is important that counselors adapt their strategies and interventions to cultural differences. Eye contact and attention patterns can be interpreted variously as resistance, passivity, or aggression, depending on the client's culture (Hall, 1976).

8. Counseling can be viewed as one form of social control because its goals are most often to help deviants better adjust to the cultural norms of the majority. For the minority client this sort of adjustment presents special problems, since more conflict can result from the clash between subcultural values and those of the majority.

Hall & Maloney (1983) suggest that it would be effective to minimize conflicts that result from a clash of values by reducing dominance factors. Sue (1983) recommends recognizing our cultural biases as only the first of several steps to ensure effective treatment of minority clients. Counselors must also be highly motivated to educate themselves about other cultural groups. Finally, counselors must develop cross-cultural intervention skills to work with each client as an individual. By endlessly focusing on the differences among various ethnic groups we can fall into the trap of neglecting the uniqueness of each member of the group. A person's ethnic identity is only one of several contextual variables to help us understand and work with him or her as a client. "Knowing that Americans tend to be open, competitive, verbally direct, independent minded, or whatever, provides very few clues to the conduct of therapy with clients" (Sue, 1983, p. 589). Similarly, understanding the cultural heritage of clients is a necessary but insufficient condition for attaining true empathic contact.

Counseling the Aged

At the turn of the 21st century, when most of us will be at our peaks of professional productivity, a disproportionate part of the North American population will be considered elderly citizens. In just one century the single specialty within the helping professions that is most likely to flourish, if not explode, will be counseling older adults. The number of people over 65 has increased sevenfold: from 1 in 30 Americans in 1900 to an expected 1 in 5 Americans by 2020 (Eisdorfer, 1983). The children of the baby boom will, by the year 2000, be grandparents. Life expectancies will continue to lengthen, stretching normal lifespans well into the 80s and perhaps 90s. Age 65 will be considered a part of the productive rather than the retirement years. Older citizens will dominate the consumer markets as they will control a significant part of industry, families, and lifestyle. And with these changing roles, opportunities, and expectations will come new problems of adaptation for the aged—and important responsibilities for therapeutic counselors to aid adjustment and resolution of conflicts.

Some models of aging view older people as helpless, disabled, and a burden on society. There are special facilities where they may be cleaned, clothed, and fed until they die. Institutional environments of this type are generally depressing places where people wander about, forgetting who or where they are. The more agile can play cards, turn the channels on the television, or even shuffle along for walks outside the home.

Alternative conceptions of aging proposed by Eisdorfer (1983) view older persons as senior adults with a wealth of valuable experiences and skills accumulated over a lifetime. Elders used to be considered the wise men and women of the community to whom the young would come for advice and assistance; now they are the elderly—the shuffleboard and Geritol generation. Old age is a time of physical changes—hair thinning and turning white, skin losing its moisture and smoothness, the body actually shrinking in size, muscles becoming flabby and losing their strength. Joints become progressively stiff, bones are fragile, the heart is less efficient, and the arteries that circulate blood work like a slow train. Digestion is slowed, reaction times are diminished, lungs work at less than peak efficiency and bring less oxygen to provide energy. All the senses lose their precision, and the older person, receiving less information from vision, hearing, taste, touch, and smell, is thus more isolated, irritable, and moody.

Yet in spite of these symptoms of physical deterioration, their effects are often slight and the stereotype of the elderly person as slow moving, fragile, with dulled and distorted perceptions is hardly accurate. In a review of experimental findings of biochemical and physiological changes in the elderly, Hussian (1981) concludes that slowed intellectual, perceptual, mental behavior, particularly in those who are free of debilitating diseases, need not necessarily dramatically restrict functioning levels in major life areas. He then suggests that while a clinician may wish to alter assessment techniques, length of sessions, or the therapeutic process, highly specialized approaches are not required when working with elderly clients. The aged retain the capacity for self-awareness and insight. They respond to reinforcement. While they may be a bit more cautious in their mental and physical movements, they still think, feel, and act and wish to do so more effectively.

Traditionally, at least at the time Erik Erikson was formulating his theory of psychosocial development, later maturity was a time for resolution of the crisis of despair and for introspective integration of one's life. The elderly were supposed to be giving meaning to their life's work and preparing themselves to accept the inevitability of death. At age 81, himself engaged in this final life stage, Erikson revised many of his thoughts about old age to place much more emphasis on the creative, productive elements supposedly restricted to earlier stages (Hall, 1983). Through their roles in grandparenting, volunteer work, and maintaining intimate relationships, older people retain the playfulness, joy, and wonder that was so much a part of childhood.

B. F. Skinner, another influential thinker of this century, is also now a senior citizen. He writes about his own struggle to maintain his desired levels of effectiveness and how he has avoided growing old as a thinker even if his body stubbornly persists in its progressive decline (Skinner, 1983).

The principal developmental task of the older adult, then, is to maintain maximum levels of productivity and mental activity in the face of physical deterioration. "Old age is like fatigue, except that its effects cannot be corrected by relaxing or taking a vacation" (Skinner, 1983, p. 241). The older adult must learn to accept his or her incapacities and to find alternative ways to accomplish the same goals and to meet the same needs. Death, certain and inevitable, is a difficult issue for the older person as it looms ahead, closer and closer. Some people become crippled by their fears; others welcome their final deliverance. Yet, when old persons are given the opportunity to talk through their fears, most are able to resolve the developmental task, accept what they cannot change, and go on about the business of living fully in what little time remains. When discomfort arises in confronting the topic of death—with relatives, friends, nurses, doctors, or counselors—it is important to distinguish who exactly is uncomfortable, the older adult or the helper (Wass & Myers, 1982).

Dying is the last developmental task for everyone. Whether it comes unexpectedly, with or without pain, during sleep or sex, death is patiently waiting. Woody Allen (1976) freely admits, "It's not that I'm afraid to die. I just don't want to be there when it happens" (p. 106). If there is a "process" of dying, even beyond Elizabeth Kübler-Ross's stages of denial, rage, bargaining, depression, and acceptance, (assuming death is patient enough to wait for the complete cycle), then certainly counselors could help make the experience easier. In *Island*, his novel of a utopian society, Aldous Huxley (1962) imagines the distinct role of a death counselor, one who helps the dying in their final transition, the last exit from life:

"So now you can let go, my darling." He stroked her grey hair. "Now you can let go. Let go," he insisted. "Let go of this poor old body. You don't need it any more. Let it fall away from you. Leave it lying here like a pile of worn-out clothes" [p. 268].

For some active and productive people, youth is more a state of mind than chronological age.

Whether to aid in the client's fight against death until the last breath or to help a client accept its inevitability and to let go peacefully, the counselor can help to make the process easier.

Only 3 percent of the clientele who are currently served by community mental health centers and private clinics are over 65, and 70 percent of clinicians report they are not treating a single elderly client (Nissenson, 1984). Do the older adults not come because they feel they are incapable of changing or because administrators and clinicians believe that their problems are incurable, irreversible, and not amenable to treatment? Even Freud suggested that counseling is useless with people over 50.

Tolliver (1983) reports that three-fourths of older persons would prefer to be working rather than retired. With enforced mandatory retirement it is even more crucial for older people to feel productive after they leave their formal jobs. They must feel that they are occupied "doing something that is within their capacity, that gives them satisfaction, and that is needed by and useful to other people" (Swensen, 1983, p. 331).

Throughout history the aged have always served the important function of passing the wisdom from one generation on to the next. Whether in the role of teacher, guru, medicine man, or grandparent, the elders have taught their accumulated knowledge, experience, and skills to youth so that they too might survive life's tests. The aged are responsible, through storytelling and sharing of life experiences, for maintaining family and ethnic traditions. It is through listening to accounts of their own mistakes, failures, and weaknesses that they hope their protegees will learn to avoid similar traps.

According to Levinson (1978), the mentor role also involves several other tasks:

1. to act as an inspired leader, a model for the young to emulate;
2. to enrich the intellectual and emotional development of the young;
3. to use whatever influence is available to aid the advancement of youth;
4. to communicate the values and customs of the previous generation;
5. to provide guidance, advice, and moral support in times of expressed need;
6. to help the young believe in themselves and in their dreams.

It is in part this mentoring role that allows the elderly to remain productive and feel that their existence is still meaningful.

Handicapped Children

Apart from the problems of handicapped children themselves, the siblings and other family members of handicapped children may develop psychological symptoms (anger, guilt, resentment) that require treatment. Seligman (1983) points out that because handicapped children need excessive caretaking, the other family members must bear the responsibility and burden, often neglecting themselves and each other in the process. He reminds the counselor it is certainly not always the case that the presence of a handicapped child adversely affects the family. Often the experience encourages brothers and sisters to develop a sensitivity and caring that they will maintain their whole lives. However, it is important to realize that the "identified client"—the handicapped child—may not be the only one with problems.

This reminder is but a specific application of the principle that holds true for all presenting problems that occur in a family: when one person develops symptoms, they inevitably disrupt the daily lives of everyone else. Particularly when the handicapped individual is making a poor psychological adjustment, the added strain and stress place the other children at risk to develop problems. In addition to feeling guilt and resentment, they may also act out as a way to win attention according to family norms that emphasize being taken care of. For all these reasons, it is often advisable to work with the handicapped in the context of their families.

Summary

Although we have chosen but a few special population groups to profile, similar principles operate across the board. Counseling skills and theory remain relatively stable with any client; it is the unique way in which the practitioner uses individual personality and experience variables to work with each person that makes a difference. Background, heritage, and culture become more of an issue when working with minority and disadvantaged groups because of the significance such experiences have played in their lives. It is just another instance of the privileges of our profession (or at least that's *our* bias) that we are permitted entry into the rich complexity of all human life.

Suggested Readings

Atkinson, D. R., Morten, G., & Sue, D. W. (Eds.). (1979). *Counseling American minorities*. Dubuque, Iowa: William C. Brown.

Birren, J. E., & Sloane, R. B. (Eds.). (1980). *Handbook of mental health and aging*. Englewood Cliffs, N.J.: Prentice-Hall.

Brodsky, A. M., & Hare-Mustin, R. T. (Eds.). (1980). *Women and psychotherapy: An assessment of research and practice*. New York: Guilford Press.

Eisenberg, S., & Patterson, L. E. (Eds.). (1979). *Helping clients with special concerns*. Chicago: Rand McNally.

Harmon, L. W., Birk, J. M., Fitzgerald, L. E., & Tanney, M. F. (Eds.). (1978). *Counseling women*. Monterey, Calif.: Brooks/Cole.

Sue, D. W., Richardson, E. H., Ruiz, R. A., & Smith, E. J. (1981). *Counseling the culturally different*. New York: Wiley.

PART FOUR
PROFESSIONAL
PRACTICE

Chapter 15

Ethical and

Legal Issues

You have been working with a young client for three months. He was, at first, wary, reticent, and cautious. It has taken patience and careful use of your trust- and relationship-building skills to break through the resistance. Finally, he is beginning to talk and share something of his life with you in the counseling sessions. Yet, each time you begin to make progress, he draws back into his shell with a defensive remark: "You shrink types are all the same. You get your kicks out of prying into other people's lives." You repeatedly reassure him, reminding him of the sanctity and privacy of your office and the confidentiality of your relationship. He has tested your integrity a number of times and has attempted to probe your attitudes and values. You have responded by keeping the focus on him. You have thus spent a disproportionate amount of counseling time reaffirming your trustworthiness.

Finally your persistence and patience pay off. After much hesitation and several false starts, he slowly discloses his secret, meanwhile closely monitoring your reactions to him. He is satisfied as to your neutrality and acceptance of him (which you are consciously controlling) and so continues to describe his problem. This 16-year-old boy has quite a successful career selling various drugs—downers, speed, cocaine, pot, Quaaludes, and sometimes heroin—to other kids in the junior and senior high school. He has no intention of quitting. In fact, he loves the work. He explains that finally he has power, respect, and friends. He likes the excitement and the risks. He enjoys having his "clients" dependent on him. And he can't complain about the money. No, he certainly has no intention of quitting this lucrative "career." But he does feel a little guilty and he wants you to help him soothe his conscience. He reminds you that if you can't help him, he can always find someone who will. He notices your hesitancy and so, laughingly, throws your own words back in your face: "Remember, everything you say in here is privileged communication and nothing disclosed will ever leave this room." You have but a moment to respond, to decide upon one of several possible courses of action:

1. Since the most sacred principle of counseling is to protect the confidentiality of the client, as well as to act in his best interests, you would have no choice but to honor your commitments. It is, after all, not your purpose to tell people how to live their lives or to judge them.

2. The protection of public welfare, in this case the young victims of drug abuse, takes precedence over a vow of confidentiality to a single client, especially one who is so irresponsible and unconscionable in his acts. It would be for the greater good of the community and perhaps, ultimately, for the client's own welfare, to notify the appropriate authorities of his illegal acts so that corrective action may be taken.

3. The young man should be persuaded to stop his predatory behavior, knowing that otherwise you will be forced to notify his parents and the school authorities of his crimes.

4. The boy is obviously disturbed and not responsible for his actions. The counseling relationship ought to continue as it has been developing. It is to be hoped that he will alter his behavior as he gains insight into his self-destructive acts and learns more socially acceptable ways of earning money and social approval.

There are, naturally, a myriad of other alternatives open to the counselor, according to values, therapeutic goals, state laws, institutional policies, and even personal feelings toward the particular client. The most difficult aspect of making ethical decisions such as this is that there are rarely single, perfect solutions.

Professional Codes

There are professional codes of ethics published by a number of organizations that work with therapeutic counselors, such as the American Association for Counseling and Development, the Association for Specialists in Group Work, American Association for Marriage and Family Therapy, American Psychological Association, the National Academy of Certified Clinical Mental Health Counselors, and the American Association for Sex Educators, Counselors, and Therapists (see Appendixes A–C). However, these guidelines are often difficult to apply to individual cases, are sometimes contradictory, and are difficult for the professional organization to enforce (Talbutt, 1981). For this reason, ethical rules cannot just be memorized; rather, ethical behavior must be learned and decision-making skills developed to be internally consistent and yet compatible with acceptable societal and professional standards.

Ethics can be particularly frustrating to discuss in relation to the counseling profession. The nature of our field—its young history, conflicting theoretical base, and emphasis on the ambiguous and abstract content of the human mind—makes it difficult to define sanctioned professional behavior, much less enforce such professional standards. There are sometimes conflicts of opinion among practicing counselors about what constitutes acceptable standards of behavior. Each practitioner uses different labels and terms to describe the processes and has different goals and techniques. Depending on the state or country in which they reside, the institutions in which they work, their training, type of degree, and client needs, they can differ widely in what may be described as "ethical conduct." You would get no such impression from studying the ethical codes of our profession, wherein each point is neatly organized, numbered, and coded and set down in dignified, precise language. Many experienced practitioners spent their whole careers attempting to set forth these standards of acceptable conduct.

There *is* a distinction between the ethical decision making of the beginner and that of the experienced practitioner. Whereas the seasoned expert has logged years of therapeutic hours, the beginning counselor is starting out in a haze of confusion. It is difficult enough to track client statements, analyze underlying meanings, plan intervention strategies, and respond with accurate level empathy without having additionally to contemplate open-ended moral issues and ethical conflicts. It is for this reason that we urge you to read and study, if not memorize, your professional ethical codes and follow them to the letter. It is only with vast experience and intensive study that a scholar or practitioner can expect to improvise individual moral decisions based on solid empirical and philosophical grounds. And even those with such wisdom may believe, or publicly announce, something different from what they actually do within the privacy of their offices. The problem is further compounded by the often conflicting demands from a number of sources.

Our Divided Loyalties

Who, exactly, does a counselor work for? We learn in school that it is our clients. As professional helpers, we are to be their advocates, to hold their trust and confidence and protect their rights. However, sometimes our loyalties are divided between two or more constituents. If the client is a child, we are answerable to the parents for our actions, often a source of conflict when the parties disagree about the best course of action. If we were to comply with parental wishes and keep them informed of our work, inevitably we would lose the trust of the child. If we are uncooperative with the parents, they may sabotage the child's efforts or remove the child from counseling. To complicate matters further, counselors must answer to their school, agency, or institution for their actions. Counselors are also subject to the personal preferences of supervisors and the norms of the colleagues with whom they work. Then, there are state and federal laws that regulate behavior, sometimes against the welfare of clients and the best interests of institutions. As has been previously mentioned, there are also professional codes of various organizations. And through them all come the urgent whispers of our own inner voices.

Within ourselves are many competing loyalties. The fact that ultimately we answer to ourselves for our actions and not to the judge, the government, or our boss, would seem to simplify the matter. Yet it is further confounded by our responsibility to various parts of our own history (for instance, a client we once failed, on whose account we promised ourselves to act differently thereafter) or to the shapers of our values and formulators of our superego (parents, grandparents, mentors, teachers, and friends).

It is not unusual for a particular agency to dictate to the counselor a rule such as: "Any drug use by clients of this agency must be reported to the authorities." Fine. Your first client walks in and casually reports that she smokes marijuana on the weekends. You are obligated by contract to report this offense. But if you do, you will surely be betraying the client. Obviously, you can't consult your supervisor, who is sworn to uphold the agency's regulations. You desperately want to keep your job and may not believe the offense is serious. The professional dilemma is clear: do you follow your conscience or do you abide by the policies you agreed to uphold when you took the job? Some rules are foolish and may be judged as immoral. There comes a time when each person must choose a course of action and live with the consequences.

Areas of Ethical Difficulty

Ethics could quite legitimately be discussed under the topic of "fear." The subject is not usually given much thought until the prospect arises that something could go wrong. Ethics is the analysis of good versus bad choices, moral versus immoral motives, helpful versus harmful action. The ethical implications of a problem are considered as the last step of therapeutic decision making. Ethical consequences of behavior are usually examined only after a narrowly avoided mishap or the threat of a problem. Ethical discussions are often post-mortem autopsies, analyses of what should have been done and/or what will be done next time.

It is more useful to consider ethical issues, their implications, and possible resolutions *before* they occur, during a time when personal and professional needs and beliefs can be rationally thought out and decisions made about behavior. Predicting and identifying the conflicts that are likely to develop in the practice of counseling allows examination of implications, exploration of personal values, and an opportunity to evaluate several preferred responses. This preparation can demystify the process and diminish much of the fear and apprehension that will arise during a crisis.

Right now, what is the ethical conflict you fear most? What situation might occur within a session that would create for you a moral nightmare of confusion and frustration? To help stimulate self-exploration, we present a realistic review of some common problems that frequently present themselves in the first year of practice.

Seduction

Do you fear being seduced by a client?

F. Scott Fitzgerald's *Tender Is the Night,* a classic in American literature, popularized the theme of the inevitable magnetism between a vulnerable, idolizing young client and her omnipotent therapist, each attracted to the other during the intimacy of a therapeutic encounter. Only within the last few years have many clients had the courage to publicize their experiences of seduction with former and current helping professionals. Before you act indignant and rush to swear that it could *never* happen to you, first consider the ingredients that operate in a counseling situation: (1) a client who feels helpless, vulnerable, and confused, (2) with few satisfying relationships in his or her life, (3) who feels undying gratitude to the counselor who has provided crucial help at a desperate time, (4) to whom she or he has disclosed the most intimate details of her or his life, (5) whom he or she worships as a professional who at once appears so omnipotent, warm, affectionate, and understanding, and (6) whose attraction is magnified by the inequality in power and control of the relationship. Add to this potent mix the variables of countertransference, involvement, respect, and affection that the counselor will come to feel for some clients, and you have a potentially explosive situation.

The terms of this description are not meant to excuse or pardon unprofessional conduct that is among the most dangerous, abusive, and exploitive breaches of trust, but rather to encourage a healthy amount of legitimate apprehension about such situations. It is not altogether impossible for a counselor to find that a grateful hug has turned unexpectedly amorous. Often, in such intense situations, emotions don't respond to a half-prepared conscience. A counselor must be constantly aware of the detrimental results that are likely to follow sexually intimate entanglement with clients. The negative consequences will often cancel the previous therapeutic effects and send the client into a tailspin of mistrust for professionals who use their power to their own advantage. It may be helpful to rehearse and roleplay sexual encounters, including responses that can be made to initiations from clients; for example, "I have a confession to make. The *only* reason I keep coming to counseling is that I am so attracted to you. You have helped me *so* much. I owe it all to you. You are so different from other people I have known. How do you feel about me?"

What is your response?

A. "Ah. Our time is about up. Maybe we can continue next time."
B. "How would it be helpful to know my feelings?"
C. "You're feeling attracted to me because I've been helpful and supportive to you and you're hoping that I am attracted to you."
D. "It is not appropriate for you to think about me personally. We have a professional relationship and it is necessary that we keep our relationship nonpersonal in order to work together effectively."
E. "Since your personal feelings seem to be getting in the way of our professional relationship, perhaps we should discuss the possibility of your working with another counselor."
F. "Your place or mine?"

No matter how you look at the situation, with levity or seriousness, this incident may test the resolve of the most experienced counselor. As with all other ethical behaviors, it is insufficient merely to memorize a moral commandment: "Thou shalt not be sexually involved with thy client." You must thoroughly and genuinely believe it as a guiding principle—an internal, personal belief that certain behaviors are crucial to maintaining professional standards. The fear of being caught is *not* enough to prevent a problem. The counselor must understand the responsibilities, moral obligations, and consequences that come with the territory.

Misjudgment

Are you fearful of making a terrible mistake that hurts a client and unsure whether you would take responsibility for the consequences?

Making mistakes is inevitable in therapeutic counseling. Some of the time we are working without a clear, detailed map of the desired direction for the counseling process. Clients often don't know themselves what is troubling them and they frequently mask their true feelings as a defense. Sometimes the deception is even deliberate, part of an elaborate game-playing scheme intended to test the counselor's ability to see through the cover-up.

The counselor's judgment is further subject to error by the relatively low reliability and validity inherent in counseling techniques. Practitioners disagree as often as they agree on the diagnosis of a client, and when they do agree on the diagnosis, they may still choose different treatment plans. Consecutive consultations with different therapeutic helpers might well yield quite different diagnostic assessments. Suppose a client presents symptoms of irritability, listlessness, low energy, failed performances at work, lack of sex drive, and loss of appetite; these symptoms may be diagnosed in a number of ways, ranging from anorexia nervosa to depression to an acute stress reaction. Errors are possible not only in the conclusions drawn about a case but also in the ways chosen for working with the client.

The issue in this discussion is not whether or not mistakes and misjudgments will occur, many of which will hurt clients, but what can be done about them. What is gained by apologizing to the victim ("I'm awfully sorry. But, ah, remember when I said that it would be best to confront?—well, ah, I've thought about it and think that might not be the best alternative.")? What would be the likelihood of keeping a job if you rigorously reported every mistake to the supervisor ("Boss, I messed up again. This time, when I should have been supportive, I started confronting. I'm afraid the client won't be coming back.")? The important part of such ethical conflicts is, first, learning from mistakes to prevent repeating the same errors, and second, minimizing or reversing any negative effects on the client, possibly by seeking counsel from a peer or supervisor or perhaps by admitting to the client the problem and solutions.

It is easy to hide transgressions. No one else will ever know what goes on within the privacy of the office. Clients usually don't challenge a process so mysterious that almost anything can be viewed as potentially therapeutic from at least one theoretical point of view. It becomes all the more essential, then, to develop and internally monitor professional behavior from an ethical perspective. The individual counselor's awareness of and commitment to ethical principles will, in the final analysis, determine the ethical content of interviews.

Deception

Would you ever deliberately lie to or deceive a client, even if it were for his or her own good?

Counselors stand for truth, honesty, sincerity, and genuineness. But influence is also an important counseling skill. Is it justifiable to manipulate a client into experimenting with a new behavior? Is it ethical to disguise a trap waiting for the unsuspecting client? Is it even appropriate to water down the truth with clients? While students may respond with a resounding chorus of "NO," most experienced counselors will reluctantly admit that therapeutic deception may be necessary when it is intended for the benefit of the client.

When a client straightforwardly asks a direct question (for instance, a subnormal client asks, "Do you think I'm intelligent?"), we are confronted with the inevitable choice of whether or not to tell the truth to the client. The client might not yet be ready for the truth or, alternatively, might respond poorly to protective lies. The counselor must make a choice representative of his or her ethical standards and live with the consequences of the choice. While you are making your own decisions as to your preferred response, consider a case that occurred with one of the authors.

> The client is a young woman, inhibited, rigid, fearful, and shy. She is petrified of anything remotely spontaneous, since the outcome is not 100 percent predictable. She is also terrified of anything that might require her verbal performance, for failure (which she very loosely defines) would certainly crush her already fragile ego.
>
> The counselor quickly (and probably accurately) decides that the vicious cycle of self-defeating beliefs ("I can't do it because I'm ——") can be broken only by encouraging her, just once, to try acting differently from the way she has in the past. If she would pretend, even within the safety of the session, to be somewhat playful and spontaneous, she could not continue to use the excuse "I can't do it," since she would have revealed an exception to her self-defeating behavior.
>
> Role playing would obviously be the technique of choice to encourage the client's creativity and spontaneity, but she is vehement in her refusal to try it. The counselor agrees to back off, and discussion continues in other directions until an opportunity arises: the client, in talking about her mother's endless complaining and cackling, starts to change her voice in imitation of her mother, thus initiating spontaneous role playing. The counselor need only change roles and start imitating the client, knowing that it will provoke her continued performance as her mother. After having previously promised *not* to pressure her into roleplaying, the counselor now has an easy chance to trick her into trying it, obviously for her own therapeutic growth. Is the counselor ethically justified in proceeding, when he has said he will not, because the outcomes are so potentially desirable?

In this case, the counselor chose to stop the action, disclose aloud the temptation to be manipulative, and then deal with the reactions. The client felt so grateful for the maintenance of trust that she was then able to experiment slowly, not at the same dramatic level as would have been possible in the incident of spontaneous role playing, but well enough to make progress. For every example in which honesty produces the best results, there are also cases in which other, less direct actions might also be defensible.

Confidentiality

Are you worried that you may inadvertently or deliberately violate your client's confidence?

In a situation such as the one presented at the beginning of this chapter, a counselor may quite deliberately decide to break a previous promise because the client is committing a crime, as well as contributing to the delinquency of others. Ethical dilemmas do arise because of a conflict between what is best for the client and what is best for other people. In a landmark court case, now referred to as the Tarasoff decision, a counselor failed to warn a murder victim of potential dangers from his client and was held responsible and ordered to pay damages to the victim's parents. Although the judgment was eventually overturned, the case has brought much attention to the limitations of confidentiality.

Berger (1982) concludes that in addition to our ethical obligations to uphold a promise of confidentiality we also have an ethical and legal responsibility to breach the vow (1) when the client is a danger to himself or others, (2) when the client is engaged in criminal actions, (3) when the counselor is so ordered by the court, and (4) when it is in the best interests of a child who is a victim of abuse. Unfortunately, the courts do not offer to counselors the same protection they do to others whose communications are privileged, such as lawyers, physicians, clergy, and spouse. We must, therefore, painfully decide when our previous vow to maintain secrecy with clients should be overruled by an even more pressing moral imperative to protect human life.

Inadvertent slips that reveal confidential information are quite another matter. There is no justifiable excuse. That is not to say that we are not constantly tempted to share information with friends, spouses, or colleagues. But we must endure the isolation of not being able to talk about our work in any revealing detail because clients deserve to have their information protected by professional, ethical behavior.

Making Ethical Decisions

Counselors will be confronted on a regular basis with the necessity of making ethical decisions. When an ethical issue emerges, the counselor will have to make a virtually instantaneous decision; little opportunity will exist for careful analysis and thoughtful reflection. Thus, the first recommendation in making ethical decisions is to anticipate. It is essential to develop a reasonably clear ethical style based on analysis and reflection to guide decision making and a capacity for making sound moral decisions that are compatible with the consensual standards created by the profession. Van Hoose and Kottler (1977) present a model for making ethical decisions (Figure 15–1). It exemplifies a systematic approach in which the counselor considers the consequences of each action as it affects personal, client, and societal demands.

In addition to the introspective analysis that leads one to select a defensible moral choice, the decision-making process should also take into account the guidelines established by professional organizations and the legal system. Most of these sources mandate the following actions:

1. *Don't attempt any therapeutic intervention without sufficient knowledge, skills, training, and supervision.* You should not ever attempt helping actions that are outside the bounds of your qualifications and competence. Workshops, certification programs, postgraduate training, internships, and intensive supervision are the means by which you can legitimately augment your therapeutic skills and continue to grow as a professional. Make referrals to specialists and other helping professionals when appropriate.

2. *You should be free of all biases and prejudices that might interfere with the capacity for objectivity, neutrality, and positive regard in the therapeutic relationship.* This includes sexual and racial biases, as well as those directed toward any ethnic or religious group, special population, or belief system.

3. *Sexual involvement with clients is strictly prohibited.* Under no circumstances should you as counselor ever engage in erotic contact, act seductively, or respond to overtures made by those who have offered their trust in your professional integrity.

4. *The rights of all participants in research projects should be carefully protected.* All experimental procedures that could conceivably produce side effects must be thoroughly described and *informed* consent obtained from all subjects.

5. *You are responsible for protecting the privacy and confidentiality of all sessions.* Except in those circumstances wherein human life is in danger, you must preserve the sanctity of the therapeutic encounter. Information regarding a case may be released only with proper client authorization or under legal compulsion.

6. *The focus of counseling is to help the client reach self-determined goals.* Except in those instances in which goals appear to be destructive, self-defeating, or in violation of principles of reality, you are committed to working toward the client's greater autonomy and independence. You should therefore avoid manipulation, as well as creating dependencies or meeting your own needs in the session.

7. *You are committed to continuing professional training and growth after completing your formal education.* The knowledge and research in our field changes so rapidly that practitioners must continually update their expertise. For this reason, many professional organizations and certification/ licensing boards require annual continuing education credits of members.

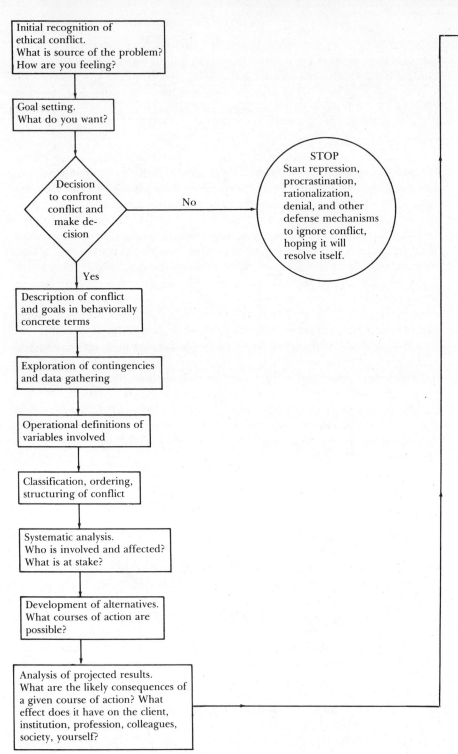

Figure 15–1. Flow chart for making ethical decisions (Van Hoose & Kottler, 1977, pp. 42–43)

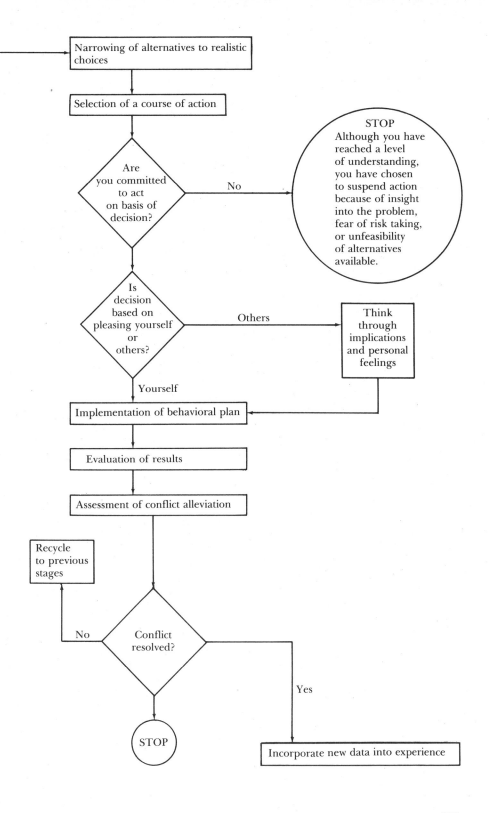

8. *You have an obligation to confront colleagues engaged in unethical, illegal, or incompetent practices.* As a professional you have a responsibility to your profession, your community, and the safety of those who seek counseling services. Your duty is to challenge directly the behavior of those who are transcending the bounds of generally accepted principles. If the problem is not sufficiently resolved, you are then required to report such behavior to appropriate authorities.

9. *You are committed to maintaining high standards of integrity, honesty, and moral fiber.* Therapeutic counselors accept their responsibility as professional helpers, recognize their powerful influence, and work toward functioning as more effective models for their clients.

10. *As a counselor you act for the general welfare of clients and society* to prevent discrimination, to help the needy and disadvantaged, to promote social justice, and to help all persons become more fully functioning.

Legal Considerations

In addition to following an ethical code, counselors must also be familiar with the ways their work intersects with the legal system. Woody (1984) identifies several broad topical areas that commonly relate to therapeutic practice. Knowledge of criminal law is important for those who will ever work with correctional programs, juvenile law for those who will work with neglect, abuse, or delinquency cases, and family law for counselors involved in cases of marital dispute, child custody, and divorce. Counselors should also be aware of personal injury law, discrimination law, and the rights of handicapped persons, children, and institutionalized patients.

With the growth in influence of therapeutic counselors, they are increasingly being called upon to give expert testimony. Divorce or custody cases, instances of employment disputes, probation violations, or clients who are offenders may necessitate visiting the courts. Their new status and power as professional experts bring greater legal liability. Accordingly, counselors should carefully study the laws of their state that apply to mental health work and learn their way around the legal system. In a review of recent court decisions that affect practicing counselors, Talbutt (1983) strongly urges that we avoid problems by keeping abreast of changes in the law and consult with legal and mental health professionals when in doubt.

Summary

The first step in making ethically sound decisions is to anticipate some possible dilemmas and to think through alternatives and preferred responses in an objective and analytical manner. These personal resolutions must be congruent with professional standards, state and federal laws, and institutional policies in order to be useful.

A systematic approach will yield ethical decisions that are personally meaningful, have a specific rationale for behavior, and are objectively defensible. With its help the counselor can respond to challenges, legal or personal, with a sense of integrity and a clear rationale for any behavior. The counselor should maintain an open, questioning attitude toward ethical decision making, recognizing the need to challenge and question decisions, values, and attitudes.

Ethical decision making is not a state we achieve but an ongoing process of learning, growth, and maturation. Ethical decision making means that we take responsibility for functioning at our highest possible level of moral behavior, both to serve our clients better and to avoid legal entanglements. Periodic reflection and a full examination of ethically challenging situations are essential factors in this process. It is often helpful to consult with colleagues and supervisors. Yet, in this profession, confusion has its healthy side; it helps us to avoid rigidity and forces us to personalize the meaning of our behavior.

Suggested Readings

Callis, R. (Ed.). (1982). *Ethical standards casebook.* Washington, D.C.: APGA Press.

Corey, G., Corey, M. S., & Callanan, P. (1984). *Issues and ethics in the helping professions.* Monterey, Calif.: Brooks/Cole.

Fried, C. (1978). *Right and wrong.* Cambridge, Mass.: Harvard University Press.

Hart, G. M. (1979). *Values clarification for counselors.* Springfield, Ill.: Charles C Thomas.

London, P. (1964). *The modes and morals of psychotherapy.* New York: Holt, Rinehart & Winston.

Rosenbaum, M. (Ed.). (1982). *Ethics and values in psychotherapy.* New York: Free Press.

Stein, H. (1982). *Ethics (and other liabilities).* New York: St. Martin's Press.

Van Hoose, W. H., & Kottler, J. A. (1985). *Ethical and legal issues in counseling and psychotherapy.* (2nd ed.). San Francisco: Jossey-Bass.

Woody, R. H. (1984). *The law and the practice of human services.* San Francisco: Jossey-Bass.

Chapter 16

Toward Closure

Advice for the Passionately Committed Counseling Student

This chapter is for those dedicated individuals who, after completing their introductory course in counseling, have decided to devote their lives to helping other people. Your commitment to the counseling profession is not to be taken lightly, nor can you realistically expect to treat your career as a mere job in which you just put in your time. Counselors are passionately committed to helping their clients to become more productive, fully functioning beings; the counseling student, too, must be intensely motivated to pursue a path of lifelong learning. It is only through your own hunger to understand, your thirst to know, your craving to find truth, and your skill in communicating your ideas that you become able to influence people in such constructive ways.

In the spirit of enthusiasm for the mission of counselors we offer the following advice to students.

Be Self-Directed

The best way to become passionate about learning is to follow your own natural curiosity to make sense of the world. So much of counseling deals with abstractions and complex queries that defy understanding. Your teachers, supervisors, and authors will only begin to tantalize you with answers to the questions that plague you the most. How does counseling work? Why does counseling work? Your assigned readings, lectures, and class discussions are but the stimulus for you to begin resolving many of these difficult issues. It is through personal reflection, self-directed study, and leisurely wandering through the library that you can really begin to educate yourself.

Read

We would encourage you, in your self-directed study, systematically to research the works that have had the most impact in the counseling profession. Make a list of classic books in the field and read them. Solicit nominations from teachers and peers. Notice in the literature those titles that are most frequently cited. Most of all, find a few reliable persons whose opinions you respect (such as a mentor) and read *everything* they recommend. Don't restrict yourself to just the books in counseling but become familiar with the literature in related fields such as psychology, social work, psychiatry, education, sociology, and philosophy.

Find a Mentor

In all chosen professions—the arts, sciences, law, medicine, business—and especially in a people-oriented career like counseling, it is important to have a model to emulate. A mentor, usually a teacher, senior colleague, or other benevolent friend/coach, helps the neophyte to learn the ropes during the period of apprenticeship. A mentor does more, much more, than give homespun advice or recommend books; she or he becomes an advocate. It is through this relationship that the beginning counselor receives support, encouragement, constructive feedback, and a guiding hand.

Select a mentor whom you admire, who has skills and knowledge you respect and wish to acquire for yourself, and who has a genuine, nonpossessive interest in you. Find someone you can trust and confide in, yet one who does not feel that such a commitment is a burden. A mentor can be a source not only of nurturance and wisdom during the formative years of professional development but also of invaluable assistance in securing a job.

Volunteer to Do Research

Getting actively involved in a research project is helpful in a number of obvious ways. It allows you to apply learning to the solution of real-life problems and personalizes the usefulness of the scientific method. Upon publication a writing credit can be a marketable commodity for gaining entrance to a doctoral program or a competitive job. Doing research also permits interaction with professors and colleagues on a level that would not be possible in the classroom. Finally, research gives one practical experience in exploring the issues, problems, and methodology of the profession. It is an opportunity to advance the growth of counseling and your own knowledge.

Ask Questions

When you don't know the answer to a question, *ASK*.

Many of the questions students ask in class are posed less to learn new ideas than to win brownie points, demonstrate what they already know, or express opinions in diplomatic ways—for example, "Aren't you saying that students are afraid to take risks by displaying their ignorance?"

Unfortunately, yes, that's what we're saying. In our experience, it is rare that a student really feels comfortable enough to ask the questions that she or he would most like to have answered. As we flash back to our graduate school days we recall that there were scores of things we didn't understand, but we felt too timid to admit our uncertainty—as if by questioning the professors we might reveal to others that we were not so bright and didn't really belong in class. It was only much later, when we were playing "I'll show you mine (ignorance) if you show me yours," that we discovered our universal passivity.

We therefore encourage you to take risks in class and ask about those things you don't understand. How, after all, can you expect your future clients to open up if *you* feel such reluctance? Right this moment, make a list of the questions you never got around to asking. Good news! There are still many opportunities left in future classes.

Challenge Your Teachers

Like questioning, but a lot more risky (and potentially more fun), is to challenge those ideas presented in class with which you disagree. This style of learning is critical to the development of your own ideas, especially with those teachers who don't react defensively.

There are many concepts central to the core of therapeutic counseling that some beginning students accept with great difficulty. For example, the notion of avoiding absolutes, shoulds, and other moralistic "rights" and "wrongs" cannot be internalized except through active dialogue with others who have reflected on the implications and tested the principles. It is through interesting debates and challenging new ideas that they can be understood and personalized.

Challenge Yourself

The most difficult task of a student is to maintain an openness to new ideas while simultaneously retaining a critical perspective. When ideas, concepts, theories are presented that at first seem threatening, rather than immediately leaping to defend yourself against other classmates or professors, *first* challenge yourself to explore the merits of the point of view. Ask yourself why you are responding so emotionally to the subject. What would it mean for you if you had to change your ideas to conform to this added information?

A related danger is that of too enthusiastically embracing a particular point of view, sowing the seeds of terminal rigidity and closing out the possibility of other ideas. Initially it *is* helpful to be suspicious and tentative. After exploring a theory that seems attractive and useful, do not fall into the destructive trap of confusing it with ultimate truth.

Experience Counseling as a Client

In the process of challenging oneself there is no vehicle more appropriate than experiencing counseling as a client. Many programs encourage participation in a form of counseling prior to graduation. For anyone who hopes to *do* counseling, it is important to know intimately the fears, joys, and apprehensions that clients experience.

Participating in counseling as a client allows you to work through inhibitions, distracting conflicts, and unresolved problems that may interfere with the ability to remain objective, focused, and therapeutic. It also helps you to believe fervently in the power of the process when you have experienced firsthand its beneficial effects.

We urge you to seek out both individual and group counseling experiences for another reason. Clearly, while a counseling student is engaged in a therapeutic relationship, there is always a part of him or her that is closely observing the process, noting the interventions that work best, and knowing, really *knowing,* the things that work best. If we truly believe that counseling is for everyone, than it is most certainly for us. All of us.

Personalize Everything

Counseling is a joy to study because all the abstract ideas, theoretical constructs, research hypotheses, clinical interpretations, class lectures, and textbook discourses can be personalized and applied to our own lives. All of a sudden, the behavior of those around us no longer appears the same. We seem more critical, yet more forgiving.

The novels we read, movies we see, conversations we participate in become wonderful opportunities to think, act, and feel differently. Learning has more meaning to us if we can make it more relevant. And that, primarily, is the student's job—to take the nucleus of an idea from one's teacher, mentor, counselor, or colleague and apply it in such a way that it becomes personally useful.

Become Active in Professional Organizations

The American Association for Counseling and Development, American Association for Marriage and Family Therapy, and the American Psychological Association are a few of the groups that advance the profession of therapeutic counseling. Through their lobbying activities, public relations and consumer education programs, and professional development courses, these organizations help support practitioners. They have also written ethical codes, work toward certification and training standards, provide referral services, sponsor national and regional conventions, fund research projects, publish professional journals, run job search programs, and provide social activities for their members.

There are many opportunities for students to get actively involved in the organizations by attending conventions, contributing articles to journals, serving on committees, presenting papers and workshops, and working on special projects of interest. Participating in state, regional, and national conventions is especially interesting because of the opportunities to make lifelong friendships with colleagues around the world. Conventions are also ideal places to receive specialized training and find jobs, since many employers are present to interview for positions. Finally, organizational activities help one to identify with counseling as a profession.

Develop a Flexible Specialty

As we have already said, the advanced degree in counseling does not guarantee employment in a specific career. It is both the plague and the privilege of graduates to market themselves in such a way that they will fit a particular position, or even to tailor-make a job to fit their own unique skills, training, and interest.

Practically everyone knows what the psychologist, psychiatrist, or social worker can and cannot do. Counseling practitioners, however, now function in many diverse settings. Five students in the same program, with the same course work, will eventually find employment in five different settings:

school counseling, industrial relations, consumer education, staff development, and a mental health center. The counseling degree, then, is education for the generalist who, through specialized training and interests, develops a unique professional identity.

We therefore suggest to the beginning student the following course of action to find eventual employment in a desired area:

1. Talk to counselors in the field about what they do and how they feel about their jobs.
2. Find excuses to talk to prospective employers to determine what they are looking for in candidates.
3. Discover a few particular types of client populations (handicapped, gifted), age groups (preschoolers, older adults), settings (hospitals, schools), and counseling skills (consultation, group interventions) in which you can gain specialized experience.
4. Use elective courses, workshop experiences, and your internship sites to help you become an expert in a few flexible specialties.
5. Volunteer your time at local community agencies to accumulate additional professional experiences.

Resist Burn-Out

In recent years there has developed a considerable body of literature describing the burn-out phenomenon, especially as it relates to counselors, psychologists, social workers, teachers, and other human services personnel (Cherniss, 1980; Freudenberger, 1974, 1983; Pines and Maslach, 1978; Spicuzza and Devoe, 1982). In a review of the literature, Maher (1983) reports some symptoms of burn-out that include fatigue, irritation, reduced work performance, apathy, boredom, and negative attitudes. The condition is caused, in part, by such factors as an excessive work load, monotony, a lack of control, and isolation.

The only antidote for burn-out is renewed enthusiasm or a job change. Counselors who are committed to their jobs and the profession may be less likely to experience the effects of burn-out and disillusionment. Marks (1977), as reported by Maher (1983), offers four conditions for encouraging commitment:

(a) intrinsic enjoyment of the activities involved in performing the role in question;
(b) loyalty to some or all of one's role partners;
(c) expectation of extrinsic rewards for the performance; and
(d) desire to avoid punishments that could result from nonperformance [p. 392].

Any one of these conditions may be sufficient for developing a commitment to a role, and that commitment will be further strengthened if all are present.

The implications for the beginning counselor are clear. It is necessary to work diligently to develop a sense of professional commitment to clients, colleagues, the profession, and ultimately ourselves as professional counselors. This sense of commitment will result in renewal and provide the energy base necessary to perform creatively and enthusiastically. The time to begin developing that sense of commitment is now.

Variations on a Theme

Naturally, we wish to leave you with the appropriate balance of healthy confusion and the eager enthusiasm to grow, to learn more, to find your own truth, and to continue in a profession that helps others to clarify their directions. Farber (1983) has concluded from interviews with practitioners that one consequence of doing counseling is an increase in the counselor's own self-awareness, self-assurance, and psychological sensitivity. This phenomenon is, perhaps, the best reason of all for feeling passionate and committed to the life of a counselor.

In the 16th century a Samurai warrior and master of Kendo ("he who wields the sword") wrote a manual of instruction for those who wished to learn his strategy. Musashi's *A Book of Five Rings* (1982) has since become a Bible for Japanese businessmen; we believe that his wisdom also speaks to prospective counselors, to those who wish to learn "the Way of Water," to become calm, unbiased, with a settled spirit, and to those who follow "the Way of Fire," who research and train diligently. Musashi prescribes the following advice for those who want to follow his way:

1. Do not think dishonestly.
2. The Way is in training.
3. Become acquainted with every art.
4. Know the Ways of all professions.
5. Distinguish between gain and loss in worldly matters.
6. Develop intuitive judgment and understanding for everything.
7. Perceive those things which cannot be seen.
8. Pay attention to trifles.
9. Do nothing which is of no use.

The greatest obstacle to any significant discovery is the illusion of knowledge. Boorstein (1983) explains that it was not ignorance that precipitated our descent into the Dark Ages of history, but rather those imaginative bold strokes that temporarily pacified fears and served hopes for simple solutions. True knowledge always advances slowly, with contradictions, conflicts, and controversy. And it is precisely these furiously passionate debates among discrepant views that produce an approximation of truth. With each course you take, with each book you read, with each workshop you attend, with each supervision session you complete, and with each client you see, greater wisdom and competence will evolve *if* (1) you learn from mistakes, (2) you passionately search for greater mastery in personal and professional skills, and (3) you retain sufficient humility to continue asking questions that have no simple answers.

In a supervision conference, one counselor lamented her frustrations and confusions about a particular case in which she felt lost, inept, discouraged. "How, after all," she pleaded, "can I work with this client when I have no idea what is going on?"

The supervisor, Dr. Williams, softly responded in a voice that rose above the chatter of advice directed to the counselor.

"Don't worry when you don't know what you're doing," he said. "Worry when you think you do."

Appendix A

Ethical Standards*

(Approved by Executive Committee upon referral of the Board of Directors, January 17, 1981.)

PREAMBLE

The American Personnel and Guidance Association is an educational, scientific, and professional organization whose members are dedicated to the enhancement of the worth, dignity, potential, and uniqueness of each individual and thus to the service of society.

The Association recognizes that the role definitions and work settings of its members include a wide variety of academic disciplines, levels of academic preparation and agency services. This diversity reflects the breadth of the Association's interest and influence. It also poses challenging complexities in efforts to set standards for the performance of members, desired requisite preparation or practice, and supporting social, legal, and ethical controls.

The specification of ethical standards enables the Association to clarify to present and future members and to those served by members, the nature of ethical responsibilities held in common by its members.

The existence of such standards serves to stimulate greater concern by members for their own professional functioning and for the conduct of fellow professionals such as counselors, guidance and student personnel workers, and others in the helping professions. As the ethical code of the Association, this document establishes principles that define the ethical behavior of Association members.

Section A: General

1. The member influences the development of the profession by continuous efforts to improve professional practices, teaching, services,

and research. Professional growth is continuous throughout the member's career and is exemplified by the development of a philosophy that explains why and how a member functions in the helping relationship. Members must gather data on their effectiveness and be guided by the findings.

2. The member has a responsibility both to the individual who is served and to the institution within which the service is performed to maintain high standards of professional conduct. The member strives to maintain the highest levels of professional services offered to the individuals to be served. The member also strives to assist the agency, organization, or institution in providing the highest caliber of professional services. The acceptance of employment in an institution implies that the member is in agreement with the general policies and principles of the institution. Therefore the professional activities of the member are also in accord with the objectives of the institution. If, despite concerted efforts, the member cannot reach agreement with the employer as to acceptable standards of conduct that allow for changes in institutional policy conducive to the positive growth and development of clients, then terminating the affiliation should be seriously considered.

3. Ethical behavior among professional associates, both members and nonmembers, must be expected at all times. When information is possessed that raises doubt as to the ethical behavior of professional colleagues, whether Association members or not, the member must take action to attempt to rectify such a condition. Such action shall use the institution's channels first and then use procedures established by the state Branch, Division, or Association.

4. The member neither claims nor implies professional qualifications exceeding those possessed and is responsible for correcting any misrepresentations of these qualifications by others.

5. In establishing fees for professional counseling services, members must consider the financial status of clients and locality. In the event that the established fee structure is inappropriate for a client, assistance must be provided in finding comparable services of acceptable cost.

6. When members provide information to the public or to subordinates, peers or supervisors, they have a responsibility to ensure that the content is general, unidentified client information that is accurate, unbiased, and consists of objective, factual data.

7. With regard to the delivery of professional services, members should accept only those positions for which they are professionally qualified.

8. In the counseling relationship the counselor is aware of the intimacy of the relationship and maintains respect for the client and avoids engaging in activities that seek to meet the counselor's personal needs at the expense of that client. Through awareness of the negative impact of both racial and sexual stereotyping and discrimination, the counselor guards the individual rights and personal dignity of the client in the counseling relationship.

Section B: Counseling Relationship

This section refers to practices and procedures of individual and/or group counseling relationships.

The member must recognize the need for client freedom of choice. Under those circumstances where this is not possible, the member must apprise clients of restrictions that may limit their freedom of choice.

1. The member's *primary* obligation is to respect the integrity and promote the welfare of the client(s), whether the client(s) is(are) assisted individually or in a group relationship. In a group setting, the member is also responsible for taking reasonable precautions to protect individuals from physical and/or psychological trauma resulting from interaction within the group.

2. The counseling relationship and information resulting therefrom [must] be kept confidential, consistent with the obligations of the member as a professional person. In a group counseling setting, the counselor must set a norm of confidentiality regarding all group participants' disclosures.

3. If an individual is already in a counseling relationship with another professional person, the member does not enter into a counseling relationship without first contacting and receiving the approval of that other professional. If the member discovers that the client is in another counseling relationship after the counseling relationship begins, the member must gain the consent of the other professional or terminate the relationship, unless the client elects to terminate the other relationship.

4. When the client's condition indicates that there is clear and imminent danger to the client or others, the member must take reasonable personal action or inform responsible authorities. Consultation with other professionals must be used where possible. The assumption of responsibility for the client's behavior must be taken only after careful deliberation. The client must be involved in the resumption of responsibility as quickly as possible.

5. Records of the counseling relationship, including interview notes, test data, correspondence, tape recordings, and other documents, are to be considered professional information for use in counseling and they should not be considered a part of the records of the institution or agency in which the counselor is employed unless specified by state statute or regulation. Revelation to others of counseling material must occur only upon the expressed consent of the client.

6. Use of data derived from a counseling relationship for purposes of counselor training or research shall be confined to content that can be disguised to ensure full protection of the identity of the subject client.

7. The member must inform the client of the purposes, goals, techniques, rules of procedure and limitations that may affect the relationship at or before the time that the counseling relationship is entered.

8. The member must screen prospective group participants, especially when the emphasis is on self-understanding and growth through self-disclosure. The member must maintain an awareness of the group participants' compatibility throughout the life of the group.

9. The member may choose to consult with any other professionally competent person about a client. In choosing a consultant, the member must avoid placing the consultant in a conflict of interest situation that would preclude the consultant's being a proper party to the member's efforts to help the client.

10. If the member determines an inability to be of professional assistance to the client, the member must either avoid initiating the counseling relationship or immediately terminate that relationship. In either event, the member must suggest appropriate alternatives. (The member must be knowledgeable about referral resources so that a satisfactory referral can be initiated.) In the event the client declines the suggested referral, the member is not obligated to continue the relationship.

11. When the member has other relationships, particularly of an administrative, supervisory and/or evaluative nature with an individual seeking counseling services, the member must not serve as the counselor but should refer the individual to another professional. Only in instances where such an alternative is unavailable and where the individual's situation warrants counseling intervention should the member enter into and/or maintain a counseling relationship. Dual relationships with clients that might impair the member's objectivity and professional judgment (e.g., as with close friends or relatives, sexual intimacies with any client) must be avoided and/or the counseling relationship terminated through referral to another competent professional.

12. All experimental methods of treatment must be clearly indicated to prospective recipients and safety precautions are to be adhered to by the member.

13. When the member is engaged in short-term group treatment/training programs (e.g., marathons and other encounter-type or growth groups), the member ensures that there is professional assistance available during and following the group experience.

14. Should the member be engaged in a work setting that calls for any variation from the above statements, the member is obligated to consult with other professionals whenever possible to consider justifiable alternatives.

Section C: Measurement and Evaluation

The primary purpose of educational and psychological testing is to provide descriptive measures that are objective and interpretable in either comparative or absolute terms. The member must recognize the need to interpret the statements that follow as applying to the whole range of appraisal techniques including test and nontest data. Test results constitute only one of a variety of pertinent sources of information for personnel, guidance, and counseling decisions.

1. The member must provide specific orientation or information to the examinee(s) prior to and following the test administration so that the results of testing may be placed in proper perspective with other relevant factors. In so doing, the member must recognize the effects of socioeconomic, ethnic and cultural factors on test scores. It is the member's professional responsibility to use additional unvalidated information carefully in modifying interpretation of the test results.

2. In selecting tests for use in a given situation or with a particular client, the member must consider carefully the specific validity, reliability, and appropriateness of the test(s). *General* validity, reliability and the like may be questioned legally as well as ethically when tests are used for vocational and educational selection, placement, or counseling.

3. When making any statements to the public about tests and testing, the member must give accurate information and avoid false claims of misconceptions. Special efforts are often required to avoid unwarranted connotations of such terms is *IQ* and *grade equivalent scores.*

4. Different tests demand different levels of competence for administration, scoring, and interpretation. Members must recognize the limits of their competence and perform only those functions for which they are prepared.

5. Tests must be administered under the same conditions that were established in their standardization. When tests are not administered under standard conditions or when unusual behavior or irregularities occur during the testing session, those conditions must be noted and the results designated as invalid or of questionable validity. Unsupervised or inadequately supervised test-taking, such as the use of tests through the mails, is considered unethical. On the other hand, the use of instruments that are so designed or standardized to be self-administered and self-scored, such as interest inventories, is to be encouraged.

6. The meaningfulness of test results used in personnel, guidance, and counseling functions generally depends on the examinee's unfamiliarity with the specific items on the test. Any prior coaching or dissemination of the test materials can invalidate test results. Therefore, test security is one of the professional obligations of the member. Conditions that produce most favorable test results must be made known to the examinee.

7. The purpose of testing and the explicit use of the results must be made known to the examinee prior to testing. The counselor must ensure that instrument limitations are not exceeded and that periodic review and/or retesting are made to prevent client stereotyping.

8. The examinee's welfare and explicit prior understanding must be the criteria for determining the recipients of the test results. The member must see that specific interpretation accompanies any release of individual or group test data. The interpretation of test data must be related to the examinee's particular concerns.

9. The member must be cautious when interpreting the results of research instruments possessing insufficient technical data. The specific pur-

poses for the use of such instruments must be stated explicitly to examinees.

10. The member must proceed with caution when attempting to evaluate and interpret the performance of minority group members or other persons who are not represented in the norm group on which the instrument was standardized.

11. The member must guard against the appropriation, reproduction, or modifications of published tests or parts thereof without acknowledgment and permission from the previous publisher.

12. Regarding the preparation, publication and distribution of tests, reference should be made to:

   a. *Standards for Educational and Psychological Tests and Manuals,* revised edition, 1974, published by the American Psychological Association on behalf of itself, the American Educational Research Association and the National Council on Measurement in Education.

   b. The responsible use of tests: A position paper of AMEG, APGA, and NCME. *Measurement and Evaluation in Guidance,* 1972, 5, 385–388.

   c. "Responsibilities of Users of Standardized Tests," APGA, *Guidepost,* October 5, 1978, pp. 5–8.

Section D: Research and Publication

1. Guidelines on research with human subjects shall be adhered to, such as:

   a. *Ethical Principles in the Conduct of Research with Human Participants,* Washington, D.C.: American Psychological Association, Inc., 1973.

   b. Code of Federal Regulations, Title 45, Subtitle A, Part 46, as currently issued.

2. In planning any research activity dealing with human subjects, the member must be aware of and responsive to all pertinent ethical principles and ensure that the research problem, design, and execution are in full compliance with them.

3. Responsibility for ethical research practice lies with the principal researcher, while others involved in the research activities share ethical obligation and full responsibility for their own actions.

4. In research with human subjects, researchers are responsible for the subjects' welfare throughout the experiment and they must take all reasonable precautions to avoid causing injurious psychological, physical, or social effects on their subjects.

5. All research subjects must be informed of the purpose of the study except when withholding information or providing misinformation to them is essential to the investigation. In such research the member must be responsible for corrective action as soon as possible following completion of the research.

6. Participation in research must be voluntary. Involuntary participation is appropriate only when it can be demonstrated that participation will have no harmful effects on subjects and is essential to the investigation.

7. When reporting research results, explicit mention must be made of all variables and conditions known to the investigator that might affect the outcome of the investigation or the interpretation of the data.

8. The member must be responsible for conducting and reporting investigations in a manner that minimizes the possibility that results will be misleading.

9. The member has an obligation to make available sufficient original research data to qualified others who may wish to replicate the study.

10. When supplying data, aiding in the research of another person, reporting research results or in making original data available, due care must be taken to disguise the identity of the subjects in the absence of specific authorization from such subjects to do otherwise.

11. When conducting and reporting research, the member must be familiar with, and give recognition to, previous work on the topic, as well as to observe all copyright laws and follow the principles of giving full credit to all to whom credit is due.

12. The member must give due credit through joint authorship, acknowledgment, footnote statements, or other appropriate means to those who have contributed significantly to the research and/or publication, in accordance with such contributions.

13. The member must communicate to other members the results of any research judged to be of professional or scientific value. Results reflecting unfavorably on institutions, programs, services, or vested interests must not be withheld for such reasons.

14. If members agree to cooperate with another individual in research and/or publication, they incur an obligation to cooperate as promised in terms of punctuality of performance and with full regard to the completeness and accuracy of the information required.

15. Ethical practice requires that authors not submit the same manuscript or one essentially similar in content, for simultaneous publication consideration by two or more journals. In addition, manuscripts published in whole or in substantial part in another journal or published work should not be submitted for publication without acknowledgment and permission from the previous publication.

Section E: Consulting

Consultation refers to a voluntary relationship between a professional helper and help-needing individual, group or social unit in which the consultant is providing help to the client(s) in defining and solving a work-related problem or potential problem with a client or client system. (This definition is adapted from Kurpius, DeWayne. Consultation theory and process: An integrated model. *Personnel and Guidance Journal,* 1978, 56.)

1. The member acting as consultant must have a high degree of self-awareness of his-her own values, knowledge, skills, limitations, and needs in entering a helping relationship that involves human and-or

organizational change and that the focus of the relationship be on the issues to be resolved and not on the person(s) presenting the problem.

2. There must be understanding and agreement between member and client for the problem definition, change goals, and predicated consequences of interventions selected.

3. The member must be reasonably certain that she/he or the organization represented has the necessary competencies and resources for giving the kind of help that is needed now or may develop later and that appropriate referral resources are available to the consultant.

4. The consulting relationship must be one in which client adaptability and growth toward self-direction are encouraged and cultivated. The member must maintain this role consistently and not become a decision maker for the client or create a future dependency on the consultant.

5. When announcing consultant availability for services, the member conscientiously adheres to the Association's *Ethical Standards*.

6. The member must refuse a private fee or other remuneration for consultation with persons who are entitled to these services through the member's employing institution or agency. The policies of a particular agency may make explicit provisions for private practice with agency clients by members of its staff. In such instances, the clients must be apprised of other options open to them should they seek private counseling services.

Section F: Private Practice

1. The member should assist the profession by facilitating the availability of counseling services in private as well as public settings.

2. In advertising services as a private practitioner, the member must advertise the services in such a manner so as to accurately inform the public as to services, expertise, profession, and techniques of counseling in a professional manner. A member who assumes an executive leadership role in the organization shall not permit his/her name to be used in professional notices during periods when not actively engaged in the private practice of counseling.

   The member may list the following: highest relevant degree, type and level of certification or license, type and/or description of services, and other relevant information. Such information must not contain false, inaccurate, misleading, partial, out-of-context, or deceptive material or statements.

3. Members may join in partnership/corporation with other members and-or other professionals provided that each member of the partnership or corporation makes clear the separate specialties by name in compliance with the regulations of the locality.   –

4. A member has an obligation to withdraw from a counseling relationship if it is believed that employment will result in violation of the *Ethical Standards*. If the mental or physical condition of the member renders it difficult to carry out an effective professional relationship or if the

member is discharged by the client because the counseling relationship is no longer productive for the client, then the member is obligated to terminate the counseling relationship.

5. A member must adhere to the regulations for private practice of the locality where the services are offered.

6. It is unethical to use one's institutional affiliation to recruit clients for one's private practice.

Section G: Personnel Administration

It is recognized that most members are employed in public or quasi-public institutions. The functioning of a member within an institution must contribute to the goals of the institution and vice versa if either is to accomplish their respective goals or objectives. It is therefore essential that the member and the institution function in ways to (a) make the institution's goals explicit and public; (b) make the member's contribution to institutional goals specific; and (c) foster mutual accountability for goal achievement.

To accomplish these objectives, it is recognized that the member and the employer must share responsibilities in the formulation and implementation of personnel policies.

1. Members must define and describe the parameters and levels of their professional competency.

2. Members must establish interpersonal relations and working agreements with supervisors and subordinates regarding counseling or clinical relationships, confidentiality, distinction between public and private material, maintenance, and dissemination of recorded information, work load and accountability. Working agreements in each instance must be specified and made known to those concerned.

3. Members must alert their employers to conditions that may be potentially disruptive or damaging.

4. Members must inform employers of conditions that may limit their effectiveness.

5. Members must submit regularly to professional review and evaluation.

6. Members must be responsible for inservice development of self and-or staff.

7. Members must inform their staff of goals and programs.

8. Members must provide personnel practices that guarantee and enhance the rights and welfare of each recipient of their service.

9. Members must select competent persons and assign responsibilities compatible with their skills and experiences.

Section H: Preparation Standards

Members who are responsible for training others must be guided by the preparation standards of the Association and relevant Division(s). The member who functions in the capacity of trainer assumes unique ethical responsibilities that frequently go beyond that of the member who does not function in a training capacity. These ethical responsibilities are outlined as follows:

1. Members must orient students to program expectations, basic skills development, and employment prospects prior to admission to the program.
2. Members in charge of learning experiences must establish programs that integrate academic study and supervised practice.
3. Members must establish a program directed toward developing students' skills, knowledge, and self-understanding, stated whenever possible in competency or performance terms.
4. Members must identify the levels of competencies of their students in compliance with relevant Division standards. These competencies must accommodate the para-professional as well as the professional.
5. Members, through continual student evaluation and appraisal, must be aware of the personal limitations of the learner that might impede future performance. The instructor must not only assist the learner in securing remedial assistance but also screen from the program those individuals who are unable to provide competent services.
6. Members must provide a program that includes training in research commensurate with levels of role functioning. Para-professional and techniques level personnel must be trained as consumers of research. In addition, these personnel must learn how to evaluate their own and their program's effectiveness. Graduate training, especially at the doctoral level, would include preparation for ongoing research by the member.
7. Members must make students aware of the ethical responsibilities and standards of the profession.
8. Preparatory programs must encourage student to value the ideals of service to individuals and to society. In this regard, direct financial remuneration or lack thereof must not influence the quality of service rendered. Monetary considerations must not be allowed to overshadow professional and humanitarian needs.
9. Members responsible for educational programs must be skilled as teachers and practitioners.
10. Members must present thoroughly varied theoretical positions so that students may make comparisons and have the opportunity to select a position.
11. Members must develop clear policies within their educational institutions regarding field placement and the roles of the student and the instructor in such placements.
12. Members must ensure that forms of learning focusing on self-understanding or growth are voluntary, or if required as part of the education program, are made known to prospective students prior to entering the program. When the education program offers a growth experience with an emphasis on self-disclosure or other relatively inti-

mate or personal involvement, the member must have no administrative, supervisory, or evaluating authority regarding the participant.

13. Members must conduct an educational program in keeping with the current relevant guidelines of the American Personnel and Guidance Association and its Divisions.

Appendix B

Code of Professional Ethics*

Section I: Code and Personal Conduct

1. A therapist provides professional service to anyone regardless of race, religion, sex, political affiliation, social or economic status, or choice of lifestyle. When a therapist cannot offer service for any reason, he or she will make proper referral. Therapists are encouraged to devote a portion of their time to work for which there is little or no financial return.
2. A therapist will not use his or her counseling relationship to further personal, religious, political, or business interests.
3. A therapist will neither offer nor accept payment for referrals, and will actively seek all significant information from the source of referral.
4. A therapist will not knowingly offer service to a client who is in treatment with another clinical professional without consultation among the parties involved.
5. A therapist will not disparage the qualifications of any colleague.
6. Every member of the AAMFT has an obligation to continuing education and professional growth in all possible ways, including active participation in the meetings and affairs of the Association.
7. A therapist will not attempt to diagnose, prescribe for, treat, or advise on problems outside the recognized boundaries of the therapist's competence.
8. A therapist will attempt to avoid relationships with clients which might impair professional judgment or increase the risks of exploiting clients. Examples of such relationships include: treatment of family members, close friends, employees, or supervisees. Sexual intimacy with clients is unethical.
9. The AAMFT encourages its members to affiliate with professional groups, clinics, or agencies operating in the field of marriage and family life. Similarly, interdisciplinary contact and cooperation are encouraged.

*Code of Professional Ethics, by the American Association for Marriage and Family Therapy. Copyright by the American Association for Marriage and Family Therapy (no date). Reprinted by permission.

Section II: Relations with Clients

1. A therapist, while offering dignified and reasonable support, is cautious in prognosis and will not exaggerate the efficacy of his or her services.
2. The therapist recognizes the importance of clear understandings on financial matters with clients. Arrangements for payments are settled at the beginning of a therapeutic relationship.
3. A therapist keeps records of each case and stores them in such a way as to ensure safety and confidentiality in accordance with the highest professional and legal standards.
   a. Information shall be revealed only to professional persons concerned with the case. Written and oral reports should present only data germane to the purposes of the inquiry; every effort should be made to avoid undue invasion of privacy.
   b. The therapist is responsible for informing clients of the limits of confidentiality.
   c. Written permission shall be granted by the clients involved before data may be divulged.
   d. Information is not communicated to others without consent of the client unless there is clear and immediate danger to an individual or to society, and then only to the appropriate family members, professional workers, or public authorities.
4. A therapist deals with relationships at varying stages of their history. While respecting at all times the rights of clients to make their own decisions, the therapist has a duty to assess the situation according to the highest professional standards. In all circumstances, the therapist will clearly advise a client that the decision to separate or divorce is the responsibility solely of the client. In such an event, the therapist has the continuing responsibility to offer support and counsel during the period of readjustment.

Section III: Research and Publication

1. The therapist is obligated to protect the welfare of his or her research subjects. The conditions of the Human Subjects Experimentation shall prevail, as specified by the Department of Health, Education and Welfare guidelines.
2. Publication credit is assigned to those who have contributed to a publication, in proportion to their contribution, and in accordance with customary publication practices.

Section IV: Implementation

1. In accepting membership in the Association, each member binds himself or herself to accept the judgment of fellow members as to standards of professional ethics, subject to the safeguards provided in this section. Acceptance of membership implies consent to abide by the acts of

discipline herein set forth and as enumerated in the Bylaws of the Association. It is the duty of each member to safeguard these standards of ethical practice. Should a fellow member appear to violate this Code, he or she may be cautioned through friendly remonstrance, colleague consultation with the party in question, or formal complaint may be filed in accordance with the following procedure:

a. Complaint of unethical practice shall be made in writing to the Chairperson of the Standing Committee on Ethics and Professional Practices and to the Executive Director. A copy of the complaint shall be furnished to the person or persons against whom it is directed.

b. Should the Standing Committee decide the complaint warrants investigation, it shall so notify the charged party(ies) in writing. When investigation is indicated, the Standing Committee shall constitute itself an Investigating Committee and shall include in its membership at least one member of the Board and at least two members (other than the charging or charged parties or any possible witnesses) from the local area involved. This Investigating Committee or representatives thereof shall make one or more local visits of investigation of the complaint. After full investigation following due process and offering the charged party(ies) opportunity to defend him or herself, the Committee shall report its findings and recommendations to the Board of Directors for action.

c. The charged party(ies) shall have free access to all charges and evidence cited against him or her, and shall have full freedom to defend himself or herself before the Investigating Committee and the Board, including the right to legal counsel.

d. Recommendation made by the Committee shall be:
   1. Advice that the charges be dropped as unfounded.
   2. Specified admonishment.
   3. Reprimand.
   4. Dismissal from membership.

2. Should a member of this Association be expelled, he or she shall at once surrender his or her membership certificate to the Board of Directors. Failure to do so shall result in such action as legal counsel may recommend.

3. Should a member of this Association be expelled from another recognized professional association or have his/her state license revoked for unethical conduct, the Standing Committee on Ethics shall investigate the matter and, where appropriate, act in the manner provided above respecting charges of unethical conduct.

4. The Committee will also give due consideration to a formal complaint by a non-member.

Section V: Public Information and advertising

All professional presentations to the public will be governed by the Standards on Public Information and Advertising.

Standards on Public Information and Advertising

Section I: General Principles

The practice of marriage and family therapy as a mental health profession is in the public interest. Therefore, it is appropriate for the well-trained and qualified practitioner to inform the public of the availability of his/her services. However, much needs to be done to educate the public as to the services available from qualified marriage and family therapists. Therefore, the clinical members of AAMFT have a responsibility to the public to engage in appropriate informational activities and to avoid misrepresentation or misleading statements in keeping with the following general principles and specific regulations.

Selection of a marriage and family therapist

A. At a time when the Human Services field is burgeoning and becoming increasingly complex and specialized, few marriage and family therapists are willing and competent to deal with every kind of marital or family problem, and many laypersons have difficulty in determining the competence of psycho-therapists in general and marriage and family therapists in particular to render different types of services. The selection of a marriage and family therapist is particularly difficult for transients, persons moving into new areas, persons of limited education or means, and others who have had no previous experience or the degree of sophistication required to evaluate training and competence or because they are in some sort of crisis.

B. Selection of a marriage and family therapist by a layperson should be made on an informed basis. Advice and recommendation of third parties—physicians, other professionals, relatives, friends, acquaintances, business associates—and restrained publicity may be helpful. A marriage and family therapist should not compensate another person for recommending him/her, for influencing a prospective client to employ him/her, or to encourage future recommendations. Advertisements and public communications, whether in directories, announcement cards, newspapers, or on radio or television, should be formulated to convey information that is necessary to make an appropriate selection. Self-praising should be avoided. Information that may be helpful in some situations would include: (1) office information, such as name, including a group name and names of professional associates, address, telephone number, credit card acceptability, languages spoken and written, and office hours; (2) earned degrees, state licensure and/or certification, and AAMFT clinical membership status; (3) description of practice, including a statement that practice is limited to one or more fields of marriage and family therapy; and (4) permitted fee information.

C. The proper motivation for commercial publicity by marriage and family therapists lies in the need to inform the public of the availability of competent, independent marriage and family therapists. The public benefit derived from advertising depends upon the usefulness of the information provided to the community to which it is directed. Advertising marked by excesses of content, volume, scope, or frequency, or which unduly emphasizes unrepresentative biographical information, does not provide that public benefit. The use of media whose scope or nature clearly suggests that the use is intended for self-praising of the therapist without concomitant benefit to the public distorts the legitimate purpose of informing the public and is clearly improper. Indeed, this and other improper advertising may hinder informed selection of a competent, independent professional and advertising that involves excessive cost may unnecessarily increase fees for marriage and family therapy.

D. Advertisements and other communications should make it apparent that the necessity [for] and advisability of marriage and family therapy depend on variant factors that must be evaluated individually. Because fee information frequently may be incomplete and misleading to a layperson, a marriage and family therapist should exercise great care to assure that fee information is complete and accurate. Because of the individuality of each problem, public statements regarding average, minimum, or estimated fees may be deceiving as will commercial publicity conveying information as to results previously achieved, general or average solutions, or expected outcomes. It would be misleading to advertise a set fee for a specific type of case without adhering to the stated fee in charging clients. Advertisements or public claims that use statistical data or other information based on past performance or prediction of future success may be deceptive if they ignore important variables. Only factual assertions, and not opinions, should be made in public communications. Not only must commercial publicity be truthful but its accurate meaning must be apparent to the average layperson. No guarantees about the outcomes of therapy should be made or implied. Any commerical publicity or advertising for which payment is made should so indicate unless it is apparent from the context that it is paid publicity or an advertisement.

E. The desirability of affording the public access to information relevant to their needs and problems has resulted in some relaxation of the former restrictions against advertising by marriage and family therapists. Historically, those restrictions were imposed to prevent deceptive publicity that would mislead laypersons, cause distrust of the profession, and undermine public confidence in the profession, and all marriage and family therapists should remain vigilant to prevent such results. Ambiguous information relevant to a layperson's decision regarding his/her selection of a marriage and family therapist, provided in ways that do not comport with the dignity of the profession or which demean the amelioration of human problems, is inappropriate in public communications. The regulation of advertising by marriage and family therapists is rooted in the public interest. Advertising through which a marriage and family therapist seeks business by use of extravagant or brash statements or appeals to fears could mislead and harm the layperson. Furthermore, public communications that would produce unrealistic expectations in particular cases and bring about distrust of the profession would be harmful to society. Thus, public confidence in our profession would be impaired by such advertisements of professional services. The therapist-client relationship, being personal and unique, should not be established as the result of pressures, deceptions, or exploitation of the vulnerability of clients frequently experiencing significant stresss at the time they seek help.

F. The Regulations recognize the value of giving assistance in the selection process through forms of advertising that furnish identification of a marriage and family therapist while avoiding falsity, deception, and misrepresentation. All publicity should be evaluated with regard to its effects on the layperson. The layperson is best served if advertisements contain no misleading information or emotional appeals, and emphasize the necessity of an individualized evaluation of the situation before conclusions as to need for a particular type of therapy and probable expenses can be made. The therapist-client relationship should result from a free and informed choice by the layperson. Unwarranted promises of benefits, over-persuasion, or vexatious or harassing conduct is improper.

G. The name under which a marriage and family therapist conducts his/her practice may be a factor in the selection process. The use of a name which could mislead laypersons concerning the identity, responsibility, source, and status of those practicing thereunder is not proper. Likewise, one should not hold oneself out as being a partner or associate of a firm if he/she is not one in fact.

H. In order to avoid the possibility of misleading persons with whom he/she deals, a marriage and family therapist should be scrupulous in the representation of his/her professional background, training, and status. In some instances a marriage and family therapist confines his/her practice to a particular area within the field of marriage and family therapy. However, a member should not hold himself/herself out as a specialist without evidence of training, education, and supervised experience in settings which meet recognized professional standards. A marriage and family therapist may, however, indicate, if it is factual, a limitation of his/her practice or that he/she practices within one or more particular areas of marriage and family treatment in public pronouncements which will assist laypersons in selecting a marriage and family therapist and accurately describe the limited area in which the member practices.

I. The marriage and family therapist should support the creation and evolution of ethical, approved plans (such as marriage and family therapist referral systems) which aid in the selection of qualified therapists.

Section II: Regulations

A. The American Association for Marriage and Family Therapy is the sole owner of its name, its logo, and the abbreviated initials AAMFT. Use of the name, logo, and initials is restricted to the following conditions.

1. Only individual clinical members may identify their membership in AAMFT in public information or advertising materials, not associates or students of organizations.
2. The initials AAMFT may not be used following one's name in the manner of an academic degree because this is misleading.
3. Use of the logo is limited to the association, its committees and regional divisions when they are engaged in bona fide activities as units or divisions of AAMFT.
4. A regional division or chapter of AAMFT may use the AAMFT insignia to list its individual members as a group (e.g., in the Yellow Pages). When all Clinical Members practicing within a directory district have been invited to list, any one or more member may do so.

B. A marriage and family therapist shall not knowingly make a representation about his/her ability, background, or experience, or that of a partner or associate, or about the fee or any other aspect of a proposed professional engagement, that is false, fraudulent, misleading, or deceptive, and that might reasonably be expected to induce reliance by a member of the public.

C. Without limitation, a false, fraudulent, misleading, or deceptive statement or claim includes a statement or claim which:

1. Contains a material misrepresentation of fact;
2. Omits to state any material fact necessary to make the statement, in light of all circumstances, not misleading;
3. Is intended or is likely to create an unjustified expectation;
4. Relates to professional fees other than:
   a. a statement of the fee for an initial consultation; a statement of the fee charges for a specific service, the description of which would not be misunderstood or be deceptive;
   b. a statement of the range of fees for specifically described services, provided there is a reasonable disclosure of all relevant variables and considerations so that the statement would not be misunderstood or be deceptive;
   c. a statement of specified hourly rates, provided the statement makes clear that the total charge will vary according to the number of hours devoted to the matter;
   d. the availability of credit arrangements; or
5. Contains a representation or implication that is likely to cause an ordinary prudent person to misunderstand or be deceived or fails to contain reasonable warnings or disclaimers necessary to make a representation or implication not deceptive.

D. A member shall not, on his/her own behalf or on behalf of a partner or associate or any other therapist associated with the firm, use or participate in the use of any form of advertising of services which:

1. Contains statistical data or other information based on past performance or prediction of future success;
2. Contains a testimonial about or endorsement of a therapist;
3. Contains a statement of opinion as to the quality of the services or contains a representation or implication regarding the quality of services, whether therapeutic or educational, which is not susceptible or reasonable verification by the public;
4. Is intended or is likely to attract clients by use of showmanship or self-praising.

E. A member shall not compensate or give anything of value to a representative of the press, radio, television, or other communication medium in anticipation of or in return for professional publicity in a news item. A paid advertisement must be identified as such unless it is apparent from the context that it is a paid advertisement. If the paid advertisement is communicated to the public by use of radio or television, it shall be prerecorded, approved for broadcast by the therapist, and a recording of the actual transmission shall be retained by the therapist.

Professional Notices, Letterheads, Offices, and Directory Listings

F. A member or group of members shall not use or participate in the use of a professional card, professional announcement card, office sign, letterhead, telephone directory listing, association directory listing, or a similar professional notice or device if it includes a statement or claim that is false, fraudulent, misleading, or deceptive within the meaning of Section II, C or that violates the regulations contained in Section II, D.

G. A member shall not practice under a name that is misleading as to the identity, responsibility, or status of those practicing thereunder, or is otherwise false, fraudulent, misleading, or deceptive within the meaning of Section II, C or is contrary to law. However, the name of a professional corporation or professional association may contain "P.C." or "P.A." or similar symbols indicating the nature of the organization.

H. A member shall not hold himself/herself out as having a partnership with one or more other qualified therapists unless they are in fact partners.

I. A partnership shall not be formed or continued between or among members in different geographical locations unless all enumerations of the members or associates of the firm on its letterhead and in other permissible listings make clear the limitations due to geographical separation of the members or associates of the firm.

J. Academic degrees earned from institutions accredited by regionally or nationally recognized accrediting agencies or associations may be used or permitted to be used provided that the statement or claim is neither false, fraudulent, misleading, or deceptive within the meaning of Section II, C.

Solicitation of Professional Employment

K. A member shall not seek, by in-person contact, his/her employment as a therapist (or employment of a partner or associate) by a client who has not sought his/her advice regarding employment of a marriage and family therapist if:
1. The solicitation involves use of a statement or claim that is false, fraudulent, misleading, or deceptive within the meaning of Section II, C; or
2. The solicitation involves the use of undue influence; or
3. The potential client is apparently in a physical or mental condition which would make it unlikely that he or she could exercise reasonable, considered judgment as to the selection of a marriage and family therapist.

L. A member shall not compensate or give anything of value to a person or organization to recommend or secure his/her employment by a claim or as a reward for having made a recommendation resulting in his/her employment by a client.

M. A member shall not accept employment when he/she knows or it is obvious that the person who seeks his/her service does so as a result of conduct prohibited by this Section.

Suggestion of Need of Marriage or Family Therapy

N. A member who has given unsolicited advice to a layperson that he/she/they should obtain marriage or family therapy shall not accept employment results from that advice if:
1. The advice embodies or implies a statement or claim that is false, fraudulent, misleading, or deceptive within the meaning of Section II, C or that violates the regulations contained in Section II, D; or
2. The advice involves the use by the marriage and family therapist of coercion, duress, compulsion, intimidation, unwarranted promises of benefits, overreaching, [or] vexatious or harassing conduct.

Appendix C

Ethical Principles of

Psychologists*

PREAMBLE

Psychologists respect the dignity and worth of the individual and strive for the preservation and protection of fundamental human rights. They are committed to increasing knowledge of human behavior and of people's understanding of themselves and others and to the utilization of such knowledge for the promotion of human

Ethical Principles of Psychologists (revised edition), by the American Psychological Association. Copyright 1981 by the American Psychological Association. Reprinted by permission of the publisher.

This version of the *Ethical Principles of Psychologists* (formerly entitled *Ethical Standards of Psychologists*) was adopted by the American Psychological Association's Council of Representatives on January 24, 1981. The revised *Ethical Principles* contain both substantive and grammatical changes in each of the nine ethical principles constituting the *Ethical Standards of Psychologists* previously adopted by the Council of Representatives in 1979, plus a new tenth principle entitled "Care and Use of Animals." Inquiries concerning the *Ethical Principles of Psychologists* should be addressed to the Administrative Officer for Ethics, American Psychological Association, 1200 Seventeenth Street, N.W., Washington, D.C., 20036.

These revised *Ethical Principles* apply to psychologists, to students of psychology, and to others who do work of a psychological nature under the supervision of a psychologist. They are also intended for the guidance of nonmembers of the Association who are engaged in psychological research or practice.

Any complaints of unethical conduct filed after January 24, 1981, shall be governed by this 1981 revision. However, conduct (a) complained about after January 24, 1981, but which occurred prior to that date, and (b) not considered unethical under prior versions of the principles but considered unethical under the 1981 revision, shall not be deemed a violation of ethical principles. Any complaints pending as of January 24, 1981, shall be governed either by the 1979 or by the 1981 version of the *Ethical Principles*, at the sound discretion of the Committee on Scientific and Professional Ethics and Conduct.

310

welfare. While pursuing these objectives, they make every effort to protect the welfare of those who seek their services and of the research participants that may be the object of study. They use their skills only for purposes consistent with these values and do not knowingly permit their misuse by others. While demanding for themselves freedom of inquiry and communication, psychologists accept the responsibility this freedom requires: competence, objectivity in the application of skills, and concern for the best interests of clients, colleagues, students, research participants, and society. In the pursuit of these ideals, psychologists subscribe to principles in the following areas: 1. Responsibility, 2. Competence, 3. Moral and Legal Standards, 4. Public Statements, 5. Confidentiality, 6. Welfare of the Consumer, 7. Professional Relationships, 8. Assessment Techniques, 9. Research with Human Participants, and 10. Care and Use of Animals.

Acceptance of membership in the American Psychological Association commits the member to adherence to these principles.

Psychologists cooperate with duly constituted committees of the American Psychological Association, in particular, the Committee on Scientific and Professional Ethics and Conduct, by responding to inquiries promptly and completely. Members also respond promptly and completely to inquiries from duly constituted state association ethics committees and professional standards review committees.

Principle 1: Responsibility

In providing services, psychologists maintain the highest standards of their profession. They accept responsibility for the consequences of their acts and make every effort to ensure that their services are used appropriately.

a. As scientists, psychologists accept responsibility for the selection of their research topics and the methods used in investigation, analysis, and reporting. They plan their research in ways to minimize the possibility that their findings will be misleading. They provide thorough discussion of the limitations of their data, especially where their work touches on social policy or might be construed to the detriment of persons in specific age, sex, ethnic, socioeconomic, or other social groups. In publishing reports of their work, they never suppress disconfirming data, and they acknowledge the existence of alternative hypotheses and explanations of their findings. Psychologists take credit only for work they have actually done.

b. Psychologists clarify in advance with all appropriate persons and agencies the expectations for sharing and utilizing research data. They avoid relationships that may limit their objectivity or create a conflict of interest. Interference with the milieu in which data are collected is kept to a minimum.

c. Psychologists have the responsibility to attempt to prevent distortion, misuse, or suppression of psychological findings by the institution or agency of which they are employees.

d. As members of governmental or other organizational bodies, psychologists remain accountable as individuals to the highest standards of their profession.

e. As teachers, psychologists recognize their primary obligation to help others acquire knowledge and skill. They maintain high standards of scholarship by presenting psychological information objectively, fully, and accurately.

f. As practitioners, psychologists know that they bear a heavy social responsibility because their recommendations and professional actions may alter the lives of others. They are alert to personal, social, organizational, financial, or political situations and pressures that might lead to misuse of their influence.

Principle 2: Competence

The maintenance of high standards of competence is a responsibility shared by all psychologists in the interest of the public and the profession as a whole. Psychologists recognize the boundaries of their competence and the limitations of their techniques. They only provide services and only use techniques for which they are qualified by training and experience. In those areas in which recognized standards do not yet exist, psychologists take whatever precautions are necessary to protect the welfare of their clients. They maintain knowledge of current scientific and professional information related to the services they render.

a. Psychologists accurately represent their competence, education, training, and experience. They claim as evidence of educational qualifications only those degrees obtained from institutions acceptable under the Bylaws and Rules of Council of the American Psychological Association.

b. As teachers, psychologists perform their duties on the basis of careful preparation so that their instruction is accurate, current, and scholarly.

c. Psychologists recognize the need for continuing education and are open to new procedures and changes in expectations and values over time.

d. Psychologists recognize differences among people, such as those that may be associated with age, sex, socioeconomic, and ethnic backgrounds. When necessary, they obtain training, experience, or counsel to assure competent service or research relating to such persons.

e. Psychologists responsible for decisions involving individuals or policies based on test results have an understanding of psychological or educational measurement, validation problems, and test research.

f. Psychologists recognize that personal problems and conflicts may interfere with professional effectiveness. Accordingly, they refrain from undertaking any activity in which their personal problems are likely to lead to inadequate performance or harm to a client, colleague, student, or research participant. If engaged in such activity when they become aware of their personal problems, they seek competent professional assistance to determine whether they should suspend, terminate, or limit the scope of their professional and/or scientific activities.

Principle 3: Moral and Legal Standards

Psychologists' moral and ethical standards of behavior are a personal matter to the same degree as they are for any other citizen, except as these may compromise the fulfillment of their professional responsibilities or reduce the public trust in psychology and psychologists. Regarding their own behavior, psychologists are sensitive to prevailing community standards and to the possible impact that conformity to or deviation from these standards may have upon the quality of their performance as psychologists. Psychologists are also aware of the possible impact of their public behavior upon the ability of colleagues to perform their professional duties.

a. As teachers, psychologists are aware of the fact that their personal values may affect the selection and presentation of instructional materials. When dealing with topics that may give offense, they recognize and respect the diverse attitudes that students may have toward such materials.

b. As employees or employers, psychologists do not engage in or condone practices that are inhumane or that result in illegal or unjustifiable actions. Such practices include, but are not limited to, those based on considerations of race, handicap, age, gender, sexual preference, religion, or national origin in hiring, promotion, or training.

c. In their professional roles, psychologists avoid any action that will violate or diminish the legal and civil rights of clients or of others who may be affected by their actions.

d. As practitioners and researchers, psychologists act in accord with Association standards and guidelines related to practice and to the conduct of research with human beings and animals. In the ordinary course of events, psychologists adhere to relevant governmental laws and institutional regulations. When federal, state, provincial, organizational, or institutional laws, regulations, or practices are in conflict with Association standards and guidelines, psychologists make known their commitment to Association standards and guidelines and, wherever possible, work toward a resolution of the conflict. Both practitioners and researchers are concerned with the development of such legal and quasi-legal regulations as best serve the public interest, and they work toward changing existing regulations that are not beneficial to the public interest.

Principle 4: Public Statements

Public statements, announcements of services, advertising, and promotional activities of psychologists serve the purpose of helping the public make informed judgments and choices. Psychologists represent accurately and objectively their professional qualifications, affiliations, and functions, as well as those of the institutions or organizations with which they or the statements may be associated. In public statements providing psychological information or professional opinions or providing information about the availability of psychological products, publications, and services, psychologists base their statements on scientifically acceptable psychological findings and techniques with full recognition of the limits and uncertainties of such evidence.

a. When announcing or advertising professional services, psychologists may list the following information to describe the provider and services provided: name, highest relevant academic degree earned from a regionally accredited institution, date, type, and level of certification or licensure, diplomate status, APA membership status, address, telephone number, office hours, a brief listing of the type of psychological services offered, an appropriate presentation of fee information, foreign languages spoken, and policy with regard to third-party payments. Additional relevant or important consumer information may be included if not prohibited by other sections of these Ethical Principles.

b. In announcing or advertising the availability of psychological products, publications, or services, psychologists do not present their affiliation with any organization in a manner that falsely implies sponsorship or certification by that organization. In particular and for example, psychologists do not state APA membership or fellow status in a way to suggest that such status implies specialized professional competence or qualifications. Public statements include, but are not limited to, communication by means of periodical, book, list, directory, television, radio, or motion picture. They do not contain (i) a false, fraudulent, misleading, deceptive, or unfair statement; (ii) a misinterpretation of fact or a statement likely to mislead or deceive because in context it makes only a partial disclosure of relevant facts; (iii) a testimonial from a patient regarding the quality of a psychologist's services or products; (iv) a statement intended or likely to create false or unjustified expectations of favorable results; (v) a statement implying unusual, unique, or one-of-a-kind abilities; (vi) a statement intended or likely to appeal to a client's fears, anxieties, or emotions concerning the possible results of failure to obtain the offered services; (vii) a statement concerning the comparative desirability of offered services; (viii) a statement of direct solicitation of individual clients.

c. Psychologists do not compensate or give anything of value to a representative of the press, radio, television, or other communication medium in anticipation of or in return for professional publicity in a news item. A paid advertisement must be identified as such, unless it is apparent from the context that it is a paid advertisement. If communicated to the public by use of radio or television, an advertisement is prerecorded and approved for broadcast by the psychologist, and a recording of the actual transmission is retained by the psychologist.

d. Announcements or advertisements of "personal growth groups," clinics, and agencies give a clear statement of purpose and a clear description of the experiences to be provided. The education, training, and experience of the staff members are appropriately specified.

e. Psychologists associated with the development or promotion of psychological devices, books, or other products offered for commercial sale make reasonable efforts to ensure that announcements and advertisements are presented in a professional, scientifically acceptable, and factually informative manner.

f. Psychologists do not participate for personal gain in commercial announcements or advertisements recommending to the public the purchase or use of proprietary or single-source products or services when that participation is based solely upon their identification as psychologists.

g. Psychologists present the science of psychology and offer their services, products, and publications fairly and accurately, avoiding misrepresentation through sensationalism, exaggeration, or superficiality. Psychologists are guided by the primary obligation to aid the public in developing informed judgments, opinions, and choices.

h. As teachers, psychologists ensure that statements in catalogs and course outlines are accurate and not misleading, particularly in terms of subject matter to be covered, bases for evaluating progress, and the nature of course experiences. Announcements, brochures, or advertisements describing workshops, seminars, or other educational programs accurately describe the audience for which the program is intended as well as eligibility requirements, educational objectives, and nature of the materials to be covered. These announcements also accurately represent the education, training, and experience of the psychologists presenting the programs and any fees involved.

i. Public announcements or advertisements soliciting research participants in which clinical services or other professional services are offered as an inducement make clear the nature of the services as well as the costs and other obligations to be accepted by participants in the research.

j. A psychologist accepts the obligation to correct others who represent the psychologist's professional qualifications, or associations with products or services, in a manner incompatible with these guidelines.

k. Individual diagnostic and therapeutic services are provided only in the context of a professional psychological relationship. When personal advice is given by means of public lectures or demonstrations, newspaper or magazine articles, radio or television programs, mail, or similar media, the psychologist utilizes the most current relevant data and exercises the highest level of professional judgment.

l. Products that are described or presented by means of public lectures or demonstrations, newspaper or magazine articles, radio or television programs, or similar media meet the same recognized standards as exist for products used in the context of a professional relationship.

Principle 5: Confidentiality

Psychologists have a primary obligation to respect the confidentiality of information obtained from persons in the course of their work as psychologists. They reveal such information to others only with the consent of the person or the person's legal representative, except in those unusual circumstances in which not to do so would result in clear danger to the person or to others. Where appropriate, psychologists inform their clients of the legal limits of confidentiality.

a. Information obtained in clinical or consulting relationships, or evaluative data concerning children, students, employees, and others, is discussed only for professional purposes and only with persons clearly concerned with the case. Written and oral reports present only data germane to the purposes of the evaluation, and every effort is made to avoid undue invasion of privacy.

b. Psychologists who present personal information obtained during the course of professional work in writings, lectures, or other public forums either obtain adequate prior consent to do so or adequately disguise all identifying information.

c. Psychologists make provisions for maintaining confidentiality in the storage and disposal of records.

d. When working with minors or other persons who are unable to give voluntary, informed consent, psychologists take special care to protect these persons' best interests.

Principle 6: Welfare of the Consumer

Psychologists respect the integrity and protect the welfare of the people and groups with whom they work. When conflicts of interest arise between clients and psychologists' employing institutions, psychologists clarify the nature and direction of their loyalties and responsibilities and keep all parties informed of their commitments. Psychologists fully inform consumers as to the purpose and nature of an evaluative, treatment, educational, or training procedure, and they freely acknowledge that clients, students, or participants in research have freedom of choice with regard to participation.

a. Psychologists are continually cognizant of their own needs and of their potentially influential position vis-à-vis persons such as clients, students, and subordinates. They avoid exploiting the trust and dependency of such persons. Psychologists make every effort to avoid dual relationships that could impair their professional judgment or increase the risk of exploitation. Examples of such dual relationships include, but are not limited to, research with and treatment of employees, students, supervisees, close friends, or relatives. Sexual intimacies with clients are unethical.

b. When a psychologist agrees to provide services to a client at the request of a third party, the psychologist assumes the responsibility of clarifying the nature of the relationships to all parties concerned.

c. Where the demands of an organization require psychologists to violate these Ethical Principles, psychologists clarify the nature of the conflict between the demands and these principles. They inform all parties of psychologists' ethical responsibilities and take appropriate action.

d. Psychologists make advance financial arrangements that safeguard the best interests of and are clearly understood by their clients. They neither give nor receive any remuneration for referring clients for professional services. They contribute a portion of their services to work for which they receive little or no financial return.

e. Psychologists terminate a clinical or consulting relationship when it is reasonably clear that the consumer is not benefiting from it. They offer to help the consumer locate alternative sources of assistance.

Principle 7: Professional Relationships

Psychologists act with due regard for the needs, special competencies, and obligations of their colleagues in psychology and other professions. They respect the prerogatives and obligations of the institutions or organizations with which these other colleagues are associated.

a. Psychologists understand the areas of competence of related professions. They make full use of all the professional, technical, and administrative resources that serve the best interests of consumers. The absence of formal relationships with other professional workers does not relieve psychologists of the responsibility of securing for their clients the best possible professional service, nor does it relieve them of the obligation to exercise foresight, diligence, and tact in obtaining the complementary or alternative assistance needed by clients.

b. Psychologists know and take into account the traditions and practices of other professional groups with whom they work and cooperate fully with such groups. If a person is receiving similar services from another professional, psychologists do not offer their own services directly to such a person. If a psychologist is contacted by a person who is already receiving similar services from another professional, the psychologist carefully considers that professional relationship and proceeds with caution and sensitivity to the therapeutic issues as well as the client's welfare. The psychologist discusses these issues with the client so as to minimize the risk of confusion and conflict.

c. Psychologists who employ or supervise other professionals or professionals in training accept the obligation to facilitate the further professional development of these individuals. They provide appropriate working conditions, timely evaluations, constructive consultation, and experience opportunities.

d. Psychologists do not exploit their professional relationships with clients, supervisees, students, employees, or research participants sexually or otherwise. Psychologists do not condone or engage in sexual harassment. Sexual harassment is defined as deliberate or repeated comments, gestures, or physical contacts of a sexual nature that are unwanted by the recipient.

e. In conducting research in institutions or organizations, psychologists secure appropriate authorization to conduct such research. They are aware of their obligations to future research workers and ensure that host institutions receive adequate information about the research and proper acknowledgment of their contributions.

f. Publication credit is assigned to those who have contributed to a publication in proportion to their professional contributions. Major contributions of a professional character made by several persons to a common project are recognized by joint authorship, with the individual who made the principal contribution listed first. Minor contributions of a professional character and extensive clerical or similar nonprofessional assistance may be acknowledged in footnotes or in an introductory statement. Acknowledgment through specific citations is made for unpublished as well as published material that has directly influenced the research or writing. Psychologists who compile and edit material of others for publication publish the material in the name of the originating group, if appropriate, with their own name appearing as chairperson or editor. All contributors are to be acknowledged and named.

g. When psychologists know of an ethical violation by another psychologist, and it seems appropriate, they informally attempt to resolve the issue by bringing the behavior to the attention of the psychologist. If the misconduct is of a minor nature and/or appears to be due to lack of sensitivity, knowledge, or experience, such an informal solution is usually appropriate. Such informal corrective efforts are made with sensitivity to any rights to confidentiality involved. If the violation does not seem amenable to an informal solution, or is of a more serious nature, psychologists bring it to the attention of the appropriate local, state, and/or national committee on professional ethics and conduct.

Principle 8: Assessment Techniques

In the development, publication, and utilization of psychological assessment techniques, psychologists make every effort to promote the welfare and best interests of the client. They guard against the misuse of assessment results. They respect the client's right to know the results, the interpretations made, and the bases for their conclusions and recommendations. Psychologists make every effort to maintain the security of tests and other assessment techniques within limits of legal mandates. They strive to ensure the appropriate use of assessment techniques by others.

a. In using assessment techniques, psychologists respect the right of clients to have full explanations of the nature and purpose of the techniques in language the clients can understand, unless an explicit exception to this right has been agreed upon in advance. When the explanations are to be provided by others, psychologists establish procedures for ensuring the adequacy of these explanations.

b. Psychologists responsible for the development and standardization of psychological tests and other assessment techniques utilize established scientific procedures and observe the relevant APA standards.

c. In reporting assessment results, psychologists indicate any reservations that exist regarding validity or reliability because of the circumstances of the assessment or the inappropriateness of the norms for the person tested. Psychologists strive to ensure that the results of assessments and their interpretations are not misused by others.

d. Psychologists recognize that assessment results may become obsolete. They make every effort to avoid and prevent the misuse of obsolete measures.

e. Psychologists offering scoring and interpretation services are able to produce appropriate evidence for the validity of the programs and procedures used in arriving at interpretations. The public offering of an automated interpretation service is considered a professional-to-professional consultation. Psychologists make every effort to avoid misuse of assessment reports.

f. Psychologists do not encourage or promote the use of psychological assessment techniques by inappropriately trained or otherwise unqualified persons through teaching, sponsorship, or supervision.

Principle 9: Research with Human Participants

The decision to undertake research rests upon a considered judgment by the individual psychologist about how best to contribute to psychological science and human welfare. Having made the decision to conduct research, the psychologist considers alternative directions in which research energies and resources might be invested. On the basis of this consideration, the psychologist carries out the investigation with respect and concern for the dignity and welfare of the people who participate and with cognizance of federal and state regulations and professional standards governing the conduct of research with human participants.

a. In planning a study, the investigator has the responsibility to make a careful evaluation of its ethical acceptability. To the extent that the weighing of scientific and human values suggests a compromise of any principle, the investigator incurs a correspondingly serious obligation to seek ethical advice and to observe stringent safeguards to protect the rights of human participants.

b. Considering whether a participant in a planned study will be a "subject at risk" or a "subject at minimal risk," according to recognized standards, is of primary ethical concern to the investigator.

c. The investigator always retains the responsibility for ensuring ethical practice in research. The investigator is also responsible for the ethical treatment of research participants by collaborators, assistants, students, and employees, all of whom, however, incur similar obligations.

d. Except in minimal-risk research, the investigator establishes a clear and fair agreement with research participants, prior to their participation, that clarifies the obligations and responsibilities of each. The investigator has the obligation to honor all promises and commitments included in that agreement. The investigator informs the participants of all aspects of the research that might reasonably be expected to influence willingness to participate and explains all other aspects of the research about which the participants inquire. Failure to make full disclosure prior to obtaining informed consent requires additional safeguards to protect the welfare and dignity of the research participants. Research with children or with participants who have impairments that would limit understanding and/or communication requires special safeguarding procedures.

e. Methodological requirements of a study may make the use of concealment or deception necessary. Before conducting such a study, the investigator has a special responsibility to (i) determine whether the use of such techniques is justified by the study's prospective scientific, educational, or applied value; (ii) determine whether alternative procedures are available that do not use concealment or deception; and (iii) ensure that the participants are provided with sufficient explanation as soon as possible.

f. The investigator respects the individual's freedom to decline to participate in or to withdraw from the research at any time. The obligation to protect this freedom requires careful thought and consideration when the investigator is in a position of authority or influence over the participant. Such positions of authority include, but are not limited to, situations in which research participation is required as part of employment or in which the participant is a student, client, or employee of the investigator.

g. The investigator protects the participant from physical and mental discomfort, harm, and danger that may arise from research procedures. If risks of such consequences exist, the investigator informs the participant of that fact. Research procedures likely to cause serious or lasting harm to a participant are not used unless the failure to use the procedures might expose the participant to risk of greater harm, or unless the research has great potential benefit and fully informed and voluntary consent is obtained from each participant. The participant should be informed of procedures for contacting the investigator within a reasonable time period following participation should stress, potential harm, or related questions or concerns arise.

h. After the data are collected, the investigator provides the participant with information about the nature of the study and attempts to remove any misconceptions that may have arisen. When scientific or humane values justify delaying or withholding this information, the investigator incurs a special responsibility to monitor the research and to ensure that there are no damaging consequences for the participant.

i. Where research procedures result in undesirable consequences for the individual participant, the investigator has the responsibility to detect and remove or correct these consequences, including long-term effects.

j. Information obtained about a research participant during the course of an investigation is confidential unless otherwise agreed upon in advance. When the possibility exists that others may obtain access to such information, this possibility, together with the plans for protecting confidentiality, is explained to the participant as part of the procedure for obtaining informed consent.

Principle 10: Care and Use of Animals

An investigator of animal behavior strives to advance understanding of basic behavioral principles and/or to contribute to the improvement of human health and welfare. In seeking these ends, the investigator ensures the welfare of animals and treats them humanely. Laws and regulations notwithstanding, an animal's immediate protection depends upon the scientist's own conscience.

a. The acquisition, care, use, and disposal of all animals are in compliance with current federal, state or provincial, and local laws and regulations.

b. A psychologist trained in research methods and experienced in the care of laboratory animals closely supervises all procedures involving animals and is responsible for ensuring appropriate consideration of their comfort, health, and humane treatment.

c. Psychologists ensure that all individuals using animals under their supervision have received explicit instruction in experimental methods and in the care, maintenance, and handling of the species being used. Responsibilities and activities of individuals participating in a research project are consistent with their respective competencies.

d. Psychologists make every effort to minimize discomfort, illness, and pain of animals. A procedure subjecting animals to pain, stress, or privation is used only when an alternative procedure is unavailable and the goal is justified by its prospective scientific, educational, or applied value. Surgical procedures are performed under appropriate anesthesia; techniques to avoid infection and minimize pain are followed during and after surgery.

e. When it is appropriate that the animal's life be terminated, it is done rapidly and painlessly.

References

Adler, A. (1929). *The practice and theory of individual psychology* (2nd ed.) (P. Radin, Trans.). New York: Humanities Press.

Adler, A. (1958). *What life should mean to you.* New York: Putnam.

Alexander, F. G., & Selesnick, S. T. (1966). *The history of psychiatry.* New York: Mentor.

Alibrandi, T. (1978). *Young alcoholics.* Minneapolis: CompCare Publications.

Allen, W. (1976). *Without feathers.* New York: Warner.

Amatea, E., & Fabrick, F. (1981). Family systems counseling: A positive alternative to traditional counseling. *Elementary School Guidance and Counseling, 15,* 223–236.

American Association for Counseling and Development. (1981). *Ethical standards.* Falls Church, Va.: AACD.

American Psychiatric Association. (1980). *Diagnostic and statistical manual of mental disorders* (3rd ed.). Washington, D.C.: A.P.A.

American Psychological Association. (1981). Ethical principles of psychologists. *American Psychologist, 36,* 633–638.

Anastasi, A. (1982). *Psychological testing* (5th ed.). New York: Macmillan.

Anderson, P. (1981, November). Substance abuse and the disabled. *Paraplegia News,* p. 8.

Argyris, C. (1974). *Theory in practice: Increasing professional effectiveness.* San Francisco: Jossey-Bass.

Armor, D. J., Polick, M. J., & Stambul, H. B. (1978). *Alcoholism and treatment,* New York: Wiley.

Association for Specialists in Group Work. (1982). Ethical guidelines for group leaders. *Journal for Specialists in Group Work, 7*(3), 174–181.

Atkinson, D. R., & Carskadden, G. (1975). A prestigious introduction, psychological jargon, and perceived counselor credibility. *Journal of Counseling Psychology, 22,* 180–186.

Avila, D. L., Combs, A. W., & Purkey, W. W. (Eds.) (1977). *The helping relationship sourcebook* (2nd ed.). Boston: Allyn & Bacon.

Baird, J. E., Jr., & Weinberg, S. B. (1981). *Group communication* (2nd ed.). Dubuque, Iowa: William C. Brown.

Bandler, R., & Grinder, J. (1975). *The structure of magic* (Vol. 1). Palo Alto: Science and Behavior Books.

Bandler, R., & Grinder, J. (1979). *Frogs into princes.* Moab, Utah: Real People Press.

Bandura, A. (1969). *Principles of behavior modification.* New York: Holt, Rinehart & Winston.

Bandura, A. (1971). Psychotherapy based upon modeling principles. In A. E. Bergin & S. L. Garfield (Eds.), *Handbook of psychotherapy and behavior change* (pp. 653–708). New York: Wiley.

Bandura, A. (1977). *Social learning theory.* Englewood Cliffs, N.J.: Prentice-Hall.

Bandura, A., Blanchare, E. B., & Ritter, R. (1969). The relative efficacy of desensitization and modeling approaches for inducing behavioral, affective, and attitudinal changes. *Journal of Personality and Social Psychology, 13,* 173–199.

Barkley, W. M. (1982). Introducing research to graduate students in the helping professions. *Counselor Education and Supervision, 21*(4), 327–331.

Bateson, G. (1972). *Steps to an ecology of the mind.* New York: Ballantine.

Bateson, G. (1979). *Mind and nature.* New York: Bantam Books.

Bateson, G., Jackson, D. D., Haley, J., & Weakland, J. (1956). Toward a theory of schizophrenia. *Behavioral Science, 1,* 251–264.

Bauer, G. P., & Kobos, J. C. (1984). Short-term psychodynamic psychotherapy: Reflections on the past and current practice. *Psychotherapy: Theory, Research, and Practice, 21*(2), 153–170.

Beck, A. T. (1976). *Cognitive therapy and the emotional disorders.* New York: International Universities Press.

Belkin, G. (1980). *Contemporary psychotherapies.* Chicago: Rand McNally.

Belkin, G. (1981). *Practical counseling in the schools* (2nd ed.). Dubuque, Iowa: William C. Brown.

Benn, D. J. (1970). *Beliefs, attitudes, and human affairs.* Monterey, Calif.: Brooks/Cole.

Bennett, M. J. (1984). Brief psychotherapy and adult development. *Psychotherapy: Theory, Research, and Practice, 21*(2), 171–177.

Berger, M. (1982). Ethics and the therapeutic relationship. In M. Rosenbaum (Ed.), *Ethics and values in psychotherapy,* (pp. 67–95). New York: Free Press.

Bergin, A. E. (1971). The evaluation of therapeutic outcomes. In A. E. Bergin & S. L. Garfield (Eds.), *Handbook of psychotherapy and behavior change.* New York: Wiley.

Bergin, A. E., & Garfield, S. L. (Eds.). (1971). *Handbook of psychotherapy and behavior change.* New York: Wiley.

Berne, E. (1961). *Transactional analysis in psychotherapy.* New York: Grove Press.

Berne, E. (1964). *Games people play.* New York: Grove Press.

Berne, E. (1972). *What do you say after you say hello?* New York: Grove Press.

Biddle, B. J., Bank, B. J., & Marlin, M. M. (1980, March). Social determinants of adolescent drinking: What they think, what they do and what I think and do. *Journal Studies on Alcohol, 41*(3), 215–241.

Biggs, D., & Keller, K. (1982). A cognitive approach to using tests in counseling. *Personnel and Guidance Journal, 60,* 528–532.

Blocher, D. H. (1966). *Developmental counseling.* New York: Ronald Press.

Blocher, D. H., & Siegal, R. (1981). Toward a cognitive developmental theory of leisure and work. *The Counseling Psychologist, 9*(3), 33–44.

Boorstein, D. (1983). *The discoverers.* New York: Random House.

Bordin, E. S. (1968). *Psychological counseling.* New York: Appleton-Century-Crofts.

Boy, A. V., & Pine, G. J. (1982). *Client-centered counseling: A renewal.* Boston: Allyn & Bacon.

Boy, A. V., & Pine, G. J. (1982). The effectiveness of a counseling theory. *Michigan Personnel and Guidance Journal, 4,* 39–42.

Boy, A. V., & Pine, G. J. (1983). Counseling: Fundamentals of theoretical renewal. *Counseling and Values, 27,* 248–255.

Brammer, L. M., & Shostrum, E. L. (1977). *Therapeutic psychology: Fundamentals of counseling and psychotherapy* (3rd ed.). Englewood Cliffs, N.J.: Prentice-Hall.

Brammer, L. M., & Shostrum, E. L. (1982). *Therapeutic psychology: Fundamentals of counseling and psychotherapy.* Englewood Cliffs, N.J.: Prentice-Hall.

Brilhart, J., & Jochem, L. (1964). Effects of different patterns on outcomes of problem-solving discussions. *Journal of Applied Psychology, 48,* 175–179.

Brown, R. W. (1978). Choosing and evaluating group techniques: A systematic framework. *Journal for Specialists in Group Work, 3,* 146–153.

Brown, R. W., & Kottler, J. A. (1979). Increasing client employability through skill development. *Journal of Employment Counseling, 16,* 164–171.

Burks, H. M., Jr., & Stefflre, B. (1979). *Theories of counseling* (3rd ed.). McGraw-Hill.

Burnett, M. (1979). Understanding and overcoming addictions. In S. Eisenberg & L. E. Patterson (Eds.), *Helping clients with special concerns* (pp. 343–362). Chicago: Rand McNally.

Buros, O. (Ed.). (1978). *Mental measurements yearbook* (8th ed.). Lincoln: University of Nebraska Press.

Butler, R. N., & Lewis, M. I. (1973). *Aging and mental health.* St. Louis: C.V. Mosby.

Caplow, T. (1954). *The sociology of work.* Minneapolis: University of Minnesota Press.

Capuzzi, D., & Lecoq, L. L. (1983, December). Social and personal determinants of adolescent use and abuse of alcohol and marijuana. *Personnel and Guidance Journal,* 199–205.

Carkhuff, R. R. (1969). *Helping and human relations* (Vols. 1–2). New York: Holt, Rinehart & Winston.

Carkhuff, R. R. (1971). Training as a preferred mode of treatment. *Journal of Counseling Psychology, 18,* 123–131.

Carkhuff, R. R., & Anthony, W. A. (1979). *The skills of helping: An introduction to counseling.* Amherst, Mass.: Human Resources Development Press.

Carkhuff, R. R., & Berenson, B. G. (1967). *Beyond counseling and therapy.* New York: Holt, Rinehart & Winston.

Carkhuff, R. R., & Berenson, B. G. (1977). *Beyond counseling and therapy* (2nd ed.). New York: Holt, Rinehart & Winston.

Carter, J. A. (1978). Impressions of counselors as a function of counselor physical attractiveness. *Journal of Counseling Psychology, 25,* 28–34.

Cash, T. F., Begley, P. J., McCown, D. A., & Weise, B. C. (1975). When counselors are heard but not seen: Initial impact of physical attractiveness. *Journal of Counseling Psychology, 22,* 273–279.

Castaneda, C. (1971). *A separate reality.* New York: Pocket Books.

Cherniss, C. (1980). *Staff burnout: Job stress in the human services.* Beverly Hills, Calif.: Sage Publications.

Choate, O., & Epstein, N. (1982, May 9). Workers in the future retool: Nothing to lose but your jobs. *Washington Post.*

Cianni-Surridge, M. (1983). Technology and work: Future issues for career guidance. *Personnel and Guidance Journal, 61,* 413–416.

Claiborn, C. D. (1979). Counselor verbal intervention, non-verbal behavior, and social power. *Journal of Counseling Psychology, 26,* 378–383.

Claiborn, C. D., & Schmidt, L. D. (1977). Effects of presession information on the perception of the counselor in the interview. *Journal of Counseling Psychology, 24,* 259–263.

Coleman, S. (1979, July). People who read people. *Psychology Today,* pp. 66–78.

Combs, A. W., Avila, D. L., & Purkey, W. W. (1971). *Helping relationships: Basic concepts for the helping professions.* Boston: Allyn & Bacon.

Conroy, P. (1982). *The lords of discipline.* New York: Bantam Books.

Corazzini, J. G., & Anderson, S. M. (1980). An apprentice model for training group leaders: Revitalizing group treatment. *Journal for Specialists in Group Work, 5,* 29–35.

Corey, G. (1982). *Theory and practice of counseling and psychotherapy.* Monterey, Calif.: Brooks/Cole.

Corey, G., & Corey, M. S. (1977). *Groups: Process and practice.* Monterey, Calif.: Brooks/Cole.

Corey, G., & Corey, M. S. (1982). *Groups: Process and practice* (2nd ed.). Monterey, Calif.: Brooks/Cole.

Cormier, W. H., & Cormier, L. S. (1979). *Interviewing strategies for helpers: A guide to assessment, treatment, and evaluation.* Monterey, Calif.: Brooks/Cole.

Cornacchia, H. J., Smith, D. E., & Bentel, D. J. (1978). *Drugs in the classroom.* St. Louis: C.V. Mosby.

Cronbach, L. (1970). *Essentials of psychological testing* (3rd ed.). New York: Harper & Row.

Dasberg, H., & Winoker, M. (1984). Teaching and learning short-term dynamic psychotherapy: Parallel processes. *Psychotherapy: Theory, Research, and Practice, 21*(2), 184–188.

Davanloo, H. (1978). *Basic principles and techniques in short-term dynamic psychotherapy.* New York: Spectrum.

Dimond, R. E., Havens, R. A., & Jones, A. C. (1978). A conceptual framework for the practice of prescriptive eclecticism in psychotherapy. *American Psychologist, 33,* 239–248.

Doherty, M. A. (1978). Sexual bias in personality theory. In L. Harmon, J. M. Birk, L. E. Fitzgerald, & M. F. Tanney (Eds.), *Counseling Women* (pp. 94–105). Monterey, Calif.: Brooks/Cole.

Dollard, J., & Miller, N. (1950). *Personality and psychotherapy.* New York: McGraw-Hill.

Drane, J. F. (1982). Ethics and psychotherapy: A philosophical perspective. In M. Rosenbaum (Ed.), *Ethics and values in psychotherapy* (pp. 15–50). New York: Free Press.

Dreikurs, R. (1950). *Fundamentals of Adlerian psychology.* Chicago: Alfred Adler Institute.

Dye, A. (1980). Thoughts on training. *Journal for Specialists in Group Work, 5,* 5–7.

Dyer, W. W., & Vriend, J. (1974). Vital components in conducting the initial interview. *Educational Technology, 14,* 24–32.

Dyer, W. W., & Vriend, J. (1977). *Counseling techniques that work.* New York: Funk & Wagnalls.

Dyer, W. W., & Vriend, J. (1980). *Group counseling for personal mastery.* New York: Sovereign.

Eber, M., & O'Brien, J. M. (1982). Psychotherapy in the movies. *Psychotherapy: Theory, Research, and Practice, 19*(1), 116–120.

Edgerton, R. B., & Karno, M. (1971). Mexican-American bilingualism and the perception of mental illness. *Archives of General Psychiatry, 24,* 286–290.

Edwards, R. B. (1982). Mental health as rational autonomy. In R. B. Edwards (Ed.), *Psychiatry and ethics* (pp. 68–78). Buffalo: Prometheus Books.

Egan, G. (1975). *Exercises in helping skills.* Monterey, Calif.: Brooks/Cole.

Egan, G. (1982). *The skilled helper: A model for systematic helping and interpersonal relating* (2nd ed.). Monterey, Calif.: Brooks/Cole.

Eisdorfer, C. (1983). Conceptual models of aging. *American Psychologist, 38,* 197–202.

Eldridge, W. D. (1982). A perspective on the similarities among selected concepts of traditional scientific research and clinical counseling. *Journal of Clinical Psychology, 38*(2), 452–460.

Ellis, A. (1962). *Reason and emotion in psychotherapy.* New York: Lyle Stuart.

Ellis, A. (1973). *Humanistic psychotherapy.* New York: Julian Press.

Ellis, A. (1977). The basic clinical theory of rational-emotive therapy. In A. Ellis & R. Grieger (Eds.), *Handbook of rational emotive therapy.* New York: Springer.

Ellis, A. (1977). Rational-emotive therapy: Research data that supports the clinical and personality hypothesis of RET and other modes of cognitive behavior therapy. *Journal of Counseling Psychology, 7,* 5–42.

Ellis, A., & Grieger, R. (Eds.). (1977). *Handbook of rational emotive therapy.* New York: Springer.

Ellis, A., & Harper, R. (1975). *A new guide to rational living.* Hollywood: Wilshire Books.

Ellis, A., & Whitely, J. M. (Eds.). (1979). *Theoretical and empirical foundations of rational-emotive therapy.* Monterey, Calif.: Brooks/Cole.

Erikson, E. (1950). *Childhood and society.* New York: Norton.

Eysenck, H. (1952). The effects of psychotherapy: An evaluation. *Journal of Consulting Psychology, 16,* 319–324.

Farber, B. A. (1983). The effects of psychotherapeutic practice upon psychotherapists. *Psychotherapy: Theory, Research, and Practice, 20* (2), 174–182.

Festinger, L. (1957). *A Theory of Cognitive Dissonance.* Stanford, Calif.: Stanford University Press.

Festinger, L. (1964). Behavioral support for opinion change. *Public Opinion Quarterly, 28,* 404–417.

Fiedler, F. E. (1950). A comparison of therapeutic relationships in psychoanalytic, nondirective, and Adlerian therapy. *Journal of Consulting Psychology, 14,* 436–445.

Fisch, R., Weakland, J. H., & Segal, L. (1982). *The tactics of change.* San Francisco: Jossey-Bass.

Fish, J. (1973). *Placebo therapy.* San Francisco: Jossey-Bass.

Fish, W. C. (1981). The intrinsic connection between ethics and psychotherapy. *Counseling and Values, 25,* 269–278.

Flaherty, J. A., & Meagher, R. (1980). Measuring racial bias on impatient treatment. *American Journal of Psychiatry, 137,* 679–682.

Framo, J. L. (1981). Family theory and therapy. *Elementary School Guidance and Counseling, 15,* 205–213.

Frank, P. (1949). *Modern science and its philosophy.* Cambridge, Mass.: Harvard University Press.

Frankl, V. (1962). *Man's search for meaning.* Boston: Beacon Press.

Frankl, V. (1978). *The unheard cry for meaning.* New York: Simon & Schuster.

Fraser, J. S. (1982). Structural and strategic family therapy: A basis for marriage, or grounds for divorce. *Journal of Marital and Family Therapy, 8*(2), 13–22.

Fretz, B. R. (1981). Evaluating the effectiveness of career intervention. *Journal of Counseling Psychology, 28,* 77–90.

Fretz, B. R., Corn, R., Tuemmler, J. M., & Bellet, W. (1979). Counselor nonverbal behaviors and client evaluations. *Journal of Counseling Psychology, 26,* 304–311.

Fretz, B. R., & Mills, D. H. (1980). *Licensing and certification of psychologists and counselors.* San Francisco: Jossey-Bass.

Freud, S. (1924). *A general introduction to psychoanalysis.* New York: Washington Square Press.

Freud, S. (1954). *The origins of psycho-analysis.* New York: Basic Books.

Freudenberger, H. J. (1974). Staff burnout. *Journal of Social Issues, 30,* 159–165.

Freudenberger, H. J. (1983). Hazards of psychotherapeutic practice. *Psychotherapy in Private Practice, 1,* 83–89.

Fromm-Reichmann, F. (1952). Some aspects of psychoanalysis and schizophrenics. In F. C. Redlich & E. R. Brody (Eds.), *Psychotherapy with schizophrenics.* New York: International Universities Press.

Fuhrmann, B. S., & Washington, C. S. (1984). Substance abuse: An overview. *Journal for Specialists in Group Work, 9*(1), 2–6.

Fuqua, D. R., & Hartman, B. W. (1983). Differential diagnosis and treatment of career indecision. *Personnel and Guidance Journal, 62,* 27–30.

Galvin, M., & Ivey, A. E. (1981). Researching one's own interviewing style: Does your theory of choice match your actual practice? *Personnel and Guidance Journal, 59,* 536–541.

Geis, H. J. (1973). Effectively leading a group in the present moment. *Educational Technology, 13*(1), 76–88.

Gelman, D. (1984). The switch is on. *Newsweek,* May 28, 1984, 93–95.

Gendlin, E. T. (1973). *Experiential psychotherapy.* In R. Corsini (Ed.), *Current Psychotherapies.* Itasca, Ill.: F.E. Peacock.

Gill, S. J., & Barry, R. A. (1982). Group-focused counseling: Classifying the essential skills. *Personnel and Guidance Journal, 60,* 302–305.

Ginzberg, E. (1972). Toward a theory of occupational choice: A restatement. *Vocational Guidance Quarterly, 20,* 169–176.

Glasser, W. (1965). *Reality therapy.* New York: Harper & Row.

Glasser, W. (1976). *Positive addition.* New York: Harper & Row.

Goldberg, C. (1977). *Therapeutic partnership: Ethical concerns in psychotherapy.* New York: Springer.

Goldman, L. (1972). Tests and counseling: The marriage that failed. *Measurement and Evaluation in Guidance, 4,* 213–220.

Goldstein, A. P. (1972). Drug education worthy of the name. *Impact, 1*(4), 18–24.

Goldstein, A. P. (1980). Relationship-enhancement methods. In F. H. Kanfer & A. P. Goldstein, (Eds.), *Helping people change.* New York: Pergamon Press.

Gordon, T. G. (1970). *Parent effectiveness training.* New York: Peter Wyden Publishing.

Gordon, T. G. (1974). *Teacher effectiveness training.* New York: Peter Wyden Publishing.

Gottman, J. M., & Leiblum, S. R. (1974). *How to do psychotherapy and how to evaluate it.* New York: Holt, Rinehart & Winston.

Greenspan, S. I., & Wieder, S. (1984). Dimensions and levels of the therapeutic process. *Psychotherapy: Theory, Research, and Practice, 21*(1), 5–23.

Groden, G., & Cautela, J. R. (1981). Behavior therapy: A survey of procedures for counselors. *Personnel and Guidance Journal, 60,* 175–180.

Haber, R. A. (1983). The family dance around drug abuse. *Personnel and Guidance Journal, 61,* 428–431.

Haley, J. (1969). The art of being a failure as a therapist. *American Journal of Orthopsychiatry, 39*(1), 691–695.

Haley, J. (Ed.). (1971). *Changing families.* New York: Grune & Stratton.

Haley, J. (1973). *Uncommon therapy.* New York: Norton.

Haley, J. (1976). *Problem solving therapy.* New York: Harper & Row.

Haley, J. (1980). How to be a marriage therapist without knowing practically anything. *Journal of Marital and Family Counseling, 6*(4), 385–392.

Haley, J. (1984). *Ordeal therapy: Unusual ways to change behavior.* San Francisco: Jossey-Bass.

Hall, C. (1954). *A primer of Freudian psychology.* New York: New American Library.

Hall, E. (1983, June). A conversation with Erik Erikson. *Psychology Today,* pp. 22–30.

Hall, E. T. (1976). *Beyond culture.* New York: Anchor Press.

Hall, G. C. N., & Maloney, H. N. (1983). Cultural control in psychotherapy with minority clients. *Psychotherapy: Theory, Research, and Practice, 20*(2), 131–142.

Hammond, R. I. (1981). *Almost all you wanted to know about alcoholism but didn't know to ask* (Rev. ed.). Lansing, Mich.: Michigan Clearinghouse for Substance Abuse Information.

Hansen, J. C., Stevic, R. R., & Warner, R. W., Jr. (1982). *Counseling: Theory and process* (3rd ed.). Boston: Allyn & Bacon.

Hare-Mustin, R. (1983). An appraisal of the relationship between women and psychotherapy. *American Psychologist, 38,* 593–601.

Harris, T. A. (1969). *I'm OK, You're OK.* New York: Avon.

Harvill, R., Masson, R. L., & Jacobs, E. (1983). Systematic group leader training: A skills development approach. *Journal for Specialists in Group Work, 8,* 226–232.

Hazler, R. J., & Roberts, G. (1984). Decision making in vocational theory: Evolution and implications. *Personnel and Guidance Journal, 62,* 408–410.

Held, B. S. (1984). Toward a strategic eclecticism. *Psychotherapy: Theory, Research, and Practice, 21*(2), 232–241.

Hepner, R., Kershbaum, H., & Landes, D. (1980). Counseling substance abusers with additional disabilities: The Center for Independent Living. *Alcohol Health and Research World, 5*(2), 11–15.

Heppner, P. P., & Dixon, D. N. (1981). A review of the interpersonal influence process in counseling. *Personnel and Guidance Journal, 59,* 542–550.

Herr, E., & Watts, A. (1981). The implications of youth employment for career education and for counseling. *Journal of Career Education, 7,* 184–202.

Herron, W. G., & Rouslin, S. (1984). *Issues in psychotherapy.* Washington, D.C.: Oryn.

Hindman, M., & Widem, P. (1980). The multidisabled: Emerging responses. *Alcohol Health and Research World, 5*(2), 11–15.

Ho, M. K., & Shipley, A. (1974). The culturally different counselor. *Elementary School Guidance and Counseling, 8,* 286–289.

Hoffman-Graff, M. A. (1977). Interviewer use of positive and negative self-disclosure and interviewer–subject sex pairing. *Journal of Counseling Psychology, 24,* 184–190.

Holland, J. (1966). *The psychology of vocational choice.* Waltham, Mass.: Blaisdell.

Holland, J. (1972). *Self-directed search: Professional manual.* Palo Alto, Calif.: Consulting Psychologists Press.

Holland, J. (1973). *Making vocational choices: A theory of careers.* Englewood Cliffs, N.J.: Prentice-Hall.

Hoppock, R. (1976). *Occupational information* (4th ed.). New York: McGraw-Hill.

Horan, J. (1979). *Counseling for effective decision making.* North Scituate, Mass.: Duxbury Press.

Horney, K. (1950). *Neurosis and human growth.* New York: Norton.

Hosford, R. E. (1969). Behavioral counseling: A contemporary overview. *Counseling Psychologist, 1,* 1–33.

Hoyt, K., Evans, R., Mackin, E., & Mangum, G. (1972). *Career education: What it is and how to do it.* Salt Lake City: Olympus.

Hussian, R. A. (1981). *Geriatric psychology: A behavioral perspective.* New York: Van Nostrand Reinhold.

Huxley, A. (1962). *Island.* New York: Harper & Row.

Isaacson, L. E. (1977). *Career information in counseling and teaching* (2nd ed.). Boston: Allyn & Bacon.

Ivey, A. (1971) *Microcounseling: Innovations in interviewing training.* Springfield, Ill.: Charles C Thomas.

Ivey, A. (1983). *Intentional interviewing and counseling.* Monterey, Calif.: Brooks/Cole.

Ivey, A., & Authier, J. (1978). *Micro-counseling* (2nd ed.). Springfield, Ill.: Charles C Thomas.

Ivey, A., & Simek-Downing, L. (1980). *Counseling and psychotherapy: Skills, theories, and practice.* Englewood Cliffs, N.J.: Prentice-Hall.

James, M., & Jongeward, D. (1971). *Born to win: Transactional analysis with gestalt experiments.* Reading, Mass.: Addison-Wesley.

James, W. (1907). *Pragmatism.* New York: New American Library.

Jones, W. T., Sontag, F., Becker, M. O., & Fogelin, R. J. (1969). *Approaches to ethics.* New York: McGraw-Hill.

Kagan, N. (1973). Can technology help us toward reliability in influencing human interaction? In J. Vriend & W. Dyer (Eds.), *Counseling effectively in groups*. Englewood Cliffs, N.J.: Educational Technology Publications.

Kaiser, H. (1965). *Effective psychotherapy: The contribution of Hellmuth Kaiser*, L. Fierman (Ed.). New York: Free Press.

Kanfer, F. H., & Goldstein, A. P. (1980). *Helping people change* (2nd ed.). New York: Pergamon Press.

Kanfer, F. H., & Phillips, J. S. (1970). *Learning foundations of behavior therapy*. New York: Wiley.

Kaplan, H. S. (1974). *The new sex therapy*. New York: Brunner/Mazel.

Kaplan, M. (1983). A woman's view of DSM III. *American Psychologist, 38*(7), 786–792.

Kass, F., Spitzer, R. L., & Williams, J. B. W. (1983). An empirical study of the issue of sex bias in the diagnostic criteria of DSM III—Axis II personality disorders. *American Psychologist, 38,* 799–801.

Katkin, E. S., & Goldband, S. (1980). Biofeedback. In F. H. Kanfer and A. P. Goldstein (Eds.), *Helping people change* (pp. 537–578). New York: Pergamon Press.

Kaul, T. J., & Schmidt, L. D. (1971). Dimensions of interviewer trustworthiness. *Journal of Counseling Psychology, 18,* 542–548.

Keith-Spiegel, P. (1977, August). Violation of ethical principles due to ignorance or poor professional judgment versus willful disregard. *Professional Psychology,* 288–296.

Kempler, W. (1973) Gestalt therapy. In R. Corsini (Ed.), *Current psychotherapies*. Itasca, Ill.: F.E. Peacock.

Koffka, K. (1935). *Principles of Gestalt psychology*. New York: Harcourt Brace & World.

Kohlberg, L. (1969). *Stages in the development of moral thought and action*. New York: Holt, Rinehart & Winston.

Kohler, W. (1929). *Gestalt psychology*. New York: Liveright.

Konner, M. (1982). *The tangled wing: Biological constraints on the human spirit*. New York: Harper & Row.

Kottler, J. A. (1983). *Pragmatic group leadership*. Monterey, Calif.: Brooks/Cole.

Kovacs, A. L. (1982). Survival in the 1980s on the theory and practice of brief psychotherapy. *Psychotherapy: Theory, Research, and Practice, 19*(2), 142–159.

Krumboltz, J. D. (1965). Behavioral counseling: Rationale and research. *Personnel and Guidance Journal, 44,* 373–387.

Krumboltz, J. D. (Ed.). (1966). *Revolution in counseling: Implications of behavioral science*. Boston: Houghton Mifflin.

Krumboltz, J. D. (1978). A social learning theory of career selection. In J. M. Whiteley & A. Resnikoff (Eds.), *Career counseling*. Monterey, Calif.: Brooks/Cole.

LaCrosse, M. B. (1975). Nonverbal behavior and perceived counselor attractiveness and persuasiveness. *Journal of Counseling Psychology, 22,* 563–566.

Lambert, M. J., Christensen, E. R., & DeJulio, S. S. (1984). *The assessment of psychotherapy outcome*. New York: Wiley.

Lazarus, A. A. (1981). *The practice of multi-modal therapy*. New York: McGraw-Hill.

Levinson, D. J. (1978). *The seasons of a man's life*. New York: Ballantine.

Levitt, E. E. (1957). The results of psychotherapy with children: An evaluation. *Journal of Consulting Psychology, 21,* 189–196.

Lieberman, M., Yalom, I., & Miles, M. (1973). *Encounter groups: First facts*. New York: Basic Books.

Loevinger, J. (1976). *Ego development*. San Francisco: Jossey-Bass.

Lowenthal, A., & Anderson, P. (1980). Network development: Linking the disabled community to alcoholism and drug abuse programs. *Alcohol Health and Research World, 5*(2), 16–19.

Madanes, C. (1983). *Strategic family therapy*. San Francisco: Jossey-Bass.

Madanes, C. (1984). *Beyond the one way mirror*. San Francisco: Jossey-Bass.

Maher, E. L. (1983). Burnout and commitment: A theoretical alternative. *Personnel and Guidance Journal, 61,* 390–393.

Mahoney, J. J. (1974). *Cognition and behavior therapy*. Cambridge, Mass.: Ballinger.

Malan, D. (1963). *A study of brief psychotherapy*. New York: Plenum.

Marks, S. R. (1977). Multiple roles and role strain: Some notes on human energy, time, and commitment. *American Sociological Review, 42,* 921–936.

Maslow, A. (1954). *Motivation and personality.* New York: Harper & Row.

Maultsby, M. C. (1975). *Help yourself to happiness.* New York: Institute for Rational Emotive Therapy.

May, R. (1958). *Existence.* New York: Simon & Schuster.

May, R. (1967). *The art of counseling.* Nashville: Abingdon Press.

May, R. (1981). *Freedom and destiny.* New York: Norton.

May, R. (1983). *The discovery of being.* New York: Norton.

McDowell, D. F. (1981). Leisure: Consciousness, well-being, and counseling. *The Counseling Psychologist, 9*(3), 3–31.

Meador, B. D., & Rogers, C. R. (1973). *Client centered therapy.* In R. Corsini (Ed.), *Current psychotherapies.* Itasca, Ill.: F.E. Peacock.

Meadow, A., Parnes, S., & Reese, J. (1959). Influence of brainstorming instructions and problem sequence on creative problem solving. *Journal of Applied Psychology, 43,* 413–436.

Mehrabian, A. (1970). *Tactics of social influence.* Englewood Cliffs, N.J.: Prentice-Hall.

Meichenbaum, D. H. (1974). *Cognitive behavior modification.* Morristown, N.J.: General Learning Press.

Meichenbaum, D. H. (1977). *Cognitive-behavior modification: An integrative approach.* New York: Plenum.

Merluzzi, T. V., Banikiotes, P. G., & Missbach, J. W. (1978). Perceptions of counselor sex, experience, and disclosure level. *Journal of Counseling Psychology, 25,* 479–482.

Milby, J. B. (1981). *Addictive behavior and its treatment.* New York: Springer.

Miller, G. M. (1982). Deriving meaning from standardized tests: Interpreting results to clients. *Measurement and Evaluation in Guidance, 15,* 87–94.

Miller, R. B. (1983). A call to armchairs. *Psychotherapy: Theory, Research, and Practice, 20*(2), 208–219.

Minuchin, S. (1974). *Families and family therapy.* Cambridge, Mass.: Harvard University Press.

Minuchin, S., & Fishman, H. C. (1981). *Family therapy techniques.* Cambridge, Mass.: Harvard University Press.

Minuchin, S., Rosman, B., & Baker, L. (1978). *Psychosomatic families: Anorexia nervosa in context.* Cambridge, Mass.: Harvard University Press.

Murphy, J. P. (1984). Substance abuse and the family. *Journal for Specialists in Group Work, 9*(2), 106–112.

Musashi, M. (1982). *A book of five rings.* Woodstock, N.Y.: Overlook Press.

Napier, R. W., & Gershenfeld, M. K. (1983). *Groups: Theory and experience.* Boston: Houghton Mifflin.

Neugarten, B. (1968). *Middle age and aging.* Chicago: University of Chicago Press.

Newman, B., & Newman, P. (1984). *Development through life* (3rd ed.). Homewood, Ill.: Dorsey Press.

Nissenson, M. (1984, January). Therapy after sixty. *Psychology Today,* pp. 22–26.

North, R., & Orange, R., Jr. (1980). *Teenage drinking: The #1 drug threat to young people today.* New York: Collier Books.

Oakley, R. (1983). *Drugs, society and human behavior.* St. Louis: C.V. Mosby.

Ohlsen, M. (1977). *Group counseling* (2nd ed.). New York: Holt, Rinehart & Winston.

Okun, B. F., & Rappaport, L. J. (1980). *Working with families.* North Scituate, Mass.: Duxbury Press.

Osipow, S. H. (1973). *Theories of career development* (2nd ed.). New York: Appleton-Century-Crofts.

Osipow, S. H., Walsh, W. B., & Tosi, D. J. (1984). *A survey of counseling methods.* Homewood, Ill.: Dorsey Press.

Palmer, J. O. (1980). *A primer of eclectic psychotherapy.* Belmont, Calif.: Wadsworth.

Paritzky, R. S., & Magoon, T. M. (1982). Goal attainment scaling models for assessing group counseling. *Personnel and Guidance Journal, 60,* 381–384.

Parloff, M. (1956). Some factors affecting the quality of therapeutic relationships. *Journal of Abnormal and Social Psychology, 52,* 5–10.

Pascarelli, E. F. (1981). Drug abuse and the elderly. In J. H. Lowinson & P. Ruiz (Eds.), *Substance abuse: Clinical problems and perspectives.* Baltimore: Williams & Wilkins.

Patterson, C. H. (1972). Ethical standards for groups. *The Counseling Psychologist, 3,* 93–101.

Patterson, C. H. (1980). *Theories of counseling and psychotherapy* (3rd ed.). New York: Harper & Row.

Patterson, L. E., & Eisenberg, S. (1983). *The counseling process.* Boston: Houghton Mifflin.

Perls, F. (1969a). *Gestalt therapy verbatim.* Lafayette, Calif.: Real People Press.

Perls, F. (1969b). *In and out of the garbage pail.* Lafayette, Calif.: Real People Press.

Pfeiffer, J. W., & Jones, J. E. (1973–1977). *A handbook of structured experiences for human relations training* (Vols. 1–11). Iowa City: University Publications.

Phillips, B. N. (1982). Regulations and control in psychology. *American Psychologist, 37*(8), 919–926.

Piaget, J. (1926). *The language and thought of the child.* New York: Harcourt Brace Jovanovich.

Pietrofesa, J., Hoffman, A., & Splete, H. (1984). *Counseling: An introduction.* Boston: Houghton Mifflin.

Pines, A., & Maslach, C. (1978). Characteristics of staff burnout in mental health settings. *Hospital and Community Psychiatry, 29,* 223–237.

Rachman, S. (1971). *The effects of psychotherapy.* London: Pergamon Press.

Remer, R. (1981). The counselor and research: An introduction. *Personnel and Guidance Journal, 59,* 567–571.

Robertiello, R. C. (1978). The occupational disease of psychotherapists. *Journal of Contemporary Psychotherapy,* 123–129.

Roe, A. (1957). Early determinants of vocational choice. *Journal of Counseling Psychology, 4,* 212–217.

Rogers, C. R. (1942). *Counseling and psychotherapy.* Boston: Houghton Mifflin.

Rogers, C. R. (1951). *Client-centered therapy.* Boston: Houghton Mifflin.

Rogers, C. R. (1957). The necessary and sufficient conditions of therapeutic personality change. *Journal of Consulting Psychology, 21,* 93–103.

Rogers, C. R. (1958). Characteristics of a helping relationship. *Personnel and Guidance Journal, 37,* 6–16.

Rogers, C. R. (1959). A theory of therapy, personality, and interpersonal relationships as developed in the client-centered framework. In S. Koch (Ed.), *Psychology: A study of a science:* Vol. 3. *Formulations of the person and the social content.* New York: McGraw-Hill.

Rogers, C. R. (1961). *On becoming a person.* Boston: Houghton Mifflin.

Rogers, C. R. (1969). *Freedom to learn.* Columbus, Ohio: Charles E. Merrill.

Rogers, C. R. (1970). *On encounter groups.* New York: Harper & Row.

Rogers, C. R. (1980) *A way of being.* Palo Alto: Houghton Mifflin.

Rogers, C. R., & Truax, C. B. (1967). The therapeutic conditions antecedent to change: A theoretical view. In C. R. Rogers (Ed.), *The therapeutic relationship and its impact.* Madison: University of Wisconsin Press.

Sachs, M. L., & Buffone, G. W. (1984). (Eds.), *Running as therapy.* Lincoln: University of Nebraska Press.

Sampson, J. P., Jr. (1983). Computer-assisted testing and assessment: Current status and implications for the future. *Measurement and Evaluation in Guidance, 15,* 293–299.

Sartre, J.-P. (1957). *Existentialism and human emotions.* New York: The Wisdom Library.

Satir, V. (1972). *Peoplemaking.* Palo Alto, Calif.: Science and Behavior Books.

Schlaadt, R. G., & Shannon, P. T. (1982). *Drugs of choice.* Englewood Cliffs, N.J.: Prentice-Hall.

Schlossberg, N. K. (1984). *Counseling adults in transition.* New York: Springer.

Schlossberg, N. K., & Kent, L. (1979). Effective helping in women. In S. Eisenberg & L. E. Patterson (Eds.), *Helping clients with special concerns* (pp. 263–286). Chicago: Rand McNally.

Schlossberg, N. K., & Pietrofesa, J. (1973). Perspectives on counseling bias: Implications for counselor education. *Counseling Psychologist, 4,* 44–54.

Schofield, W. (1964). *Psychotherapy: The purchase of friendship.* Englewood Cliffs, N.J.: Prentice-Hall.

Seligman, L. (1983). An introduction to the new DSM-II. *Personnel and Guidance Journal, 61*(10), 601–605.

Seligman, M. (1983). Sources of psychological disturbance among siblings of handicapped children. *Personnel and Guidance Journal, 61,* 529–531.

Shertzer, B., & Linden, J. (1979) *Fundamentals of individual appraisal: Assessment techniques for counselors.* Boston: Houghton Mifflin.

Shertzer, B., & Stone, S. (1980). *Fundamentals of counseling.* Boston: Houghton Mifflin.

Siegel, J. C., & Sell, J. M. (1978). Effects of objective evidence of expertness and nonverbal behavior on client perceived expertness. *Journal of Counseling Psychology, 25,* 188–192.

Sifneos, P. (1967). Two different kinds of psychotherapy of short duration. *American Journal of Psychiatry, 123,* 1069–1073.

Singer, P. (1981). *The expanding circle: Ethics and sociobiology.* New York: New American Library.

Skinner, B. F. (1938). *The behavior of organisms: An experimental analysis.* New York: Appleton-Century-Crofts.

Skinner, B. F. (1953). *Science and human behavior.* New York: Macmillan.

Skinner, B. F. (1983). Intellectual self-management in old age. *American Psychologist, 38,* 239–244.

Smith, M. C., & Glass, G. V. (1977). Meta-analysis of psychotherapy outcome studies. *American Psychologist, 32,* 752–761.

Smith, M. C., Glass, G. V., & Miller, T. J. (1980). *The benefits of psychotherapy.* Baltimore: Johns Hopkins University Press.

Spicuzza, F. J., & Devoe, M. W. (1982). Burnout in the helping professions: Mutual aid groups as self-help. *Personnel and Guidance Journal, 61,* 95–99.

Spitzer, R. L., Skodol, A. E., Gibbon, M., & Williams, J. (1981). *DSM-III case book.* Washington, D.C.: APA.

Stanton, M. D. (1981). One integrated structural/strategic approach to family therapy. *Journal of Marital and Family Therapy,* 427–439.

Stein, H. (1982). *Ethics (and other liabilities).* New York: St. Martin's Press.

Strong, S. R. (1968). Counseling: An interpersonal influence process. *Journal of Counseling Psychology, 15,* 215–224.

Strong, S. R., & Claiborn, C. D. (1982). *Change through interaction.* New York: Wiley-Interscience.

Strong, S. R., & Dixon, D. N. (1971). Expertness, attractiveness, and influence in counseling. *Journal of Counseling Psychology, 18,* 562–570.

Strong, S. R., & Schmidt, L. D. (1970). Expertness influence in counseling. *Journal of Counseling Psychology, 17,* 81–87.

Strupp, H. H., & Hadley, W. S. (1977). A tripartite model of mental health and therapeutic outcome. *American Psychologist, 32,* 187–197.

Stuart, R. B. (1970). *Trick or treatment: How and when psychotherapy fails.* Champaign, Ill.: Research Press.

Sue, S. (1977). Community health services to minority groups: Some optimism, some pessimism. *American Psychologist, 32,* 616–624.

Sue, S. (1983). Ethnic minority issues in psychology. *American Psychologist, 38,* 583–592.

Super, D. E. (1953). A theory of vocational development. *American Psychologist, 8,* 185–190.

Super, D. E. (1954). Career patterns as a basis for vocational counseling. *Journal of Counseling Psychology, 1,* 12–19.

Super, D. E. (1957). *The psychology of careers.* New York: Harper & Row.

Swensen, C. H. (1983). A respectable old age. *American Psychologist, 38,* 327–334.

Talbutt, L. C. (1981). Ethical standards: Assets and limitations. *Personnel and Guidance Journal, 60,* 110–112.

Talbutt, L. C. (1983). Recent court decisions: A quiz for APGA members. *Personnel and Guidance Journal, 61*(6), 355–357.

Task Force on Prescription Drugs. (1968). *The drug users.* Washington, D.C.: U.S. Government Printing Office.

Temerlin, M. K. (1968). Suggestion effects in psychiatric diagnosis. *The Journal of Nervous and Mental Disease, 147,* 349–353.

Terkel, S. (1972). *Working.* New York: Avon.

Thomas, A. H., & Stewart, N. R. (1971). Counselor response to female clients with deviate and conforming career goals. *Journal of Counseling Psychology, 18,* 352–357.

Thomas, L. (1979). *The medusa and the snail.* New York: Viking.

Thompson, C. (1950). *Psychoanalysis: Evolution and development.* New York: Grove Press.

Thoresen, C. E. (1969). The counselor as an applied behavioral scientist. *Personnel and Guidance Journal, 47,* 841–848.

Thorne, F. C. (1967). *Integrative psychology.* Brandon, Vt.: Clinical Psychology Publishing.

Tiedeman, D. V., & O'Hara, R. P. (1963). *Career development: Choice and adjustment.* New York: College Entrance Examination Board.

Toffler, A. (1970). *Future shock.* New York: Bantam Books.

Tolliver, L. M. (1983). Social and mental health needs of the aged. *American Psychologist, 38,* 316–318.

Tramel, D. (1981). A lesson from the physicists. *Personnel and Guidance Journal, 59,* 425–429.

Troll, L. (1975). *Early and middle adulthood.* Monterey, Calif.: Brooks/Cole.

Trotzer, J. P. (1977). *The counselor and the group.* Monterey, Calif.: Brooks/Cole.

Trotzer, J. P. (1979). Developmental tasks in group counseling: The basis for structure. *Journal for Specialists in Group Work, 4,* 177–185.

Truax, C. B. (1963). Effective ingredients in psychotherapy: An approach to unraveling the patient–therapist interaction. *Journal of Counseling Psychology, 10,* 256–263.

Truax, C. B., & Carkhuff, R. R. (1965). The experimental manipulation of therapeutic conditions. *Journal of Consulting Psychology, 29,* 119–124.

Truax, C. B., & Carkhuff, R. R. (1967). *Toward effective counseling and psychotherapy.* Chicago: Aldine.

Turkington, C. (1984, January). Ideology affects approach taken to alleviate PMS. *APA Monitor,* pp. 28–29.

Tyler, L. (1970). Thoughts about theory. In W. H. Van Hoose & J. J. Pietrofesa (Eds.), *Counseling and guidance in the twentieth century* (pp. 298–305). Boston: Houghton Mifflin.

Umbarger, C. C. (1983). *Structural family therapy.* New York: Grune & Stratton.

Van Hoose, W. H., & Kottler, J. A. (1985). *Ethical and legal issues in counseling and psychotherapy* (2nd ed.). San Francisco: Jossey-Bass.

Vash, C. (1981). *The psychology of disability.* New York: Springer.

Vriend, J., & Kottler, J. A. (1980). Initial interview checklist increases counselor effectiveness. *Canadian Counsellor, 14*(3), 153–155.

Wallace, M. E. (1982). A common base for psychotherapy and family therapy. *Psychotherapy: Theory, Research, and Practice, 19,* 297–306.

Wass, H., & Myers, J. E. (1982). Psychosocial aspects of death among the elderly: A review of the literature. *Personnel and Guidance Journal, 61,* 131–137.

Watson, J. B., & Rayner, R. (1920). Conditioned emotional reactions. *Journal of Experimental Psychology, 3,* 1–14.

Watzlawick, P., Weakland, J. H., & Fisch, R. (1974). *Change: Principles of problem formation and problem resolution.* New York: Norton.

Weil, A. (1972). *The natural mind.* Boston: Houghton Mifflin.

Weissman, M., & Klerman, G. (1977). Sex differences in epidemiology of depression. *Archives of General Psychiatry, 34,* 98–111.

White, L. C. (1980). Competences counselor educators value. *Personnel and Guidance Journal, 59,* 31–36.

White, T. H. (1939). *The once and future king.* New York: Berkley Books.

Whitehorn, J., & Betz, B. (1954). A study of psychotherapeutic relationships between physicians and schizophrenic patients. *American Journal of Psychiatry, 3,* 321–331.

Whiteley, J. M. (1980). Counseling psychology in the year 2000 A.D. *The Counseling Psychologist, 8,* 2–16.

Whiteley, J. M. (1980). *History of counseling psychology.* Washington, D.C.: AACD Press.

Whiteley, J. M., & Fretz, B. R. (1980). *The present and future of counseling psychology.* Washington, D.C.: AACD Press.

Whiteley, J. M., & Resnikoff, A. (1978). *Career counseling.* Monterey, Calif.: Brooks/Cole.

Wiener, E. A., & Stewart, B. J. (1984). *Assessing individuals.* Boston: Little, Brown.

Williams, J. B. W., & Spitzer, R. L. (1983). The issue of sex bias in DSM-III. *American Psychologist,* 793–798.

Williamson, E. G. (1939). *How to counsel students: A manual for clinical counselors.* New York: McGraw-Hill.

Williamson, E. G. (1950) *Counseling adolescents.* New York: McGraw-Hill.

Williamson, E. G., & Biggs, D. A. (1979). Trait-factor theory and individual differences. In H. M. Burks & B. Stefflre, *Theories of counseling* (3rd ed.). New York: McGraw-Hill.

Wilson, E. O. (1978). *On human nature.* New York: Bantam Books.

Wolberg, L. R. (1967). *The technique of psychotherapy.* New York: Grune & Stratton.

Wolpe, J. (1958). *Psychotherapy by reciprocal inhibition.* Stanford, Calif.: Stanford University Press.

Wolpe, J. (1969). *The practice of behavior therapy.* Elmsford, N.Y.: Pergamon Press.

Wolpe, J. (1982). *The practice of behavior therapy* (2nd ed.). Elmsford, N.Y.: Pergamon Press.

Woody, R. H. (1984). *The law and the practice of human services.* San Francisco: Jossey-Bass.

Yalom, I. (1975). *The theory and practice of group psychotherapy.* New York: Basic Books.

Yalom, I. (1980). *Existential psychotherapy.* New York: Basic Books.

Index

Credits

CHAPTER 10

194–196, Quotations and Tables 10–1 and 10–2 from "Group Focused Counseling: Classifying the Essential Skills," by S. J. Gill and R. A. Barry, 1982, *Personnel and Guidance Journal, 60,* pp. 302–305. Copyright 1982 American Association for Counseling and Development. Reprinted with permission.

CHAPTER 11

202, Quotations from *Working* by L. Terkel. Copyright 1974 by Pantheon Books, a Division of Random House, Inc. Reprinted by permission. **207–209,** Quotations from John Holland, *Making Vocational Choices: A Theory of Careers,* © 1973. Reprinted by permission of Prentice-Hall, Inc., Englewood Cliffs, N.J. **210–211,** Quotations from *Occupational Information,* 4th Ed., by R. Hoppock. Copyright 1976 by McGraw-Hill Book Company. Reprinted by permission. **214,** Figure 11–2 from "A Social Learning Theory of Career Selection," by J. Krumboltz. In Whiteley and Resnikoff (Eds.), *Career Counseling.* Copyright 1978 by Wadsworth, Inc. Reprinted by permission of Brooks/Cole Publishing Company, Monterey, California.

CHAPTER 12

222, Figure 12–1 from "Family Systems Counseling: A Positive Alternative to Traditional Counseling," by E. Amata and F. Fabrick, 1981, *Elementary School Guidance and Counseling, 15,* pp. 223-236. Copyright 1981 American Association for Counseling and Development. Reprinted with permission.

CHAPTER 15

278–279, Figure 15–1 from *Ethical and Legal Issues in Counseling and Psychotherapy,* by W. Van Hoose and J. Kottler. Copyright © 1977 by Jossey-Bass Inc., Publishers. Reprinted by permission.